W9-CDO-655

PRAISE FOR THE FIRST EDITION OF *ELOQUENT JAVASCRIPT*

"I became a better architect, author, mentor and developer because of this book. It deserves to share shelf space with Flannagan and Crockford."
—ANGUS CROLL, TWITTER DEVELOPER

"This is the book I give out when people ask me how to learn proper JavaScript."
—CHRIS WILLIAMS, ORGANIZER OF JSCONF US

"One of the best JavaScript books I've read."
—REY BANGO, JQUERY TEAM MEMBER AND CLIENT-WEB COMMUNITY PROGRAM MANAGER AT MICROSOFT

"A really good guide to JavaScript; but even more than that, this book is a great guide to programming."
—BEN NADEL, CHIEF SOFTWARE ENGINEER AT EPICENTER CONSULTING

"A good book, suitable for those without experience in JavaScript and even those without programming experience."
—NICHOLAS ZAKAS, AUTHOR OF *HIGH PERFORMANCE JAVASCRIPT* AND *THE PRINCIPLES OF OBJECT-ORIENTED JAVASCRIPT*

"Does a good job of detailing the fundamentals and explaining concepts like the stack and the environment. This attention to detail is what sets the book apart from other JavaScript books."
—DESIGNORATI

"If you're new to JavaScript, the first thing I'd recommend you do is visit *Eloquent JavaScript* and check out Marijn Haverbeke's introduction to the language."
—CNET UK

ELOQUENT JAVASCRIPT

2ND EDITION

A Modern Introduction to Programming

by Marijn Haverbeke

no starch press

San Francisco

ELOQUENT JAVASCRIPT, 2ND EDITION. Copyright © 2015 by Marijn Haverbeke.

All rights reserved. No part of this work may be reproduced or transmitted in any form or by any means, electronic or mechanical, including photocopying, recording, or by any information storage or retrieval system, without the prior written permission of the copyright owner and the publisher.

Printed in USA
Fourth printing

20 19 18 17 16   4 5 6 7 8 9

ISBN-10: 1-59327-584-6
ISBN-13: 978-1-59327-584-6

Publisher: William Pollock
Production Editor: Serena Yang
Cover Illustration: Wasif Hyder
Developmental Editor: Jennifer Griffith-Delgado
Technical Reviewers: Alex Cash, Angus Croll, and Peter van der Zee
Copyeditor: Kim Wimpsett
Compositor: Serena Yang
Proofreader: James M. Fraleigh

The illustrations are contributed by various artists: computer (introduction) and unicycle people (Chapter 21) by Max Xiantu. Sea of bits (Chapter 1) and weresquirrel (Chapter 4) by Margarita Martínez and José Menor. Octopuses (Chapter 2 and 4) by Jim Tierney. Object with on/off switch (Chapter 6) by Dyle MacGregor. Regular expression diagrams in Chapter 9 generated with Regexper by Jeff Avallone. Game concept for Chapter 15 by Thomas Palef. Pixel art in Chapter 16 by Antonio Perdomo Pastor.

For information on distribution, translations, or bulk sales, please contact No Starch Press, Inc. directly:

No Starch Press, Inc.
245 8th Street, San Francisco, CA 94103
phone: 415.863.9900; info@nostarch.com
www.nostarch.com

The Library of Congress has catalogued the first edition as follows:

Haverbeke, Marijn.
  Eloquent JavaScript: a modern introduction to programming / by Marijn Haverbeke.
       p. cm.
  Includes index.
  ISBN-13: 978-1-59327-282-1
  ISBN-10: 1-59327-282-0
  1. JavaScript (Computer program language) I. Title.
  QA76.73.J39H38 2009
  005.13'3--dc22
                                          2010032246

No Starch Press and the No Starch Press logo are registered trademarks of No Starch Press, Inc. Other product and company names mentioned herein may be the trademarks of their respective owners. Rather than use a trademark symbol with every occurrence of a trademarked name, we are using the names only in an editorial fashion and to the benefit of the trademark owner, with no intention of infringement of the trademark.

The information in this book is distributed on an "As Is" basis, without warranty. While every precaution has been taken in the preparation of this work, neither the author nor No Starch Press, Inc. shall have any liability to any person or entity with respect to any loss or damage caused or alleged to be caused directly or indirectly by the information contained in it.

For Lotte and Jan

BRIEF CONTENTS

CONTENTS IN DETAIL

PART I: LANGUAGE

1
VALUES, TYPES, AND OPERATORS   11

2
PROGRAM STRUCTURE   23

3
FUNCTIONS
41

4
DATA STRUCTURES: OBJECTS AND ARRAYS
59

5
HIGHER-ORDER FUNCTIONS 81

6
THE SECRET LIFE OF OBJECTS 99

7
PROJECT: ELECTRONIC LIFE 119

8
BUGS AND ERROR HANDLING 139

9
REGULAR EXPRESSIONS

10
MODULES

11
PROJECT: A PROGRAMMING LANGUAGE   191

PART II: BROWSER

12
JAVASCRIPT AND THE BROWSER   207

13
THE DOCUMENT OBJECT MODEL   215

14
HANDLING EVENTS 235

15
PROJECT: A PLATFORM GAME 253

16
DRAWING ON CANVAS   275

17
HTTP   299

21
PROJECT: SKILL-SHARING WEBSITE   367

22
JAVASCRIPT AND PERFORMANCE   389

EXERCISE HINTS   407

INTRODUCTION

This is a book about getting computers to do what you want them to do. Computers are about as common as screwdrivers today, but they contain a lot more hidden complexity and thus are harder to operate and understand. To many, they remain alien, slightly threatening things.

We've found two effective ways of bridging the communication gap between us, squishy biological organisms with a talent for social and spatial reasoning, and computers, unfeeling manipulators of meaningless data. The first is to appeal to our sense of the physical world and build interfaces that mimic that world and allow us to manipulate shapes on a screen with our fingers. This works very well for casual machine interaction.

But we have not yet found a good way to use the point-and-click approach to communicate things to the computer that the designer of the interface did not anticipate. For open-ended interfaces, such as instructing the computer to perform arbitrary tasks, we've had more luck with an approach that makes use of our talent for language: teaching the machine a language.

Human languages allow words and phrases to be combined in many ways, which allows us to say many different things. Computer languages, though typically less grammatically flexible, follow a similar principle.

Casual computing has become much more widespread in the past 20 years, and language-based interfaces, which once were the default way in which people interacted with computers, have largely been replaced with graphical interfaces. But they are still there, if you know where to look. One such language, JavaScript, is built into almost every web browser and is thus available on just about every consumer device.

This book intends to make you familiar enough with this language to be able to make a computer do what you want.

On Programming

> I do not enlighten those who are not eager to learn, nor arouse those who are not anxious to give an explanation themselves. If I have presented one corner of the square and they cannot come back to me with the other three, I should not go over the points again.
> —Confucius

Besides explaining JavaScript, I also will introduce the basic principles of programming. Programming, it turns out, is hard. The fundamental rules are typically simple and clear. But programs built on top of these rules tend to become complex enough to introduce their own rules and complexity. You're building your own maze, in a way, and you might just get lost in it.

There will be times when reading this book will feel terribly frustrating. If you are new to programming, there will be a lot of new material to digest. Much of this material will then be *combined* in ways that require you to make additional connections.

It is up to you to make the necessary effort. When you are struggling to follow the book, do not jump to any conclusions about your own capabilities. You are fine—you just need to keep at it. Take a break, reread some material, and *always* make sure you read and understand the example programs and exercises. Learning is hard work, but everything you learn is yours and will make subsequent learning easier.

> The computer programmer is a creator of universes for which he [sic] alone is responsible. Universes of virtually unlimited complexity can be created in the form of computer programs.
> —Joseph Weizenbaum, *Computer Power and Human Reason*

A program is many things. It is a piece of text typed by a programmer; it is the directing force that makes the computer do what it does; it is data in the computer's memory, yet it controls the actions performed on this same memory. Analogies that try to compare programs to objects we are familiar with tend to fall short. A superficially fitting one is that of a machine—lots of separate parts tend to be involved, and to make the whole thing tick, we have to consider the ways in which these parts interconnect and contribute to the operation of the whole.

A computer is a machine built to act as a host for these immaterial machines. Computers themselves can do only stupidly straightforward things. The reason they are so useful is that they do these things at an incredibly high speed. A program can ingeniously combine an enormous number of these simple actions in order to do very complicated things.

To some of us, writing computer programs is a fascinating game. A program is a building of thought. It is costless to build, it is weightless, and it grows easily under our typing hands.

But without care, a program's size and complexity will grow out of control, confusing even the person who created it. Keeping programs under control is the main problem of programming. When a program works, it is beautiful. The art of programming is the skill of controlling complexity. The great program is subdued—simple in its complexity.

Many programmers believe that this complexity is best managed by using only a small set of well-understood techniques in their programs. They have composed strict rules ("best practices") prescribing the form programs should have, and the more zealous among them will consider those who go outside of this safe little zone to be *bad* programmers.

What hostility to the richness of programming—to try to reduce it to something straightforward and predictable, to place a taboo on all the weird and beautiful programs! The landscape of programming techniques is enormous, fascinating in its diversity, and still largely unexplored. It is certainly dangerous going, luring the inexperienced programmer into all kinds of confusion, but that only means you should proceed with caution and keep your wits about you. There will always be new challenges and new territory to explore. Programmers who refuse to keep exploring will stagnate, forget their joy, and get bored with their craft.

Why Language Matters

In the beginning, at the birth of computing, there were no programming languages. Programs looked something like this:

```
00110001 00000000 00000000
00110001 00000001 00000001
00110011 00000001 00000010
01010001 00001011 00000010
00100010 00000010 00001000
01000011 00000001 00000000
```

```
01000001 00000001 00000001
00010000 00000010 00000000
01100010 00000000 00000000
```

This program adds the numbers from 1 to 10 together and prints out the result: 1 + 2 + ... + 10 = 55. It could run on a simple, hypothetical machine. To program early computers, it was necessary to set large arrays of switches in the right position or punch holes in strips of cardboard and feed them to the computer. You can probably imagine how tedious and error-prone this procedure was. Even writing simple programs required much cleverness and discipline. Complex ones were nearly inconceivable.

Of course, manually entering these arcane patterns of bits (the ones and zeros) did give the programmer a profound sense of being a mighty wizard. And that has to be worth something in terms of job satisfaction.

Each line of the previous program contains a single instruction. It could be written in English like this:

```
1. Store the number 0 in memory location 0.
2. Store the number 1 in memory location 1.
3. Store the value of memory location 1 in memory location 2.
4. Subtract the number 11 from the value in memory location 2.
5. If the value in memory location 2 is the number 0,
   continue with instruction 9.
6. Add the value of memory location 1 to memory location 0.
7. Add the number 1 to the value of memory location 1.
8. Continue with instruction 3.
9. Output the value of memory location 0.
```

Although that is already more readable than the soup of bits, it is still rather unpleasant. It might help to use names instead of numbers for the instructions and memory locations.

```
Set "total" to 0.
Set "count" to 1.
[loop]
 Set "compare" to "count".
 Subtract 11 from "compare".
 If "compare" is zero, continue at [end].
 Add "count" to "total".
 Add 1 to "count".
 Continue at [loop].
[end]
 Output "total".
```

Can you see how the program works at this point? The first two lines give two memory locations their starting values: total will build up the result of the computation, and count will keep track of the number that we are currently looking at. The lines using compare are probably the weirdest ones.

The program wants to see whether count is equal to 11 in order to decide whether it can stop running. Because our hypothetical machine is rather primitive, it can only test whether a number is zero and make a decision (or jump) based on that. So it uses the memory location labeled compare to compute the value of count - 11 and makes a decision based on that value. The next two lines add the value of count to the result and increment count by 1 every time the program has decided that count is not 11 yet.

Here is the same program in JavaScript:

```
var total = 0, count = 1;
while (count <= 10) {
  total += count;
  count += 1;
}
console.log(total);
// ▷ 55
```

This version gives us a few more improvements. Most importantly, there is no need to specify the way we want the program to jump back and forth anymore. The while language construct takes care of that. It continues executing the block (wrapped in braces) below it as long as the condition it was given holds. That condition is count <= 10, which means "count is less than or equal to 10." We no longer have to create a temporary value and compare that to zero, which was an uninteresting detail. Part of the power of programming languages is that they take care of uninteresting details for us.

At the end of the program, after while has finished, the console.log operation is applied to the result in order to write it as output.

Finally, here is what the program could look like if we happened to have the convenient operations range and sum available, which create a collection of numbers within a range and compute the sum of a collection of numbers, respectively:

```
console.log(sum(range(1, 10)));
// ▷ 55
```

The moral of this story is that the same program can be expressed in long and short, unreadable and readable ways. The first version of the program was extremely obscure, whereas this last one is almost English: log the sum of the range of numbers from 1 to 10. (We will see in later chapters how to build operations like sum and range.)

A good programming language helps the programmer by allowing them to talk about the actions that the computer has to perform on a higher level. It helps omit uninteresting details, provides convenient building blocks (such as while and console.log), allows you to define your own building blocks (such as sum and range), and makes those blocks easy to compose.

What Is JavaScript?

JavaScript was introduced in 1995 as a way to add programs to web pages in the Netscape Navigator browser. The language has since been adopted by all other major graphical web browsers. It has made modern web applications possible—applications with which you can interact directly, without doing a page reload for every action. But it is also used in more traditional websites to provide various forms of interactivity and cleverness.

It is important to note that JavaScript has almost nothing to do with the programming language named Java. The similar name was inspired by marketing considerations, rather than good judgment. When JavaScript was introduced, the Java language was being heavily marketed and was gaining popularity. Someone thought it was a good idea to ride on the coattails of this success. Now we are stuck with the name.

After JavaScript's widespread adoption, a standard document was written to describe the way the language should work to make sure the various pieces of software that claimed to support JavaScript were actually talking about the same language. This is called the ECMAScript standard, after the ECMA organization that did the standardization. In practice, the terms ECMAScript and JavaScript can be used interchangeably—they are two names for the same language.

There are those who will say *terrible* things about the JavaScript language. Many of these things are true. When I was required to write something in JavaScript for the first time, I quickly came to despise it. It would accept almost anything I typed but interpret it in a way that was completely different from what I meant. This had a lot to do with the fact that I did not have a clue what I was doing, of course, but there is a real issue here: JavaScript is ridiculously liberal in what it allows. The idea behind this design was that it would make programming in JavaScript easier for beginners. In actuality, it mostly makes finding problems in your programs harder because the system will not point them out to you.

This flexibility also has its advantages, though. It leaves space for a lot of techniques that are impossible in more rigid languages, and as you will see (for example, in Chapter 10), it can be used to overcome some of JavaScript's shortcomings. After learning the language properly and working with it for a while, I have learned to actually *like* JavaScript.

There have been several versions of JavaScript. ECMAScript version 3 was the most widely supported version at the time of JavaScript's ascent to dominance, roughly between 2000 and 2010. During this time, work was underway on an ambitious version 4, which planned a number of radical improvements and extensions to the language. Changing a living, widely used language in such a radical way turned out to be politically difficult, and work on version 4 was abandoned in 2008, leading to the much less ambitious version 5 that came out in 2009. We're now at the point where all major browsers support version 5, which is the version that this book will be focusing on. Version 6 is in the process of being finalized, and some browsers are starting to support new features from this version.

Web browsers are not the only platforms on which JavaScript is used. Some databases, such as MongoDB and CouchDB, use JavaScript as their scripting and query language. Several platforms for desktop and server programming, most notably the Node.js project (the subject of Chapter 20), are providing a powerful environment for programming JavaScript outside of the browser.

Code, and What to Do with It

Code is the text that makes up programs. Most chapters in this book contain quite a lot of it. In my experience, reading code and writing code are indispensable parts of learning to program, so try to not just glance over the examples. Read them attentively and understand them. This may be slow and confusing at first, but I promise that you will quickly get the hang of it. The same goes for the exercises. Don't assume you understand them until you've actually written a working solution.

I recommend you try your solutions to exercises in an actual JavaScript interpreter. That way, you'll get immediate feedback on whether what you are doing is working, and, I hope, you'll be tempted to experiment and go beyond the exercises.

The easiest way to run the example code in the book, and to experiment with it, is to look it up in the online version of the book at *http://eloquentjavascript.net/*. There, you can click any code example to edit and run it and to see the output it produces. To work on the exercises, go to *http://eloquentjavascript.net/code/*, which provides starting code for each coding exercise and allows you to look at the solutions.

If you want to run the programs defined in this book outside of the book's sandbox, some care is required. Many examples stand on their own and should work in any JavaScript environment. But code in later chapters is mostly written for a specific environment (the browser or Node.js) and can run only there. In addition, many chapters define bigger programs, and the pieces of code that appear in them depend on each other or on external files. The sandbox on the website provides links to Zip files containing all of the scripts and data files necessary to run the code for a given chapter.

Overview of This Book

This book contains roughly three parts. The first 11 chapters discuss the JavaScript language itself. The next eight chapters are about web browsers and the way JavaScript is used to program them. Finally, two chapters are devoted to Node.js, another environment to program JavaScript in.

Throughout the book, there are five *project chapters*, which describe larger example programs to give you a taste of real programming. In order of appearance, we will work through building an artificial life simulation, a programming language, a platform game, a paint program, and a dynamic website.

The language part of the book starts with four chapters to introduce the basic structure of the JavaScript language. They introduce control structures (such as the while word you saw in this introduction), functions (writing your own operations), and data structures. After these, you will be able to write simple programs. Next, Chapters 5 and 6 introduce techniques to use functions and objects to write more *abstract* code and thus keep complexity under control.

After a first project chapter, the first part of the book continues with chapters on error handling and fixing, on regular expressions (an important tool for working with text data), and on modularity—another weapon against complexity. The second project chapter concludes the first part of the book.

The second part, Chapters 12 to 19, describes the tools that browser JavaScript has access to. You'll learn to display things on the screen (Chapters 13 and 16), respond to user input (Chapters 14 and 18), and communicate over the network (Chapter 17). There are again two project chapters in this part.

After that, Chapter 20 describes Node.js, and Chapter 21 builds a simple web system using that tool.

Finally, Chapter 22 describes some of the considerations that come up when optimizing JavaScript programs for speed.

Typographic Conventions

In this book, text written in a monospaced font will represent elements of programs—sometimes they are self-sufficient fragments, and sometimes they just refer to part of a nearby program. Programs (of which you have already seen a few), are written as follows:

```
function fac(n) {
  if (n == 0)
    return 1;
  else
    return fac(n - 1) * n;
}
```

Sometimes, in order to show the output that a program produces, the expected output is written after it, with two slashes and an arrow in front.

```
console.log(fac(8));
// ▷ 40320
```

Good luck!

PART I

LANGUAGE

"Below the surface of the machine, the program moves. Without effort, it expands and contracts. In great harmony, electrons scatter and regroup. The forms on the monitor are but ripples on the water. The essence stays invisibly below."

—Master Yuan-Ma, *The Book of Programming*

1

VALUES, TYPES, AND OPERATORS

Inside the computer's world, there is only data. You
can read data, modify data, create new data—but anything that isn't data simply does not exist. All this data
is stored as long sequences of bits and is thus fundamentally alike.

Bits are any kind of two-valued things, usually described as zeros and
ones. Inside the computer, they take forms such as a high or low electrical
charge, a strong or weak signal, or a shiny or dull spot on the surface of a
CD. Any piece of discrete information can be reduced to a sequence of zeros
and ones and thus represented in bits.

For example, think about how you might show the number 13 in bits. It
works the same way you write decimal numbers, but instead of 10 different
digits, you have only 2, and the weight of each increases by a factor of 2 from
right to left. Here are the bits that make up the number 13, with the weights
of the digits shown below them:

0	0	0	0	1	1	0	1
128	64	32	16	8	4	2	1

So that's the binary number 00001101, or 8 + 4 + 1, which equals 13.

Values

Imagine a sea of bits. An ocean of them. A typical modern computer has more than 30 billion bits in its volatile data storage. Nonvolatile storage (the hard disk or equivalent) tends to have yet a few orders of magnitude more.

To be able to work with such quantities of bits without getting lost, you can separate them into chunks that represent pieces of information. In a JavaScript environment, those chunks are called *values*. Though all values are made of bits, they play different roles. Every value has a type that determines its role. There are six basic types of values in JavaScript: numbers, strings, Booleans, objects, functions, and undefined values.

To create a value, you must merely invoke its name. This is convenient. You don't have to gather building material for your values or pay for them. You just call for one, and *woosh*, you have it. They are not created from thin air, of course. Every value has to be stored somewhere, and if you want to use a gigantic amount of them at the same time, you might run out of bits. Fortunately, this is a problem only if you need them all simultaneously. As soon as you no longer use a value, it will dissipate, leaving behind its bits to be recycled as building material for the next generation of values.

This chapter introduces the atomic elements of JavaScript programs, that is, the simple value types and the operators that can act on such values.

Numbers

Values of the *number* type are, unsurprisingly, numeric values. In a JavaScript program, they are written as follows:

13

Use that in a program, and it will cause the bit pattern for the number 13 to come into existence inside the computer's memory.

JavaScript uses a fixed number of bits, namely 64 of them, to store a single number value. There are only so many patterns you can make with 64 bits, which means that the amount of different numbers that can be represented is limited. For N decimal digits, the amount of numbers that can be represented is 10^N. Similarly, given 64 binary digits, you can represent

2^{64} different numbers, which is about 18 quintillion (an 18 with 18 zeros after it). This is a lot.

Computer memory used to be a lot smaller, and people tended to use groups of 8 or 16 bits to represent their numbers. It was easy to accidentally *overflow* such small numbers—to end up with a number that did not fit into the given amount of bits. Today, even personal computers have plenty of memory, so you are free to use 64-bit chunks, which means you need to worry about overflow only when dealing with truly astronomical numbers.

Not all whole numbers below 18 quintillion fit in a JavaScript number, though. Those bits also store negative numbers, so one bit indicates the sign of the number. A bigger issue is that nonwhole numbers must also be represented. To do this, some of the bits are used to store the position of the decimal point. The actual maximum whole number that can be stored is more in the range of 9 quadrillion (15 zeros), which is still plenty huge.

Fractional numbers are written by using a dot.

```
9.81
```

For very big or very small numbers, you can also use scientific notation by adding an "e" (for "exponent"), followed by the exponent of the number:

```
2.998e8
```

That is $2.998 \times 10^8 = 299,800,000$.

Calculations with whole numbers (also called *integers*) smaller than the aforementioned 9 quadrillion are guaranteed to always be precise. Unfortunately, calculations with fractional numbers are generally not. Just as π (pi) cannot be precisely expressed by a finite number of decimal digits, many numbers lose some precision when only 64 bits are available to store them. This is a shame, but it causes practical problems only in specific situations. The important thing is to be aware of it and treat fractional digital numbers as approximations, not as precise values.

Arithmetic

The main thing to do with numbers is arithmetic. Arithmetic operations such as addition or multiplication take two number values and produce a new number from them. Here is what they look like in JavaScript:

```
100 + 4 * 11
```

The + and * symbols are called *operators*. The first stands for addition, and the second stands for multiplication. Putting an operator between two values will apply it to those values and produce a new value.

Does the example mean "add 4 and 100, and multiply the result by 11," or is the multiplication done before the adding? As you might have guessed, the multiplication happens first. But as in mathematics, you can change this by wrapping the addition in parentheses.

```
(100 + 4) * 11
```

For subtraction, there is the - operator, and division can be done with the / operator.

When operators appear together without parentheses, the order in which they are applied is determined by the *precedence* of the operators. The example shows that multiplication comes before addition. The / operator has the same precedence as *. Likewise for + and -. When multiple operators with the same precedence appear next to each other, as in 1 - 2 + 1, they are applied left to right: (1 - 2) + 1.

These rules of precedence are not something you should worry about. When in doubt, just add parentheses.

There is one more arithmetic operator, which you might not immediately recognize. The % symbol is used to represent the *remainder* operation. X % Y is the remainder of dividing X by Y. For example, 314 % 100 produces 14, and 144 % 12 gives 0. Remainder's precedence is the same as that of multiplication and division. You'll often see this operator referred to as *modulo*, though technically *remainder* is more accurate.

Special Numbers

There are three special values in JavaScript that are considered numbers but don't behave like normal numbers.

The first two are Infinity and -Infinity, which represent the positive and negative infinities. Infinity - 1 is still Infinity, and so on. Don't put too much trust in infinity-based computation. It isn't mathematically solid, and it will quickly lead to our next special number: NaN.

NaN stands for "not a number," even though it is a value of the number type. You'll get this result when you, for example, try to calculate 0 / 0 (zero divided by zero), Infinity - Infinity, or any number of other numeric operations that don't yield a precise, meaningful result.

Strings

The next basic data type is the *string*. Strings are used to represent text. They are written by enclosing their content in quotes.

```
"Patch my boat with chewing gum"
'Monkeys wave goodbye'
```

Both single and double quotes can be used to mark strings as long as the quotes at the start and the end of the string match.

Almost anything can be put between quotes, and JavaScript will make a string value out of it. But a few characters are more difficult. You can imagine how putting quotes between quotes might be hard. *Newlines* (the characters you get when you press ENTER) also can't be put between quotes. The string has to stay on a single line.

To include such characters in a string, the following notation is used: whenever a backslash (\) is found inside quoted text, it indicates that the character after it has a special meaning. This is called *escaping* the character. A quote that is preceded by a backslash will not end the string but be part of it. When an n character occurs after a backslash, it is interpreted as a newline. Similarly, a t after a backslash means a tab character. Take the following string:

```
"This is the first line\nAnd this is the second"
```

The actual text contained is this:

```
This is the first line
And this is the second
```

There are, of course, situations where you want a backslash in a string to be just a backslash, not a special code. If two backslashes follow each other, they will collapse together, and only one will be left in the resulting string value. This is how the string "A newline character is written like "\n"." can be expressed:

```
"A newline character is written like \"\\n\"."
```

Strings cannot be divided, multiplied, or subtracted, but the + operator *can* be used on them. It does not add, but rather *concatenates*—it glues two strings together. The following line will produce the string "concatenate":

```
"con" + "cat" + "e" + "nate"
```

There are more ways of manipulating strings, which we will discuss when we get to methods in Chapter 4.

Unary Operators

Not all operators are symbols. Some are written as words. One example is the typeof operator, which produces a string value naming the type of the value you give it.

```
console.log(typeof 4.5)
// ▷ number
console.log(typeof "x")
// ▷ string
```

We will use console.log in example code to indicate that we want to see the result of evaluating something. When you run such code, the value produced should be shown on the screen, though how it appears will depend on the JavaScript environment you use to run it.

The other operators we saw all operated on two values, but typeof takes only one. Operators that use two values are called *binary* operators, while those that take one are called *unary* operators. The minus operator can be used both as a binary operator and as a unary operator.

```
console.log(- (10 - 2))
// ▷ -8
```

Boolean Values

Often, you will need a value that simply distinguishes between two possibilities, like "yes" and "no" or "on" and "off." For this, JavaScript has a *Boolean* type, which has just two values: true and false (which are written simply as those words).

Comparisons

Here is one way to produce Boolean values:

```
console.log(3 > 2)
// ▷ true
console.log(3 < 2)
// ▷ false
```

The > and < signs are the traditional symbols for "is greater than" and "is less than," respectively. They are binary operators. Applying them results in a Boolean value that indicates whether they hold true in this case.

Strings can be compared in the same way.

```
console.log("Aardvark" < "Zoroaster")
// ▷ true
```

The way strings are ordered is more or less alphabetic: uppercase letters are always "less" than lowercase ones, so "Z" < "a" is true, and nonalphabetic characters (!, -, and so on) are also included in the ordering. The actual comparison is based on the *Unicode* standard. This standard assigns a number to virtually every character you would ever need, including characters from Greek, Arabic, Japanese, Tamil, and so on. Having such numbers is useful for storing strings inside a computer because it makes it possible to represent them as a sequence of numbers. When comparing strings, Java-Script goes over them from left to right, comparing the numeric codes of the characters one by one.

Other similar operators are >= (greater than or equal to), <= (less than or equal to), == (equal to), and != (not equal to).

```
console.log("Itchy" != "Scratchy")
// ▷ true
```

There is only one value in JavaScript that is not equal to itself, and that is NaN ("not a number").

```
console.log(NaN == NaN)
// ▷ false
```

NaN is supposed to denote the result of a nonsensical computation, and as such, it isn't equal to the result of any *other* nonsensical computations.

Logical Operators

There are also some operations that can be applied to Boolean values themselves. JavaScript supports three logical operators: *and*, *or*, and *not*. These can be used to "reason" about Booleans.

The && operator represents logical *and*. It is a binary operator, and its result is true only if both the values given to it are true.

```
console.log(true && false)
// ▷ false
console.log(true && true)
// ▷ true
```

The || operator denotes logical *or*. It produces true if either of the values given to it is true.

```
console.log(false || true)
// ▷ true
console.log(false || false)
// ▷ false
```

Not is written as an exclamation mark (!). It is a unary operator that flips the value given to it—!true produces false and !false gives true.

When mixing these Boolean operators with arithmetic and other operators, it is not always obvious when parentheses are needed. In practice, you can usually get by with knowing that of the operators we have seen so far, || has the lowest precedence, then comes &&, then the comparison operators (>, ==, and so on), and then the rest. This order has been chosen such that, in typical expressions like the following one, as few parentheses as possible are necessary:

```
1 + 1 == 2 && 10 * 10 > 50
```

The last logical operator I will discuss is not unary, not binary, but *ternary*, operating on three values. It is written with a question mark and a colon, like this:

```
console.log(true ? 1 : 2);
// ▷ 1
```

```
console.log(false ? 1 : 2);
// ▷ 2
```

This one is called the *conditional* operator (or sometimes just *ternary* operator since it is the only such operator in the language). The value on the left of the question mark "picks" which of the other two values will come out. When it is true, the middle value is chosen, and when it is false, the value on the right comes out.

Undefined Values

There are two special values, written `null` and `undefined`, that are used to denote the absence of a meaningful value. They are themselves values, but they carry no information.

Many operations in the language that don't produce a meaningful value (you'll see some later) yield `undefined` simply because they have to yield *some* value.

The difference in meaning between `undefined` and `null` is an accident of JavaScript's design, and it doesn't matter most of the time. In the cases where you actually have to concern yourself with these values, I recommend treating them as interchangeable (more on that in a moment).

Automatic Type Conversion

In the introduction, I mentioned that JavaScript goes out of its way to accept almost any program you give it, even programs that do odd things. This is nicely demonstrated by the following expressions:

```
console.log(8 * null)
// ▷ 0
console.log("5" - 1)
// ▷ 4
console.log("5" + 1)
// ▷ 51
console.log("five" * 2)
// ▷ NaN
console.log(false == 0)
// ▷ true
```

When an operator is applied to the "wrong" type of value, JavaScript will quietly convert that value to the type it wants, using a set of rules that often aren't what you want or expect. This is called *type coercion*. So the `null` in the first expression becomes 0, and the `"5"` in the second expression becomes 5 (from string to number). Yet in the third expression, + tries string concatenation before numeric addition, so the 1 is converted to `"1"` (from number to string).

When something that doesn't map to a number in an obvious way (such as "five" or undefined) is converted to a number, the value NaN is produced. Further arithmetic operations on NaN keep producing NaN, so if you find yourself getting one of those in an unexpected place, look for accidental type conversions.

When comparing values of the same type using ==, the outcome is easy to predict: you should get true when both values are the same, except in the case of NaN. But when the types differ, JavaScript uses a complicated and confusing set of rules to determine what to do. In most cases, it just tries to convert one of the values to the other value's type. However, when null or undefined occurs on either side of the operator, it produces true only if both sides are one of null or undefined.

```
console.log(null == undefined);
// ▷ true
console.log(null == 0);
// ▷ false
```

That last piece of behavior is often useful. When you want to test whether a value has a real value instead of null or undefined, you can simply compare it to null with the == (or !=) operator.

But what if you want to test whether something refers to the precise value false? The rules for converting strings and numbers to Boolean values state that 0, NaN, and the empty string ("") count as false, while all the other values count as true. Because of this, expressions like 0 == false and "" == false are also true. For cases like this, where you do *not* want any automatic type conversions to happen, there are two extra operators: === and !==. The first tests whether a value is precisely equal to the other, and the second tests whether it is not precisely equal. So "" === false is false as expected.

I recommend using the three-character comparison operators defensively to prevent unexpected type conversions from tripping you up. But when you're certain the types on both sides will be the same, there is no problem with using the shorter operators.

Short-Circuiting of Logical Operators

The logical operators && and || handle values of different types in a peculiar way. They will convert the value on their left side to Boolean type in order to decide what to do, but depending on the operator and the result of that conversion, they return either the *original* left-hand value or the right-hand value.

The || operator, for example, will return the value to its left when that can be converted to true and will return the value on its right otherwise. This conversion works as you'd expect for Boolean values and should do something analogous for values of other types.

```
console.log(null || "user")
// ▷ user
console.log("Karl" || "user")
// ▷ Karl
```

This functionality allows the || operator to be used as a way to fall back on a default value. If you give it an expression that might produce an empty value on the left, the value on the right will be used as a replacement in that case.

The && operator works similarly, but the other way around. When the value to its left is something that converts to false, it returns that value, and otherwise it returns the value on its right.

Another important property of these two operators is that the expression to their right is evaluated only when necessary. In the case of true || X, no matter what X is—even if it's an expression that does something *terrible*—the result will be true, and X is never evaluated. The same goes for false && X, which is false and will ignore X. This is called *short-circuit evaluation*.

The conditional operator works in a similar way. The first expression is always evaluated, but the second or third value, the one that is not picked, is not.

Summary

We looked at four types of JavaScript values in this chapter: numbers, strings, Booleans, and undefined values.

Such values are created by typing in their name (true, null) or value (13, "abc"). You can combine and transform values with operators. We saw binary operators for arithmetic (+, -, *, /, and %), string concatenation (+), comparison (==, !=, ===, !==, <, >, <=, >=), and logic (&&, ||), as well as several unary operators (- to negate a number, ! to negate logically, and typeof to find a value's type).

This gives you enough information to use JavaScript as a pocket calculator, but not much more. The next chapter will start tying these expressions together into basic programs.

"And my heart glows bright red under my filmy, translucent skin and they have to administer 10cc of JavaScript to get me to come back. (I respond well to toxins in the blood.) Man, that stuff will kick the peaches right out your gills!"

—why, *Why's (Poignant) Guide to Ruby*

2

PROGRAM STRUCTURE

In this chapter, we will start to do things that can actually be called *programming*. We will expand our command of the JavaScript language beyond the nouns and sentence fragments we've seen so far, to the point where we can express some meaningful prose.

Expressions and Statements

In Chapter 1, we made some values and then applied operators to them to get new values. Creating values like this is an essential part of every JavaScript program, but it is only a part.

A fragment of code that produces a value is called an *expression*. Every value that is written literally (such as 22 or "psychoanalysis") is an expression. An expression between parentheses is also an expression, as is a binary operator applied to two expressions or a unary operator applied to one.

This shows part of the beauty of a language-based interface. Expressions can nest in a way very similar to the way subsentences in human languages are nested—a subsentence can contain its own subsentences, and so on. This allows us to combine expressions to express arbitrarily complex computations.

If an expression corresponds to a sentence fragment, a JavaScript *statement* corresponds to a full sentence in a human language. A program is simply a list of statements.

The simplest kind of statement is an expression with a semicolon after it. This is a program:

```
1;
!false;
```

It is a useless program, though. An expression can be content to just produce a value, which can then be used by the enclosing expression. A statement stands on its own and amounts to something only if it affects the world. It could display something on the screen—that counts as changing the world—or it could change the internal state of the machine in a way that will affect the statements that come after it. These changes are called *side effects*. The statements in the previous example just produce the values 1 and true and then immediately throw them away. This leaves no impression on the world at all. When executing the program, nothing observable happens.

In some cases, JavaScript allows you to omit the semicolon at the end of a statement. In other cases, it has to be there, or the next line will be treated as part of the same statement. The rules for when it can be safely omitted are somewhat complex and error-prone. In this book, every statement that needs a semicolon will always be terminated by one. I recommend you do the same in your own programs, at least until you've learned more about subtleties involved in leaving out semicolons.

Variables

How does a program keep an internal state? How does it remember things? We have seen how to produce new values from old values, but this does not change the old values, and the new value has to be immediately used or it will dissipate again. To catch and hold values, JavaScript provides a thing called a *variable*.

```
var caught = 5 * 5;
```

And that gives us our second kind of statement. The special word (*keyword*) var indicates that this sentence is going to define a variable. It is followed by the name of the variable and, if we want to immediately give it a value, by an = operator and an expression.

The previous statement creates a variable called caught and uses it to grab hold of the number that is produced by multiplying 5 by 5.

After a variable has been defined, its name can be used as an expression. The value of such an expression is the value the variable currently holds. Here's an example:

```
var ten = 10;
console.log(ten * ten);
// ▷ 100
```

Variable names can be any word that isn't reserved as a keyword (such as var). They may not include spaces. Digits can also be part of variable names—catch22 is a valid name, for example—but the name must not start with a digit. A variable name cannot include punctuation, except for the characters $ and _.

When a variable points at a value, that does not mean it is tied to that value forever. The = operator can be used at any time on existing variables to disconnect them from their current value and have them point to a new one.

```
var mood = "light";
console.log(mood);
// ▷ light
mood = "dark";
console.log(mood);
// ▷ dark
```

You should imagine variables as tentacles, rather than boxes. They do not *contain* values; they *grasp* them—two variables can refer to the same value. A program can access only the values that it still has a hold on. When you need to remember something, you grow a tentacle to hold on to it or reattach one of your existing tentacles to it.

Let's look at an example. To remember the number of dollars that Luigi still owes you, you create a variable. And then when he pays back $35, you give this variable a new value.

```
var luigisDebt = 140;
luigisDebt = luigisDebt - 35;
console.log(luigisDebt);
// ▷ 105
```

When you define a variable without giving it a value, the tentacle has nothing to grasp, so it ends in thin air. If you ask for the value of an empty variable, you'll get the value undefined.

A single var statement may define multiple variables. The definitions must be separated by commas.

```
var one = 1, two = 2;
console.log(one + two);
// ▷ 3
```

Keywords and Reserved Words

Words with a special meaning, such as var, are *keywords*, and they may not be used as variable names. There are also a number of words that are "reserved for use" in future versions of JavaScript. These are also officially not allowed to be used as variable names, though some JavaScript environments do allow them. The full list of keywords and reserved words is rather long.

```
break case catch continue debugger default delete
do else false finally for function if implements
in instanceof interface let new null package private
protected public return static switch throw true
try typeof var void while with yield this
```

Don't worry about memorizing these, but remember that this might be the problem when a variable definition does not work as expected.

The Environment

The collection of variables and their values that exist at a given time is called the *environment*. When a program starts up, this environment is not empty. It always contains variables that are part of the language standard, and most of the time, it has variables that provide ways to interact with the surrounding system. For example, in a browser, there are variables and functions to inspect and influence the currently loaded website and to read mouse and keyboard input.

Functions

A lot of the values provided in the default environment have the type *function*. A function is a piece of program wrapped in a value. Such values can be *applied* in order to run the wrapped program. For example, in a browser environment, the variable `alert` holds a function that shows a little dialog box with a message. It is used like this:

```
alert("Good morning!");
```

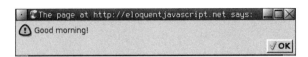

Executing a function is called *invoking, calling,* or *applying* it. You can call a function by putting parentheses after an expression that produces a function value. Usually you'll directly use the name of the variable that holds the function. The values between the parentheses are given to the program inside the function. In the example, the alert function uses the string that we give it as the text to show in the dialog box. Values given to functions are called *arguments*. The alert function needs only one of them, but other functions might need a different number or different types of arguments.

The console.log Function

The alert function can be useful as an output device when experimenting, but clicking away all those little windows will get on your nerves. In past examples, we've used `console.log` to output values. Most JavaScript systems (including all modern web browsers and Node.js) provide a `console.log` function that writes out its arguments to *some* text output device. In browsers, the output lands in the JavaScript console. This part of the browser interface is hidden by default, but most browsers open it when you press F12 or, on Mac, when you press COMMAND-OPTION-I. If that does not work, search through the menus for an item named "web console" or "developer tools."

```
var x = 30;
console.log("the value of x is", x);
// ▷ the value of x is 30
```

Though variable names cannot contain period characters, `console.log` clearly has one. This is because `console.log` isn't a simple variable. It is actually an expression that retrieves the `log` property from the value held by the `console` variable. We will find out exactly what this means in Chapter 4.

Return Values

Showing a dialog box or writing text to the screen is a *side effect*. A lot of functions are useful because of the side effects they produce. Functions may also produce values, and in that case, they don't need to have a side effect to be useful. For example, the function Math.max takes any number of number values and gives back the greatest.

```
console.log(Math.max(2, 4));
// ▷ 4
```

When a function produces a value, it is said to *return* that value. Anything that produces a value is an expression in JavaScript, which means function calls can be used within larger expressions. Here a call to Math.min, which is the opposite of Math.max, is used as an input to the plus operator:

```
console.log(Math.min(2, 4) + 100);
// ▷ 102
```

The next chapter explains how to write your own functions.

Prompt and Confirm

Browser environments contain other functions besides alert for popping up windows. You can ask the user an OK/Cancel question using confirm. This returns a Boolean: true if the user clicks OK and false if the user clicks Cancel.

```
confirm("Shall we, then?");
```

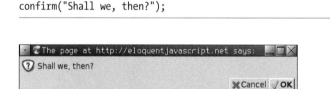

The prompt function can be used to ask an "open" question. The first argument is the question, the second one is the text that the user starts with. A line of text can be typed into the dialog window, and the function will return this text as a string.

```
prompt("Tell me everything you know.", "...");
```

These two functions aren't used much in modern web programming, mostly because you have no control over the way the resulting windows look, but they are useful for toy programs and experiments.

Control Flow

When your program contains more than one statement, the statements are executed, predictably, from top to bottom. As a basic example, this program has two statements. The first one asks the user for a number, and the second, which is executed afterward, shows the square of that number.

```
var theNumber = Number(prompt("Pick a number", ""));
alert("Your number is the square root of " +
      theNumber * theNumber);
```

The function `Number` converts a value to a number. We need that conversion because the result of `prompt` is a string value, and we want a number. There are similar functions called `String` and `Boolean` that convert values to those types.

Here is the rather trivial schematic representation of straight control flow:

Conditional Execution

Executing statements in straight-line order isn't the only option we have. An alternative is *conditional execution*, where we choose between two different routes based on a Boolean value, like this:

Conditional execution is written with the `if` keyword in JavaScript. In the simple case, we just want some code to be executed if, and only if, a certain condition holds. For example, in the previous program, we might want to show the square of the input only if the input is actually a number.

```
var theNumber = prompt("Pick a number", "");
if (!isNaN(theNumber))
  alert("Your number is the square root of " +
        theNumber * theNumber);
```

With this modification, if you enter "cheese," no output will be shown.

The keyword if executes or skips a statement depending on the value of a Boolean expression. The deciding expression is written after the keywords, between parentheses, followed by the statement to execute.

The isNaN function is a standard JavaScript function that returns true only if the argument it is given is NaN. The Number function happens to return NaN when you give it a string that doesn't represent a valid number. Thus, the condition translates to "unless theNumber is not-a-number, do this."

You often won't just have code that executes when a condition holds true, but also code that handles the other case. This alternate path is represented by the second arrow in the diagram. The else keyword can be used, together with if, to create two separate, alternative execution paths.

```
var theNumber = Number(prompt("Pick a number", ""));
if (!isNaN(theNumber))
  alert("Your number is the square root of " +
        theNumber * theNumber);
else
  alert("Hey. Why didn't you give me a number?");
```

If we have more than two paths to choose from, multiple if/else pairs can be "chained" together. Here's an example:

```
var num = Number(prompt("Pick a number", "0"));

if (num < 10)
  alert("Small");
else if (num < 100)
  alert("Medium");
else
  alert("Large");
```

The program will first check whether num is less than 10. If it is, it chooses that branch, shows "Small", and is done. If it isn't, it takes the else branch, which itself contains a second if. If the second condition (< 100) holds, that means the number is between 10 and 100, and "Medium" is shown. If it doesn't, the second, and last, else branch is chosen.

The flow chart for this program looks something like this:

while and do Loops

Consider a program that prints all even numbers from 0 to 12. One way to write this is as follows:

```
console.log(0);
console.log(2);
console.log(4);
console.log(6);
console.log(8);
console.log(10);
console.log(12);
```

That works, but the idea of writing a program is to make something *less* work, not more. If we needed all even numbers less than 1,000, the previous would be unworkable. What we need is a way to repeat some code. This form of control flow is called a loop.

Looping control flow allows us to go back to some point in the program where we were before and repeat it with our current program state. If we combine this with a variable that counts, we can do something like this:

```
var number = 0;
while (number <= 12) {
  console.log(number);
  number = number + 2;
}
// ▷ 0
// ▷ 2
//   ... etcetera
```

A statement starting with the keyword while creates a loop. The word while is followed by an expression in parentheses and then a statement, much like if. The loop executes that statement as long as the expression produces a value that is true when converted to Boolean type.

In this loop, we want to both print the current number and add two to our variable. Whenever we need to execute multiple statements inside a loop, we wrap them in braces, { and }. Braces do for statements what parentheses do for expressions: they group them together, making them count as a single statement. A sequence of statements wrapped in braces is called a *block*.

Many JavaScript programmers wrap every single loop or if body in braces. They do this both for the sake of consistency and to avoid having to add or remove braces when changing the number of statements in the body later.

In this book, I will write most single-statement bodies without braces, since I value brevity. You are free to go with whichever style you prefer.

The variable `number` demonstrates the way a variable can track the progress of a program. Every time the loop repeats, `number` is incremented by 2. Then, at the beginning of every repetition, it is compared with the number 12 to decide whether the program has done all the work it intended to do.

As an example that actually does something useful, we can now write a program that calculates and shows the value of 2^{10} (2 to the 10th power). We use two variables: one to keep track of our result and one to count how often we have multiplied this result by 2. The loop tests whether the second variable has reached 10 yet and then updates both variables.

```
var result = 1;
var counter = 0;
while (counter < 10) {
  result = result * 2;
  counter = counter + 1;
}
console.log(result);
// ▷ 1024
```

The counter could also start at 1 and check for `<= 10`, but, for reasons that will become apparent in Chapter 4, it is a good idea to get used to counting from 0.

The do loop is a control structure similar to the `while` loop. It differs only on one point: a do loop always executes its body at least once, and it starts testing whether it should stop only after that first execution. To reflect this, the test appears after the body of the loop:

```
do {
  var yourName = prompt("Who are you?");
} while (!yourName);
console.log(yourName);
```

This program will force you to enter a name. It will ask again and again until it gets something that is not an empty string. Applying the ! operator will convert a value to Boolean type before negating it, and all strings except "" convert to true.

Indenting Code

You've probably noticed the spaces I put in front of some statements. In JavaScript, these are not required—the computer will accept the program just fine without them. In fact, even the line breaks in programs are optional. You could write a program as a single long line if you felt like it. The role of the indentation inside blocks is to make the structure of the code stand out. In complex code, where new blocks are opened inside other blocks, it can become hard to see where one block ends and another begins. With proper indentation, the visual shape of a program corresponds to the shape of the blocks inside it. I like to use two spaces for every open block, but tastes differ—some people use four spaces, and some people use tab characters.

for Loops

Many loops follow the pattern seen in the previous while examples. First, a "counter" variable is created to track the progress of the loop. Then comes a while loop, whose test expression usually checks whether the counter has reached some boundary yet. At the end of the loop body, the counter is updated to track progress.

Because this pattern is so common, JavaScript and similar languages provide a slightly shorter and more comprehensive form, the for loop.

```
for (var number = 0; number <= 12; number = number + 2)
  console.log(number);
// ▷ 0
// ▷ 2
//   ... etcetera
```

This program is exactly equivalent to the earlier even number printing example. The only change is that all the statements that are related to the "state" of the loop are now grouped together.

The parentheses after a for keyword must contain two semicolons. The part before the first semicolon *initializes* the loop, usually by defining a variable. The second part is the expression that *checks* whether the loop must continue. The final part *updates* the state of the loop after every iteration. In most cases, this is shorter and clearer than a while construct.

Here is the code that computes 2^{10}, using for instead of while:

```
var result = 1;
for (var counter = 0; counter < 10; counter = counter + 1)
  result = result * 2;
console.log(result);
// ▷ 1024
```

Note that even though no block is opened with a {, the statement in the loop is still indented two spaces to make it clear that it "belongs" to the line before it.

Breaking Out of a Loop

Having the loop's condition produce false is not the only way a loop can finish. There is a special statement called break that has the effect of immediately jumping out of the enclosing loop.

This program illustrates the break statement. It finds the first number that is both greater than or equal to 20 and divisible by 7.

```
for (var current = 20; ; current++) {
  if (current % 7 == 0)
    break;
}
console.log(current);
// ▷ 21
```

Using the remainder (%) operator is an easy way to test whether a number is divisible by another number. If it is, the remainder of their division is zero.

The for construct in the example does not have a part that checks for the end of the loop. This means that the loop will never stop unless the break statement inside is executed.

If you were to leave out that break statement or accidentally write a condition that always produces true, your program would get stuck in an *infinite loop*. A program stuck in an infinite loop will never finish running, which is usually a bad thing.

The continue keyword is similar to break, in that it influences the progress of a loop. When continue is encountered in a loop body, control jumps out of the body and continues with the loop's next iteration.

Updating Variables Succinctly

Especially when looping, a program often needs to "update" a variable to hold a value based on that variable's previous value.

```
counter = counter + 1;
```

JavaScript provides a shortcut for this:

```
counter += 1;
```

Similar shortcuts work for many other operators, such as result *= 2 to double result or counter -= 1 to count downward.

This allows us to shorten our counting example a little more.

```
for (var number = 0; number <= 12; number += 2)
  console.log(number);
```

For counter += 1 and counter -= 1, there are even shorter equivalents: counter++ and counter- -.

Dispatching on a Value with switch

It is common for code to look like this:

```
if (variable == "value1") action1();
else if (variable == "value2") action2();
else if (variable == "value3") action3();
else defaultAction();
```

There is a construct called switch that is intended to solve such a "dispatch" in a more direct way. Unfortunately, the syntax JavaScript uses for this (which it inherited from the C/Java line of programming languages) is somewhat awkward—a chain of if statements often looks better. Here is an example:

```
switch (prompt("What is the weather like?")) {
  case "rainy":
    console.log("Remember to bring an umbrella.");
    break;
  case "sunny":
    console.log("Dress lightly.");
  case "cloudy":
    console.log("Go outside.");
    break;
  default:
    console.log("Unknown weather type!");
    break;
}
```

You may put any number of case labels inside the block opened by switch. The program will jump to the label that corresponds to the value that switch was given or to default if no matching value is found. It starts executing statements there, even if they're under another label, until it reaches a break statement. In some cases, such as the "sunny" case in the example, this can be used to share some code between cases (it recommends going outside for both sunny and cloudy weather). But beware: it is easy to forget such a break, which will cause the program to execute code you do not want executed.

Capitalization

Variable names may not contain spaces, yet it is often helpful to use multiple words to clearly describe what the variable represents. These are pretty much your choices for writing a variable name with several words in it:

```
fuzzylittleturtle
fuzzy_little_turtle
FuzzyLittleTurtle
fuzzyLittleTurtle
```

The first style can be hard to read. Personally, I like the look of the underscores, though that style is a little painful to type. The standard JavaScript functions, and most JavaScript programmers, follow the bottom style—they capitalize every word except the first. It is not hard to get used to little things like that, and code with mixed naming styles can be jarring to read, so we will just follow this convention.

In a few cases, such as the Number function, the first letter of a variable is also capitalized. This was done to mark this function as a constructor. What a constructor is will become clear in Chapter 6. For now, the important thing is not to be bothered by this apparent lack of consistency.

Comments

Often, raw code does not convey all the information you want a program to convey to human readers, or it conveys it in such a cryptic way that people might not understand it. At other times, you might just feel poetic or want to include some thoughts as part of your program. This is what *comments* are for.

A comment is a piece of text that is part of a program but is completely ignored by the computer. JavaScript has two ways of writing comments. To write a single-line comment, you can use two slash characters (//) and then the comment text after it.

```
var accountBalance = calculateBalance(account);
// It's a green hollow where a river sings
accountBalance.adjust();
// Madly catching white tatters in the grass.
var report = new Report();
// Where the sun on the proud mountain rings:
addToReport(accountBalance, report);
// It's a little valley, foaming like light in a glass.
```

A // comment goes only to the end of the line. A section of text between /* and */ will be ignored, regardless of whether it contains line breaks. This is often useful for adding blocks of information about a file or a chunk of program.

```
/*
I first found this number scrawled on the back of one of
my notebooks a few years ago. Since then, it has often
dropped by, showing up in phone numbers and the serial
numbers of products that I've bought. It obviously likes
me, so I've decided to keep it.
*/
var myNumber = 11213;
```

Summary

You now know that a program is built out of statements, which themselves sometimes contain more statements. Statements tend to contain expressions, which themselves can be built out of smaller expressions.

Putting statements after one another gives you a program that is executed from top to bottom. You can introduce disturbances in the flow of control by using conditional (if, else, and switch) and looping (while, do, and for) statements.

Variables can be used to file pieces of data under a name, and they are useful for tracking states in your program. The environment is the set of variables that are defined. JavaScript systems always put a number of useful standard variables into your environment.

Functions are special values that encapsulate a piece of a program. You can invoke them by writing functionName(argument1, argument2). Such a function call is an expression, and may produce a value.

Exercises

If you are unsure how to check your solutions to the exercises, refer to the introduction.

Each exercise starts with a problem description. Read that and try to solve the exercise. If you run into problems, consider reading the hints at the end of the book. Full solutions to the exercises are not included in this book, but you can find them online at *http://eloquentjavascript.net/code/*. If you want to learn something from the exercises, I recommend looking at the solutions only after you've solved the exercise, or at least after you've attacked it long and hard enough to have a slight headache.

Looping a Triangle

Write a loop that makes seven calls to console.log to output the following triangle:

```
#
##
###
####
#####
######
#######
```

It may be useful to know that you can find the length of a string by writing .length after it.

```
var abc = "abc";
console.log(abc.length);
// ▷ 3
```

FizzBuzz

Write a program that uses `console.log` to print all the numbers from 1 to 100, with two exceptions. For numbers divisible by 3, print "Fizz" instead of the number, and for numbers divisible by 5 (and not 3), print "Buzz" instead.

When you have that working, modify your program to print "FizzBuzz" for numbers that are divisible by both 3 and 5.

(This is actually an interview question that has been claimed to weed out a significant percentage of programmer candidates. So if you solved it, you're now allowed to feel good about yourself.)

Chess Board

Write a program that creates a string that represents an 8×8 grid, using newline characters to separate lines. At each position of the grid there is either a space or a "#" character. The characters should form a chess board.

Passing this string to `console.log` should show something like this:

```
# # # #
 # # # #
# # # #
 # # # #
# # # #
 # # # #
# # # #
 # # # #
```

When you have a program that generates this pattern, define a variable size = 8 and change the program so that it works for any size, outputting a grid of the given width and height.

"People think that computer science is the art of geniuses but the actual reality is the opposite, just many people doing things that build on each other, like a wall of mini stones."

—Donald Knuth

3

FUNCTIONS

You've seen function values, such as alert, and how
to call them. Functions are the bread and butter of
JavaScript programming. The concept of wrapping a
piece of program in a value has many uses. It is a tool
to structure larger programs, to reduce repetition, to
associate names with subprograms, and to isolate these
subprograms from each other.

The most obvious application of functions is defining new vocabulary.
Creating new words in regular, human-language prose is usually bad style.
But in programming, it is indispensable.

Typical adult English speakers have some 20,000 words in their vocabulary. Few programming languages come with 20,000 commands built in.
And the vocabulary that *is* available tends to be more precisely defined, and
thus less flexible, than in human language. Therefore, we usually *have* to
add some of our own vocabulary to avoid repeating ourselves too much.

Defining a Function

A function definition is just a regular variable definition where the value given to the variable happens to be a function. For example, the following code defines the variable square to refer to a function that produces the square of a given number:

```
var square = function(x) {
  return x * x;
};

console.log(square(12));
// ▷ 144
```

A function is created by an expression that starts with the keyword function. Functions have a set of *parameters* (in this case, only x) and a *body*, which contains the statements that are to be executed when the function is called. The function body must always be wrapped in braces, even when it consists of only a single statement (as in the previous example).

A function can have multiple parameters or no parameters at all. In the following example, makeNoise does not list any parameter names, whereas power lists two:

```
var makeNoise = function() {
  console.log("Pling!");
};

makeNoise();
// ▷ Pling!

var power = function(base, exponent) {
  var result = 1;
  for (var count = 0; count < exponent; count++)
    result *= base;
  return result;
};

console.log(power(2, 10));
// ▷ 1024
```

Some functions produce a value, such as power and square, and some don't, such as makeNoise, which produces only a side effect. A return statement determines the value the function returns. When control comes across such a statement, it immediately jumps out of the current function and gives the returned value to the code that called the function. The return keyword without an expression after it will cause the function to return undefined.

Parameters and Scopes

The parameters to a function behave like regular variables, but their initial values are given by the *caller* of the function, not the code in the function itself.

An important property of functions is that the variables created inside of them, including their parameters, are *local* to the function. This means, for example, that the result variable in the power example will be newly created every time the function is called, and these separate incarnations do not interfere with each other.

This "localness" of variables applies only to the parameters and to variables declared with the var keyword inside the function body. Variables declared outside of any function are called *global*, because they are visible throughout the program. It is possible to access such variables from inside a function, as long as you haven't declared a local variable with the same name.

The following code demonstrates this. It defines and calls two functions that both assign a value to the variable x. The first one declares the variable as local and thus changes only the local variable. The second does not declare x locally, so references to x inside of it refer to the global variable x defined at the top of the example.

```
var x = "outside";

var f1 = function() {
  var x = "inside f1";
};
f1();
console.log(x);
// ▷ outside

var f2 = function() {
  x = "inside f2";
};
f2();
console.log(x);
// ▷ inside f2
```

This behavior helps prevent accidental interference between functions. If all variables were shared by the whole program, it'd take a lot of effort to make sure no name is ever used for two different purposes. And if you *did* reuse a variable name, you might see strange effects from unrelated code messing with the value of your variable. By treating function-local variables as existing only within the function, the language makes it possible to read and understand functions as small universes, without having to worry about all the code at once.

Nested Scopes

JavaScript distinguishes not just between *global* and *local* variables. Functions can be created inside other functions, producing several degrees of locality.

For example, this rather nonsensical function has two functions inside of it:

```
var landscape = function() {
  var result = "";
  var flat = function(size) {
    for (var count = 0; count < size; count++)
      result += "_";
  };
  var mountain = function(size) {
    result += "/";
    for (var count = 0; count < size; count++)
      result += "'";
    result += "\\";
  };

  flat(3);
  mountain(4);
  flat(6);
  mountain(1);
  flat(1);
  return result;
};

console.log(landscape());
// ▷ ___/''''_____/'\_
```

The flat and mountain functions can "see" the variable called result, since they are inside the function that defines it. But they cannot see each other's count variables since they are outside each other's scope. The environment outside of the landscape function doesn't see any of the variables defined inside landscape.

In short, each local scope can also see all the local scopes that contain it. The set of variables visible inside a function is determined by the place of that function in the program text. All variables from blocks *around* a function's definition are visible—meaning both those in function bodies that enclose it and those at the top level of the program. This approach to variable visibility is called *lexical scoping*.

People who have experience with other programming languages might expect that any block of code between braces produces a new local environment. But in JavaScript, functions are the only things that create a new scope. You are allowed to use free-standing blocks.

```
var something = 1;
{
  var something = 2;
  // Do stuff with variable something...
}
// Outside of the block again...
```

But the something inside the block refers to the same variable as the one outside the block. In fact, although blocks like this are allowed, they are useful only to group the body of an if statement or a loop.

If you find this odd, you're not alone. The next version of JavaScript will introduce a let keyword, which works like var but creates a variable that is local to the enclosing *block*, not the enclosing *function*.

Functions as Values

Function variables usually simply act as names for a specific piece of the program. Such a variable is defined once and never changed. This makes it easy to start confusing the function and its name.

But the two are different. A function value can do all the things that other values can do—you can use it in arbitrary expressions, not just call it. It is possible to store a function value in a new place, pass it as an argument to a function, and so on. Similarly, a variable that holds a function is still just a regular variable and can be assigned a new value, like so:

```
var launchMissiles = function(value) {
  missileSystem.launch("now");
};
if (safeMode)
  launchMissiles = function(value) {/* do nothing */};
```

In Chapter 5, we will discuss the wonderful things that can be done by passing around function values to other functions.

Declaration Notation

There is a slightly shorter way to say "var square = function...". The function keyword can also be used at the start of a statement, as in the following:

```
function square(x) {
  return x * x;
}
```

This is a function *declaration*. The statement defines the variable square and points it at the given function. So far so good. There is one subtlety with this form of function definition, however.

```
console.log("The future says:", future());

function future() {
  return "We STILL have no flying cars.";
}
```

This code works, even though the function is defined *below* the code that uses it. This is because function declarations are not part of the regular top-to-bottom flow of control. They are conceptually moved to the top of their scope and can be used by all the code in that scope. This is sometimes useful because it gives us the freedom to order code in a way that seems meaningful, without worrying about having to define all functions above their first use.

What happens when you put such a function definition inside a conditional (if) block or a loop? Well, don't do that. Different JavaScript platforms in different browsers have traditionally done different things in that situation, and the latest standard actually forbids it. If you want your programs to behave consistently, only use this form of function-defining statements in the outermost block of a function or program.

```
function example() {
  function a() {} // Okay
  if (something) {
    function b() {} // Danger!
  }
}
```

The Call Stack

It will be helpful to take a closer look at the way control flows through functions. Here is a simple program that makes a few function calls:

```
function greet(who) {
  console.log("Hello " + who);
}
greet("Harry");
console.log("Bye");
```

A run through this program goes roughly like this: the call to greet causes control to jump to the start of that function (line 2). It calls console .log (a built-in browser function), which takes control, does its job, and then returns control to line 2. Then it reaches the end of the greet function, so it returns to the place that called it, at line 4. The line after that calls console .log again.

We could show the flow of control schematically like this:

```
top
   greet
         console.log
   greet
top
   console.log
top
```

Because a function has to jump back to the place of the call when it returns, the computer must remember the context from which the function was called. In one case, console.log has to jump back to the greet function. In the other case, it jumps back to the end of the program.

The place where the computer stores this context is the *call stack*. Every time a function is called, the current context is put on top of this "stack." When the function returns, it removes the top context from the stack and uses it to continue execution.

Storing this stack requires space in the computer's memory. When the stack grows too big, the computer will fail with a message like "out of stack space" or "too much recursion." The following code illustrates this by asking the computer a really hard question, which causes an infinite back-and-forth between two functions. Rather, it *would* be infinite, if the computer had an infinite stack. As it is, we will run out of space, or "blow the stack."

```
function chicken() {
  return egg();
}
function egg() {
  return chicken();
}
console.log(chicken() + " came first.");
// ▷ ??
```

Optional Arguments

The following code is allowed and executes without any problem:

```
alert("Hello", "Good Evening", "How do you do?");
```

The function alert officially accepts only one argument. Yet when you call it like this, it doesn't complain. It simply ignores the other arguments and shows you "Hello."

JavaScript is extremely broad-minded about the number of arguments you pass to a function. If you pass too many, the extra ones are ignored. If you pass too few, the missing parameters simply get assigned the value undefined.

The downside of this is that it is possible—likely, even—that you'll accidentally pass the wrong number of arguments to functions and no one will tell you about it.

The upside is that this behavior can be used to have a function take "optional" arguments. For example, the following version of power can be called either with two arguments or with a single argument, in which case the exponent is assumed to be two, and the function behaves like square.

```
function power(base, exponent) {
  if (exponent == undefined)
    exponent = 2;
  var result = 1;
  for (var count = 0; count < exponent; count++)
    result *= base;
  return result;
}

console.log(power(4));
// ▷ 16
console.log(power(4, 3));
// ▷ 64
```

In the next chapter, we will see a way in which a function body can get at the exact list of arguments that were passed. This is helpful because it makes it possible for a function to accept any number of arguments. For example, console.log makes use of this—it outputs all of the values it is given.

```
console.log("R", 2, "D", 2);
// ▷ R 2 D 2
```

Closure

The ability to treat functions as values, combined with the fact that local variables are "re-created" every time a function is called, brings up an interesting question. What happens to local variables when the function call that created them is no longer active?

The following code shows an example of this. It defines a function, wrapValue, which creates a local variable. It then returns a function that accesses and returns this local variable.

```
function wrapValue(n) {
  var localVariable = n;
  return function() { return localVariable; };
}
```

```
var wrap1 = wrapValue(1);
var wrap2 = wrapValue(2);
console.log(wrap1());
// ▷ 1
console.log(wrap2());
// ▷ 2
```

This is allowed and works as you'd hope—the variable can still be accessed. In fact, multiple instances of the variable can be alive at the same time, which is another good illustration of the concept that local variables really are re-created for every call—different calls can't trample on one another's local variables.

This feature—being able to reference a specific instance of local variables in an enclosing function—is called *closure*. A function that "closes over" some local variables is called *a* closure. This behavior not only frees you from having to worry about lifetimes of variables but also allows for some creative use of function values.

With a slight change, we can turn the previous example into a way to create functions that multiply by an arbitrary amount.

```
function multiplier(factor) {
  return function(number) {
    return number * factor;
  };
}

var twice = multiplier(2);
console.log(twice(5));
// ▷ 10
```

The explicit localVariable from the wrapValue example isn't needed since a parameter is itself a local variable.

Thinking about programs like this takes some practice. A good mental model is to think of the function keyword as "freezing" the code in its body and wrapping it into a package (the function value). So when you read return function(...) {...}, think of it as returning a handle to a piece of computation, frozen for later use.

In the example, multiplier returns a frozen chunk of code that gets stored in the twice variable. The last line then calls the value in this variable, causing the frozen code (return number * factor;) to be activated. It still has access to the factor variable from the multiplier call that created it, and in addition it gets access to the argument passed when unfreezing it, 5, through its number parameter.

Recursion

It is perfectly okay for a function to call itself, as long as it takes care not to overflow the stack. A function that calls itself is called *recursive*. Recursion allows some functions to be written in a different style. Take, for example, this alternative implementation of power:

```
function power(base, exponent) {
  if (exponent == 0)
    return 1;
  else
    return base * power(base, exponent - 1);
}

console.log(power(2, 3));
// ▷ 8
```

This is rather close to the way mathematicians define exponentiation and arguably describes the concept in a more elegant way than the looping variant does. The function calls itself multiple times with different arguments to achieve the repeated multiplication.

But this implementation has one important problem: in typical JavaScript implementations, it's about 10 times slower than the looping version. Running through a simple loop is a lot cheaper than calling a function multiple times.

The dilemma of speed versus elegance is an interesting one. You can see it as a kind of continuum between human-friendliness and machine-friendliness. Almost any program can be made faster by making it bigger and more convoluted. The programmer must decide on an appropriate balance.

In the case of the earlier power function, the inelegant (looping) version is still fairly simple and easy to read. It doesn't make much sense to replace it with the recursive version. Often, though, a program deals with such complex concepts that giving up some efficiency in order to make the program more straightforward becomes an attractive choice.

The basic rule, which has been repeated by many programmers and with which I wholeheartedly agree, is to not worry about efficiency until you know for sure that the program is too slow. If it is, find out which parts are taking up the most time, and start exchanging elegance for efficiency in those parts.

Of course, this rule doesn't mean one should start ignoring performance altogether. In many cases, like the power function, not much simplicity is gained from the "elegant" approach. And sometimes an experienced programmer can see right away that a simple approach is never going to be fast enough.

The reason I'm stressing this is that, surprisingly, many beginning programmers focus fanatically on efficiency, even in the smallest details. The result is bigger, more complicated, and often less correct programs, that take longer to write than their more straightforward equivalents and that usually run only marginally faster.

But recursion is not always just a less-efficient alternative to looping. Some problems are much easier to solve with recursion than with loops. Most often these are problems that require exploring or processing several "branches," each of which might branch out again into more branches.

Consider this puzzle: by starting from the number 1 and repeatedly either adding 5 or multiplying by 3, an infinite amount of new numbers can be produced. How would you write a function that, given a number, tries to find a sequence of such additions and multiplications that produce that number? For example, the number 13 could be reached by first multiplying by 3 and then adding 5 twice, whereas the number 15 cannot be reached at all.

Here is a recursive solution:

```
function findSolution(target) {
  function find(start, history) {
    if (start == target)
      return history;
    else if (start > target)
      return null;
    else
      return find(start + 5, "(" + history + " + 5)") ||
             find(start * 3, "(" + history + " * 3)");
  }
  return find(1, "1");
}

console.log(findSolution(24));
// ▷ (((1 * 3) + 5) * 3)
```

Note that this program doesn't necessarily find the *shortest* sequence of operations. It is satisfied when it finds any sequence at all.

I don't necessarily expect you to see how it works right away. But let's work through it, since it makes for a great exercise in recursive thinking.

The inner function find does the actual recursing. It takes two arguments—the current number and a string that records how we reached this number—and returns either a string that shows how to get to the target or null.

To do this, the function performs one of three actions. If the current number is the target number, the current history is a way to reach that target, so it is simply returned. If the current number is greater than the target, there's no sense in further exploring this history since both adding and multiplying will only make the number bigger. And finally, if we're still below the target, the function tries both possible paths that start from the current number, by calling itself twice, once for each of the allowed next steps. If the first call returns something that is not null, it is returned. Otherwise, the second call is returned—regardless of whether it produces a string or null.

To better understand how this function produces the effect we're looking for, let's look at all the calls to find that are made when searching for a solution for the number 13.

```
find(1, "1")
  find(6, "(1 + 5)")
    find(11, "((1 + 5) + 5)")
      find(16, "(((1 + 5) + 5) + 5)")
        too big
      find(33, "(((1 + 5) + 5) * 3)")
        too big
    find(18, "((1 + 5) * 3)")
      too big
  find(3, "(1 * 3)")
    find(8, "((1 * 3) + 5)")
      find(13, "(((1 * 3) + 5) + 5)")
        found!
```

The indentation suggests the depth of the call stack. The first time find is called, it calls itself twice to explore the solutions that start with (1 + 5) and (1 * 3). The first call tries to find a solution that starts with (1 + 5) and, using recursion, explores *every* solution that yields a number less than or equal to the target number. Since it doesn't find a solution that hits the target, it returns null back to the first call. There the || operator causes the call that explores (1 * 3) to happen. This search has more luck because its first recursive call, through yet *another* recursive call, hits upon the target number, 13. This innermost recursive call returns a string, and each of the || operators in the intermediate calls pass that string along, ultimately returning our solution.

Growing Functions

There are two more or less natural ways for functions to be introduced into programs.

The first is that you find yourself writing very similar code multiple times. We want to avoid doing that since having more code means more space for mistakes to hide and more material to read for people trying to understand the program. So we take the repeated functionality, find a good name for it, and put it into a function.

The second way is that you find you need some functionality that you haven't written yet and that sounds like it deserves its own function. You'll start by naming the function, and you'll then write its body. You might even start writing code that uses the function before you actually define the function itself.

How difficult it is to find a good name for a function is a good indication of how clear a concept it is that you're trying to wrap. Let's go through an example.

We want to write a program that prints two numbers, the numbers of cows and chickens on a farm, with the words Cows and Chickens after them, and zeros padded before both numbers so that they are always three digits long.

```
007 Cows
011 Chickens
```

That clearly asks for a function of two arguments. Let's get coding.

```
function printFarmInventory(cows, chickens) {
  var cowString = String(cows);
  while (cowString.length < 3)
    cowString = "0" + cowString;
  console.log(cowString + " Cows");
  var chickenString = String(chickens);
  while (chickenString.length < 3)
    chickenString = "0" + chickenString;
  console.log(chickenString + " Chickens");
}
printFarmInventory(7, 11);
```

Adding .length after a string value will give us the length of that string. Thus, the while loops keep adding zeros in front of the number strings until they are at least three characters long.

Mission accomplished! But just as we are about to send the farmer the code (along with a hefty invoice, of course), he calls and tells us he's also started keeping pigs, and couldn't we please extend the software to also print pigs?

We sure can. But just as we're in the process of copying and pasting those four lines one more time, we stop and reconsider. There has to be a better way. Here's a first attempt:

```
function printZeroPaddedWithLabel(number, label) {
  var numberString = String(number);
  while (numberString.length < 3)
    numberString = "0" + numberString;
  console.log(numberString + " " + label);
}

function printFarmInventory(cows, chickens, pigs) {
  printZeroPaddedWithLabel(cows, "Cows");
  printZeroPaddedWithLabel(chickens, "Chickens");
  printZeroPaddedWithLabel(pigs, "Pigs");
}

printFarmInventory(7, 11, 3);
```

It works! But that name, `printZeroPaddedWithLabel`, is a little awkward. It conflates three things—printing, zero-padding, and adding a label—into a single function.

Instead of lifting out the repeated part of our program wholesale, let's try to pick out a single *concept*.

```
function zeroPad(number, width) {
  var string = String(number);
  while (string.length < width)
    string = "0" + string;
  return string;
}

function printFarmInventory(cows, chickens, pigs) {
  console.log(zeroPad(cows, 3) + " Cows");
  console.log(zeroPad(chickens, 3) + " Chickens");
  console.log(zeroPad(pigs, 3) + " Pigs");
}

printFarmInventory(7, 16, 3);
```

A function with a nice, obvious name like `zeroPad` makes it easier for someone who reads the code to figure out what it does. And it is useful in more situations than just this specific program. For example, you could use it to help print nicely aligned tables of numbers.

How smart and versatile should our function be? We could write anything from a terribly simple function that simply pads a number so that it's three characters wide to a complicated generalized number-formatting system that handles fractional numbers, negative numbers, alignment of dots, padding with different characters, and so on.

A useful principle is not to add cleverness unless you are absolutely sure you're going to need it. It can be tempting to write general "frameworks" for every little bit of functionality you come across. Resist that urge. You won't get any real work done, and you'll end up writing a lot of code that no one will ever use.

Functions and Side Effects

Functions can be roughly divided into those that are called for their side effects and those that are called for their return value. (Though it is definitely also possible to have both side effects and return a value.)

The first helper function in the farm example, `printZeroPaddedWithLabel`, is called for its side effect: it prints a line. The second version, `zeroPad`, is called for its return value. It is no coincidence that the second is useful in more situations than the first. Functions that create values are easier to combine in new ways than functions that directly perform side effects.

A *pure* function is a specific kind of value-producing function that not only has no side effects but also doesn't rely on side effects from other code—for example, it doesn't read global variables that are occasionally changed by other code. A pure function has the pleasant property that, when called with the same arguments, it always produces the same value (and doesn't do anything else). This makes it easy to reason about. A call to such a function can be mentally substituted by its result, without changing the meaning of the code. When you are not sure that a pure function is working correctly, you can test it by simply calling it, and know that if it works in that context, it will work in any context. Nonpure functions might return different values based on all kinds of factors and have side effects that might be hard to test and think about.

Still, there's no need to feel bad when writing functions that are not pure or to wage a holy war to purge them from your code. Side effects are often useful. There'd be no way to write a pure version of console.log, for example, and console.log is certainly useful. Some operations are also easier to express in an efficient way when we use side effects, so computing speed can be a reason to avoid purity.

Summary

This chapter taught you how to write your own functions. The function keyword, when used as an expression, can create a function value. When used as a statement, it can be used to declare a variable and give it a function as its value.

```
// Create a function value f
var f = function(a) {
  console.log(a + 2);
};

// Declare g to be a function
function g(a, b) {
  return a * b * 3.5;
}
```

A key aspect in understanding functions is understanding local scopes. Parameters and variables declared inside a function are local to the function, re-created every time the function is called, and not visible from the outside. Functions declared inside another function have access to the outer function's local scope.

Separating the tasks your program performs into different functions is helpful. You won't have to repeat yourself as much, and functions can make a program more readable by grouping code into conceptual chunks, in the same way that chapters and sections help organize regular text.

Exercises

Minimum

The previous chapter introduced the standard function Math.min that returns its smallest argument. We can do that ourselves now. Write a function min that takes two arguments and returns their minimum.

Recursion

We've seen that % (the remainder operator) can be used to test whether a number is even or odd by using % 2 to check whether it's divisible by two. Here's another way to define whether a positive whole number is even or odd:

- Zero is even.

- One is odd.

- For any other number N, its evenness is the same as $N - 2$.

Define a recursive function isEven corresponding to this description. The function should accept a number parameter and return a Boolean.

Test it on 50 and 75. See how it behaves on -1. Why? Can you think of a way to fix this?

Bean Counting

You can get the Nth character, or letter, from a string by writing "string" .charAt(N), similar to how you get its length with "s".length. The returned value will be a string containing only one character (for example, "b"). The first character has position zero, which causes the last one to be found at position string.length - 1. In other words, a two-character string has length 2, and its characters have positions 0 and 1.

Write a function countBs that takes a string as its only argument and returns a number that indicates how many uppercase "B" characters are in the string.

Next, write a function called countChar that behaves like countBs, except it takes a second argument that indicates the character that is to be counted (rather than counting only uppercase "B" characters). Rewrite countBs to make use of this new function.

"On two occasions I have been asked, 'Pray, Mr. Babbage, if you put into the machine wrong figures, will the right answers come out?' . . . I am not able rightly to apprehend the kind of confusion of ideas that could provoke such a question."

—Charles Babbage,
Passages from the Life of a Philosopher (1864)

4

DATA STRUCTURES: OBJECTS AND ARRAYS

Numbers, Booleans, and strings are the bricks that data structures are built from. But you can't make much of a house out of a single brick. *Objects* allow us to group values—including other objects—together and thus build more complex structures.

The programs we have built so far have been seriously hampered by the fact that they were operating only on simple data types. This chapter will add a basic understanding of data structures to your toolkit. By the end of it, you'll know enough to start writing some useful programs.

The chapter will work through a more or less realistic programming example, introducing concepts as they apply to the problem at hand. The example code will often build on functions and variables that were introduced earlier in the text.

The online coding sandbox for the book (*http://eloquentjavascript.net/ code/*) provides a way to run code in the context of a specific chapter. If you decide to work through the examples in another environment, be sure to first download the full code for this chapter from the sandbox page.

The Weresquirrel

Every now and then, usually between eight and ten in the evening, Jacques finds himself transforming into a small furry rodent with a bushy tail.

On one hand, Jacques is quite glad that he doesn't have classic lycanthropy. Turning into a squirrel tends to cause fewer problems than turning into a wolf. Instead of having to worry about accidentally eating the neighbor (*that* would be awkward), he worries about being eaten by the neighbor's cat. After two occasions where he woke up on a precariously thin branch in the crown of an oak, naked and disoriented, he has taken to locking the doors and windows of his room at night and putting a few walnuts on the floor to keep himself busy.

That takes care of the cat and oak problems. But Jacques still suffers from his condition. The irregular occurrences of the transformation make him suspect that they might be triggered by something. For a while, he believed that it happened only on days when he had touched trees. So he stopped touching trees entirely and even avoided going near them. But the problem persisted.

Switching to a more scientific approach, Jacques intends to start keeping a daily log of everything he did that day and whether he changed form. With this data he hopes to narrow down the conditions that trigger the transformations.

The first thing he does is design a data structure to store this information.

Data Sets

To work with a chunk of digital data, we'll first have to find a way to represent it in our machine's memory. Say, as a simple example, that we want to represent a collection of numbers: 2, 3, 5, 7, and 11.

We could get creative with strings—after all, strings can be any length, so we can put a lot of data into them—and use "2 3 5 7 11" as our representation. But this is awkward. You'd have to somehow extract the digits and convert them back to numbers to access them.

Fortunately, JavaScript provides a data type specifically for storing sequences of values. It is called an *array* and is written as a list of values between square brackets, separated by commas.

```
var listOfNumbers = [2, 3, 5, 7, 11];
console.log(listOfNumbers[1]);
// ▷ 3
console.log(listOfNumbers[1 - 1]);
// ▷ 2
```

The notation for getting at the elements inside an array also uses square brackets. A pair of square brackets immediately after an expression, with another expression inside of them, will look up the element in the left-hand expression that corresponds to the *index* given by the expression in the brackets.

The first index of an array is zero, not one. So the first element can be read with listOfNumbers[0]. If you don't have a programming background, this convention might take some getting used to. But zero-based counting has a long tradition in technology, and as long as this convention is followed consistently (which it is, in JavaScript), it works well.

Properties

We've seen a few suspicious-looking expressions like myString.length (to get the length of a string) and Math.max (the maximum function) in past examples. These are expressions that access a *property* of some value. In the first case, we access the length property of the value in myString. In the second, we access the property named max in the Math object (which is a collection of mathematics-related values and functions).

Almost all JavaScript values have properties. The exceptions are null and undefined. If you try to access a property on one of these nonvalues, you get an error.

```
null.length;
// ▷ TypeError: Cannot read property 'length' of null
```

The two most common ways to access properties in JavaScript are with a dot and with square brackets. Both value.x and value[x] access a property on value—but not necessarily the same property. The difference is in how x is interpreted. When using a dot, the part after the dot must be a valid variable name, and it directly names the property. When using square brackets, the expression between the brackets is *evaluated* to get the property name. Whereas value.x fetches the property of value named "x," value[x] tries to evaluate the expression x and uses the result as the property name.

So if you know that the property you are interested in is called "length," you say value.length. If you want to extract the property named by the value held in the variable i, you say value[i]. And because property names can be any string, if you want to access a property named "0" or "John Doe," you must use square brackets: value[0] or value["John Doe"]. This is the case even though you know the precise name of the property in advance, because neither "0" nor "John Doe" is a valid variable name and so cannot be accessed through dot notation.

The elements in an array are stored in properties. Because the names of these properties are numbers and we often need to get their name from a variable, we have to use the bracket syntax to access them. The length property of an array tells us how many elements it contains. This property name is a valid variable name, and we know its name in advance, so to find the length of an array, you typically write array.length because that is easier to write than array["length"].

Methods

Both string and array objects contain, in addition to the length property, a number of properties that refer to function values.

```
var doh = "Doh";
console.log(typeof doh.toUpperCase);
// ▷ function
console.log(doh.toUpperCase());
// ▷ DOH
```

Every string has a toUpperCase property. When called, it will return a copy of the string, in which all letters have been converted to uppercase. There is also toLowerCase. You can guess what that does.

Interestingly, even though the call to toUpperCase does not pass any arguments, the function somehow has access to the string "Doh", the value whose property we called. How this works is described in Chapter 6.

Properties that contain functions are generally called *methods* of the value they belong to. As in, "toUpperCase is a method of a string."

This example demonstrates some methods that array objects have:

```
var mack = [];
mack.push("Mack");
mack.push("the", "Knife");
console.log(mack);
// ▷ ["Mack", "the", "Knife"]
console.log(mack.join(" "));
// ▷ Mack the Knife
console.log(mack.pop());
// ▷ Knife
console.log(mack);
// ▷ ["Mack", "the"]
```

The push method can be used to add values to the end of an array. The pop method does the opposite: it removes the value at the end of the array and returns it. An array of strings can be flattened to a single string with the join method. The argument given to join determines the text that is glued between the array's elements.

Objects

Back to the weresquirrel. A set of daily log entries can be represented as an array. But the entries do not consist of just a number or a string—each entry needs to store a list of activities and a Boolean value that indicates whether Jacques turned into a squirrel. Ideally, we would like to group these values together into a single value and then put these grouped values into an array of log entries.

Values of the type *object* are arbitrary collections of properties, and we can add or remove these properties as we please. One way to create an object is by using a brace notation.

```
var day1 = {
  squirrel: false,
  events: ["work", "touched tree", "pizza", "running",
           "television"]
};
console.log(day1.squirrel);
// ▷ false
console.log(day1.wolf);
// ▷ undefined
day1.wolf = false;
console.log(day1.wolf);
// ▷ false
```

Inside the braces, we can give a list of properties separated by commas. Each property is written as a name, followed by a colon, followed by an expression that provides a value for the property. Spaces and line breaks are not significant. When an object spans multiple lines, indenting it like in the previous example improves readability. Properties whose names are not valid variable names or valid numbers have to be quoted.

```
var descriptions = {
  work: "Went to work",
  "touched tree": "Touched a tree"
};
```

This means that braces have *two* meanings in JavaScript. At the start of a statement, they start a block of statements. In any other position, they describe an object. Fortunately, it is almost never useful to start a statement with a brace object, and in typical programs, there is no ambiguity between these two uses.

Reading a property that doesn't exist will produce the value undefined, which happens the first time we try to read the wolf property in the previous example.

It is possible to assign a value to a property expression with the = operator. This will replace the property's value if it already existed or create a new property on the object if it didn't.

To briefly return to our tentacle model of variable bindings—property bindings are similar. They *grasp* values, but other variables and properties might be holding onto those same values. You may think of objects as octopuses with any number of tentacles, each of which has a name inscribed on it.

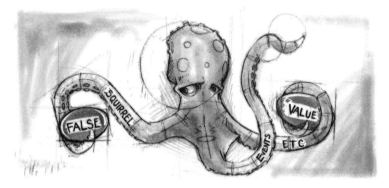

The delete operator cuts off a tentacle from such an octopus. It is a unary operator that, when applied to a property access expression, will remove the named property from the object. This is not a common thing to do, but it is possible.

```
var anObject = {left: 1, right: 2};
console.log(anObject.left);
// ▷ 1
delete anObject.left;
console.log(anObject.left);
// ▷ undefined
console.log("left" in anObject);
// ▷ false
console.log("right" in anObject);
// ▷ true
```

The binary in operator, when applied to a string and an object, returns a Boolean value that indicates whether that object has that property. The difference between setting a property to undefined and actually deleting it is that, in the first case, the object still *has* the property (it just doesn't have a very interesting value), whereas in the second case the property is no longer present and in will return false.

Arrays, then, are just a kind of object specialized for storing sequences of things. If you evaluate typeof [1, 2], this produces "object". You can see them as long, flat octopuses with all their arms in a neat row, labeled with numbers.

So we can represent Jacques's journal as an array of objects.

```
var journal = [
  {events: ["work", "touched tree", "pizza",
            "running", "television"],
   squirrel: false},
  {events: ["work", "ice cream", "cauliflower",
            "lasagna", "touched tree", "brushed teeth"],
   squirrel: false},
  {events: ["weekend", "cycling", "break",
            "peanuts", "beer"],
   squirrel: true},
  /* and so on... */
];
```

Mutability

We will get to actual programming *real* soon now. But first, there's one last piece of theory to understand.

We've seen that object values can be modified. The types of values discussed in earlier chapters, such as numbers, strings, and Booleans, are all *immutable*—it is impossible to change an existing value of those types. You can combine them and derive new values from them, but when you take a specific string value, that value will always remain the same. The text inside it cannot be changed. If you have reference to a string that contains "cat", it is not possible for other code to change a character in *that* string to make it spell "rat".

With objects, on the other hand, the content of a value *can* be modified by changing its properties.

When we have two numbers, 120 and 120, we can consider them precisely the same number, whether or not they refer to the same physical bits. But with objects, there is a difference between having two references to the same object and having two different objects that contain the same properties. Consider the following code:

```
var object1 = {value: 10};
var object2 = object1;
var object3 = {value: 10};

console.log(object1 == object2);
// ▷ true
console.log(object1 == object3);
// ▷ false

object1.value = 15;
console.log(object2.value);
// ▷ 15
console.log(object3.value);
// ▷ 10
```

The object1 and object2 variables grasp the *same* object, which is why changing object1 also changes the value of object2. The variable object3 points to a different object, which initially contains the same properties as object1 but lives a separate life.

JavaScript's == operator, when comparing objects, will return true only if both objects are precisely the same value. Comparing different objects will return false, even if they have identical contents. There is no deep comparison operation built into JavaScript, which looks at object's contents, but it is possible to write it yourself (which will be one of the exercises at the end of this chapter).

The Lycanthrope's Log

So Jacques starts up his JavaScript interpreter and sets up the environment he needs to keep his journal.

```
var journal = [];

function addEntry(events, didITurnIntoASquirrel) {
  journal.push({
    events: events,
    squirrel: didITurnIntoASquirrel
  });
}
```

And then, every evening at ten—or sometimes the next morning, after climbing down from the top shelf of his bookcase—he records the day.

```
addEntry(["work", "touched tree", "pizza", "running",
          "television"], false);
addEntry(["work", "ice cream", "cauliflower", "lasagna",
          "touched tree", "brushed teeth"], false);
addEntry(["weekend", "cycling", "break", "peanuts",
          "beer"], true);
```

Once he has enough data points, he intends to compute the correlation between his squirrelification and each of the day's events and ideally learn something useful from those correlations.

Correlation is a measure of dependence between variables ("variables" in the statistical sense, not the JavaScript sense). It is usually expressed as a coefficient that ranges from −1 to 1. Zero correlation means the variables are not related, whereas a correlation of one indicates that the two are perfectly related—if you know one, you also know the other. Negative one also means that the variables are perfectly related but that they are opposites—when one is true, the other is false.

For binary (Boolean) variables, the *phi* coefficient (φ) provides a good measure of correlation and is relatively easy to compute. To compute φ, we need a table n that contains the number of times the various combinations of the two variables were observed. For example, we could take the event of eating pizza and put that in a table like this:

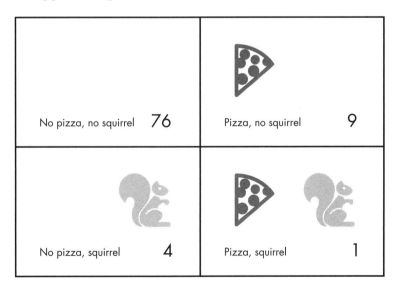

| No pizza, no squirrel | 76 | Pizza, no squirrel | 9 |
| No pizza, squirrel | 4 | Pizza, squirrel | 1 |

φ can be computed using the following formula, where n refers to the numbers in the table:

$$\phi = \frac{n_{11}n_{00} - n_{10}n_{01}}{\sqrt{n_{1\bullet}n_{0\bullet}n_{\bullet1}n_{\bullet0}}} \tag{4.1}$$

The notation n_{01} indicates the number of measurements where the first measurement (pizza) is false (0) and the second measurement (squirrelness) is true (1). In this example, n_{01} is 4.

The value $n_{1\bullet}$ refers to the sum of all measurements where the first variable is true, which is 10 in the example table. Likewise, $n_{\bullet 0}$ refers to the sum of the measurements where the squirrel variable is false.

So for the pizza table, the part above the division line (the dividend) would be $1 \times 76 - 9 \times 4 = 40$, and the part below it (the divisor) would be the square root of $10 \times 80 \times 5 \times 85$, or $\sqrt{340000}$. This comes out to $\varphi \approx 0.069$, which is tiny. Eating pizza does not appear to have influence on the transformations.

Computing Correlation

We can represent a two-by-two table in JavaScript with a four-element array ([76, 9, 4, 1]). We could also use other representations, such as an array containing two two-element arrays ([[76, 9], [4, 1]]) or an object with property names like "11" and "01", but the flat array is simple and makes the expressions that access the table pleasantly short. We'll interpret the indices to the array as a two-bit binary number, where the leftmost (most significant) digit refers to the squirrel variable and the rightmost (least significant) digit refers to the event variable. For example, the binary number 10 refers to the case where Jacques did turn into a squirrel, but the event (say, "pizza") didn't occur. This happened four times. And since binary 10 is 2 in decimal notation, we will store this value at index 2 in the array.

This is the function that computes the φ coefficient from such an array:

```
function phi(table) {
  return (table[3] * table[0] - table[2] * table[1]) /
    Math.sqrt((table[2] + table[3]) *
              (table[0] + table[1]) *
              (table[1] + table[3]) *
              (table[0] + table[2]));
}

console.log(phi([76, 9, 4, 1]));
// ▷ 0.068599434
```

This is simply a direct translation of the φ formula into JavaScript. Math .sqrt is the square root function, as provided by the Math object in a standard JavaScript environment. We have to sum two fields from the table to get fields like $n_{1\bullet}$ because the sums of rows or columns are not stored directly in our data structure.

Jacques kept his journal for three months. The resulting data set is available in the coding sandbox for this chapter (*http://eloquentjavascript.net/code/*), where it is stored in the JOURNAL variable and in a downloadable file.

To extract a two-by-two table for a specific event from this journal, we must loop over all the entries and tally up how many times the event occurs in relation to squirrel transformations.

```
function hasEvent(event, entry) {
  return entry.events.indexOf(event) != -1;
}

function tableFor(event, journal) {
  var table = [0, 0, 0, 0];
  for (var i = 0; i < journal.length; i++) {
    var entry = journal[i], index = 0;
    if (hasEvent(event, entry)) index += 1;
    if (entry.squirrel) index += 2;
    table[index] += 1;
  }
  return table;
}

console.log(tableFor("pizza", JOURNAL));
// ▷ [76, 9, 4, 1]
```

The hasEvent function tests whether an entry contains a given event. Arrays have an indexOf method that tries to find a given value (in this case, the event name) in the array and returns the index at which it was found or −1 if it wasn't found. So if the call to indexOf doesn't return −1, then we know the event was found in the entry.

The body of the loop in tableFor figures out which box in the table each journal entry falls into by checking whether the entry contains the specific event it's interested in and whether the event happens alongside a squirrel incident. The loop then adds one to the number in the array that corresponds to this box on the table.

We now have the tools we need to compute individual correlations. The only step remaining is to find a correlation for every type of event that was recorded and see whether anything stands out. But how should we store these correlations once we compute them?

Objects as Maps

One possible way is to store all the correlations in an array, using objects with name and value properties. But that makes looking up the correlation for a given event somewhat cumbersome: you'd have to loop over the whole array to find the object with the right name. We could wrap this lookup process in a function, but we would still be writing more code, and the computer would be doing more work than necessary.

A better way is to use object properties named after the event types. We can use the square bracket access notation to create and read the properties and can use the in operator to test whether a given property exists.

```
var map = {};
function storePhi(event, phi) {
  map[event] = phi;
}

storePhi("pizza", 0.069);
storePhi("touched tree", -0.081);
console.log("pizza" in map);
// ▷ true
console.log(map["touched tree"]);
// ▷ -0.081
```

A *map* is a way to go from values in one domain (in this case, event names) to corresponding values in another domain (in this case, φ coefficients).

There are a few potential problems with using objects like this, which we will discuss in Chapter 6, but for the time being, we won't worry about those.

What if we want to find all the events for which we have stored a coefficient? The properties don't form a predictable series, like they would in an array, so we cannot use a normal for loop. JavaScript provides a loop construct specifically for going over the properties of an object. It looks a little like a normal for loop but distinguishes itself by the use of the word in.

```
for (var event in map)
  console.log("The correlation for '" + event + "' is " + map[event]);
// ▷ The correlation for 'pizza' is 0.069
// ▷ The correlation for 'touched tree' is -0.081
```

The Final Analysis

To find all the types of events that are present in the data set, we simply process each entry in turn and then loop over the events in that entry. We keep an object phis that has correlation coefficients for all the event types we have seen so far. Whenever we run across a type that isn't in the phis object yet, we compute its correlation and add it to the object.

```
function gatherCorrelations(journal) {
  var phis = {};
  for (var entry = 0; entry < journal.length; entry++) {
    var events = journal[entry].events;
    for (var i = 0; i < events.length; i++) {
      var event = events[i];
```

```
    if (!(event in phis))
      phis[event] = phi(tableFor(event, journal));
  }
}
return phis;
}

var correlations = gatherCorrelations(JOURNAL);
console.log(correlations.pizza);
// ▷ 0.068599434
```

Let's see what came out.

```
for (var event in correlations)
  console.log(event + ": " + correlations[event]);
// ▷ carrot:    0.0140970969
// ▷ exercise: 0.0685994341
// ▷ weekend:  0.1371988681
// ▷ bread:    -0.0757554019
// ▷ pudding: -0.0648203724
// and so on...
```

Most correlations seem to lie close to zero. Eating carrots, bread, or pudding apparently does not trigger squirrel-lycanthropy. It *does* seem to occur somewhat more often on weekends, however. Let's filter the results to show only correlations greater than 0.1 or less than −0.1.

```
for (var event in correlations) {
  var correlation = correlations[event];
  if (correlation > 0.1 || correlation < -0.1)
    console.log(event + ": " + correlation);
}
// ▷ weekend:         0.1371988681
// ▷ brushed teeth: -0.3805211953
// ▷ candy:           0.1296407447
// ▷ work:           -0.1371988681
// ▷ spaghetti:       0.2425356250
// ▷ reading:         0.1106828054
// ▷ peanuts:         0.5902679812
```

A-ha! There are two factors whose correlation is clearly stronger than the others. Eating peanuts has a strong positive effect on the chance of turning into a squirrel, whereas brushing his teeth has a significant negative effect.

Interesting. Let's try something.

```
for (var i = 0; i < JOURNAL.length; i++) {
  var entry = JOURNAL[i];
  if (hasEvent("peanuts", entry) &&
      !hasEvent("brushed teeth", entry))
    entry.events.push("peanut teeth");
}
console.log(phi(tableFor("peanut teeth", JOURNAL)));
// ▷ 1
```

Well, that's unmistakable! The phenomenon occurs precisely when Jacques eats peanuts and fails to brush his teeth. If only he weren't such a slob about dental hygiene, he'd have never even noticed his affliction.

Knowing this, Jacques simply stops eating peanuts altogether and finds that this completely puts an end to his transformations.

All is well with Jacques for a while. But a few years later, he loses his job and is eventually forced to take employment with a circus, where he performs as *The Incredible Squirrelman* by stuffing his mouth with peanut butter before every show. One day, fed up with this pitiful existence, Jacques fails to change back into his human form, hops through a crack in the circus tent, and vanishes into the forest. He is never seen again.

Further Arrayology

Before finishing up this chapter, I want to introduce you to a few more object-related concepts. We'll start by introducing some generally useful array methods.

We saw push and pop, which add and remove elements at the end of an array, earlier in this chapter. The corresponding methods for adding and removing things at the start of an array are called unshift and shift.

```
var todoList = [];
function rememberTo(task) {
  todoList.push(task);
}
function whatIsNext() {
  return todoList.shift();
}
function urgentlyRememberTo(task) {
  todoList.unshift(task);
}
```

The previous program manages lists of tasks. You add tasks to the end of the list by calling rememberTo("eat"), and when you're ready to do something, you call whatIsNext() to get (and remove) the front item from the list. The urgentlyRememberTo function also adds a task but adds it to the front instead of the back of the list.

The indexOf method has a sibling called lastIndexof, which starts searching for the given element at the end of the array instead of the front.

```
console.log([1, 2, 3, 2, 1].indexOf(2));
// ▷ 1
console.log([1, 2, 3, 2, 1].lastIndexOf(2));
// ▷ 3
```

Both indexOf and lastIndexOf take an optional second argument that indicates where to start searching from.

Another fundamental method is slice, which takes a start index and an end index and returns an array that has only the elements between those indices. The start index is inclusive, the end index exclusive.

```
console.log([0, 1, 2, 3, 4].slice(2, 4));
// ▷ [2, 3]
console.log([0, 1, 2, 3, 4].slice(2));
// ▷ [2, 3, 4]
```

When the end index is not given, slice will take all of the elements after the start index. Strings also have a slice method, which has a similar effect.

The concat method can be used to glue arrays together, similar to what the + operator does for strings. The following example shows both concat and slice in action. It takes an array and an index, and it returns a new array that is a copy of the original array with the element at the given index removed.

```
function remove(array, index) {
  return array.slice(0, index)
    .concat(array.slice(index + 1));
}
console.log(remove(["a", "b", "c", "d", "e"], 2));
// ▷ ["a", "b", "d", "e"]
```

Strings and Their Properties

We can read properties like length and toUpperCase from string values. But if you try to add a new property, it doesn't stick.

```
var myString = "Fido";
myString.myProperty = "value";
console.log(myString.myProperty);
// ▷ undefined
```

Values of type string, number, and Boolean are not objects, and though the language doesn't complain if you try to set new properties on them, it doesn't actually store those properties. The values are immutable and cannot be changed.

But these types do have some built-in properties. Every string value has a number of methods. The most useful ones are probably slice and indexOf, which resemble the array methods of the same name.

```
console.log("coconuts".slice(4, 7));
// ▷ nut
console.log("coconut".indexOf("u"));
// ▷ 5
```

One difference is that a string's indexOf can take a string containing more than one character, whereas the corresponding array method looks only for a single element.

```
console.log("one two three".indexOf("ee"));
// ▷ 11
```

The trim method removes whitespace (spaces, newlines, tabs, and similar characters) from the start and end of a string.

```
console.log("  okay \n ".trim());
// ▷ okay
```

We have already seen the string type's length property. Accessing the individual characters in a string can be done with the charAt method but also by simply reading numeric properties, like you'd do for an array.

```
var string = "abc";
console.log(string.length);
// ▷ 3
console.log(string.charAt(0));
// ▷ a
console.log(string[1]);
// ▷ b
```

The arguments Object

Whenever a function is called, a special variable named arguments is added to the environment in which the function body runs. This variable refers to an object that holds all of the arguments passed to the function. Remember that in JavaScript you are allowed to pass more (or fewer) arguments to a function than the number of parameters the function itself declares.

```
function noArguments() {}
noArguments(1, 2, 3); // This is okay
```

```
function threeArguments(a, b, c) {}
threeArguments(); // And so is this
```

The arguments object has a length property that tells us the number of
arguments that were really passed to the function. It also has a property for
each argument, named 0, 1, 2, and so on.

If that sounds a lot like an array to you, you're right, it *is* a lot like an
array. But this object, unfortunately, does not have any array methods (like
slice or indexOf), so it is a little harder to use than a real array.

```
function argumentCounter() {
  console.log("You gave me", arguments.length, "arguments.");
}
argumentCounter("Straw man", "Tautology", "Ad hominem");
// ▷ You gave me 3 arguments.
```

Some functions can take any number of arguments, like console.log.
These typically loop over the values in their arguments object. They can be
used to create very pleasant interfaces. For example, remember how we
created the entries to Jacques's journal.

```
addEntry(["work", "touched tree", "pizza", "running",
         "television"], false);
```

Since he is going to be calling this function a lot, we could create an alternative that is easier to call.

```
function addEntry(squirrel) {
  var entry = {events: [], squirrel: squirrel};
  for (var i = 1; i < arguments.length; i++)
    entry.events.push(arguments[i]);
  journal.push(entry);
}
addEntry(true, "work", "touched tree", "pizza",
         "running", "television");
```

This version reads its first argument (squirrel) in the normal way and
then goes over the rest of the arguments (the loop starts at index 1, skipping
the first) to gather them into an array.

The Math Object

As we've seen, Math is a grab-bag of number-related utility functions, such as
Math.max (maximum), Math.min (minimum), and Math.sqrt (square root).

The Math object is used simply as a container to group a bunch of related
functionality. There is only one Math object, and it is almost never useful as

a value. Rather, it provides a *namespace* so that all these functions and values do not have to be global variables.

Having too many global variables "pollutes" the namespace. The more names that have been taken, the more likely you are to accidentally overwrite the value of some variable. For example, it's not unlikely that you'll want to name something max in one of your programs. Since JavaScript's built-in max function is tucked safely inside the Math object, we don't have to worry about overwriting it.

Many languages will stop you, or at least warn you, when you are defining a variable with a name that is already taken. JavaScript does neither, so be careful.

Back to the Math object. If you need to do trigonometry, Math can help. It contains cos (cosine), sin (sine), and tan (tangent), as well as their inverse functions, acos, asin, and atan, respectively. The number π (pi)—or at least the closest approximation that fits in a JavaScript number—is available as Math.PI. (There is an old programming tradition of writing the names of constant values in all caps.)

```
function randomPointOnCircle(radius) {
  var angle = Math.random() * 2 * Math.PI;
  return {x: radius * Math.cos(angle),
          y: radius * Math.sin(angle)};
}
console.log(randomPointOnCircle(2));
// ▷ {x: 0.3667, y: 1.966}
```

If sines and cosines are not something you are very familiar with, don't worry. When they are used in this book, in Chapter 13, I'll explain them.

The previous example uses Math.random. This is a function that returns a new pseudorandom number between zero (inclusive) and one (exclusive) every time you call it.

```
console.log(Math.random());
// ▷ 0.36993729369714856
console.log(Math.random());
// ▷ 0.727367032552138
console.log(Math.random());
// ▷ 0.40180766698904335
```

Though computers are deterministic machines—they always react the same way if given the same input—it is possible to have them produce numbers that appear random. To do this, the machine keeps a number (or a bunch of numbers) in its internal state. Then, every time a random number is requested, it performs some complicated deterministic computations on this internal state and returns part of the result of those computations. The machine also uses the outcome to change its own internal state so that the next "random" number produced will be different.

If we want a whole random number instead of a fractional one, we can use `Math.floor` (which rounds down to the nearest whole number) on the result of `Math.random`.

```
console.log(Math.floor(Math.random() * 10));
// ▷ 2
```

Multiplying the random number by 10 gives us a number greater than or equal to zero, and below 10. Since `Math.floor` rounds down, this expression will produce, with equal chance, any number from 0 through 9.

There are also the functions `Math.ceil` (for "ceiling," which rounds up to a whole number) and `Math.round` (to the nearest whole number).

The Global Object

The global scope, the space in which global variables live, can also be approached as an object in JavaScript. Each global variable is present as a property of this object. In browsers, the global scope object is stored in the `window` variable.

```
var myVar = 10;
console.log("myVar" in window);
// ▷ true
console.log(window.myVar);
// ▷ 10
```

Summary

Objects and arrays (which are a specific kind of object) provide ways to group several values into a single value. Conceptually, this allows us to put a bunch of related things in a bag and run around with the bag, instead of trying to wrap our arms around all of the individual things and trying to hold on to them separately.

Most values in JavaScript have properties, the exceptions being `null` and `undefined`. Properties are accessed using `value.propName` or `value["propName"]`. Objects tend to use names for their properties and store more or less a fixed set of them. Arrays, on the other hand, usually contain varying numbers of conceptually identical values and use numbers (starting from 0) as the names of their properties.

There *are* some named properties in arrays, such as `length` and a number of methods. Methods are functions that live in properties and (usually) act on the value they are a property of.

Objects can also serve as maps, associating values with names. The `in` operator can be used to find out whether an object contains a property with a given name. The same keyword can also be used in a `for` loop (`for (var name in object)`) to loop over an object's properties.

Exercises

The Sum of a Range

The introduction of this book alluded to the following as a nice way to compute the sum of a range of numbers:

```
console.log(sum(range(1, 10)));
```

Write a range function that takes two arguments, start and end, and returns an array containing all the numbers from start up to (and including) end.

Next, write a sum function that takes an array of numbers and returns the sum of these numbers. Run the previous program and see whether it does indeed return 55.

As a bonus assignment, modify your range function to take an optional third argument that indicates the "step" value used to build up the array. If no step is given, the array elements go up by increments of one, corresponding to the old behavior. The function call range(1, 10, 2) should return [1, 3, 5, 7, 9]. Make sure it also works with negative step values so that range(5, 2, -1) produces [5, 4, 3, 2].

Reversing an Array

Arrays have a method reverse, which changes the array by inverting the order in which its elements appear. For this exercise, write two functions, reverseArray and reverseArrayInPlace. The first, reverseArray, takes an array as an argument and produces a *new* array that has the same elements in the inverse order. The second, reverseArrayInPlace, does what the reverse method does: it modifies the array given as argument in order to reverse its elements. Neither may use the standard reverse method.

Thinking back to the notes about side effects and pure functions in the previous chapter, which variant do you expect to be useful in more situations? Which one is more efficient?

A List

Objects, as generic blobs of values, can be used to build all sorts of data structures. A common data structure is the *list* (not to be confused with the array). A list is a nested set of objects, with the first object holding a reference to the second, the second to the third, and so on.

```
var list = {
  value: 1,
  rest: {
    value: 2,
```

```
    rest: {
      value: 3,
      rest: null
    }
  }
};
```

The resulting objects form a chain, like this:

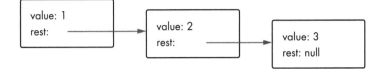

A nice thing about lists is that they can share parts of their structure. For example, if I create two new values {value: 0, rest: list} and {value: -1, rest: list} (with list referring to the variable defined earlier), they are both independent lists, but they share the structure that makes up their last three elements. In addition, the original list is also still a valid three-element list.

Write a function arrayToList that builds up a data structure like the previous one when given [1, 2, 3] as an argument, and write a listToArray function that produces an array from a list. Also write the helper functions prepend, which takes an element and a list and creates a new list that adds the element to the front of the input list, and nth, which takes a list and a number and returns the element at the given position in the list, or undefined when there is no such element.

If you haven't already, also write a recursive version of nth.

Deep Comparison

The == operator compares objects by identity. But sometimes, you would prefer to compare the values of their actual properties.

Write a function, deepEqual, that takes two values and returns true only if they are the same value or are objects with the same properties whose values are also equal when compared with a recursive call to deepEqual.

To find out whether to compare two things by identity (use the === operator for that) or by looking at their properties, you can use the typeof operator. If it produces "object" for both values, you should do a deep comparison. But you have to take one silly exception into account: by a historical accident, typeof null also produces "object".

"There are two ways of constructing a software design: One way is to make it so simple that there are obviously no deficiencies, and the other way is to make it so complicated that there are no obvious deficiencies"

—C.A.R. Hoare,
1980 ACM Turing Aware Lecture

5

HIGHER-ORDER FUNCTIONS

A large program is a costly program, and not just because of the time it takes to build. Size almost always involves complexity, and complexity confuses programmers. Confused programmers, in turn, tend to introduce mistakes (*bugs*) into programs. A large program also provides a lot of space for these bugs to hide, making them hard to find.

Let's briefly go back to the final two example programs in the introduction. The first is self-contained and six lines long.

```
var total = 0, count = 1;
while (count <= 10) {
  total += count;
  count += 1;
}
console.log(total);
```

The second relies on two external functions and is one line long.

```
console.log(sum(range(1, 10)));
```

Which one is more likely to contain a bug?

If we count the size of the definitions of sum and range, the second program is also big—even bigger than the first. But still, I'd argue that it is more likely to be correct.

It is more likely to be correct because the solution is expressed in a vocabulary that corresponds to the problem being solved. Summing a range of numbers isn't about loops and counters. It is about ranges and sums.

The definitions of this vocabulary (the functions sum and range) will still involve loops, counters, and other incidental details. But because they are expressing simpler concepts than the program as a whole, they are easier to get right.

Abstraction

In the context of programming, these kinds of vocabularies are usually called *abstractions*. Abstractions hide details and give us the ability to talk about problems at a higher (or more abstract) level.

As an analogy, compare these two recipes for pea soup:

> Put 1 cup of dried peas per person into a container. Add water until the peas are well covered. Leave the peas in water for at least 12 hours. Take the peas out of the water and put them in a cooking pan. Add 4 cups of water per person. Cover the pan and keep the peas simmering for two hours. Take half an onion per person. Cut it into pieces with a knife. Add it to the peas. Take a stalk of celery per person. Cut it into pieces with a knife. Add it to the peas. Take a carrot per person. Cut it into pieces. With a knife! Add it to the peas. Cook for 10 more minutes.

And the second recipe:

> Per person: 1 cup dried split peas, half a chopped onion, a stalk of celery, and a carrot.
>
> Soak peas for 12 hours. Simmer for 2 hours in 4 cups of water (per person). Chop and add vegetables. Cook for 10 more minutes.

The second is shorter and easier to interpret. But you do need to understand a few more cooking-related words—*soak, simmer, chop*, and, I guess, *vegetable*.

When programming, we can't rely on all the words we need to be waiting for us in the dictionary. Thus, you might fall into the pattern of the first recipe—work out the precise steps the computer has to perform, one by one, blind to the higher-level concepts that they express.

It has to become second nature, for a programmer, to notice when a concept is begging to be abstracted into a new word.

Abstracting Array Traversal

Plain functions, as we've seen them so far, are a good way to build abstractions. But sometimes they fall short.

In the previous chapter, this type of for loop made several appearances:

```
var array = [1, 2, 3];
for (var i = 0; i < array.length; i++) {
  var current = array[i];
  console.log(current);
}
```

It's trying to say, "For each element in the array, log it to the console." But it uses a roundabout way that involves a counter variable i, a check against the array's length, and an extra variable declaration to pick out the current element. Apart from being a bit of an eyesore, this provides a lot of space for potential mistakes. We might accidentally reuse the i variable, misspell length as lenght, confuse the i and current variables, and so on.

So let's try to abstract this into a function. Can you think of a way?

Well, it's easy to write a function that goes over an array and calls console.log on every element.

```
function logEach(array) {
  for (var i = 0; i < array.length; i++)
    console.log(array[i]);
}
```

But what if we want to do something other than logging the elements? Since "doing something" can be represented as a function and functions are just values, we can pass our action as a function value.

```
function forEach(array, action) {
  for (var i = 0; i < array.length; i++)
    action(array[i]);
}

forEach(["Wampeter", "Foma", "Granfalloon"], console.log);
// ▷ Wampeter
// ▷ Foma
// ▷ Granfalloon
```

Often, you don't pass a predefined function to forEach but create a function value on the spot instead.

```
var numbers = [1, 2, 3, 4, 5], sum = 0;
forEach(numbers, function(number) {
  sum += number;
});
```

```
console.log(sum);
// ▷ 15
```

This looks quite a lot like the classical for loop, with its body written as a block below it. However, now the body is inside the function value, as well as inside the parentheses of the call to forEach. This is why it has to be closed with the closing brace *and* closing parenthesis.

Using this pattern, we can specify a variable name for the current element (number), rather than having to pick it out of the array manually.

In fact, we don't need to write forEach ourselves. It is available as a standard method on arrays. Since the array is already provided as the thing the method acts on, forEach takes only one required argument: the function to be executed for each element.

To illustrate how helpful this is, let's look back at a function from the previous chapter. It contains two array-traversing loops.

```
function gatherCorrelations(journal) {
  var phis = {};
  for (var entry = 0; entry < journal.length; entry++) {
    var events = journal[entry].events;
    for (var i = 0; i < events.length; i++) {
      var event = events[i];
      if (!(event in phis))
        phis[event] = phi(tableFor(event, journal));
    }
  }
  return phis;
}
```

Working with forEach makes it slightly shorter and quite a bit cleaner.

```
function gatherCorrelations(journal) {
  var phis = {};
  journal.forEach(function(entry) {
    entry.events.forEach(function(event) {
      if (!(event in phis))
        phis[event] = phi(tableFor(event, journal));
    });
  });
  return phis;
}
```

Higher-Order Functions

Functions that operate on other functions, either by taking them as arguments or by returning them, are called *higher-order functions*. If you have already accepted the fact that functions are regular values, there is nothing particularly remarkable about the fact that such functions exist. The term comes from mathematics, where the distinction between functions and other values is taken more seriously.

Higher-order functions allow us to abstract over *actions*, not just values. They come in several forms. For example, you can have functions that create new functions.

```
function greaterThan(n) {
  return function(m) { return m > n; };
}
var greaterThan10 = greaterThan(10);
console.log(greaterThan10(11));
// ▷ true
```

And you can have functions that change other functions.

```
function noisy(f) {
  return function(arg) {
    console.log("calling with", arg);
    var val = f(arg);
    console.log("called with", arg, "- got", val);
    return val;
  };
}
noisy(Boolean)(0);
// ▷ calling with 0
// ▷ called with 0 - got false
```

You can even write functions that provide new types of control flow.

```
function unless(test, then) {
  if (!test) then();
}
function repeat(times, body) {
  for (var i = 0; i < times; i++) body(i);
}

repeat(3, function(n) {
  unless(n % 2, function() {
    console.log(n, "is even");
  });
});
// ▷ 0 is even
// ▷ 2 is even
```

The lexical scoping rules that we discussed in Chapter 3 work to our advantage when using functions in this way. In the previous example, the n variable is a parameter to the outer function. Because the inner function lives inside the environment of the outer one, it can use n. The bodies of such inner functions can access the variables around them. They can play a role similar to the {} blocks used in regular loops and conditional statements. An important difference is that variables declared inside inner functions do not end up in the environment of the outer function. And that is usually a good thing.

Passing Along Arguments

The noisy function defined earlier, which wraps its argument in another function, has a rather serious deficit.

```
function noisy(f) {
  return function(arg) {
    console.log("calling with", arg);
    var val = f(arg);
    console.log("called with", arg, "- got", val);
    return val;
  };
}
```

If f takes more than one parameter, it gets only the first one. We could add a bunch of arguments to the inner function (arg1, arg2, and so on) and pass them all to f, but it is not clear how many would be enough. This solution would also deprive f of the information in arguments.length. Since we'd always pass the same number of arguments, it wouldn't know how many arguments were originally given.

For these kinds of situations, JavaScript functions have an apply method. You pass it an array (or array-like object) of arguments, and it will call the function with those arguments.

```
function transparentWrapping(f) {
  return function() {
    return f.apply(null, arguments);
  };
}
```

That's a useless function, but it shows the pattern we are interested in—the function it returns passes all of the given arguments, and only those arguments, to f. It does this by passing its own arguments object to apply. The first argument to apply, for which we are passing null here, can be used to simulate a method call. We will come back to that in the next chapter.

JSON

Higher-order functions that somehow apply a function to the elements of an array are widely used in JavaScript. The forEach method is the most primitive such function. There are a number of other variants available as methods on arrays. To familiarize ourselves with them, let's play around with another data set.

A few years ago, someone crawled through a lot of archives and put together a book on the history of my family name (Haverbeke—meaning Oatbrook). I opened it hoping to find knights, pirates, and alchemists ... but the book turns out to be mostly full of Flemish farmers. For my amusement, I extracted the information on my direct ancestors and put it into a computer-readable format.

The file I created looks something like this:

```
[
  {"name": "Emma de Milliano", "sex": "f",
   "born": 1876, "died": 1956,
   "father": "Petrus de Milliano",
   "mother": "Sophia van Damme"},
  {"name": "Carolus Haverbeke", "sex": "m",
   "born": 1832, "died": 1905,
   "father": "Carel Haverbeke",
   "mother": "Maria van Brussel"},
  ... and so on
]
```

This format is called JSON (pronounced "Jason"), which stands for JavaScript Object Notation. It is widely used as a data storage and communication format on the Web.

JSON is similar to JavaScript's way of writing arrays and objects, with a few restrictions. All property names have to be surrounded by double quotes, and only simple data expressions are allowed—no function calls, variables, or anything that involves actual computation. Comments are not allowed in JSON.

JavaScript gives us functions, JSON.stringify and JSON.parse, that convert data from and to this format. The first takes a JavaScript value and returns a JSON-encoded string. The second takes such a string and converts it to the value it encodes.

```
var string = JSON.stringify({name: "X", born: 1980});
console.log(string);
// ▷ {"name":"X","born":1980}
console.log(JSON.parse(string).born);
// ▷ 1980
```

The variable `ANCESTRY_FILE`, available in the sandbox for this chapter and in a downloadable file on the website (*http://eloquentjavascript.net/code/*), contains the content of my JSON file as a string. Let's decode it and see how many people it contains.

```
var ancestry = JSON.parse(ANCESTRY_FILE);
console.log(ancestry.length);
// ▷ 39
```

Filtering an Array

To find the people in the ancestry data set who were young in 1924, the following function might be helpful. It filters out the elements in an array that don't pass a test.

```
function filter(array, test) {
  var passed = [];
  for (var i = 0; i < array.length; i++) {
    if (test(array[i]))
      passed.push(array[i]);
  }
  return passed;
}

console.log(filter(ancestry, function(person) {
  return person.born > 1900 && person.born < 1925;
}));
// ▷ [{name: "Philibert Haverbeke", ...}, ...]
```

This uses the argument named test, a function value, to fill in a "gap" in the computation. The test function is called for each element, and its return value determines whether an element is included in the returned array.

Three people in the file were alive and young in 1924: my grandfather, grandmother, and great-aunt.

Note how the `filter` function, rather than deleting elements from the existing array, builds up a new array with only the elements that pass the test. This function is *pure*. It does not modify the array it is given.

Like forEach, `filter` is also a standard method on arrays. The example defined the function only in order to show what it does internally. From now on, we'll use it like this instead:

```
console.log(ancestry.filter(function(person) {
  return person.father == "Carel Haverbeke";
}));
// ▷ [{name: "Carolus Haverbeke", ...}]
```

Transforming with map

Say we have an array of objects representing people, produced by filtering the ancestry array somehow. But we want an array of names, which is easier to read.

The map method transforms an array by applying a function to all of its elements and building a new array from the returned values. The new array will have the same length as the input array, but its content will have been "mapped" to a new form by the function.

```
function map(array, transform) {
  var mapped = [];
  for (var i = 0; i < array.length; i++)
    mapped.push(transform(array[i]));
  return mapped;
}

var overNinety = ancestry.filter(function(person) {
  return person.died - person.born > 90;
});
console.log(map(overNinety, function(person) {
  return person.name;
}));
// ▷ ["Clara Aernoudts", "Emile Haverbeke",
//    "Maria Haverbeke"]
```

Interestingly, the people who lived to at least 90 years of age are the same three people who we saw before—the people who were young in the 1920s, which happens to be the most recent generation in my data set. I guess medicine has come a long way.

Like forEach and filter, map is also a standard method on arrays.

Summarizing with reduce

Another common pattern of computation on arrays is computing a single value from them. Our recurring example, summing a collection of numbers, is an instance of this. Another example would be finding the person with the earliest year of birth in the data set.

The higher-order operation that represents this pattern is called *reduce* (or sometimes *fold*). You can think of it as folding up the array, one element at a time. When summing numbers, you'd start with the number zero and, for each element, combine it with the current sum by adding the two.

The parameters to the reduce function are, apart from the array, a combining function and a start value. This function is a little less straightforward than filter and map, so pay careful attention.

```
function reduce(array, combine, start) {
  var current = start;
  for (var i = 0; i < array.length; i++)
    current = combine(current, array[i]);
  return current;
}

console.log(reduce([1, 2, 3, 4], function(a, b) {
  return a + b;
}, 0));
// ▷ 10
```

The standard array method reduce, which of course corresponds to this function, has an added convenience. If your array contains at least one element, you are allowed to leave off the start argument. The method will take the first element of the array as its start value and start reducing at the second element.

To use reduce to find my most ancient known ancestor, we can write something like this:

```
console.log(ancestry.reduce(function(min, cur) {
  if (cur.born < min.born) return cur;
  else return min;
}));
// ▷ {name: "Pauwels van Haverbeke", born: 1535, ...}
```

Composability

Consider how we would have written the previous example (finding the person with the earliest year of birth) without higher-order functions. The code is not that much worse.

```
var min = ancestry[0];
for (var i = 1; i < ancestry.length; i++) {
  var cur = ancestry[i];
  if (cur.born < min.born)
    min = cur;
}
console.log(min);
// ▷ {name: "Pauwels van Haverbeke", born: 1535, ...}
```

There are a few more variables, and the program is two lines longer but still quite easy to understand.

Higher-order functions start to shine when you need to *compose* functions. As an example, let's write code that finds the average age for men and for women in the data set.

```
function average(array) {
  function plus(a, b) { return a + b; }
  return array.reduce(plus) / array.length;
}
function age(p) { return p.died - p.born; }
function male(p) { return p.sex == "m"; }
function female(p) { return p.sex == "f"; }

console.log(average(ancestry.filter(male).map(age)));
// ▷ 61.67
console.log(average(ancestry.filter(female).map(age)));
// ▷ 54.56
```

(It's a bit silly that we have to define plus as a function, but operators in JavaScript, unlike functions, are not values, so you can't pass them as arguments.)

Instead of tangling the logic into a big loop, it is neatly composed into the concepts we are interested in—determining sex, computing age, and averaging numbers. We can apply these one by one to get the result we are looking for.

This is *fabulous* for writing clear code. Unfortunately, this clarity comes at a cost.

The Cost

In the happy land of elegant code and pretty rainbows, there lives a spoil-sport monster called *inefficiency*.

A program that processes an array is most elegantly expressed as a sequence of cleanly separated steps that each do something with the array and produce a new array. But building up all those intermediate arrays is somewhat expensive.

Likewise, passing a function to forEach and letting that method handle the array iteration for us is convenient and easy to read. But function calls in JavaScript are costly compared to simple loop bodies.

And so it goes with a lot of techniques that help improve the clarity of a program. Abstractions add layers between the raw things the computer is doing and the concepts we are working with and thus cause the machine to perform more work. This is not an iron law—there are programming languages that have better support for building abstractions without adding inefficiencies, and even in JavaScript, an experienced programmer can find ways to write abstract code that is still fast. But it is a problem that comes up a lot.

Fortunately, most computers are insanely fast. If you are processing a modest set of data or doing something that has to happen only on a human time scale (say, every time the user clicks a button), then it *does not matter* whether you wrote a pretty solution that takes half a millisecond or a super-optimized solution that takes a tenth of a millisecond.

It is helpful to roughly keep track of how often a piece of your program is going to run. If you have a loop inside a loop (either directly or through the outer loop calling a function that ends up performing the inner loop), the code inside the inner loop will end up running $N \times M$ times, where N is the number of times the outer loop repeats and M is the number of times the inner loop repeats within each iteration of the outer loop. If that inner loop contains another loop that makes P rounds, its body will run $M \times N \times P$ times, and so on. This can add up to large numbers, and when a program is slow, the problem can often be traced to only a small part of the code, which sits inside an inner loop.

Great-great-great-great-...

My grandfather, Philibert Haverbeke, is included in the data file. By starting with him, I can trace my lineage to find out whether the most ancient person in the data, Pauwels van Haverbeke, is my direct ancestor. And if he is, I would like to know how much DNA I theoretically share with him.

To be able to go from a parent's name to the actual object that represents this person, we first build up an object that associates names with people.

```
var byName = {};
ancestry.forEach(function(person) {
  byName[person.name] = person;
});

console.log(byName["Philibert Haverbeke"]);
// ▷ {name: "Philibert Haverbeke", ...}
```

Now, the problem is not entirely as simple as following the father properties and counting how many we need to reach Pauwels. There are several cases in the family tree where people married their second cousins (tiny villages and all that). This causes the branches of the family tree to rejoin in a few places, which means I share more than $1/2^G$ of my genes with this person, where G for the number of generations between Pauwels and me. This formula comes from the idea that each generation splits the gene pool in two.

A reasonable way to think about this problem is to look at it as being analogous to reduce, which condenses an array to a single value by repeatedly combining values, left to right. In this case, we also want to condense our data structure to a single value but in a way that follows family lines. The *shape* of the data is that of a family tree, rather than a flat list.

The way we want to reduce this shape is by computing a value for a given person by combining values from their ancestors. This can be done recursively: if we are interested in person A, we have to compute the values for A's parents, which in turn requires us to compute the value for A's grandparents, and so on. In principle, that'd require us to look at an infinite number of people, but since our data set is finite, we have to stop some-where. We'll allow a default value to be given to our reduction function, which will be used for people who are not in the data. In our case, that value is simply zero, on the assumption that people not in the list don't share DNA with the ancestor we are looking at.

Given a person, a function to combine values from the two parents of a given person, and a default value, reduceAncestors condenses a value from a family tree.

```
function reduceAncestors(person, f, defaultValue) {
  function valueFor(person) {
    if (person == null)
      return defaultValue;
    else
      return f(person, valueFor(byName[person.mother]),
                       valueFor(byName[person.father]));
  }
  return valueFor(person);
}
```

The inner function (valueFor) handles a single person. Through the magic of recursion, it can simply call itself to handle the father and the mother of this person. The results, along with the person object itself, are passed to f, which returns the actual value for this person.

We can then use this to compute the amount of DNA my grandfather shared with Pauwels van Haverbeke and divide that by four.

```
function sharedDNA(person, fromMother, fromFather) {
  if (person.name == "Pauwels van Haverbeke")
    return 1;
  else
    return (fromMother + fromFather) / 2;
}
var ph = byName["Philibert Haverbeke"];
console.log(reduceAncestors(ph, sharedDNA, 0) / 4);
// ▷ 0.00049
```

The person with the name Pauwels van Haverbeke obviously shared 100 percent of his DNA with Pauwels van Haverbeke (there are no people who share names in the data set), so the function returns 1 for him. All other people share the average of the amounts that their parents share.

So, statistically speaking, I share about 0.05 percent of my DNA with this 16th-century person. It should be noted that this is only a statistical approximation, not an exact amount. It is a rather small number, but given how much genetic material we carry (about 3 billion base pairs), there's still probably some aspect in the biological machine that is me that originates with Pauwels.

We could also have computed this number without relying on reduceAncestors. But separating the general approach (condensing a family tree) from the specific case (computing shared DNA) can improve the clarity of the code and allows us to reuse the abstract part of the program for other cases. For example, the following code finds the percentage of known ancestors, for a given person, who lived past 70:

```
function countAncestors(person, test) {
  function combine(person, fromMother, fromFather) {
    var thisOneCounts = test(person);
    return fromMother + fromFather + (thisOneCounts ? 1 : 0);
  }
  return reduceAncestors(person, combine, 0);
}
function longLivingPercentage(person) {
  var all = countAncestors(person, function(person) {
    return true;
  });
  var longLiving = countAncestors(person, function(person) {
    return (person.died - person.born) >= 70;
  });
  return longLiving / all;
}
console.log(longLivingPercentage(byName["Emile Haverbeke"]));
// ▷ 0.145
```

Such numbers are not to be taken too seriously, given that our data set contains a rather arbitrary collection of people. But the code illustrates the fact that reduceAncestors gives us a useful piece of vocabulary for working with the family tree data structure.

Binding

The bind method, which all functions have, creates a new function that will call the original function but with some of the arguments already fixed.

The following code shows an example of bind in use. It defines a function isInSet that tells us whether a person is in a given set of strings. To call filter in order to collect those person objects whose names are in a specific set, we can either write a function expression that makes a call to isInSet with our set as its first argument or *partially apply* the isInSet function.

```
var theSet = ["Carel Haverbeke", "Maria van Brussel",
              "Donald Duck"];
function isInSet(set, person) {
  return set.indexOf(person.name) > -1;
}
```

```
console.log(ancestry.filter(function(person) {
  return isInSet(theSet, person);
}));
// ▷ [{name: "Maria van Brussel", ...},
//    {name: "Carel Haverbeke", ...}]
console.log(ancestry.filter(isInSet.bind(null, theSet)));
// ▷ ... same result
```

The call to bind returns a function that will call isInSet with theSet as the first argument, followed by any remaining arguments given to the bound function.

The first argument, where the example passes null, is used for method calls, similar to the first argument to apply. I'll describe this in more detail in the next chapter.

Summary

Being able to pass function values to other functions is not just a gimmick but a deeply useful aspect of JavaScript. It allows us to write computations with "gaps" in them as functions and have the code that calls these functions fill in those gaps by providing function values that describe the missing computations.

Arrays provide a number of useful higher-order methods—forEach to do something with each element in an array, filter to build a new array with some elements filtered out, map to build a new array where each element has been put through a function, and reduce to combine all an array's elements into a single value.

Functions have an apply method that can be used to call them with an array specifying their arguments. They also have a bind method, which is used to create a partially applied version of the function.

Exercises

Flattening

Use the reduce method in combination with the concat method to "flatten" an array of arrays into a single array that has all the elements of the input arrays.

Mother-Child Age Difference

Using the example data set from this chapter, compute the average age difference between mothers and children (the age of the mother when the child is born). You can use the average function defined earlier in this chapter.

Note that not all the mothers mentioned in the data are themselves present in the array. The byName object, which makes it easy to find a person's object from their name, might be useful here.

Historical Life Expectancy

When we looked up all the people in our data set that lived more than 90 years, only the latest generation in the data came out. Let's take a closer look at that phenomenon.

Compute and output the average age of the people in the ancestry data set per century. A person is assigned to a century by taking their year of death, dividing it by 100, and rounding it up, as in Math.ceil(person.died / 100).

For bonus points, write a function groupBy that abstracts the grouping operation. It should accept as arguments an array and a function that computes the group for an element in the array and returns an object that maps group names to arrays of group numbers.

Every and Then Some

Arrays also come with the standard methods every and some. Both take a predicate function that, when called with an array element as argument, returns true or false. Just like && returns a true value only when the expressions on both sides are true, every returns true only when the predicate returns true for *all* elements of the array. Similarly, some returns true as soon as the predicate returns true for *any* of the elements. They do not process more elements than necessary—for example, if some finds that the predicate holds for the first element of the array, it will not look at the values after that.

Write two functions, every and some, that behave like these methods, except that they take the array as their first argument rather than being a method.

"The problem with object-oriented languages
is they've got all this implicit environment that
they carry around with them. You wanted a
banana but what you got was a gorilla holding
the banana and the entire jungle."

—Joe Armstrong,
interviewed in *Coders at Work*

6

THE SECRET LIFE OF OBJECTS

When a programmer says "object," this is a loaded term.
In my profession, objects are a way of life, the subject
of holy wars, and a beloved buzzword that still hasn't
quite lost its power.

To an outsider, this is probably a little confusing. Let's start with a brief
history of objects as a programming construct.

History

This story, like most programming stories, starts with the problem of complexity. One philosophy is that complexity can be made manageable by separating it into small compartments that are isolated from each other. These
compartments have ended up with the name *objects*.

An object is a hard shell that hides the gooey complexity inside it and
instead offers us a few knobs and connectors (such as methods) that present
an *interface* through which the object is to be used. The idea is that the interface is relatively simple and all the complex things going on *inside* the object
can be ignored when working with it.

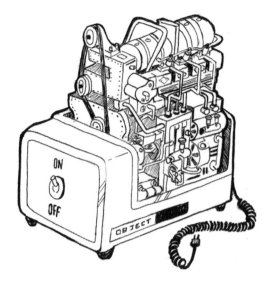

As an example, you can imagine an object that provides an interface to an area on your screen. It provides a way to draw shapes or text onto this area but hides all the details of how these shapes are converted to the actual pixels that make up the screen. You'd have a set of methods—for example, drawCircle—and those are the only things you need to know in order to use such an object.

These ideas were initially worked out in the 1970s and 1980s and, in the 1990s, were carried up by a huge wave of hype—the object-oriented programming revolution. Suddenly, there was a large tribe of people declaring that objects were the *right* way to program—and that anything that did not involve objects was outdated nonsense.

That kind of zealotry always produces a lot of impractical silliness, and there has been a sort of counter-revolution since then. In some circles, objects have a rather bad reputation nowadays.

I prefer to look at the issue from a practical, rather than ideological, angle. There are several useful concepts, most importantly that of *encapsulation* (distinguishing between internal complexity and external interface), that the object-oriented culture has popularized. These are worth studying.

This chapter describes JavaScript's rather eccentric take on objects and the way they relate to some classical object-oriented techniques.

Methods

Methods are simply properties that hold function values. This is a simple method:

```
var rabbit = {};
rabbit.speak = function(line) {
  console.log("The rabbit says '" + line + "'");
};
```

```
rabbit.speak("I'm alive.");
// ▷ The rabbit says 'I'm alive.'
```

Usually a method needs to do something with the object it was called on. When a function is called as a method—looked up as a property and immediately called, as in object.method()—the special variable this in its body will point to the object that it was called on.

```
function speak(line) {
  console.log("The " + this.type + " rabbit says '" +
              line + "'");
}
var whiteRabbit = {type: "white", speak: speak};
var fatRabbit = {type: "fat", speak: speak};

whiteRabbit.speak("Oh my ears and whiskers, " +
                  "how late it's getting!");
// ▷ The white rabbit says 'Oh my ears and whiskers, how
//   late it's getting!'
fatRabbit.speak("I could sure use a carrot right now.");
// ▷ The fat rabbit says 'I could sure use a carrot
//   right now.'
```

The code uses the this keyword to output the type of rabbit that is speaking. Recall that the apply and bind methods both take a first argument that can be used to simulate method calls. This first argument is in fact used to give a value to this.

There is a method similar to apply, called call. It also calls the function it is a method of but takes its arguments normally, rather than as an array. Like apply and bind, call can be passed a specific this value.

```
speak.apply(fatRabbit, ["Burp!"]);
// ▷ The fat rabbit says 'Burp!'
speak.call({type: "old"}, "Oh my.");
// ▷ The old rabbit says 'Oh my.'
```

Prototypes

Watch closely.

```
var empty = {};
console.log(empty.toString);
// ▷ function toString(){...}
console.log(empty.toString());
// ▷ [object Object]
```

I just pulled a property out of an empty object. Magic!

Well, not really. I have simply been withholding information about the way JavaScript objects work. In addition to their set of properties, almost all objects also have a *prototype*. A prototype is another object that is used as a fallback source of properties. When an object gets a request for a property that it does not have, its prototype will be searched for the property, then the prototype's prototype, and so on.

So who is the prototype of that empty object? It is the great ancestral prototype, the entity behind almost all objects, `Object.prototype`.

```
console.log(Object.getPrototypeOf({}) ==
            Object.prototype);
// ▷ true
console.log(Object.getPrototypeOf(Object.prototype));
// ▷ null
```

As you might expect, the `Object.getPrototypeOf` function returns the prototype of an object.

The prototype relations of JavaScript objects form a tree-shaped structure, and at the root of this structure sits `Object.prototype`. It provides a few methods that show up in all objects, such as `toString`, which converts an object to a string representation.

Many objects don't directly have `Object.prototype` as their prototype, but instead have another object, which provides its own default properties. Functions derive from `Function.prototype`, and arrays derive from `Array.prototype`.

```
console.log(Object.getPrototypeOf(isNaN) ==
            Function.prototype);
// ▷ true
console.log(Object.getPrototypeOf([]) ==
            Array.prototype);
// ▷ true
```

Such a prototype object will itself have a prototype, often `Object.prototype`, so that it still indirectly provides methods like toString.

The `Object.getPrototypeOf` function obviously returns the prototype of an object. You can use `Object.create` to create an object with a specific prototype.

```
var protoRabbit = {
  speak: function(line) {
    console.log("The " + this.type + " rabbit says '" +
                line + "'");
  }
};
```

```
var killerRabbit = Object.create(protoRabbit);
killerRabbit.type = "killer";
killerRabbit.speak("SKREEEE!");
// ▷ The killer rabbit says 'SKREEEE!'
```

The "proto" rabbit acts as a container for the properties that are shared by all rabbits. An individual rabbit object, like the killer rabbit, contains properties that apply only to itself—in this case its type—and derives shared properties from its prototype.

Constructors

A more convenient way to create objects that derive from some shared prototype is to use a *constructor*. In JavaScript, calling a function with the new keyword in front of it causes it to be treated as a constructor. The constructor will have its this variable bound to a fresh object, and unless it explicitly returns another object value, this new object will be returned from the call.

An object created with new is said to be an *instance* of its constructor.

Here is a simple constructor for rabbits. It is a convention to capitalize the names of constructors so that they are easily distinguished from other functions.

```
function Rabbit(type) {
  this.type = type;
}

var killerRabbit = new Rabbit("killer");
var blackRabbit = new Rabbit("black");
console.log(blackRabbit.type);
// ▷ black
```

Constructors (in fact, all functions) automatically get a property named prototype, which by default holds a plain, empty object that derives from Object.prototype. Every instance created with this constructor will have this object as its prototype. So to add a speak method to rabbits created with the Rabbit constructor, we can simply do this:

```
Rabbit.prototype.speak = function(line) {
  console.log("The " + this.type + " rabbit says '" +
              line + "'");
};
blackRabbit.speak("Doom...");
// ▷ The black rabbit says 'Doom...'
```

It is important to note the distinction between the way a prototype is associated with a constructor (through its prototype property) and the way objects *have* a prototype (which can be retrieved with Object.getPrototypeOf). The actual prototype of a constructor is Function.prototype since constructors are functions. Its prototype *property* will be the prototype of instances created through it but is not its *own* prototype.

Overriding Derived Properties

When you add a property to an object, whether it is present in the prototype or not, the property is added to the object *itself*, which will henceforth have it as its own property. If there *is* a property by the same name in the prototype, this property will no longer affect the object. The prototype itself is not changed.

```
Rabbit.prototype.teeth = "small";
console.log(killerRabbit.teeth);
// ▷ small
killerRabbit.teeth = "long, sharp, and bloody";
console.log(killerRabbit.teeth);
// ▷ long, sharp, and bloody
console.log(blackRabbit.teeth);
// ▷ small
console.log(Rabbit.prototype.teeth);
// ▷ small
```

The following diagram sketches the situation after this code has run. The Rabbit and Object prototypes lie behind killerRabbit as a kind of backdrop, where properties that are not found in the object itself can be looked up.

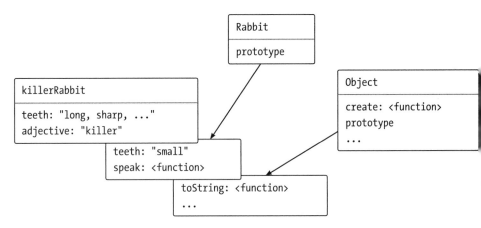

Overriding properties that exist in a prototype is often a useful thing to do. As the rabbit teeth example shows, it can be used to express exceptional properties in instances of a more generic class of objects, while letting the nonexceptional objects simply take a standard value from their prototype.

It is also used to give the standard function and array prototypes a different toString method than the basic object prototype.

```
console.log(Array.prototype.toString ==
           Object.prototype.toString);
// ▷ false
console.log([1, 2].toString());
// ▷ 1,2
```

Calling toString on an array gives a result similar to calling .join(",") on it—it puts commas between the values in the array. Directly calling Object.prototype.toString with an array produces a different string. That function doesn't know about arrays, so it simply puts the word "object" and the name of the type between square brackets.

```
console.log(Object.prototype.toString.call([1, 2]));
// ▷ [object Array]
```

Prototype Interference

A prototype can be used at any time to add new properties and methods to all objects based on it. For example, it might become necessary for our rabbits to dance.

```
Rabbit.prototype.dance = function() {
  console.log("The " + this.type + " rabbit dances a jig.");
};
killerRabbit.dance();
// ▷ The killer rabbit dances a jig.
```

That's convenient. But there are situations where it causes problems. In previous chapters, we used an object as a way to associate values with names by creating properties for the names and giving them the corresponding value as their value. Here's an example from Chapter 4:

```
var map = {};
function storePhi(event, phi) {
  map[event] = phi;
}

storePhi("pizza", 0.069);
storePhi("touched tree", -0.081);
```

We can iterate over all phi values in the object using a for/in loop and test whether a name is in there using the regular in operator. But unfortunately, the object's prototype gets in the way.

```
Object.prototype.nonsense = "hi";
for (var name in map)
  console.log(name);
// ▷ pizza
// ▷ touched tree
// ▷ nonsense
console.log("nonsense" in map);
// ▷ true
console.log("toString" in map);
// ▷ true

// Delete the problematic property again
delete Object.prototype.nonsense;
```

That's all wrong. There is no event called "nonsense" in our data set. And there *definitely* is no event called "toString."

Oddly, toString did not show up in the for/in loop, but the in operator returned true for it. This is because JavaScript distinguishes between *enumerable* and *nonenumerable* properties.

All properties that we create by simply assigning to them are enumerable. The standard properties in Object.prototype are all nonenumerable, which is why they do not show up in such a for/in loop.

It is possible to define our own nonenumerable properties by using the Object.defineProperty function, which allows us to control the type of property we are creating.

```
Object.defineProperty(Object.prototype, "hiddenNonsense",
                      {enumerable: false, value: "hi"});
for (var name in map)
  console.log(name);
// ▷ pizza
// ▷ touched tree
console.log(map.hiddenNonsense);
// ▷ hi
```

So now the property is there, but it won't show up in a loop. That's good. But we still have the problem with the regular in operator claiming that the Object.prototype properties exist in our object. For that, we can use the object's hasOwnProperty method.

```
console.log(map.hasOwnProperty("toString"));
// ▷ false
```

This method tells us whether the object *itself* has the property, without looking at its prototypes. This is often a more useful piece of information than what the in operator gives us.

When you are worried that someone (some other code you loaded into your program) might have messed with the base object prototype, I recommend you write your for/in loops like this:

```
for (var name in map) {
  if (map.hasOwnProperty(name)) {
    // ... this is an own property
  }
}
```

Prototype-less Objects

But the rabbit hole doesn't end there. What if someone registered the name hasOwnProperty in our map object and set it to the value 42? Now the call to map.hasOwnProperty will try to call the local property, which holds a number, not a function.

In such a case, prototypes just get in the way, and we would actually prefer to have objects without prototypes. We saw the Object.create function, which allows us to create an object with a specific prototype. You are allowed to pass null as the prototype to create a fresh object with no prototype. For objects like map, where the properties could be anything, this is exactly what we want.

```
var map = Object.create(null);
map["pizza"] = 0.069;
console.log("toString" in map);
// ▷ false
console.log("pizza" in map);
// ▷ true
```

Much better! We no longer need the hasOwnProperty kludge because all the properties the object has are its own properties. Now we can safely use for/in loops, no matter what people have been doing to Object.prototype.

Polymorphism

When you call the String function, which converts a value to a string, on an object, it will call the toString method on that object to try to create a meaningful string to return. I mentioned that some of the standard prototypes define their own version of toString so they can create a string that contains more useful information than "[object Object]".

This is a simple instance of a powerful idea. When a piece of code is written to work with objects that have a certain interface—in this case, a toString method—any kind of object that happens to support this interface can be plugged into the code, and it will just work.

This technique is called *polymorphism*—though no actual shape-shifting is involved. Polymorphic code can work with values of different shapes, as long as they support the interface it expects.

Laying Out a Table

I am going to work through a slightly more involved example in an attempt to give you a better idea what polymorphism, as well as object-oriented programming in general, looks like. The project is this: we will write a program that, given an array of arrays of table cells, builds up a string that contains a nicely laid out table—meaning that the columns are straight and the rows are aligned. Something like this:

```
name           height country
-----------    ------ -------------
Kilimanjaro     5895  Tanzania
Everest         8848  Nepal
Mount Fuji      3776  Japan
Mont Blanc      4808  Italy/France
Vaalserberg      323  Netherlands
Denali          6168  United States
Popocatepetl    5465  Mexico
```

The way our table-building system will work is that the builder function will ask each cell how wide and high it wants to be and then use this information to determine the width of the columns and the height of the rows. The builder function will then ask the cells to draw themselves at the correct size and assemble the results into a single string.

The layout program will communicate with the cell objects through a well-defined interface. That way, the types of cells that the program supports is not fixed in advance. We can add new cell styles later—for example, underlined cells for table headers—and if they support our interface, they will just work, without requiring changes to the layout program.

This is the interface:

- `minHeight()` returns a number indicating the minimum height this cell requires (in lines).

- `minWidth()` returns a number indicating this cell's minimum width (in characters).

- `draw(width, height)` returns an array of length `height`, which contains a series of strings that are each `width` characters wide. This represents the content of the cell.

I'm going to make heavy use of higher-order array methods in this example since it lends itself well to that approach.

The first part of the program computes arrays of minimum column widths and row heights for a grid of cells. The rows variable will hold an array of arrays, with each inner array representing a row of cells.

```
function rowHeights(rows) {
  return rows.map(function(row) {
    return row.reduce(function(max, cell) {
      return Math.max(max, cell.minHeight());
    }, 0);
  });
}

function colWidths(rows) {
  return rows[0].map(function(_, i) {
    return rows.reduce(function(max, row) {
      return Math.max(max, row[i].minWidth());
    }, 0);
  });
}
```

Using a variable name starting with an underscore (_) or consisting entirely of a single underscore is a way to indicate (to human readers) that this argument is not going to be used.

The rowHeights function shouldn't be too hard to follow. It uses reduce to compute the maximum height of an array of cells and wraps that in map in order to do it for all rows in the rows array.

Things are slightly harder for the colWidths function because the outer array is an array of rows, not of columns. I have failed to mention so far that map (as well as forEach, filter, and similar array methods) passes a second argument to the function it is given: the index of the current element. By mapping over the elements of the first row and only using the mapping function's second argument, colWidths builds up an array with one element for every column index. The call to reduce runs over the outer rows array for each index and picks out the width of the widest cell at that index.

Here's the code to draw a table:

```
function drawTable(rows) {
  var heights = rowHeights(rows);
  var widths = colWidths(rows);

  function drawLine(blocks, lineNo) {
    return blocks.map(function(block) {
      return block[lineNo];
    }).join(" ");
  }
```

```
function drawRow(row, rowNum) {
  var blocks = row.map(function(cell, colNum) {
    return cell.draw(widths[colNum], heights[rowNum]);
  });
  return blocks[0].map(function(_, lineNo) {
    return drawLine(blocks, lineNo);
  }).join("\n");
}

return rows.map(drawRow).join("\n");
}
```

The drawTable function uses the internal helper function drawRow to draw all rows and then joins them together with newline characters.

The drawRow function itself first converts the cell objects in the row to *blocks*, which are arrays of strings representing the content of the cells, split by line. A single cell containing simply the number 3776 might be represented by a single-element array like ["3776"], whereas an underlined cell might take up two lines and be represented by the array ["name", "---"].

The blocks for a row, which all have the same height, should appear next to each other in the final output. The second call to map in drawRow builds up this output line by line by mapping over the lines in the leftmost block and, for each of those, collecting a line that spans the full width of the table. These lines are then joined with newline characters to provide the whole row as drawRow's return value.

The function drawLine extracts lines that should appear next to each other from an array of blocks and joins them with a space character to create a one-character gap between the table's columns.

Now let's write a constructor for cells that contain text, which implements the interface for table cells. The constructor splits a string into an array of lines using the string method split, which cuts up a string at every occurrence of its argument and returns an array of the pieces. The minWidth method finds the maximum line width in this array.

```
function repeat(string, times) {
  var result = "";
  for (var i = 0; i < times; i++)
    result += string;
  return result;
}

function TextCell(text) {
  this.text = text.split("\n");
}
TextCell.prototype.minWidth = function() {
  return this.text.reduce(function(width, line) {
    return Math.max(width, line.length);
  }, 0);
```

```
};
TextCell.prototype.minHeight = function() {
  return this.text.length;
};
TextCell.prototype.draw = function(width, height) {
  var result = [];
  for (var i = 0; i < height; i++) {
    var line = this.text[i] || "";
    result.push(line + repeat(" ", width - line.length));
  }
  return result;
};
```

The code uses a helper function called repeat, which builds a string whose value is the string argument repeated times number of times. The draw method uses it to add "padding" to lines so that they all have the required length.

Let's try everything we've written so far by building up a 5×5 checkerboard.

```
var rows = [];
for (var i = 0; i < 5; i++) {
  var row = [];
  for (var j = 0; j < 5; j++) {
    if ((j + i) % 2 == 0)
      row.push(new TextCell("##"));
    else
      row.push(new TextCell("  "));
  }
  rows.push(row);
}
console.log(drawTable(rows));
// ▷ ##    ##    ##
//      ##    ##
//   ##    ##    ##
//      ##    ##
//   ##    ##    ##
```

It works! But since all cells have the same size, the table-layout code doesn't really do anything interesting.

The source data for the table of mountains that we are trying to build is available in the MOUNTAINS variable in the sandbox and also downloadable from the list of data sets on the website (*http://eloquentjavascript.net/code/*).

We will want to highlight the top row, which contains the column names, by underlining the cells with a series of dash characters. No problem—we simply write a cell type that handles underlining.

```
function UnderlinedCell(inner) {
  this.inner = inner;
};
UnderlinedCell.prototype.minWidth = function() {
  return this.inner.minWidth();
};
UnderlinedCell.prototype.minHeight = function() {
  return this.inner.minHeight() + 1;
};
UnderlinedCell.prototype.draw = function(width, height) {
  return this.inner.draw(width, height - 1)
    .concat([repeat("-", width)]);
};
```

An underlined cell *contains* another cell. It reports its minimum size as being the same as that of its inner cell (by calling through to that cell's minWidth and minHeight methods) but adds one to the height to account for the space taken up by the underline.

Drawing such a cell is quite simple—we take the content of the inner cell and concatenate a single line full of dashes to it.

Having an underlining mechanism, we can now write a function that builds up a grid of cells from our data set.

```
function dataTable(data) {
  var keys = Object.keys(data[0]);
  var headers = keys.map(function(name) {
    return new UnderlinedCell(new TextCell(name));
  });
  var body = data.map(function(row) {
    return keys.map(function(name) {
      return new TextCell(String(row[name]));
    });
  });
  return [headers].concat(body);
}

console.log(drawTable(dataTable(MOUNTAINS)));
// ▷ name          height country
//    ------------ ------ -------------
//    Kilimanjaro  5895   Tanzania
//    ... etcetera
```

The standard Object.keys function returns an array of property names in an object. The top row of the table must contain underlined cells that give the names of the columns. Below that, the values of all the objects in the data set appear as normal cells—we extract them by mapping over the keys array so that we are sure that the order of the cells is the same in every row.

The resulting table resembles the example shown before, except that it does not right-align the numbers in the height column. We will get to that in a moment.

Getters and Setters

When specifying an interface, it is possible to include properties that are not methods. We could have defined minHeight and minWidth to simply hold numbers. But that'd have required us to compute them in the constructor, which adds code there that isn't strictly relevant to *constructing* the object. It would cause problems if, for example, the inner cell of an underlined cell was changed, at which point the size of the underlined cell should also change.

This has led some people to adopt a principle of never including non-method properties in interfaces. Rather than directly access a simple value property, they'd use getSomething and setSomething methods to read and write the property. This approach has the downside that you will end up writing—and reading—a lot of additional methods.

Fortunately, JavaScript provides a technique that gets us the best of both worlds. We can specify properties that, from the outside, look like normal properties but secretly have methods associated with them.

```
var pile = {
  elements: ["eggshell", "orange peel", "worm"],
  get height() {
    return this.elements.length;
  },
  set height(value) {
    console.log("Ignoring attempt to set height to", value);
  }
};

console.log(pile.height);
// ▷ 3
pile.height = 100;
// ▷ Ignoring attempt to set height to 100
```

In object literal, the get or set notation for properties allows you to specify a function to be run when the property is read or written. You can also add such a property to an existing object, for example a prototype, using the Object.defineProperty function (which we previously used to create nonenumerable properties).

```
Object.defineProperty(TextCell.prototype, "heightProp", {
  get: function() { return this.text.length; }
});
```

```
var cell = new TextCell("no\nway");
console.log(cell.heightProp);
// ▷ 2
cell.heightProp = 100;
console.log(cell.heightProp);
// ▷ 2
```

You can use a similar set property, in the object passed to defineProperty, to specify a setter method. When a getter but no setter is defined, writing to the property is simply ignored.

Inheritance

We are not quite done yet with our table layout exercise. It helps readability to right-align columns of numbers. We should create another cell type that is like TextCell, but rather than padding the lines on the right side, it pads them on the left side so that they align to the right.

We could simply write a whole new constructor with all three methods in its prototype. But prototypes may themselves have prototypes, and this allows us to do something clever.

```
function RTextCell(text) {
  TextCell.call(this, text);
}
RTextCell.prototype = Object.create(TextCell.prototype);
RTextCell.prototype.draw = function(width, height) {
  var result = [];
  for (var i = 0; i < height; i++) {
    var line = this.text[i] || "";
    result.push(repeat(" ", width - line.length) + line);
  }
  return result;
};
```

We reuse the constructor and the minHeight and minWidth methods from the regular TextCell. An RTextCell is now basically equivalent to a TextCell, except that its draw method contains a different function.

This pattern is called *inheritance*. It allows us to build slightly different data types from existing data types with relatively little work. Typically, the new constructor will call the old constructor (using the call method in order to be able to give it the new object as its this value). Once this constructor has been called, we can assume that all the fields that the old object type is supposed to contain have been added. We arrange for the constructor's prototype to derive from the old prototype so that instances of this type will also have access to the properties in that prototype. Finally, we can override some of these properties by adding them to our new prototype.

Now, if we slightly adjust the dataTable function to use RTextCells for cells whose value is a number, we get the table we were aiming for.

```
function dataTable(data) {
  var keys = Object.keys(data[0]);
  var headers = keys.map(function(name) {
    return new UnderlinedCell(new TextCell(name));
  });
  var body = data.map(function(row) {
    return keys.map(function(name) {
      var value = row[name];
      // This was changed:
      if (typeof value == "number")
        return new RTextCell(String(value));
      else
        return new TextCell(String(value));
    });
  });
  return [headers].concat(body);
}

console.log(drawTable(dataTable(MOUNTAINS)));
// ▷ ... beautifully aligned table
```

Inheritance is a fundamental part of the object-oriented tradition, alongside encapsulation and polymorphism. But while the latter two are now generally regarded as wonderful ideas, inheritance is somewhat controversial.

The main reason for this is that it is often confused with polymorphism, sold as a more powerful tool than it really is, and subsequently overused in all kinds of ugly ways. Whereas encapsulation and polymorphism can be used to *separate* pieces of code from each other, reducing the tangledness of the overall program, inheritance fundamentally ties types together, creating *more* tangle.

You can have polymorphism without inheritance, as we saw. I am not going to tell you to avoid inheritance entirely—I use it regularly in my own programs. But you should see it as a slightly dodgy trick that can help you define new types with little code, not as a grand principle of code organization. A preferable way to extend types is through composition, such as how UnderlinedCell builds on another cell object by simply storing it in a property and forwarding method calls to it in its own methods.

The instanceof Operator

It is occasionally useful to know whether an object was derived from a specific constructor. For this, JavaScript provides a binary operator called instanceof.

```
console.log(new RTextCell("A") instanceof RTextCell);
// ▷ true
console.log(new RTextCell("A") instanceof TextCell);
// ▷ true
console.log(new TextCell("A") instanceof RTextCell);
// ▷ false
console.log([1] instanceof Array);
// ▷ true
```

The operator will see through inherited types. An RTextCell is an instance of TextCell because RTextCell.prototype derives from TextCell.prototype. The operator can be applied to standard constructors like Array. Almost every object is an instance of Object.

Summary

So objects are more complicated than I initially portrayed them. They have prototypes, which are other objects, and will act as if they have properties they don't have as long as the prototype has that property. Simple objects have Object.prototype as their prototype.

Constructors, which are functions whose names usually start with a capital letter, can be used with the new operator to create new objects. The new object's prototype will be the object found in the prototype property of the constructor function. You can make good use of this by putting the properties that all values of a given type share into their prototype. The instanceof operator can, given an object and a constructor, tell you whether that object is an instance of that constructor.

One useful thing to do with objects is to specify an interface for them and tell everybody that they are supposed to talk to your object only through that interface. The rest of the details that make up your object are now *encapsulated*, hidden behind the interface.

Once you are talking in terms of interfaces, who says that only one kind of object may implement this interface? Having different objects expose the same interface and then writing code that works on any object with the interface is called polymorphism. It is very useful.

When implementing multiple types that differ in only some details, it can be helpful to simply make the prototype of your new type derive from the prototype of your old type and have your new constructor call the old one. This gives you an object type similar to the old type but for which you can add and override properties as you see fit.

Exercises

A Vector Type

Write a constructor Vector that represents a vector in two-dimensional space. It takes x and y parameters (numbers), which it should save to properties of the same name.

Give the Vector prototype two methods, plus and minus, that take another vector as a parameter and return a new vector that has the sum or difference of the two vectors' (the one in this and the parameter) *x* and *y* values.

Add a getter property length to the prototype that computes the length of the vector—that is, the distance of the point (*x*, *y*) from the origin (0, 0).

Another Cell

Implement a cell type named StretchCell(inner, width, height) that conforms to the table cell interface described earlier in the chapter. It should wrap another cell (like UnderlinedCell does) and ensure that the resulting cell has at least the given width and height, even if the inner cell would naturally be smaller.

Sequence Interface

Design an *interface* that abstracts iteration over a collection of values. An object that provides this interface represents a sequence, and the interface must somehow make it possible for code that uses such an object to iterate over the sequence, looking at the element values it is made up of and having some way to find out when the end of the sequence is reached.

When you have specified your interface, try to write a function logFive that takes a sequence object and calls console.log on its first five elements—or fewer, if the sequence has fewer than five elements.

Then implement an object type ArraySeq that wraps an array and allows iteration over the array using the interface you designed. Implement another object type RangeSeq that iterates over a range of integers (taking from and to arguments to its constructor) instead.

"The question of whether
Machines Can Think . . . is about as
relevant as the question of whether
Submarines Can Swim."

—Edsger Dijkstra,
The Threats to Computing Science

7

PROJECT: ELECTRONIC LIFE

In "project" chapters, I'll stop pummeling you with new
theory for a brief moment and instead work through a
program with you. Theory is indispensable when learning to program, but it should also be accompanied by
reading and understanding nontrivial programs.

Our project in this chapter is to build a virtual ecosystem, a little world
populated with critters that move around and struggle for survival.

Definition

To make this task manageable, we will radically simplify the concept of a
world. Namely, a world will be a two-dimensional grid where each entity takes
up one full square of the grid. On every *turn*, the critters all get a chance to
take some action.

Thus, we chop both time and space into units with a fixed size: squares
for space and turns for time. Of course, this is a somewhat crude and inac-
curate approximation. But our simulation is intended to be amusing, not
accurate, so we can freely cut such corners.

We can define a world with a *plan*, an array of strings that lays out the
world's grid using one character per square.

```
var plan =
  ["############################",
   "#      #    #      o      ##",
   "#                          #",
   "#          #####            #",
   "##         #    #    ##      #",
   "###           ##    #       #",
   "#           ###     #       #",
   "#    ####                   #",
   "#    ##       o            #",
   "# o  #         o      ###  #",
   "#    #                     #",
   "############################"];
```

The # characters in this plan represent walls and rocks, and the o characters represent critters. The spaces, as you might have guessed, are empty space.

A plan array can be used to create a world object. Such an object keeps track of the size and content of the world. It has a toString method, which converts the world back to a printable string (similar to the plan it was based on) so that we can see what's going on inside. The world object also has a turn method, which allows all the critters in it to take one turn and updates the world to reflect their actions.

Representing Space

The grid that models the world has a fixed width and height. Squares are identified by their x- and y-coordinates. We use a simple type, Vector (as seen in the exercises for the previous chapter), to represent these coordinate pairs.

```
function Vector(x, y) {
  this.x = x;
  this.y = y;
}
Vector.prototype.plus = function(other) {
  return new Vector(this.x + other.x, this.y + other.y);
};
```

Next, we need an object type that models the grid itself. A grid is part of a world, but we are making it a separate object (which will be a property of a world object) to keep the world object itself simple. The world should concern itself with world-related things, and the grid should concern itself with grid-related things.

To store a grid of values, we have several options. We can use an array of row arrays and use two property accesses to get to a specific square, like this:

```
var grid = [["top left",    "top middle",    "top right"],
            ["bottom left", "bottom middle", "bottom right"]];
console.log(grid[1][2]);
// ▷ bottom right
```

Or we can use a single array, with size width × height, and decide that the element at (x,y) is found at position $x + (y \times width)$ in the array.

```
var grid = ["top left",    "top middle",    "top right",
            "bottom left", "bottom middle", "bottom right"];
console.log(grid[2 + (1 * 3)]);
// ▷ bottom right
```

Since the actual access to this array will be wrapped in methods on the grid object type, it doesn't matter to outside code which approach we take. I chose the second representation because it makes it much easier to create the array. When calling the Array constructor with a single number as an argument, it creates a new empty array of the given length.

This code defines the Grid object, with some basic methods:

```
function Grid(width, height) {
  this.space = new Array(width * height);
  this.width = width;
  this.height = height;
}
Grid.prototype.isInside = function(vector) {
  return vector.x >= 0 && vector.x < this.width &&
         vector.y >= 0 && vector.y < this.height;
};
Grid.prototype.get = function(vector) {
  return this.space[vector.x + this.width * vector.y];
};
Grid.prototype.set = function(vector, value) {
  this.space[vector.x + this.width * vector.y] = value;
};
```

And here is a trivial test:

```
var grid = new Grid(5, 5);
console.log(grid.get(new Vector(1, 1)));
// ▷ undefined
grid.set(new Vector(1, 1), "X");
console.log(grid.get(new Vector(1, 1)));
// ▷ X
```

A Critter's Programming Interface

Before we can start on the World constructor, we must get more specific about the critter objects that will be living inside it. I mentioned that the world will ask the critters what actions they want to take. This works as follows: each critter object has an act method that, when called, returns an *action*. An action is an object with a type property, which names the type of action the critter wants to take, for example "move". The action may also contain extra information, such as the direction the critter wants to move in.

Critters are terribly myopic and can see only the squares directly around them on the grid. But even this limited vision can be useful when deciding which action to take. When the act method is called, it is given a view object that allows the critter to inspect its surroundings. We name the eight surrounding squares by their compass directions: "n" for north, "ne" for northeast, and so on. Here's the object we will use to map from direction names to coordinate offsets:

```
var directions = {
  "n":  new Vector( 0, -1),
  "ne": new Vector( 1, -1),
  "e":  new Vector( 1,  0),
  "se": new Vector( 1,  1),
  "s":  new Vector( 0,  1),
  "sw": new Vector(-1,  1),
  "w":  new Vector(-1,  0),
  "nw": new Vector(-1, -1)
};
```

The view object has a method look, which takes a direction and returns a character, for example "#" when there is a wall in that direction, or " " (space) when there is nothing there. The object also provides the convenient methods find and findAll. Both take a map character as an argument. The first returns a direction in which the character can be found next to the critter or returns null if no such direction exists. The second returns an array containing all directions with that character. For example, a creature sitting left (west) of a wall will get ["ne", "e", "se"] when calling findAll on its view object with the "#" character as argument.

Here is a simple, stupid critter that just follows its nose until it hits an obstacle and then bounces off in a random open direction:

```
function randomElement(array) {
  return array[Math.floor(Math.random() * array.length)];
}

var directionNames = "n ne e se s sw w nw".split(" ");

function BouncingCritter() {
  this.direction = randomElement(directionNames);
};
```

```
BouncingCritter.prototype.act = function(view) {
  if (view.look(this.direction) != " ")
    this.direction = view.find(" ") || "s";
  return {type: "move", direction: this.direction};
};
```

The `randomElement` helper function simply picks a random element from an array, using `Math.random` plus some arithmetic to get a random index. We'll use this again later because randomness can be useful in simulations.

To pick a random direction, the `BouncingCritter` constructor calls `randomElement` on an array of direction names. We could also have used `Object.keys` to get this array from the `directions` object we defined earlier, but that provides no guarantees about the order in which the properties are listed. In most situations, modern JavaScript engines will return properties in the order they were defined, but they are not required to.

The `|| "s"` in the act method is there to prevent `this.direction` from getting the value `null` if the critter is somehow trapped with no empty space around it (for example when crowded into a corner by other critters).

The World Object

Now we can start on the `World` object type. The constructor takes a plan (the array of strings representing the world's grid, described earlier) and a *legend* as arguments. A legend is an object that tells us what each character in the map means. It contains a constructor for every character—except for the space character, which always refers to `null`, the value we'll use to represent empty space.

```
function elementFromChar(legend, ch) {
  if (ch == " ")
    return null;
  var element = new legend[ch]();
  element.originChar = ch;
  return element;
}

function World(map, legend) {
  var grid = new Grid(map[0].length, map.length);
  this.grid = grid;
  this.legend = legend;

  map.forEach(function(line, y) {
    for (var x = 0; x < line.length; x++)
      grid.set(new Vector(x, y),
               elementFromChar(legend, line[x]));
  });
}
```

In `elementFromChar`, first we create an instance of the right type by looking up the character's constructor and applying `new` to it. Then we add an `originChar` property to it to make it easy to find out what character the element was originally created from.

We need this `originChar` property when implementing the world's `toString` method. This method builds up a maplike string from the world's current state by performing a two-dimensional loop over the squares on the grid.

```
function charFromElement(element) {
  if (element == null)
    return " ";
  else
    return element.originChar;
}

World.prototype.toString = function() {
  var output = "";
  for (var y = 0; y < this.grid.height; y++) {
    for (var x = 0; x < this.grid.width; x++) {
      var element = this.grid.get(new Vector(x, y));
      output += charFromElement(element);
    }
    output += "\n";
  }
  return output;
};
```

A wall is a simple object—it is used only for taking up space and has no act method.

```
function Wall() {}
```

When we try the `World` object by creating an instance based on the plan from earlier in the chapter and then calling `toString` on it, we get a string very similar to the plan we put in.

```
var world = new World(plan,
                      {"#": Wall,
                       "o": BouncingCritter});
console.log(world.toString());
// ▷ ############################
// #      #    #      o      ##
// #                          #
// #          #####           #
// ##         #   #    ##      #
// ###           ##    #       #
// #             ###   #       #
// #   ####                    #
```

```
//     #   ##       o           #
//     # o #           o       ### #
//     #   #                     #
//     ############################
```

this and Its Scope

The World constructor contains a call to forEach. One interesting thing to note is that inside the function passed to forEach, we are no longer directly in the function scope of the constructor. Each function call gets its own this binding, so the this in the inner function does *not* refer to the newly constructed object that the outer this refers to. In fact, when a function isn't called as a method, this will refer to the global object.

This means that we can't write this.grid to access the grid from inside the loop. Instead, the outer function creates a normal local variable, grid, through which the inner function gets access to the grid.

This is a bit of a design blunder in JavaScript. Fortunately, the next version of the language provides a solution for this problem. Meanwhile, there are workarounds. A common pattern is to say var self = this and from then on refer to self, which is a normal variable and thus visible to inner functions.

Another solution is to use the bind method, which allows us to provide an explicit this object to bind to.

```
var test = {
  prop: 10,
  addPropTo: function(array) {
    return array.map(function(elt) {
      return this.prop + elt;
    }.bind(this));
  }
};
console.log(test.addPropTo([5]));
// ▷ [15]
```

The function passed to map is the result of the bind call and thus has its this bound to the first argument given to bind—the outer function's this value (which holds the test object).

Most standard higher-order methods on arrays, such as forEach and map, take an optional second argument that can also be used to provide a this for the calls to the iteration function. So you could express the previous example in a slightly simpler way.

```
var test = {
  prop: 10,
  addPropTo: function(array) {
    return array.map(function(elt) {
```

```
      return this.prop + elt;
    }, this); // ← no bind
  }
};
console.log(test.addPropTo([5]));
// ▷ [15]
```

This works only for higher-order functions that support such a *context* parameter. When they don't, you'll need to use one of the other approaches.

In our own higher-order functions, we can support such a context parameter by using the call method to call the function given as an argument. For example, here is a forEach method for our Grid type, which calls a given function for each element in the grid that isn't null or undefined:

```
Grid.prototype.forEach = function(f, context) {
  for (var y = 0; y < this.height; y++) {
    for (var x = 0; x < this.width; x++) {
      var value = this.space[x + y * this.width];
      if (value != null)
        f.call(context, value, new Vector(x, y));
    }
  }
};
```

Animating Life

The next step is to write a turn method for the World object that gives the critters a chance to act. It will go over the grid using the forEach method we just defined, looking for objects with an act method. When it finds one, turn calls that method to get an action object and carries out the action when it is valid. For now, only "move" actions are understood.

There is one potential problem with this approach. Can you spot it? If we let critters move as we come across them, they may move to a square that we haven't looked at yet, and we'll allow them to move *again* when we reach that square. Thus, we have to keep an array of critters that have already had their turn and ignore them when we see them again.

```
World.prototype.turn = function() {
  var acted = [];
  this.grid.forEach(function(critter, vector) {
    if (critter.act && acted.indexOf(critter) == -1) {
      acted.push(critter);
      this.letAct(critter, vector);
    }
  }, this);
};
```

We use the second parameter to the grid's forEach method to be able to access the correct this inside the inner function. The letAct method contains the actual logic that allows the critters to move.

```
World.prototype.letAct = function(critter, vector) {
  var action = critter.act(new View(this, vector));
  if (action && action.type == "move") {
    var dest = this.checkDestination(action, vector);
    if (dest && this.grid.get(dest) == null) {
      this.grid.set(vector, null);
      this.grid.set(dest, critter);
    }
  }
};

World.prototype.checkDestination = function(action, vector) {
  if (directions.hasOwnProperty(action.direction)) {
    var dest = vector.plus(directions[action.direction]);
    if (this.grid.isInside(dest))
      return dest;
  }
};
```

First, we simply ask the critter to act, passing it a view object that knows about the world and the critter's current position in that world (we'll define View in a moment). The act method returns an action of some kind.

If the action's type is not "move", it is ignored. If it *is* "move", if it has a direction property that refers to a valid direction, *and* if the square in that direction is empty (null), we set the square where the critter used to be to hold null and store the critter in the destination square.

Note that letAct takes care to ignore nonsense input—it doesn't assume that the action's direction property is valid or that the type property makes sense. This kind of *defensive* programming makes sense in some situations. The main reason for doing it is to validate inputs coming from sources you don't control (such as user or file input), but it can also be useful to isolate subsystems from each other. In this case, the intention is that the critters themselves can be programmed sloppily—they don't have to verify if their intended actions make sense. They can just request an action, and the world will figure out whether to allow it.

These two methods are not part of the external interface of a World object. They are an internal detail. Some languages provide ways to explicitly declare certain methods and properties *private* and signal an error when you try to use them from outside the object. JavaScript does not, so you will have to rely on some other form of communication to describe what is part of an object's interface. Sometimes it can help to use a naming scheme to distinguish between external and internal properties, for example by prefixing all internal ones with an underscore character (_). This will make accidental uses of properties that are not part of an object's interface easier to spot.

The one missing part, the View type, looks like this:

```
function View(world, vector) {
  this.world = world;
  this.vector = vector;
}
View.prototype.look = function(dir) {
  var target = this.vector.plus(directions[dir]);
  if (this.world.grid.isInside(target))
    return charFromElement(this.world.grid.get(target));
  else
    return "#";
};
View.prototype.findAll = function(ch) {
  var found = [];
  for (var dir in directions)
    if (this.look(dir) == ch)
      found.push(dir);
  return found;
};
View.prototype.find = function(ch) {
  var found = this.findAll(ch);
  if (found.length == 0) return null;
  return randomElement(found);
};
```

The look method figures out the coordinates that we are trying to look at and, if they are inside the grid, finds the character corresponding to the element that sits there. For coordinates outside the grid, look simply pretends that there is a wall there so that if you define a world that isn't walled in, the critters still won't be tempted to try to walk off the edges.

It Moves

We instantiated a World object earlier. Now that we've added all the necessary methods, it should be possible to actually make the world move.

```
for (var i = 0; i < 5; i++) {
  world.turn();
  console.log(world.toString());
}
// ▷ ... five turns of moving critters
```

The first two maps that are displayed will look something like this (depending on the random direction the critters picked):

```
###############################   ###############################
#      #    #              ## #   #      #    #              ##
#                  o       # #    #                          #
#          #####           # #    #          #####    o      #
##         #    #    ##     # ##         #    #    ##       #
###             ##    #     # ###             ##    #       #
#               ###   #     # #               ###   #       #
#     ####                 # #    ####                      #
#     ##                   # #    ##                        #
#     #    o         ### #  #o    #                   ### #
#o    #         o         # #    #    #         o  o        #
###############################   ###############################
```

They move! To get a more interactive view of these critters crawling around and bouncing off the walls, open this chapter in the online version of the book at *http://eloquentjavascript.net/*.

More Life-forms

The dramatic highlight of our world, if you watch for a bit, is when two critters bounce off each other. Can you think of another interesting form of behavior?

The one I came up with is a critter that moves along walls. Conceptually, the critter keeps its left hand (paw, tentacle, whatever) to the wall and follows along. This turns out to be not entirely trivial to implement.

We need to be able to "compute" with compass directions. Since directions are modeled by a set of strings, we need to define our own operation (dirPlus) to calculate relative directions. So dirPlus("n", 1) means one 45-degree turn clockwise from north, giving "ne". Similarly, dirPlus("s", -2) means 90 degrees counterclockwise from south, which is east.

```
function dirPlus(dir, n) {
  var index = directionNames.indexOf(dir);
  return directionNames[(index + n + 8) % 8];
}

function WallFollower() {
  this.dir = "s";
}
```

```
WallFollower.prototype.act = function(view) {
  var start = this.dir;
  if (view.look(dirPlus(this.dir, -3)) != " ")
    start = this.dir = dirPlus(this.dir, -2);
  while (view.look(this.dir) != " ") {
    this.dir = dirPlus(this.dir, 1);
    if (this.dir == start) break;
  }
  return {type: "move", direction: this.dir};
};
```

The act method only has to "scan" the critter's surroundings, starting from its left side and going clockwise until it finds an empty square. It then moves in the direction of that empty square.

What complicates things is that a critter may end up in the middle of empty space, either as its start position or as a result of walking around another critter. If we apply the approach I just described in empty space, the poor critter will just keep on turning left at every step, running in circles.

So there is an extra check (the if statement) to start scanning to the left only if it looks like the critter has just passed some kind of obstacle—that is, if the space behind and to the left of the critter is not empty. Otherwise, the critter starts scanning directly ahead, so that it'll walk straight when in empty space.

And finally, there's a test comparing this.dir to start after every pass through the loop to make sure that the loop won't run forever when the critter is walled in or crowded in by other critters and can't find an empty square.

A More Lifelike Simulation

To make life in our world more interesting, we will add the concepts of food and reproduction. Each living thing in the world gets a new property, energy, which is reduced by performing actions and increased by eating things. When the critter has enough energy, it can reproduce, generating a new critter of the same kind. To keep things simple, the critters in our world reproduce asexually, all by themselves.

If critters only move around and eat one another, the world will soon succumb to the law of increasing entropy, run out of energy, and become a lifeless wasteland. To prevent this from happening (too quickly, at least), we add plants to the world. Plants do not move. They just use photosynthesis to grow (that is, increase their energy) and reproduce.

To make this work, we'll need a world with a different letAct method. We could just replace the method of the World prototype, but I've become very attached to our simulation with the wall-following critters and would hate to break that old world.

One solution is to use inheritance. We create a new constructor, LifelikeWorld, whose prototype is based on the World prototype but which overrides the letAct method. The new letAct method delegates the work of actually performing an action to various functions stored in the actionTypes object.

```
function LifelikeWorld(map, legend) {
  World.call(this, map, legend);
}
LifelikeWorld.prototype = Object.create(World.prototype);

var actionTypes = Object.create(null);

LifelikeWorld.prototype.letAct = function(critter, vector) {
  var action = critter.act(new View(this, vector));
  var handled = action &&
    action.type in actionTypes &&
    actionTypes[action.type].call(this, critter,
                                  vector, action);
  if (!handled) {
    critter.energy -= 0.2;
    if (critter.energy <= 0)
      this.grid.set(vector, null);
  }
};
```

The new letAct method first checks whether an action was returned at all, then whether a handler function for this type of action exists, and finally whether that handler returned true, indicating that it successfully handled the action. Note the use of call to give the handler access to the world, through its this binding.

If the action didn't work for whatever reason, the default action is for the critter to simply wait. It loses one-fifth point of energy, and if its energy level drops to zero or below, the critter dies and is removed from the grid.

Action Handlers

The simplest action a critter can perform is "grow", used by plants. When an action object like {type: "grow"} is returned, the following handler method will be called:

```
actionTypes.grow = function(critter) {
  critter.energy += 0.5;
  return true;
};
```

Growing always succeeds and adds half a point to the plant's energy level.

Moving is more involved.

```
actionTypes.move = function(critter, vector, action) {
  var dest = this.checkDestination(action, vector);
  if (dest == null ||
      critter.energy <= 1 ||
      this.grid.get(dest) != null)
    return false;
  critter.energy -= 1;
  this.grid.set(vector, null);
  this.grid.set(dest, critter);
  return true;
};
```

This action first checks, using the checkDestination method defined earlier, whether the action provides a valid destination. If not, or if the destination isn't empty, or if the critter lacks the required energy, move returns false to indicate no action was taken. Otherwise, it moves the critter and subtracts the energy cost.

In addition to moving, critters can eat.

```
actionTypes.eat = function(critter, vector, action) {
  var dest = this.checkDestination(action, vector);
  var atDest = dest != null && this.grid.get(dest);
  if (!atDest || atDest.energy == null)
    return false;
  critter.energy += atDest.energy;
  this.grid.set(dest, null);
  return true;
};
```

Eating another critter also involves providing a valid destination square. This time, the destination must not be empty and must contain something with energy, like a critter (but not a wall—walls are not edible). If so, the energy from the eaten is transferred to the eater, and the victim is removed from the grid.

And finally, we allow our critters to reproduce.

```
actionTypes.reproduce = function(critter, vector, action) {
  var baby = elementFromChar(this.legend,
                             critter.originChar);
  var dest = this.checkDestination(action, vector);
  if (dest == null ||
      critter.energy <= 2 * baby.energy ||
      this.grid.get(dest) != null)
    return false;
  critter.energy -= 2 * baby.energy;
  this.grid.set(dest, baby);
```

```
    return true;
};
```

Reproducing costs twice the energy level of the newborn critter. So we first create a (hypothetical) baby using elementFromChar on the critter's own origin character. Once we have a baby, we can find its energy level and test whether the parent has enough energy to successfully bring it into the world. We also require a valid (and empty) destination.

If everything is okay, the baby is put onto the grid (it is now no longer hypothetical), and the energy is spent.

Populating the New World

We now have a framework to simulate these more lifelike creatures. We could put the critters from the old world into it, but they would just die since they don't have an energy property. So let's make new ones. First we'll write a plant, which is a rather simple life-form.

```
function Plant() {
  this.energy = 3 + Math.random() * 4;
}
Plant.prototype.act = function(context) {
  if (this.energy > 15) {
    var space = context.find(" ");
    if (space)
      return {type: "reproduce", direction: space};
  }
  if (this.energy < 20)
    return {type: "grow"};
};
```

Plants start with an energy level between 3 and 7, randomized so that they don't all reproduce in the same turn. When a plant reaches 15 energy points and there is empty space nearby, it reproduces into that empty space. If a plant can't reproduce, it simply grows until it reaches energy level 20.

We now define a plant eater.

```
function PlantEater() {
  this.energy = 20;
}
PlantEater.prototype.act = function(context) {
  var space = context.find(" ");
  if (this.energy > 60 && space)
    return {type: "reproduce", direction: space};
  var plant = context.find("*");
  if (plant)
    return {type: "eat", direction: plant};
```

```
  if (space)
    return {type: "move", direction: space};
};
```

We'll use the * character for plants, so that's what critters will look for when they search for food.

Bringing the World to Life

And that gives us enough elements to try our new world. Imagine the following map as a grassy valley with a herd of herbivores in it, some boulders, and lush plant life everywhere.

```
var valley = new LifelikeWorld(
  ["############################",
   "#####                 ######",
   "##    ***             **##",
   "#    *##**         ** 0 *##",
   "#    ***     0    ##**    *#",
   "#       0         ##***    #",
   "#                 ##**     #",
   "#   0       #*            #",
   "#*          #**     0     #",
   "#***        ##**    0   **#",
   "##****    #####**      *###",
   "############################"],
  {"#": Wall,
   "0": PlantEater,
   "*": Plant}
);
```

Let's see what happens if we run this. These snapshots illustrate a typical run of this world.

```
############################   ############################
#####                 ######   ##### **             ######
##    ***  0         *##        ##  ** *          0     ##
#    *##*           **    *##    #   **##                ##
#    **             ##*    *#    #  ** 0         ##0     #
#                  ##*      #    #   *0      * *  ##      #
#                 ## 0     #    #            *** ##   0 #
#           #*      0      #    #**        #***       #
#*          #**  0         #    #**    0  #****       #
#*   0   0 ##*         **#      #***       ##***   0   #
##*         ###*        ###     ##**       ###**  0  ###
############################   ############################
```

```
#############################    #############################
#####0 0            ######    ##### 0            ######
##                    ##    ##                    ##
#     ##0             ##    #    ##            0    ##
#         0  0 *##      #    #                ##     #
# 0    0     0  **##   0 #    #                ##     #
#              **##    0 #    #           0 ## *    #
#         #   *** *     #    #         #  0       #
#         # 0*****  0   #    #      0 #  0        #
#         ##*******     #    #          ##   0    0 #
##        ###*******   ###    ##      ### 0        ###
#############################    #############################


#############################    #############################
#####               ######    #####            ######
##                    ##    ##          **  *  ##
#    ##               ##    #    ##        ***** ##
#                 ##    #    #           ##****   #
#              ##* *   #    #           ##*****   #
#         0  ## *    #    #           ##******* #
#      #             # #    #      #       ** **  #
#      #             # #    #      #              #
#      ##            # #    #      ##             #
##       ###       ###    ##      ###        ###
#############################    #############################
```

Most of the time, the plants multiply and expand quite quickly, but then the abundance of food causes a population explosion of the herbivores, who proceed to wipe out all or nearly all of the plants, resulting in a mass starvation of the critters. Sometimes, the ecosystem recovers and another cycle starts. At other times, one of the species dies out completely. If it's the herbivores, the whole space will fill with plants. If it's the plants, the remaining critters starve, and the valley becomes a desolate wasteland. Ah, the cruelty of nature.

Exercises

Artificial Stupidity

Having the inhabitants of our world go extinct after a few minutes is kind of depressing. To deal with this, we could try to create a smarter plant eater.

There are several obvious problems with our herbivores. First, they are terribly greedy, stuffing themselves with every plant they see until they have wiped out the local plant life. Second, their randomized movement (recall that the view.find method returns a random direction when multiple directions match) causes them to stumble around ineffectively and starve if there don't happen to be any plants nearby. And finally, they breed very fast, which makes the cycles between abundance and famine quite intense.

Write a new critter type that tries to address one or more of these points and substitute it for the old `PlantEater` type in the valley world. See how it fares. Tweak it some more if necessary.

Predators

Any serious ecosystem has a food chain longer than a single link. Write another critter that survives by eating the herbivore critter. You'll notice that stability is even harder to achieve now that there are cycles at multiple levels. Try to find a strategy to make the ecosystem run smoothly for at least a little while.

One thing that will help is to make the world bigger. This way, local population booms or busts are less likely to wipe out a species entirely, and there is space for the relatively large prey population needed to sustain a small predator population.

"Debugging is twice as hard as writing the code in the first place. Therefore, if you write the code as cleverly as possible, you are, by definition, not smart enough to debug it."

—Brian Kernighan and P.J. Plauger, *The Elements of Programming Style*

8

BUGS AND ERROR HANDLING

A program is crystallized thought. Sometimes those thoughts are confused. Other times, mistakes are introduced when converting thought into code. Either way, the result is a flawed program.

Flaws in a program are usually called bugs. Bugs can be programmer errors or problems in other systems that the program interacts with. Some bugs are immediately apparent, while others are subtle and might remain hidden in a system for years.

Often, problems surface only when a program encounters a situation that the programmer didn't originally consider. Sometimes such situations are unavoidable. When the user is asked to input their age and types *orange*, this puts our program in a difficult position. The situation has to be anticipated and handled somehow.

Programmer Mistakes

When it comes to programmer mistakes, our aim is simple. We want to find them and fix them. Such mistakes can range from simple typos that cause the computer to complain as soon as it lays eyes on our program to subtle mistakes in our understanding of the way the program operates, causing incorrect outcomes only in specific situations. Bugs of the latter type can take weeks to diagnose.

The degree to which languages help you find such mistakes varies. Unsurprisingly, JavaScript is at the "hardly helps at all" end of that scale. Some languages want to know the types of all your variables and expressions before even running a program and will tell you right away when a type is used in an inconsistent way. JavaScript considers types only when actually running the program, and even then, it allows you to do some clearly nonsensical things without complaint, such as x = true * "monkey".

There are some things that JavaScript does complain about, though. Writing a program that is not syntactically valid will immediately trigger an error. Other things, such as calling something that's not a function or looking up a property on an undefined value, will cause an error to be reported when the program is running and encounters the nonsensical action.

But often, your nonsense computation will simply produce a NaN (not a number) or undefined value. And the program happily continues, convinced that it's doing something meaningful. The mistake will manifest itself only later, after the bogus value has traveled though several functions. It might not trigger an error at all but silently cause the program's output to be wrong. Finding the source of such problems can be difficult.

The process of finding mistakes—bugs—in programs is called *debugging*.

Strict Mode

JavaScript can be made a *little* more strict by enabling *strict mode*. This is done by putting the string "use strict" at the top of a file or a function body. Here's an example:

```
function canYouSpotTheProblem() {
  "use strict";
  for (counter = 0; counter < 10; counter++)
    console.log("Happy happy");
}

canYouSpotTheProblem();
// ▷ ReferenceError: counter is not defined
```

Normally, when you forget to put var in front of your variable, as with counter in the example, JavaScript quietly creates a global variable and uses that. In strict mode, however, an error is reported instead. This is very helpful. It should be noted, though, that this doesn't work when the variable in question already exists as a global variable, but only when assigning to it would have created it.

Another change in strict mode is that the this binding holds the value undefined in functions that are not called as methods. When making such a call outside of strict mode, this refers to the global scope object. So if you accidentally call a method or constructor incorrectly in strict mode, JavaScript will produce an error as soon as it tries to read something from this, rather than happily working with the global object, creating and reading global variables.

For example, consider the following code, which calls a constructor without the new keyword so that its this will *not* refer to a newly constructed object:

```
function Person(name) { this.name = name; }
var ferdinand = Person("Ferdinand"); // oops
console.log(name);
// ▷ Ferdinand
```

So the bogus call to Person succeeded but returned an undefined value and created the global variable name. In strict mode, the result is different.

```
"use strict";
function Person(name) { this.name = name; }
// Oops, forgot 'new'
var ferdinand = Person("Ferdinand");
// ▷ TypeError: Cannot set property 'name' of undefined
```

We are immediately told that something is wrong. This is helpful.

Strict mode does a few more things. It disallows giving a function multiple parameters with the same name and removes certain problematic language features entirely (such as the with statement, which is so misguided it is not further discussed in this book).

In short, putting a "use strict" at the top of your program rarely hurts and might help you spot a problem.

Testing

If the language is not going to do much to help us find mistakes, we'll have to find them the hard way: by running the program and seeing whether it does the right thing.

Doing this by hand, again and again, is a sure way to drive yourself insane. Fortunately, it is often possible to write a second program that automates testing your actual program.

As an example, we once again use the Vector type.

```
function Vector(x, y) {
  this.x = x;
  this.y = y;
}
Vector.prototype.plus = function(other) {
  return new Vector(this.x + other.x, this.y + other.y);
};
```

We will write a program to check that our implementation of Vector works as intended. Then, every time we change the implementation, we follow up by running the test program so that we can be reasonably confident that we didn't break anything. When we add extra functionality (for example, a new method) to the Vector type, we also add tests for the new feature.

```
function testVector() {
  var p1 = new Vector(10, 20);
  var p2 = new Vector(-10, 5);
  var p3 = p1.plus(p2);

  if (p1.x !== 10) return "fail: x property";
  if (p1.y !== 20) return "fail: y property";
  if (p2.x !== -10) return "fail: negative x property";
  if (p3.x !== 0) return "fail: x from plus";
  if (p3.y !== 25) return "fail: y from plus";
  return "everything ok";
}
console.log(testVector());
// ▷ everything ok
```

Writing tests like this tends to produce rather repetitive, awkward code. Fortunately, there exist pieces of software that help you build and run collections of tests (*test suites*) by providing a language (in the form of functions and methods) suited to expressing tests and by outputting informative information when a test fails. These are called *testing frameworks*.

Debugging

Once you notice that there is something wrong with your program because it misbehaves or produces errors, the next step is to figure out *what* the problem is.

Sometimes it is obvious. The error message will point at a specific line of your program, and if you look at the error description and that line of code, you can often see the problem.

But not always. Sometimes the line that triggered the problem is simply the first place where a bogus value produced elsewhere gets used in an invalid way. And sometimes there is no error message at all—just an invalid result. If you have been solving the exercises in the earlier chapters, you will probably have already experienced such situations.

The following example program tries to convert a whole number to a string in any base (decimal, binary, and so on) by repeatedly picking out the last digit and then dividing the number to get rid of this digit. But the insane output that it currently produces suggests that it has a bug.

```
function numberToString(n, base) {
  var result = "", sign = "";
  if (n < 0) {
    sign = "-";
    n = -n;
  }
  do {
    result = String(n % base) + result;
    n /= base;
  } while (n > 0);
  return sign + result;
}
console.log(numberToString(13, 10));
// ▷ 1.5e-3231.3e-3221.3e-3211.3e-3201.3e-3191.3e-3181.3...
```

Even if you see the problem already, pretend for a moment that you don't. We know that our program is malfunctioning, and we want to find out why.

This is where you must resist the urge to start making random changes to the code. Instead, *think*. Analyze what is happening and come up with a theory of why it might be happening. Then, make additional observations to test this theory—or, if you don't yet have a theory, make additional observations that might help you come up with one.

Putting a few strategic console.log calls into the program is a good way to get additional information about what the program is doing. In this case, we want n to take the values 13, 1, and then 0. Let's write out its value at the start of the loop.

```
13
1.3
0.13
0.013
...
1.5e-323
```

Right. Dividing 13 by 10 does not produce a whole number. Instead of n /= base, what we actually want is n = Math.floor(n / base) so that the number is properly "shifted" to the right.

An alternative to using console.log is to use the *debugger* capabilities of your browser. Modern browsers come with the ability to set a *breakpoint* on a specific line of your code. This will cause the execution of the program to pause every time the line with the breakpoint is reached and allow you to inspect the values of variables at that point. I won't go into details here since debuggers differ from browser to browser, but look in your browser's developer tools and search the Web for more information. Another way to set a breakpoint is to include a `debugger` statement (consisting of simply that keyword) in your program. If the developer tools of your browser are active, the program will pause whenever it reaches that statement, and you will be able to inspect its state.

Error Propagation

Not all problems can be prevented by the programmer, unfortunately. If your program communicates with the outside world in any way, there is a chance that the input it gets will be invalid or that other systems that it tries to talk to are broken or unreachable.

Simple programs, or programs that run only under your supervision, can afford to just give up when such a problem occurs. You'll look into the problem and try again. "Real" applications, on the other hand, are expected to not simply crash. Sometimes the right thing to do is take the bad input in stride and continue running. In other cases, it is better to report to the user what went wrong and then give up. But in either situation, the program has to actively do something in response to the problem.

Say you have a function `promptInteger` that asks the user for a whole number and returns it. What should it return if the user inputs *orange*?

One option is to make it return a special value. Common choices for such values are `null` and `undefined`.

```
function promptNumber(question) {
  var result = Number(prompt(question, ""));
  if (isNaN(result)) return null;
  else return result;
}

console.log(promptNumber("How many trees do you see?"));
```

This is a sound strategy. Now any code that calls `promptNumber` must check whether an actual number was read and, failing that, must somehow recover—maybe by asking again or by filling in a default value. Or it could again return a special value to *its* caller to indicate that it failed to do what it was asked.

In many situations, mostly when errors are common and the caller should be explicitly taking them into account, returning a special value is a perfectly fine way to indicate an error. It does, however, have its downsides. First, what if the function can already return every possible kind of value? For such a function, it is hard to find a special value that can be distinguished from a valid result.

The second issue with returning special values is that it can lead to some very cluttered code. If a piece of code calls `promptNumber` 10 times, it has to check 10 times whether `null` was returned. And if its response to finding `null` is to simply return `null` itself, the caller will in turn have to check for it, and so on.

Exceptions

When a function cannot proceed normally, what we would *like* to do is just stop what we are doing and immediately jump back to a place that knows how to handle the problem. This is what *exception handling* does.

Exceptions are a mechanism that make it possible for code that runs into a problem to *raise* (or *throw*) an exception, which is simply a value. Raising an exception somewhat resembles a super-charged return from a function: it jumps out of not just the current function but also out of its callers, all the way down to the first call that started the current execution. This is called *unwinding the stack*. You may remember the stack of function calls that was mentioned in Chapter 3. An exception zooms down this stack, throwing away all the call contexts it encounters.

If exceptions always zoomed right down to the bottom of the stack, they would not be of much use. They would just provide a novel way to blow up your program. Their power lies in the fact that you can set "obstacles" along the stack to *catch* the exception as it is zooming down. Then you can do something with it, after which the program continues running at the point where the exception was caught.

Here's an example:

```
function promptDirection(question) {
  var result = prompt(question, "");
  if (result.toLowerCase() == "left") return "L";
  if (result.toLowerCase() == "right") return "R";
  throw new Error("Invalid direction: " + result);
}

function look() {
  if (promptDirection("Which way?") == "L")
    return "a house";
  else
    return "two angry bears";
}

try {
  console.log("You see", look());
} catch (error) {
  console.log("Something went wrong: " + error);
}
```

The throw keyword is used to raise an exception. Catching one is done by wrapping a piece of code in a try block, followed by the keyword catch. When the code in the try block causes an exception to be raised, the catch block is evaluated. The variable name (in parentheses) after catch will be bound to the exception value. After the catch block finishes—or if the try block finishes without problems—control proceeds beneath the entire try/catch statement.

In this case, we used the `Error` constructor to create our exception value. This is a standard JavaScript constructor that creates an object with a `message` property. In modern JavaScript environments, instances of this constructor also gather information about the call stack that existed when the exception was created, a so-called *stack trace*. This information is stored in the stack property and can be helpful when trying to debug a problem: it tells us the precise function where the problem occurred and which other functions led up to the call that failed.

Note that the function `look` completely ignores the possibility that `promptDirection` might go wrong. This is the big advantage of exceptions—error-handling code is necessary only at the point where the error occurs and at the point where it is handled. The functions in between can forget all about it.

Well, almost...

Cleaning Up After Exceptions

Consider the following situation: a function, `withContext`, wants to make sure that, during its execution, the top-level variable context holds a specific context value. After it finishes, it restores this variable to its old value.

```
var context = null;

function withContext(newContext, body) {
  var oldContext = context;
  context = newContext;
  var result = body();
  context = oldContext;
  return result;
}
```

What if body raises an exception? In that case, the call to `withContext` will be thrown off the stack by the exception, and context will never be set back to its old value.

There is one more feature that try statements have. They may be followed by a `finally` block either instead of or in addition to a catch block. A `finally` block means "No matter *what* happens, run this code after trying to run the code in the try block." If a function has to clean something up, the cleanup code should usually be put into a `finally` block.

```
function withContext(newContext, body) {
  var oldContext = context;
  context = newContext;
  try {
    return body();
```

```
  } finally {
    context = oldContext;
  }
}
```

Note that we no longer have to store the result of body (which we want to return) in a variable. Even if we return directly from the try block, the finally block will be run. Now we can do this and be safe:

```
try {
  withContext(5, function() {
    if (context < 10)
      throw new Error("Not enough context!");
  });
} catch (e) {
  console.log("Ignoring: " + e);
}
// ▷ Ignoring: Error: Not enough context!

console.log(context);
// ▷ null
```

Even though the function called from withContext exploded, withContext itself still properly cleaned up the context variable.

Selective Catching

When an exception makes it all the way to the bottom of the stack without being caught, it gets handled by the environment. What this means differs between environments. In browsers, a description of the error typically gets written to the JavaScript console (reachable through the browser's Tools or Developer menu).

For programmer mistakes or problems that the program cannot possibly handle, just letting the error go through is often okay. An unhandled exception is a reasonable way to signal a broken program, and the JavaScript console will, on modern browsers, provide you with some information about which function calls were on the stack when the problem occurred.

For problems that are *expected* to happen during routine use, crashing with an unhandled exception is not a very friendly response.

Invalid uses of the language, such as referencing a nonexistent variable, looking up a property on null, or calling something that's not a function, will also result in exceptions being raised. Such exceptions can be caught just like your own exceptions.

When a catch body is entered, all we know is that *something* in our try body caused an exception. But we don't know *what*, or *which* exception it caused.

JavaScript (in a rather glaring omission) doesn't provide direct support for selectively catching exceptions: either you catch them all or you don't catch any. This makes it very easy to *assume* that the exception you get is the one you were thinking about when you wrote the catch block.

But it might not be. Some other assumption might be violated, or you might have introduced a bug somewhere that is causing an exception. Here is an example, which *attempts* to keep on calling promptDirection until it gets a valid answer:

```
for (;;) {
  try {
    var dir = promtDirection("Where?"); // ← typo!
    console.log("You chose ", dir);
    break;
  } catch (e) {
    console.log("Not a valid direction. Try again.");
  }
}
```

The for (;;) construct is a way to intentionally create a loop that doesn't terminate on its own. We break out of the loop only when a valid direction is given. *But* we misspelled promptDirection, which will result in an "undefined variable" error. Because the catch block completely ignores its exception value (e), assuming it knows what the problem is, it wrongly treats the variable error as indicating bad input. Not only does this cause an infinite loop, but it also "buries" the useful error message about the misspelled variable.

As a general rule, don't blanket-catch exceptions unless it is for the purpose of "routing" them somewhere—for example, over the network to tell another system that our program crashed. And even then, think carefully about how you might be hiding information.

So we want to catch a *specific* kind of exception. We can do this by checking in the catch block whether the exception we got is the one we are interested in and by rethrowing it otherwise. But how do we recognize an exception?

Of course, we could match its message property against the error message we happen to expect. But that's a shaky way to write code—we'd be using information that's intended for human consumption (the message) to make a programmatic decision. As soon as someone changes (or translates) the message, the code will stop working.

Rather, let's define a new type of error and use instanceof to identify it.

```
function InputError(message) {
  this.message = message;
  this.stack = (new Error()).stack;
}
InputError.prototype = Object.create(Error.prototype);
InputError.prototype.name = "InputError";
```

The prototype is made to derive from `Error.prototype` so that `instanceof Error` will also return true for `InputError` objects. It's also given a `name` property since the standard error types (`Error`, `SyntaxError`, `ReferenceError`, and so on) also have such a property.

The assignment to the stack property tries to give this object a somewhat useful stack trace, on platforms that support it, by creating a regular error object and then using that object's stack property as its own.

Now `promptDirection` can throw such an error.

```
function promptDirection(question) {
  var result = prompt(question, "");
  if (result.toLowerCase() == "left") return "L";
  if (result.toLowerCase() == "right") return "R";
  throw new InputError("Invalid direction: " + result);
}
```

And the loop can catch it more carefully.

```
for (;;) {
  try {
    var dir = promptDirection("Where?");
    console.log("You chose ", dir);
    break;
  } catch (e) {
    if (e instanceof InputError)
      console.log("Not a valid direction. Try again.");
    else
      throw e;
  }
}
```

This will catch only instances of `InputError` and let unrelated exceptions through. If you reintroduce the typo, the undefined variable error will be properly reported.

Assertions

Assertions are a tool to do basic sanity checking for programmer errors. Consider this helper function, assert:

```
function AssertionFailed(message) {
  this.message = message;
}
AssertionFailed.prototype = Object.create(Error.prototype);

function assert(test, message) {
  if (!test)
    throw new AssertionFailed(message);
}
```

```
function lastElement(array) {
  assert(array.length > 0, "empty array in lastElement");
  return array[array.length - 1];
}
```

This provides a compact way to enforce expectations, helpfully blowing up the program if the stated condition does not hold. For instance, the lastElement function, which fetches the last element from an array, would return undefined on empty arrays if the assertion was omitted. Fetching the last element from an empty array does not make much sense, so it is almost certainly a programmer error to do so.

Assertions are a way to make sure mistakes cause failures at the point of the mistake, rather than silently producing nonsense values that may go on to cause trouble in an unrelated part of the system.

Summary

Mistakes and bad input are facts of life. Bugs in programs need to be found and fixed. They can become easier to notice by having automated test suites and adding assertions to your programs.

Problems caused by factors outside the program's control should usually be handled gracefully. Sometimes, when the problem can be handled locally, special return values are a sane way to track them. Otherwise, exceptions are preferable.

Throwing an exception causes the call stack to be unwound until the next enclosing try/catch block or until the bottom of the stack. The exception value will be given to the catch block that catches it, which should verify that it is actually the expected kind of exception and then do something with it. To deal with the unpredictable control flow caused by exceptions, finally blocks can be used to ensure a piece of code is *always* run when a block finishes.

Exercises

Retry

Say you have a function primitiveMultiply that, in 50 percent of cases, multiplies two numbers and, in the other 50 percent, raises an exception of type MultiplicatorUnitFailure. Write a function that wraps this clunky function and just keeps trying until a call succeeds and returns the result.

Make sure you handle only the exceptions you are trying to handle.

The Locked Box

Consider the following (rather contrived) object:

```
var box = {
  locked: true,
  unlock: function() { this.locked = false; },
  lock: function() { this.locked = true;  },
  _content: [],
  get content() {
    if (this.locked) throw new Error("Locked!");
    return this._content;
  }
};
```

It is a box with a lock. Inside is an array, but you can get at it only when the box is unlocked. Directly accessing the _content property is not allowed.

Write a function called withBoxUnlocked that takes a function value as argument, unlocks the box, runs the function, and then ensures that the box is locked again before returning, regardless of whether the argument function returned normally or threw an exception.

"Some people, when confronted
with a problem, think 'I know,
I'll use regular expressions.'
Now they have two problems."

—Jamie Zawinski

9

REGULAR EXPRESSIONS

Programming tools and techniques survive and spread in a chaotic, evolutionary way. It's not always the pretty or brilliant ones that win but rather the ones that function well enough within the right niche—for example, by being integrated with another successful piece of technology.

In this chapter, I will discuss one such tool, *regular expressions.* Regular expressions are a way to describe patterns in string data. They form a small, separate language that is part of JavaScript and many other languages and tools.

Regular expressions are both terribly awkward and extremely useful. Their syntax is cryptic, and the programming interface JavaScript provides for them is clumsy. But they are a powerful tool for inspecting and processing strings. Properly understanding regular expressions will make you a more effective programmer.

Creating a Regular Expression

A regular expression is a type of object. It can either be constructed with the RegExp constructor or written as a literal value by enclosing the pattern in forward slash (/) characters.

```
var re1 = new RegExp("abc");
var re2 = /abc/;
```

Both of these regular expression objects represent the same pattern: an *a* character followed by a *b* followed by a *c*.

When using the `RegExp` constructor, the pattern is written as a normal string, so the usual rules apply for backslashes.

The second notation, where the pattern appears between slash characters, treats backslashes somewhat differently. First, since a forward slash ends the pattern, we need to put a backslash before any forward slash that we want to be *part* of the pattern. In addition, backslashes that aren't part of special character codes (like \n) will be *preserved*, rather than ignored as they are in strings, and change the meaning of the pattern. Some characters, such as question marks and plus signs, have special meanings in regular expressions and must be preceded by a backslash if they are meant to represent the character itself.

```
var eighteenPlus = /eighteen\+/;
```

Knowing precisely what characters to backslash-escape when writing regular expressions requires you to know every character with a special meaning. For the time being, this may not be realistic, so when in doubt, just put a backslash before any character that is not a letter, number, or whitespace.

Testing for Matches

Regular expression objects have a number of methods. The simplest one is test. If you pass it a string, it will return a Boolean telling you whether the string contains a match of the pattern in the expression.

```
console.log(/abc/.test("abcde"));
// ▷ true
console.log(/abc/.test("abxde"));
// ▷ false
```

A regular expression consisting of only nonspecial characters simply represents that sequence of characters. If *abc* occurs anywhere in the string we are testing against (not just at the start), test will return true.

Matching a Set of Characters

Finding out whether a string contains *abc* could just as well be done with a call to indexOf. Regular expressions allow us to go beyond that and express more complicated patterns.

Say we want to match any number. In a regular expression, putting a set of characters between square brackets makes that part of the expression match any of the characters between the brackets.

Both of the following expressions match all strings that contain a digit:

```
console.log(/[0123456789]/.test("in 1992"));
// ▷ true
console.log(/[0-9]/.test("in 1992"));
// ▷ true
```

Within square brackets, a dash (-) between two characters can be used to indicate a range of characters, where the ordering is determined by the character's Unicode number. Characters 0 to 9 sit right next to each other in this ordering (codes 48 to 57), so [0-9] covers all of them and matches any digit.

There are a number of common character groups that have their own built-in shortcuts. Digits are one of them: \d means the same thing as [0-9].

\d Any digit character

\w An alphanumeric character ("word character")

\s Any whitespace character (space, tab, newline, and similar)

\D A character that is *not* a digit

\W A nonalphanumeric character

\S A nonwhitespace character

. Any character except for newline

So you could match a date and time format like 30-01-2003 15:20 with the following expression:

```
var dateTime = /\d\d-\d\d-\d\d\d\d \d\d:\d\d/;
console.log(dateTime.test("30-01-2003 15:20"));
// ▷ true
console.log(dateTime.test("30-jan-2003 15:20"));
// ▷ false
```

That looks completely awful, doesn't it? It has way too many backslashes, producing background noise that makes it hard to spot the actual pattern expressed. We'll see a slightly improved version of this expression later.

These backslash codes can also be used inside square brackets. For example, [\d.] means any digit or a period character. But note that the period itself, when used between square brackets, loses its special meaning. The same goes for other special characters, such as +.

To *invert* a set of characters—that is, to express that you want to match any character *except* the ones in the set—you can write a caret (^) character after the opening bracket.

```
var notBinary = /[^01]/;
console.log(notBinary.test("1100100010100110"));
// ▷ false
console.log(notBinary.test("1100100010200110"));
// ▷ true
```

Repeating Parts of a Pattern

We now know how to match a single digit. What if we want to match a whole number—a sequence of one or more digits?

When you put a plus sign (+) after something in a regular expression, it indicates that the element may be repeated more than once. Thus, /\d+/ matches one or more digit characters.

```
console.log(/'\d+'/.test("'123'"));
// ▷ true
console.log(/'\d+'/.test("''"));
// ▷ false
console.log(/'\d*'/.test("'123'"));
// ▷ true
console.log(/'\d*'/.test("''"));
// ▷ true
```

The star (*) has a similar meaning but also allows the pattern to match zero times. Something with a star after it never prevents a pattern from matching—it'll just match zero instances if it can't find any suitable text to match.

A question mark makes a part of a pattern "optional," meaning it may occur zero or one time. In the following example, the *u* character is allowed to occur, but the pattern also matches when it is missing.

```
var neighbor = /neighbou?r/;
console.log(neighbor.test("neighbour"));
// ▷ true
console.log(neighbor.test("neighbor"));
// ▷ true
```

To indicate that a pattern should occur a precise number of times, use braces. Putting {4} after an element, for example, requires it to occur exactly four times. It is also possible to specify a range this way: {2,4} means the element must occur at least twice and at most four times.

Here is another version of the date and time pattern that allows both single- and double-digit days, months, and hours. It is also slightly more readable.

```
var dateTime = /\d{1,2}-\d{1,2}-\d{4} \d{1,2}:\d{2}/;
console.log(dateTime.test("30-1-2003 8:45"));
// ▷ true
```

You can also specify open-ended ranges when using curly braces by omitting the number after the comma. So {5,} means five or more times.

Grouping Subexpressions

To use an operator like * or + on more than one element at a time, you can use parentheses. A part of a regular expression that is enclosed in parentheses counts as a single element as far as the operators following it are concerned.

```
var cartoonCrying = /boo+(hoo+)+/i;
console.log(cartoonCrying.test("Boohoooohoohooo"));
// ▷ true
```

The first and second + characters apply only to the second *o* in *boo* and *hoo*, respectively. The third + applies to the whole group (hoo+), matching one or more sequences like that.

The i at the end of the expression in the previous example makes this regular expression case insensitive, allowing it to match the uppercase *B* in the input string, even though the pattern is itself all lowercase.

Matches and Groups

The test method is the absolute simplest way to match a regular expression. It tells you only whether it matched and nothing else. Regular expressions also have an exec (execute) method that will return null if no match was found and return an object with information about the match otherwise.

```
var match = /\d+/.exec("one two 100");
console.log(match);
// ▷ ["100"]
console.log(match.index);
// ▷ 8
```

An object returned from exec has an index property that tells us *where* in the string the successful match begins. Other than that, the object looks like (and in fact is) an array of strings, whose first element is the string that was matched—in the previous example, this is the sequence of digits that we were looking for.

String values have a `match` method that behaves similarly.

```
console.log("one two 100".match(/\d+/));
// ▷ ["100"]
```

When the regular expression contains subexpressions grouped with parentheses, the text that matched those groups will also show up in the array. The whole match is always the first element. The next element is the part matched by the first group (the one whose opening parenthesis comes first in the expression), then the second group, and so on.

```
var quotedText = /'([^']*)'/;
console.log(quotedText.exec("she said 'hello'"));
// ▷ ["'hello'", "hello"]
```

When a group does not end up being matched at all (for example, when followed by a question mark), its position in the output array will hold `undefined`. Similarly, when a group is matched multiple times, only the last match ends up in the array.

```
console.log(/bad(ly)?/.exec("bad"));
// ▷ ["bad", undefined]
console.log(/(\d)+/.exec("123"));
// ▷ ["123", "3"]
```

Groups can be useful for extracting parts of a string. If we don't just want to verify whether a string contains a date but also extract it and construct an object that represents it, we can wrap parentheses around the digit patterns and directly pick the date out of the result of exec.

But first, a brief detour, in which we discuss the preferred way to store date and time values in JavaScript.

The Date Type

JavaScript has a standard object type for representing dates—or rather, points in time. It is called `Date`. If you simply create a `Date` object using `new`, you get the current date and time.

```
console.log(new Date());
// ▷ Wed Dec 04 2013 14:24:57 GMT+0100 (CET)
```

You can also create an object for a specific time.

```
console.log(new Date(2009, 11, 9));
// ▷ Wed Dec 09 2009 00:00:00 GMT+0100 (CET)
console.log(new Date(2009, 11, 9, 12, 59, 59, 999));
// ▷ Wed Dec 09 2009 12:59:59 GMT+0100 (CET)
```

JavaScript uses a convention where month numbers start at zero (so December is 11), yet day numbers start at one. This is confusing and silly. Be careful.

The last four arguments (hours, minutes, seconds, and milliseconds) are optional and taken to be zero when not given.

Timestamps are stored as the number of milliseconds since the start of 1970, using negative numbers for times before 1970 (following a convention set by "Unix time," which was invented around that time). The getTime method on a Date object returns this number. It is big, as you can imagine.

```
console.log(new Date(2013, 11, 19).getTime());
// ▷ 1387407600000
console.log(new Date(1387407600000));
// ▷ Thu Dec 19 2013 00:00:00 GMT+0100 (CET)
```

If you give the Date constructor a single argument, that argument is treated as a millisecond count. You can get the current millisecond count by creating a new Date object and calling getTime on it but also by calling the Date.now function.

Date objects provide methods like getFullYear, getMonth, getDate, getHours, getMinutes, and getSeconds to extract their components. There's also getYear, which gives you a rather useless two-digit year value (such as 93 or 14).

Putting parentheses around the parts of the expression that we are interested in, we can now easily create a Date object from a string.

```
function findDate(string) {
  var dateTime = /(\d{1,2})-(\d{1,2})-(\d{4})/;
  var match = dateTime.exec(string);
  return new Date(Number(match[3]),
                  Number(match[2]) - 1,
                  Number(match[1]));
}
console.log(findDate("30-1-2003"));
// ▷ Sun Mar 02 2003 00:00:00 GMT+0100 (CET)
```

Word and String Boundaries

Unfortunately, findDate will also happily extract the nonsensical date 00-1-3000 from the string "100-1-30000". A match may happen anywhere in the string, so in this case, it'll just start at the second character and end at the second-to-last character.

If we want to enforce that the match must span the whole string, we can add the markers ^ and $. The caret matches the start of the input string, while the dollar sign matches the end. So, /^\d+$/ matches a string consisting entirely of one or more digits, /^!/ matches any string that starts with an exclamation mark, and /x^/ does not match any string (there cannot be an *x* before the start of the string).

If, on the other hand, we just want to make sure the date starts and ends on a word boundary, we can use the marker \b. A word boundary can be the start or end of the string or any point in the string that has a word character (as in \w) on one side and a nonword character on the other.

```
console.log(/cat/.test("concatenate"));
// ▷ true
console.log(/\bcat\b/.test("concatenate"));
// ▷ false
```

Note that a boundary marker doesn't represent an actual character. It just enforces that the regular expression matches only when a certain condition holds at the place where it appears in the pattern.

Choice Patterns

Say we want to know whether a piece of text contains not only a number but a number followed by one of the words *pig*, *cow*, or *chicken*, or any of their plural forms.

We could write three regular expressions and test them in turn, but there is a nicer way. The pipe character (|) denotes a choice between the pattern to its left and the pattern to its right. So I can say this:

```
var animalCount = /\b\d+ (pig|cow|chicken)s?\b/;
console.log(animalCount.test("15 pigs"));
// ▷ true
console.log(animalCount.test("15 pigchickens"));
// ▷ false
```

Parentheses can be used to limit the part of the pattern that the pipe operator applies to, and you can put multiple such operators next to each other to express a choice between more than two patterns.

The Mechanics of Matching

Regular expressions can be thought of as flow diagrams. This is the diagram for the livestock expression in the previous example:

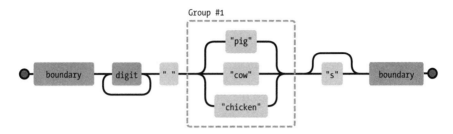

Our expression matches a string if we can find a path from the left side of the diagram to the right side. We keep a current position in the string, and every time we move through a box, we verify that the part of the string after our current position matches that box.

So if we try to match "the 3 pigs" with our regular expression, our progress through the flow chart would look like this:

- At position 4, there is a word boundary, so we can move past the first box.

- Still at position 4, we find a digit, so we can also move past the second box.

- At position 5, one path loops back to before the second (digit) box, while the other moves forward through the box that holds a single space character. There is a space here, not a digit, so we must take the second path.

- We are now at position 6 (the start of "pigs") and at the three-way branch in the diagram. We don't see "cow" or "chicken" here, but we do see "pig," so we take that branch.

- At position 9, after the three-way branch, one path skips the *s* box and goes straight to the final word boundary, while the other path matches an *s*. There is an *s* character here, not a word boundary, so we go through the *s* box.

- We're at position 10 (the end of the string) and can match only a word boundary. The end of a string counts as a word boundary, so we go through the last box and have successfully matched this string.

Conceptually, a regular expression engine looks for a match in a string as follows: it starts at the start of the string and tries a match there. In this case, there *is* a word boundary there, so it'd get past the first box—but there is no digit, so it'd fail at the second box. Then it moves on to the second character in the string and tries to begin a new match there ... and so on, until it finds a match or reaches the end of the string and decides that there really is no match.

Backtracking

The regular expression /\b([01]+b|\d+|[\da-f]+h)\b/ matches either a binary number followed by a *b*, a regular decimal number with no suffix character, or a hexadecimal number (that is, base 16, with the letters *a* to *f* standing for the digits 10 to 15) followed by an *h*. This is the corresponding diagram:

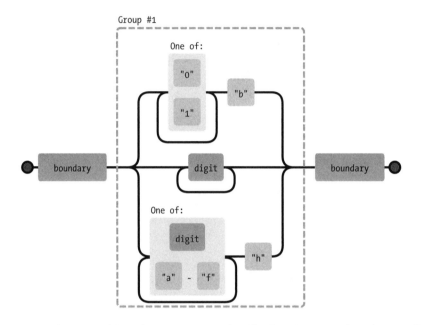

When matching this expression, it will often happen that the top (binary) branch is entered even though the input does not actually contain a binary number. When matching the string "103", for example, it becomes clear only at the 3 that we are in the wrong branch. The string *does* match the expression, just not the branch we are currently in.

So the matcher *backtracks*. When entering a branch, it remembers its current position (in this case, at the start of the string, just past the first boundary box in the diagram) so that it can go back and try another branch if the current one does not work out. After encountering the 3 character, the string "103" will start trying the branch for decimal numbers. This one matches, so a match is reported after all.

The matcher stops as soon as it finds a full match. This means that if multiple branches could potentially match a string, only the first one (ordered by where the branches appear in the regular expression) is used.

Backtracking also happens for repetition operators like + and ∗. If you match /^.∗x/ against "abcxe", the .∗ part will first try to consume the whole string. The engine will then realize that it needs an *x* to match the pattern. Since there is no *x* past the end of the string, the star operator tries to match one character less. But the matcher doesn't find an *x* after abcx either, so it backtracks again, matching the star operator to just abc. *Now* it finds an *x* where it needs it and reports a successful match from positions 0 to 4.

It is possible to write regular expressions that will do a *lot* of backtracking. This problem occurs when a pattern can match a piece of input in many different ways. For example, if we get confused while writing a binary-number regular expression, we might accidentally write something like `/([01]+)+b/`.

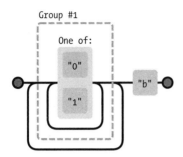

If that tries to match some long series of zeroes and ones with no trailing *b* character, the matcher will first go through the inner loop until it runs out of digits. Then it notices there is no *b*, so it backtracks one position, goes through the outer loop once, and gives up again, trying to backtrack out of the inner loop once more. It will continue to try every possible route through these two loops. This means the amount of work *doubles* with each additional character. For even just a few dozen characters, the resulting match will take practically forever.

The replace Method

String values have a `replace` method, which can be used to replace part of the string with another string.

```
console.log("papa".replace("p", "m"));
// ▷ mapa
```

The first argument can also be a regular expression, in which case the first match of the regular expression is replaced. When a g option (for *global*) is added to the regular expression, *all* matches in the string will be replaced, not just the first.

```
console.log("Borobudur".replace(/[ou]/, "a"));
// ▷ Barobudur
console.log("Borobudur".replace(/[ou]/g, "a"));
// ▷ Barabadar
```

It would have been sensible if the choice between replacing one match or all matches was made through an additional argument to `replace` or by providing a different method, `replaceAll`. But for some unfortunate reason, the choice relies on a property of the regular expression instead.

The real power of using regular expressions with `replace` comes from the fact that we can refer back to matched groups in the replacement string. For example, say we have a big string containing the names of people, one name per line, in the format `Lastname, Firstname`. If we want to swap these names and remove the comma to get a simple `Firstname Lastname` format, we can use the following code:

```
console.log(
  "Hopper, Grace\nMcCarthy, John\nRitchie, Dennis"
    .replace(/([\w ]+), ([\w ]+)/g, "$2 $1"));
// ▷ Grace Hopper
//    John McCarthy
//    Dennis Ritchie
```

The $1 and $2 in the replacement string refer to the parenthesized groups in the pattern. $1 is replaced by the text that matched against the first group, $2 by the second, and so on, up to $9. The whole match can be referred to with $&.

It is also possible to pass a function, rather than a string, as the second argument to `replace`. For each replacement, the function will be called with the matched groups (as well as the whole match) as arguments, and its return value will be inserted into the new string.

Here's a simple example:

```
var s = "the cia and fbi";
console.log(s.replace(/\b(fbi|cia)\b/g, function(str) {
  return str.toUpperCase();
}));
// ▷ the CIA and FBI
```

And here's a more interesting one:

```
var stock = "1 lemon, 2 cabbages, and 101 eggs";
function minusOne(match, amount, unit) {
  amount = Number(amount) - 1;
  if (amount == 1) // only one left, remove the 's'
    unit = unit.slice(0, unit.length - 1);
  else if (amount == 0)
    amount = "no";
  return amount + " " + unit;
}
console.log(stock.replace(/(\d+) (\w+)/g, minusOne));
// ▷ no lemon, 1 cabbage, and 100 eggs
```

This takes a string, finds all occurrences of a number followed by an alphanumeric word, and returns a string wherein every such occurrence is decremented by one.

The (\d+) group ends up as the amount argument to the function, and the (\w+) group gets bound to unit. The function converts amount to a number—which always works, since it matched \d+—and makes some adjustments in case there is only one or zero left.

Greed

It isn't hard to use replace to write a function that removes all comments from a piece of JavaScript code. Here is a first attempt:

```
function stripComments(code) {
  return code.replace(/\/\/.*|\/\*[^]*\*\//g, "");
}
console.log(stripComments("1 + /* 2 */3"));
// ▷ 1 + 3
console.log(stripComments("x = 10;// ten!"));
// ▷ x = 10;
console.log(stripComments("1 /* a */+/* b */ 1"));
// ▷ 1   1
```

The part before the *or* operator simply matches two slash characters followed by any number of non-newline characters. The part for multiline comments is more involved. We use [^] (any character that is not in the empty set of characters) as a way to match any character. We cannot just use a dot here because block comments can continue on a new line, and dots do not match the newline character.

But the output of the previous example appears to have gone wrong. Why?

The [^]* part of the expression, as I described in the section on backtracking, will first match as much as it can. If that causes the next part of the pattern to fail, the matcher moves back one character and tries again from there. In the example, the matcher first tries to match the whole rest of the string and then moves back from there. It will find an occurrence of */ after going back four characters and match that. This is not what we wanted—the intention was to match a single comment, not to go all the way to the end of the code and find the end of the last block comment.

Because of this behavior, we say the repetition operators (+, *, ?, and {}) are *greedy*, meaning they match as much as they can and backtrack from there. If you put a question mark after them (+?, *?, ??, {}?), they become nongreedy and start by matching as little as possible, matching more only when the remaining pattern does not fit the smaller match.

And that is exactly what we want in this case. By having the star match the smallest stretch of characters that brings us to a */, we consume one block comment and nothing more.

```
function stripComments(code) {
  return code.replace(/\/\/.*|\/\*[^]*?\*\//g, "");
}
console.log(stripComments("1 /* a */+/* b */ 1"));
// ▷ 1 + 1
```

A lot of bugs in regular expression programs can be traced to unintentionally using a greedy operator where a nongreedy one would work better. When using a repetition operator, consider the nongreedy variant first.

Dynamically Creating RegExp Objects

There are cases where you might not know the exact pattern you need to match against when you are writing your code. Say you want to look for the user's name in a piece of text and enclose it in underscore characters to make it stand out. Since you will know the name only once the program is actually running, you can't use the slash-based notation.

But you can build up a string and use the RegExp constructor on that. Here's an example:

```
var name = "harry";
var text = "Harry is a suspicious character.";
var regexp = new RegExp("\\b(" + name + ")\\b", "gi");
console.log(text.replace(regexp, "_$1_"));
// ▷ _Harry_ is a suspicious character.
```

When creating the \b boundary markers, we have to use two backslashes because we are writing them in a normal string, not a slash-enclosed regular expression. The second argument to the RegExp constructor contains the options for the regular expression—in this case "gi" for global and case-insensitive.

But what if the name is "dea+hl[]rd" because our user is a nerdy teenager? That would result in a nonsensical regular expression, which won't actually match the user's name.

To work around this, we can add backslashes before any character that we don't trust. Adding backslashes before alphabetic characters is a bad idea because things like \b and \n have a special meaning. But escaping everything that's not alphanumeric or whitespace is safe.

```
var name = "dea+hl[]rd";
var text = "This dea+hl[]rd guy is super annoying.";
var escaped = name.replace(/[^\w\s]/g, "\\$&");
var regexp = new RegExp("\\b(" + escaped + ")\\b", "gi");
console.log(text.replace(regexp, "_$1_"));
// ▷ This _dea+hl[]rd_ guy is super annoying.
```

The search Method

The indexOf method on strings cannot be called with a regular expression. But there is another method, search, which does expect a regular expression. Like indexOf, it returns the first index on which the expression was found, or −1 when it wasn't found.

```
console.log("  word".search(/\S/));
// ▷ 2
console.log("    ".search(/\S/));
// ▷ -1
```

Unfortunately, there is no way to indicate that the match should start at a given offset (like we can with the second argument to indexOf), which would often be useful.

The lastIndex Property

The exec method similarly does not provide a convenient way to start searching from a given position in the string. But it does provide an *inconvenient* way.

Regular expression objects have properties. One such property is source, which contains the string that expression was created from. Another property is lastIndex, which controls, in some limited circumstances, where the next match will start.

Those circumstances are that the regular expression must have the global (g) option enabled, and the match must happen through the exec method. Again, a more sane solution would have been to just allow an extra argument to be passed to exec, but sanity is not a defining characteristic of JavaScript's regular expression interface.

```
var pattern = /y/g;
pattern.lastIndex = 3;
var match = pattern.exec("xyzzy");
console.log(match.index);
// ▷ 4
console.log(pattern.lastIndex);
// ▷ 5
```

If the match was successful, the call to exec automatically updates the lastIndex property to point after the match. If no match was found, lastIndex is set back to zero, which is also the value it has in a newly constructed regular expression object.

When using a global regular expression value for multiple exec calls, these automatic updates to the lastIndex property can cause problems. Your regular expression might be accidentally starting at an index that was left over from a previous call.

```
var digit = /\d/g;
console.log(digit.exec("here it is: 1"));
// ▷ ["1"]
console.log(digit.exec("and now: 1"));
// ▷ null
```

Another interesting effect of the global option is that it changes the way the match method on strings works. When called with a global expression, instead of returning an array similar to that returned by exec, match will find *all* matches of the pattern in the string and return an array containing the matched strings.

```
console.log("Banana".match(/an/g));
// ▷ ["an", "an"]
```

So be cautious with global regular expressions. The cases where they are necessary—calls to replace and places where you want to explicitly use lastIndex—are typically the only places where you want to use them.

Looping over Matches

A common pattern is to scan through all occurrences of a pattern in a string, in a way that gives us access to the match object in the loop body, by using lastIndex and exec.

```
var input = "A string with 3 numbers in it... 42 and 88.";
var number = /\b(\d+)\b/g;
var match;
while (match = number.exec(input))
  console.log("Found", match[1], "at", match.index);
// ▷ Found 3 at 14
//   Found 42 at 33
//   Found 88 at 40
```

This makes use of the fact that the value of an assignment expression (=) is the assigned value. So by using match = re.exec(input) as the condition in the while statement, we perform the match at the start of each iteration, save its result in a variable, and stop looping when no more matches are found.

Parsing an INI File

To conclude the chapter, we'll look at a problem that calls for regular expressions. Imagine we are writing a program to automatically harvest information about our enemies from the Internet. (We will not actually write that program here, just the part that reads the configuration file. Sorry to disappoint.) The configuration file looks like this:

```
searchengine=http://www.google.com/search?q=$1
spitefulness=9.7

; comments are preceded by a semicolon...
; each section concerns an individual enemy
[larry]
fullname=Larry Doe
type=kindergarten bully
website=http://www.geocities.com/CapeCanaveral/11451

[gargamel]
fullname=Gargamel
type=evil sorcerer
outputdir=/home/marijn/enemies/gargamel
```

The exact rules for this format (which is actually a widely used format, usually called an *INI* file) are as follows:

- Blank lines and lines starting with semicolons are ignored.

- Lines wrapped in [and] start a new section.

- Lines containing an alphanumeric identifier followed by an = character add a setting to the current section.

- Anything else is invalid.

Our task is to convert a string like this into an array of objects, each with a name property and an array of settings. We'll need one such object for each section and one for the global settings at the top.

Since the format has to be processed line by line, splitting up the file into separate lines is a good start. We used string.split("\n") to do this in Chapter 6. Some operating systems, however, use not just a newline character to separate lines but a carriage return character followed by a newline ("\r\n"). Given that the split method also allows a regular expression as its argument, we can split on a regular expression like /\r?\n/ to split in a way that allows both "\n" and "\r\n" between lines.

```
function parseINI(string) {
  // Start with an object to hold the top-level fields
  var currentSection = {name: null, fields: []};
  var categories = [currentSection];

  string.split(/\r?\n/).forEach(function(line) {
    var match;
```

```
    if (/^\s*(;.*)?$/.test(line)) {
      return;
    } else if (match = line.match(/^\[(.*)\]$/)) {
      currentSection = {name: match[1], fields: []};
      categories.push(currentSection);
    } else if (match = line.match(/^(\w+)=(.*)$/)) {
      currentSection.fields.push({name: match[1],
                                 value: match[2]});
    } else {
      throw new Error("Line '" + line + "' is invalid.");
    }
  });

  return categories;
}
```

This code goes over every line in the file, updating the "current section" object as it goes along. First, it checks whether the line can be ignored, using the expression /^\s*(;.*)?$/. Do you see how it works? The part between the parentheses will match comments, and the ? will make sure it also matches lines containing only whitespace.

If the line is not a comment, the code then checks whether the line starts a new section. If so, it creates a new current section object, to which subsequent settings will be added.

The last meaningful possibility is that the line is a normal setting, which the code adds to the current section object.

If a line matches none of these forms, the function throws an error.

Note the recurring use of ^ and $ to make sure the expression matches the whole line, not just part of it. Leaving these out results in code that mostly works but behaves strangely for some input, which can be a difficult bug to track down.

The pattern if (match = string.match(...)) is similar to the trick of using an assignment as the condition for while. You often aren't sure that your call to match will succeed, so you can access the resulting object only inside an if statement that tests for this. To not break the pleasant chain of if forms, we assign the result of the match to a variable and immediately use that assignment as the test in the if statement.

International Characters

Because of JavaScript's initial simplistic implementation and the fact that this simplistic approach was later set in stone as standard behavior, JavaScript's regular expressions are rather dumb about non-English characters. For example, as far as JavaScript's regular expressions are concerned, a "word character" is only one of the 26 characters in the Latin alphabet (uppercase or lowercase) and, for some reason, the underscore character.

Things like *à* or *ß*, which most definitely are word characters, will not match \w (and *will* match uppercase \W, the nonword category).

By a strange historical accident, \s (whitespace) does not have this problem and matches all characters that the Unicode standard considers whitespace, including things like the nonbreaking space and the Mongolian vowel separator.

Some regular expression implementations in other programming languages have syntax to match specific Unicode character categories, such as "all uppercase letters," "all punctuation," or "control characters." There are plans to add support for such categories in JavaScript, but it unfortunately looks like they won't be realized in the near future.

Summary

Regular expressions are objects that represent patterns in strings. They use their own syntax to express these patterns.

/abc/   A sequence of characters

/[abc]/   Any character from a set of characters

/[^abc]/   Any character *not* in a set of characters

/[0-9]/   Any character in a range of characters

/x+/   One or more occurrences of the pattern x

/x+?/   One or more occurrences, nongreedy

/x*/   Zero or more occurrences

/x?/   Zero or one occurrence

/x{2,4}/   Between two and four occurrences

/(abc)/   A group

/a|b|c/   Any one of several patterns

/\d/   Any digit character

/\w/   An alphanumeric character ("word character")

/\s/   Any whitespace character

/./   Any character except newlines

/\b/   A word boundary

/^/   Start of input

/$/   End of input

A regular expression has a method, test, to test whether a given string matches it. It also has an exec method that, when a match is found, returns an array containing all matched groups. Such an array has an index property that indicates where the match started.

Strings have a match method to match them against a regular expression and a search method to search for one, returning only the starting position of the match. Their `replace` method can replace matches of a pattern with a replacement string. Alternatively, you can pass a function to `replace`, which will be used to build up a replacement string based on the match text and matched groups.

Regular expressions can have options, which are written after the closing slash. The `i` option makes the match case insensitive, while the `g` option makes the expression *global*, which, among other things, causes the `replace` method to replace all instances instead of just the first.

The `RegExp` constructor can be used to create a regular expression value from a string.

Regular expressions are a sharp tool with an awkward handle. They simplify some tasks tremendously but can quickly become unmanageable when applied to complex problems. Part of knowing how to use them is resisting the urge to try to shoehorn things that they cannot sanely express into them.

Exercises

It is almost unavoidable that, in the course of working on these exercises, you will get confused and frustrated by some regular expression's inexplicable behavior. Sometimes it helps to enter your expression into an online tool like *http://debuggex.com/* to see whether its visualization corresponds to what you intended and to experiment with the way it responds to various input strings.

Regexp Golf

Code golf is a term used for the game of trying to express a particular program in as few characters as possible. Similarly, *regexp golf* is the practice of writing as tiny a regular expression as possible to match a given pattern, and *only* that pattern.

For each of the following items, write a regular expression to test whether any of the given substrings occur in a string. The regular expression should match only strings containing one of the substrings described. Do not worry about word boundaries unless explicitly mentioned. When your expression works, see whether you can make it any smaller.

1. *car* and *cat*
2. *pop* and *prop*
3. *ferret*, *ferry*, and *ferrari*
4. Any word ending in *ious*
5. A whitespace character followed by a dot, comma, colon, or semicolon
6. A word longer than six letters
7. A word without the letter *e*

Refer to the table in the chapter summary for help. Test each solution with a few test strings.

Quoting Style

Imagine you have written a story and used single quotation marks through-out to mark pieces of dialogue. Now you want to replace all the dialogue quotes with double quotes, while keeping the single quotes used in contrac-tions like *aren't*.

Think of a pattern that distinguishes these two kinds of quote usage and craft a call to the `replace` method that does the proper replacement.

Numbers Again

A series of digits can be matched by the simple regular expression /\d+/.

Write an expression that matches only JavaScript-style numbers. It must support an optional minus *or* plus sign in front of the number, the decimal dot, and exponent notation—5e-3 or 1E10— again with an optional sign in front of the exponent. Also note that it is not necessary for there to be digits in front of or after the dot, but the number cannot be a dot alone. That is, .5 and 5. are valid JavaScript numbers, but a lone dot *isn't*.

10

MODULES

Every program has a shape. On a small scale, this shape is determined by its division into functions and the blocks inside those functions. Programmers have a lot of freedom in the way they structure their programs. Shape follows more from the taste of the programmer than from the program's intended functionality.

When looking at a larger program in its entirety, individual functions start to blend into the background. Such a program can be made more readable if we have a larger unit of organization.

Modules divide programs into clusters of code that, by *some* criterion, belong together. This chapter explores some of the benefits that such division provides and shows techniques for building modules in JavaScript.

Why Modules Help

There are a number of reasons why authors divide their books into chapters and sections. These divisions make it easier for a reader to see how the book is built up and to find specific parts that they are interested in. They also help the *author* by providing a clear focus for every section.

The benefits of organizing a program into several files or modules are similar. Structure helps people who aren't yet familiar with the code find what they are looking for and makes it easier for the programmer to keep things that are related close together.

Some programs are even organized along the model of a traditional text, with a well-defined order in which the reader is encouraged to go through the program and with lots of prose (comments) providing a coherent description of the code. This makes reading the program a lot less intimidating—reading unknown code is usually intimidating—but has the downside of being more work to set up. It also makes the program more difficult to change because prose tends to be more tightly interconnected than code. This style is called *literate programming*. The "project" chapters of this book can be considered literate programs.

As a general rule, structuring things costs energy. In the early stages of a project, when you are not quite sure yet what goes where or what kind of modules the program needs at all, I endorse a minimalist, structureless attitude. Just put everything wherever it is convenient to put it until the code stabilizes. That way, you won't be wasting time moving pieces of the program back and forth, and you won't accidentally lock yourself into a structure that does not actually fit your program.

Namespacing

Most modern programming languages have a scope level between *global* (everyone can see it) and *local* (only this function can see it). JavaScript does not. Thus, by default, everything that needs to be visible outside of the scope of a top-level function is visible *everywhere*.

Namespace pollution, the problem of a lot of unrelated code having to share a single set of global variable names, was mentioned in Chapter 4, where the Math object was given as an example of an object that acts like a module by grouping math-related functionality.

Though JavaScript provides no actual module construct yet, objects can be used to create publicly accessible subnamespaces, and functions can be used to create an isolated, private namespace inside of a module. Later in this chapter, I will discuss a way to build reasonably convenient, namespace-isolating modules on top of the primitive concepts that JavaScript gives us.

Reuse

In a "flat" project, which isn't structured as a set of modules, it is not apparent which parts of the code are needed to use a particular function. In my program for spying on my enemies (see Chapter 9), I wrote a function for reading configuration files. If I want to use that function in another project, I must go and copy out the parts of the old program that look like they are relevant to the functionality that I need and paste them into my new program. Then, if I find a mistake in that code, I'll fix it only in whichever program that I'm working with at the time and forget to also fix it in the other program.

Once you have lots of such shared, duplicated pieces of code, you will find yourself wasting a lot of time and energy on moving them around and keeping them up-to-date.

Putting pieces of functionality that stand on their own into separate files and modules makes them easier to track, update, and share because all the various pieces of code that want to use the module load it from the same actual file.

This idea gets even more powerful when the relations between modules—which other modules each module depends on—are explicitly stated. You can then automate the process of installing and upgrading external modules (*libraries*).

Taking this idea even further, imagine an online service that tracks and distributes hundreds of thousands of such libraries, allowing you to search for the functionality you need and, once you find it, set up your project to automatically download it.

This service exists. It is called NPM (*http://npmjs.org/*). NPM consists of an online database of modules and a tool for downloading and upgrading the modules your program depends on. It grew out of Node.js, the browser-less JavaScript environment we will discuss in Chapter 20, but can also be useful when programming for the browser.

Decoupling

Another important role of modules is isolating pieces of code from each other, in the same way that the object interfaces from Chapter 6 do. A well-designed module will provide an interface for external code to use. As the module gets updated with bug fixes and new functionality, the existing interface stays the same (it is *stable*) so that other modules can use the new, improved version without any changes to themselves.

Note that a stable interface does not mean no new functions, methods, or variables are added. It just means that existing functionality isn't removed and its meaning is not changed.

A good module interface should allow the module to grow without breaking the old interface. This means exposing as few of the module's internal concepts as possible while also making the "language" that the interface exposes powerful and flexible enough to be applicable in a wide range of situations.

For interfaces that expose a single, focused concept, such as a configuration file reader, this design comes naturally. For others, such as a text editor, which has many different aspects that external code might need to access (content, styling, user actions, and so on), it requires careful design.

Using Functions as Namespaces

Functions are the only things in JavaScript that create a new scope. So if we want our modules to have their own scope, we will have to base them on functions.

Consider this trivial module for associating names with day-of-the-week numbers, as returned by a Date object's getDay method:

```
var names = ["Sunday", "Monday", "Tuesday", "Wednesday",
             "Thursday", "Friday", "Saturday"];
function dayName(number) {
  return names[number];
}

console.log(dayName(1));
// ▷ Monday
```

The dayName function is part of the module's interface, but the names variable is not. We would prefer *not* to spill it into the global scope.

We can do this:

```
var dayName = function() {
  var names = ["Sunday", "Monday", "Tuesday", "Wednesday",
               "Thursday", "Friday", "Saturday"];
  return function(number) {
    return names[number];
  };
}();

console.log(dayName(3));
// ▷ Wednesday
```

Now names is a local variable in an (unnamed) function. This function is created and immediately called, and its return value (the actual dayName function) is stored in a variable. We could have pages and pages of code in this function, with 100 local variables, and they would all be internal to our module—visible to the module itself but not to outside code.

We can use a similar pattern to isolate code from the outside world entirely. The following module logs a value to the console but does not actually provide any values for other modules to use:

```
(function() {
  function square(x) { return x * x; }
  var hundred = 100;

  console.log(square(hundred));
})();
// ▷ 10000
```

This code simply outputs the square of 100, but in the real world it could be a module that adds a method to some prototype or sets up a widget on a web page. It is wrapped in a function to prevent the variables it uses internally from polluting the global scope.

Why did we wrap the namespace function in a pair of parentheses? This has to do with a quirk in JavaScript's syntax. If an *expression* starts with the keyword function, it is a function expression. However, if a *statement* starts with function, it is a function *declaration*, which requires a name and, not being an expression, cannot be called by writing parentheses after it. You can think of the extra wrapping parentheses as a trick to force the function to be interpreted as an expression.

Objects as Interfaces

Now imagine that we want to add another function to our day-of-the-week module, one that goes from a day name to a number. We can't simply return the function anymore but must wrap the two functions in an object.

```
var weekDay = function() {
  var names = ["Sunday", "Monday", "Tuesday", "Wednesday",
               "Thursday", "Friday", "Saturday"];
  return {
    name: function(number) { return names[number]; },
    number: function(name) { return names.indexOf(name); }
  };
}();

console.log(weekDay.name(weekDay.number("Sunday")));
// ▷ Sunday
```

For bigger modules, gathering all the *exported* values into an object at the end of the function becomes awkward since many of the exported functions are likely to be big and you'd prefer to write them somewhere else, near related internal code. A convenient alternative is to declare an object (conventionally named exports) and add properties to that whenever we are defining something that needs to be exported. In the following example, the module function takes its interface object as an argument, allowing code outside of the function to create it and store it in a variable. (Outside of a function, this refers to the global scope object.)

```
(function(exports) {
  var names = ["Sunday", "Monday", "Tuesday", "Wednesday",
               "Thursday", "Friday", "Saturday"];

  exports.name = function(number) {
    return names[number];
  };
```

```
  exports.number = function(name) {
    return names.indexOf(name);
  };
})(this.weekDay = {});

console.log(weekDay.name(weekDay.number("Saturday")));
// ▷ Saturday
```

Detaching from the Global Scope

The previous pattern is commonly used by JavaScript modules intended for the browser. The module will claim a single global variable and wrap its code in a function in order to have its own private namespace. But this pattern still causes problems if multiple modules happen to claim the same name or if you want to load two versions of a module alongside each other.

With a little plumbing, we can create a system that allows one module to directly ask for the interface object of another module, without going through the global scope. Our goal is a require function that, when given a module name, will load that module's file (from disk or the Web, depending on the platform we are running on) and return the appropriate interface value.

This approach solves the problems mentioned previously and has the added benefit of making your program's dependencies explicit, making it harder to accidentally make use of some module without stating that you need it.

For require we need two things. First, we want a function readFile, which returns the content of a given file as a string. (A single such function is not present in standard JavaScript, but different JavaScript environments, such as the browser and Node.js, provide their own ways of accessing files. For now, let's just pretend we have this function.) Second, we need to be able to actually execute this string as JavaScript code.

Evaluating Data as Code

There are several ways to take data (a string of code) and run it as part of the current program.

The most obvious way is the special operator eval, which will execute a string of code in the *current* scope. This is usually a bad idea because it breaks some of the sane properties that scopes normally have, such as being isolated from the outside world.

```
function evalAndReturnX(code) {
  eval(code);
  return x;
}
```

```
console.log(evalAndReturnX("var x = 2"));
// ▷ 2
```

A better way of interpreting data as code is to use the `Function` constructor. This takes two arguments: a string containing a comma-separated list of argument names and a string containing the function's body.

```
var plusOne = new Function("n", "return n + 1;");
console.log(plusOne(4));
// ▷ 5
```

This is precisely what we need for our modules. We can wrap a module's code in a function, with that function's scope becoming our module scope.

The require Function

The following is a minimal implementation of `require`:

```
function require(name) {
  var code = new Function("exports", readFile(name));
  var exports = {};
  code(exports);
  return exports;
}

console.log(require("weekDay").name(1));
// ▷ Monday
```

Since the `new Function` constructor wraps the module code in a function, we don't have to write a wrapping namespace function in the module file itself. And since we make `exports` an argument to the module function, the module does not have to declare it. This removes a lot of clutter from our example module.

```
var names = ["Sunday", "Monday", "Tuesday", "Wednesday",
             "Thursday", "Friday", "Saturday"];

exports.name = function(number) {
  return names[number];
};
exports.number = function(name) {
  return names.indexOf(name);
};
```

When using this pattern, a module typically starts with a few variable declarations that load the modules it depends on.

```
var weekDay = require("weekDay");
var today = require("today");

console.log(weekDay.name(today.dayNumber()));
```

The simplistic implementation of require given previously has several problems. For one, it will load and run a module every time it is required, so if several modules have the same dependency or a require call is put inside a function that will be called multiple times, time and energy will be wasted.

This can be solved by storing the modules that have already been loaded in an object and simply returning the existing value when one is loaded multiple times.

The second problem is that it is not possible for a module to directly export a value other than the exports object, such as a function. For example, a module might want to export only the constructor of the object type it defines. Right now, it cannot do that because require always uses the exports object it creates as the exported value.

The traditional solution for this is to provide modules with another variable, module, which is an object that has a property exports. This property initially points at the empty object created by require but can be overwritten with another value in order to export something else.

```
function require(name) {
  if (name in require.cache)
    return require.cache[name];

  var code = new Function("exports, module", readFile(name));
  var exports = {}, module = {exports: exports};
  code(exports, module);

  require.cache[name] = module.exports;
  return module.exports;
}
require.cache = Object.create(null);
```

We now have a module system that uses a single global variable (require) to allow modules to find and use each other without going through the global scope.

This style of module system is called *CommonJS modules*, after the pseudo-standard that first specified it. It is built into the Node.js system. Real implementations do a lot more than the example I showed. Most importantly, they have a much more intelligent way of going from a module name to an actual piece of code, allowing both pathnames relative to the current file and module names that point directly to locally installed modules.

Slow-Loading Modules

Though it is possible to use the CommonJS module style when writing Java-Script for the browser, it is somewhat involved. The reason for this is that reading a file (module) from the Web is a lot slower than reading it from the hard disk. While a script is running in the browser, nothing else can happen to the website on which it runs, for reasons that will become clear in Chapter 14. This means that if every require call went and fetched something from some faraway web server, the page would freeze for a painfully long time while loading its scripts.

One way to work around this problem is to run a program like Browserify (*http://browserify.com/*) on your code before you serve it on a web page. This will look for calls to require, resolve all dependencies, and gather the needed code into a single big file. The website itself can simply load this file to get all the modules it needs.

Another solution is to wrap the code that makes up your module in a function so that the module loader can first load its dependencies in the background and then call the function, initializing the module, when the dependencies have been loaded. That is what the Asynchronous Module Definition (AMD) module system does.

Our trivial program with dependencies would look like this in AMD:

```
define(["weekDay", "today"], function(weekDay, today) {
  console.log(weekDay.name(today.dayNumber()));
});
```

The define function is central to this approach. It takes first an array of module names and then a function that takes one argument for each dependency. It will load the dependencies (if they haven't already been loaded) in the background, allowing the page to continue working while the files are being fetched. Once all dependencies are loaded, define will call the function it was given, with the interfaces of those dependencies as arguments.

The modules that are loaded this way must themselves contain a call to define. The value used as their interface is whatever was returned by the function passed to define. Here is the weekDay module again:

```
define([], function() {
  var names = ["Sunday", "Monday", "Tuesday", "Wednesday",
               "Thursday", "Friday", "Saturday"];
  return {
    name: function(number) { return names[number]; },
    number: function(name) { return names.indexOf(name); }
  };
});
```

To be able to show a minimal implementation of `define`, we will pretend we have a `backgroundReadFile` function that takes a filename and a function and calls the function with the content of the file as soon as it has finished loading it. (Chapter 17 will explain how to write that function.)

For the purpose of keeping track of modules while they are being loaded, the implementation of `define` will use objects that describe the state of modules, telling us whether they are available yet and providing their interface when they are.

The `getModule` function, when given a name, will return such an object and ensure that the module is scheduled to be loaded. It uses a cache object to avoid loading the same module twice.

```
var defineCache = Object.create(null);
var currentMod = null;

function getModule(name) {
  if (name in defineCache)
    return defineCache[name];

  var module = {exports: null,
                loaded: false,
                onLoad: []};
  defineCache[name] = module;
  backgroundReadFile(name, function(code) {
    currentMod = module;
    new Function("", code)();
  });
  return module;
}
```

We assume the loaded file also contains a (single) call to `define`. The `currentMod` variable is used to tell this call about the module object that is currently being loaded so that it can update this object when it finishes loading. We will come back to this mechanism in a moment.

The `define` function itself uses `getModule` to fetch or create the module objects for the current module's dependencies. Its task is to schedule the `moduleFunction` (the function that contains the module's actual code) to be run whenever those dependencies are loaded. For this purpose, it defines a function `whenDepsLoaded` that is added to the `onLoad` array of all dependencies that are not yet loaded. This function immediately returns if there are still unloaded dependencies, so it will do actual work only once, when the last dependency has finished loading. It is also called immediately, from `define` itself, in case there are no dependencies that need to be loaded.

```
function define(depNames, moduleFunction) {
  var myMod = currentMod;
  var deps = depNames.map(getModule);
```

```
  deps.forEach(function(mod) {
    if (!mod.loaded)
      mod.onLoad.push(whenDepsLoaded);
  });

  function whenDepsLoaded() {
    if (!deps.every(function(m) { return m.loaded; }))
      return;

    var args = deps.map(function(m) { return m.exports; });
    var exports = moduleFunction.apply(null, args);
    if (myMod) {
      myMod.exports = exports;
      myMod.loaded = true;
      myMod.onLoad.forEach(function(f) { f(); });
    }
  }
  whenDepsLoaded();
}
```

When all dependencies are available, whenDepsLoaded calls the function that holds the module, giving it the dependencies' interfaces as arguments.

The first thing define does is store the value that currentMod had when it was called in a variable myMod. Remember that getModule, just before evaluating the code for a module, stored the corresponding module object in currentMod. This allows whenDepsLoaded to store the return value of the module function in that module's exports property, set the module's loaded property to true, and call all the functions that are waiting for the module to load.

This code is a lot harder to follow than the require function. Its execution does not follow a simple, predictable path. Instead, multiple operations are set up to happen at some unspecified time in the future, which obscures the way the code executes.

A real AMD implementation is, again, quite a lot more clever about resolving module names to actual URLs and generally more robust than the one shown previously. The RequireJS project (*http://requirejs.org/*) provides a popular implementation of this style of module loader.

Interface Design

Designing interfaces for modules and object types is one of the subtler aspects of programming. Any nontrivial piece of functionality can be modeled in various ways. Finding a way that works well requires insight and foresight.

The best way to learn the value of good interface design is to use lots of interfaces—some good, some bad. Experience will teach you what works and what doesn't. Never assume that a painful interface is "just the way it is." Fix it, or wrap it in a new interface that works better for you.

Predictability

If programmers can predict the way your interface works, they (or you) won't get sidetracked as often by the need to look up how to use it. Thus, try to follow conventions. When there is another module or part of the standard JavaScript environment that does something similar to what you are implementing, it might be a good idea to make your interface resemble the existing interface. That way, it'll feel familiar to people who know the existing interface.

Another area where predictability is important is the actual *behavior* of your code. It can be tempting to make an unnecessarily clever interface with the justification that it's more convenient to use. For example, you could accept all kinds of different types and combinations of arguments and do the "right thing" for all of them. Or you could provide dozens of specialized convenience functions that provide slightly different flavors of your module's functionality. These might make code that builds on your interface slightly shorter, but they will also make it much harder for people to build a clear mental model of the module's behavior.

Composability

In your interfaces, try to use the simplest data structures possible and make functions do a single, clear thing. Whenever practical, make them pure functions (see Chapter 3).

For example, it is not uncommon for modules to provide their own array-like collection objects, with their own interface for counting and extracting elements. Such objects won't have map or forEach methods, and any existing function that expects a real array won't be able to work with them. This is an example of poor *composability*—the module cannot be easily composed with other code.

One example would be a module for spell-checking text, which we might need when we want to write a text editor. The spell-checker could be made to operate directly on whichever complicated data structures the editor uses and directly call internal functions in the editor to have the user choose between spelling suggestions. If we go that way, the module cannot be used with any other programs. On the other hand, if we define the spell-checking interface so that you can pass it a simple string and it will return the position in the string where it found a possible misspelling, along with an array of suggested corrections, then we have an interface that could also be composed with other systems because strings and arrays are always available in JavaScript.

Layered Interfaces

When designing an interface for a complex piece of functionality—sending email, for example—you often run into a dilemma. On the one hand, you do not want to overload the user of your interface with details. They shouldn't have to study your interface for 20 minutes before they can send an email.

On the other hand, you do not want to hide all the details either—when people need to do complicated things with your module, they should be able to.

Often the solution is to provide two interfaces: a detailed *low-level* one for complex situations and a simple *high-level* one for routine use. The second can usually be built easily using the tools provided by the first. In the email module, the high-level interface could just be a function that takes a message, a sender address, and a receiver address and then sends the email. The low-level interface would allow full control over email headers, attachments, HTML mail, and so on.

Summary

Modules provide structure to bigger programs by separating the code into different files and namespaces. Giving these modules well-defined interfaces makes them easier to use and reuse and makes it possible to continue using them as the module itself evolves.

Though the JavaScript language is characteristically unhelpful when it comes to modules, the flexible functions and objects it provides make it possible to define rather nice module systems. Function scopes can be used as internal namespaces for the module, and objects can be used to store sets of exported values.

There are two popular, well-defined approaches to such modules. One is called *CommonJS Modules* and revolves around a require function that fetches a module by name and returns its interface. The other is called *AMD* and uses a define function that takes an array of module names and a function and, after loading the modules, runs the function with their interfaces as arguments.

Exercises

Month Names

Write a simple module similar to the weekDay module that can convert month numbers (zero-based, as in the Date type) to names and can convert names back to numbers. Give it its own namespace since it will need an internal array of month names, and use plain JavaScript, without any module loader system.

A Return to Electronic Life

With my hope that Chapter 7 is still somewhat fresh in your mind, think back to the system designed in that chapter and come up with a way to separate the code into modules. To refresh your memory, these are the functions and types defined in that chapter, in order of appearance:

1. Vector

2. Grid

3. `directions`

4. `randomElement`

5. `BouncingCritter`

6. `elementFromChar`

7. `World`

8. `charFromElement`

9. `Wall`

10. `View`

11. `directionNames`

12. `WallFollower`

13. `dirPlus`

14. `LifelikeWorld`

15. `Plant`

16. `PlantEater`

17. `SmartPlantEater`

18. `Tiger`

Don't exaggerate and create too many modules. A book that starts a new chapter for every page would probably get on your nerves, if only because of all the space wasted on titles. Similarly, having to open 10 files to read a tiny project isn't helpful. Aim for three to five modules.

You can choose to have some functions become internal to their module and thus inaccessible to other modules.

There is no single correct solution here. Module organization is largely a matter of taste.

Circular Dependencies

A tricky subject in dependency management is circular dependencies, where module A depends on B, and B also depends on A. Many module systems simply forbid this. CommonJS modules allow a limited form: it works as long as the modules do not replace their default exports object with another value and start accessing each other's interface only after they finish loading.

Can you think of a way in which support for this feature could be implemented? Look back to the definition of require and consider what the function would have to do to allow this.

"The evaluator, which determines the meaning
of expressions in a programming language,
is just another program."

—Hal Abelson and Gerald Sussman,
Structure and Interpretation of Computer Programs

11

PROJECT: A PROGRAMMING LANGUAGE

Building your own programming language is surprisingly easy (as long as you do not aim too high) and very enlightening.

The main thing I want to show in this chapter is that there is no magic involved in building your own language. I've often felt that some human inventions were so immensely clever and complicated that I'd never be able to understand them. But with a little reading and tinkering, such things often turn out to be quite mundane.

We will build a programming language called Egg. It will be a tiny, simple language but one that is powerful enough to express any computation you can think of. It will also allow simple abstraction based on functions.

Parsing

The most immediately visible part of a programming language is its *syntax*, or notation. A *parser* is a program that reads a piece of text and produces a data structure that reflects the structure of the program contained in that text. If the text does not form a valid program, the parser should complain and point out the error.

Our language will have a simple and uniform syntax. Everything in Egg is an expression. An expression can be a variable, a number, a string, or an *application.* Applications are used for function calls but also for constructs such as if or while.

To keep the parser simple, strings in Egg do not support anything like backslash escapes. A string is simply a sequence of characters that are not double quotes, wrapped in double quotes. A number is a sequence of digits. Variable names can consist of any character that is not whitespace and does not have a special meaning in the syntax.

Applications are written the way they are in JavaScript, by putting parentheses after an expression and having any number of arguments between those parentheses, separated by commas.

```
do(define(x, 10),
   if(>(x, 5),
      print("large"),
      print("small")))
```

The uniformity of the Egg language means that things that are operators in JavaScript (such as >) are normal variables in this language, applied just like other functions. And since the syntax has no concept of a block, we need a do construct to represent doing multiple things in sequence.

The data structure that the parser will use to describe a program will consist of expression objects, each of which has a type property indicating the kind of expression it is and other properties to describe its content.

Expressions of type "value" represent literal strings or numbers. Their value property contains the string or number value that they represent. Expressions of type "word" are used for identifiers (names). Such objects have a name property that holds the identifier's name as a string. Finally, "apply" expressions represent applications. They have an operator property that refers to the expression that is being applied, and they have an args property that refers to an array of argument expressions.

The >(x, 5) part of the previous program would be represented like this:

```
{
  type: "apply",
  operator: {type: "word", name: ">"},
  args: [
    {type: "word", name: "x"},
    {type: "value", value: 5}
  ]
}
```

Such a data structure is called a *syntax tree*. If you imagine the objects as dots and the links between them as lines between those dots, it has a treelike shape. The fact that expressions contain other expressions, which in turn might contain more expressions, is similar to the way branches split and split again.

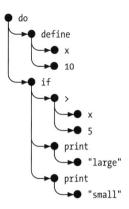

Contrast this to the parser we wrote for the configuration file format in Chapter 9, which had a simple structure: it split the input into lines and handled those lines one at a time. There were only a few simple forms that a line was allowed to have.

Here we must find a different approach. Expressions are not separated into lines, and they have a recursive structure. Application expressions *contain* other expressions.

Fortunately, this problem can be solved elegantly by writing a parser function that is recursive in a way that reflects the recursive nature of the language.

We define a function parseExpression, which takes a string as input and returns an object containing the data structure for the expression at the start of the string, along with the part of the string left after parsing this expression. When parsing subexpressions (the argument to an application, for example), this function can be called again, yielding the argument expression as well as the text that remains. This text may in turn contain more arguments or may be the closing parenthesis that ends the list of arguments.

This is the first part of the parser:

```
function parseExpression(program) {
  program = skipSpace(program);
  var match, expr;
  if (match = /^"([^"]*)"/.exec(program))
    expr = {type: "value", value: match[1]};
  else if (match = /^\d+\b/.exec(program))
    expr = {type: "value", value: Number(match[0])};
  else if (match = /^[^\s(),"]+/.exec(program))
    expr = {type: "word", name: match[0]};
  else
    throw new SyntaxError("Unexpected syntax: " + program);

  return parseApply(expr, program.slice(match[0].length));
}
```

```
function skipSpace(string) {
  var first = string.search(/\S/);
  if (first == -1) return "";
  return string.slice(first);
}
```

Because Egg allows any amount of whitespace between its elements, we have to repeatedly cut the whitespace off the start of the program string. This is what the skipSpace function helps with.

After skipping any leading space, parseExpression uses three regular expressions to spot the three simple (atomic) elements that Egg supports: strings, numbers, and words. The parser constructs a different kind of data structure depending on which one matches. If the input does not match one of these three forms, it is not a valid expression, and the parser throws an error. SyntaxError is a standard error object type, which is raised when an attempt is made to run an invalid JavaScript program.

We can then cut off the part that we matched from the program string and pass that, along with the object for the expression, to parseApply, which checks whether the expression is an application. If so, it parses a parenthesized list of arguments.

```
function parseApply(expr, program) {
  program = skipSpace(program);
  if (program[0] != "(")
    return {expr: expr, rest: program};

  program = skipSpace(program.slice(1));
  expr = {type: "apply", operator: expr, args: []};
  while (program[0] != ")") {
    var arg = parseExpression(program);
    expr.args.push(arg.expr);
    program = skipSpace(arg.rest);
    if (program[0] == ",")
      program = skipSpace(program.slice(1));
    else if (program[0] != ")")
      throw new SyntaxError("Expected ',' or ')'");
  }
  return parseApply(expr, program.slice(1));
}
```

If the next character in the program is not an opening parenthesis, this is not an application, and parseApply simply returns the expression it was given.

Otherwise, it skips the opening parenthesis and creates the syntax tree object for this application expression. It then recursively calls parseExpression to parse each argument until a closing parenthesis is found. The recursion is indirect, through parseApply and parseExpression calling each other.

Because an application expression can itself be applied (such as in `multiplier(2)(1)`), parseApply must, after it has parsed an application, call itself again to check whether another pair of parentheses follows.

This is all we need to parse Egg. We wrap it in a convenient parse function that verifies that it has reached the end of the input string after parsing the expression (an Egg program is a single expression), and that gives us the program's data structure.

```
function parse(program) {
  var result = parseExpression(program);
  if (skipSpace(result.rest).length > 0)
    throw new SyntaxError("Unexpected text after program");
  return result.expr;
}

console.log(parse("+(a, 10)"));
// ▷ {type: "apply",
//    operator: {type: "word", name: "+"},
//    args: [{type: "word", name: "a"},
//          {type: "value", value: 10}]}
```

It works! It doesn't give us very helpful information when it fails and doesn't store the line and column on which each expression starts, which might be helpful when reporting errors later, but it's good enough for our purposes.

The Evaluator

What can we do with the syntax tree for a program? Run it, of course! And that is what the evaluator does. You give it a syntax tree and an environment object that associates names with values, and it will evaluate the expression that the tree represents and return the value that this produces.

```
function evaluate(expr, env) {
  switch(expr.type) {
    case "value":
      return expr.value;

    case "word":
      if (expr.name in env)
        return env[expr.name];
      else
        throw new ReferenceError("Undefined variable: " + expr.name);

    case "apply":
      if (expr.operator.type == "word" && expr.operator.name in specialForms)
        return specialForms[expr.operator.name](expr.args, env);
```

```
      var op = evaluate(expr.operator, env);
      if (typeof op != "function")
        throw new TypeError("Applying a non-function.");
      return op.apply(null, expr.args.map(function(arg) {
        return evaluate(arg, env);
      }));
    }
  }

  var specialForms = Object.create(null);
```

The evaluator has code for each of the expression types. A literal value expression simply produces its value. (For example, the expression 100 just evaluates to the number 100.) For a variable, we must check whether it is actually defined in the environment and, if it is, fetch the variable's value.

Applications are more involved. If they are a special form, like if, we do not evaluate anything and simply pass the argument expressions, along with the environment, to the function that handles this form. If it is a normal call, we evaluate the operator, verify that it is a function, and call it with the result of evaluating the arguments.

We will use plain JavaScript function values to represent Egg's function values. We will come back to this later, when the special form called fun is defined.

The recursive structure of evaluate resembles the similar structure of the parser. Both mirror the structure of the language itself. It would also be possible to integrate the parser with the evaluator and evaluate during parsing, but splitting them up this way makes the program more readable.

This is really all that is needed to interpret Egg. It is that simple. But without defining a few special forms and adding some useful values to the environment, you can't do anything with this language yet.

Special Forms

The specialForms object is used to define special syntax in Egg. It associates words with functions that evaluate such special forms. It is currently empty. Let's add some forms.

```
specialForms["if"] = function(args, env) {
  if (args.length != 3)
    throw new SyntaxError("Bad number of args to if");

  if (evaluate(args[0], env) !== false)
    return evaluate(args[1], env);
  else
    return evaluate(args[2], env);
};
```

Egg's if construct expects exactly three arguments. It will evaluate the first, and if the result isn't the value false, it will evaluate the second. Otherwise, the third gets evaluated. This if form is more similar to JavaScript's ternary ?: operator than to JavaScript's if. It is an expression, not a statement, and it produces a value, namely, the result of the second or third argument.

Egg differs from JavaScript in how it handles the condition value to if. It will not treat things like zero or the empty string as false, but only the precise value false.

The reason we need to represent if as a special form, rather than a regular function, is that all arguments to functions are evaluated before the function is called, whereas if should evaluate only *either* its second or its third argument, depending on the value of the first.

The while form is similar.

```
specialForms["while"] = function(args, env) {
  if (args.length != 2)
    throw new SyntaxError("Bad number of args to while");

  while (evaluate(args[0], env) !== false)
    evaluate(args[1], env);

  // Since undefined does not exist in Egg, we return false,
  // for lack of a meaningful result.
  return false;
};
```

Another basic building block is do, which executes all its arguments from top to bottom. Its value is the value produced by the last argument.

```
specialForms["do"] = function(args, env) {
  var value = false;
  args.forEach(function(arg) {
    value = evaluate(arg, env);
  });
  return value;
};
```

To be able to create variables and give them new values, we also create a form called define. It expects a word as its first argument and an expression producing the value to assign to that word as its second argument. Since define, like everything, is an expression, it must return a value. We'll make it return the value that was assigned (just like JavaScript's = operator).

```
specialForms["define"] = function(args, env) {
  if (args.length != 2 || args[0].type != "word")
    throw new SyntaxError("Bad use of define");
  var value = evaluate(args[1], env);
```

```
    env[args[0].name] = value;
    return value;
};
```

The Environment

The environment accepted by evaluate is an object with properties whose names correspond to variable names and whose values correspond to the values those variables are bound to. Let's define an environment object to represent the global scope.

To be able to use the if construct we just defined, we must have access to Boolean values. Since there are only two Boolean values, we do not need special syntax for them. We simply bind two variables to the values true and false and use those.

```
var topEnv = Object.create(null);

topEnv["true"] = true;
topEnv["false"] = false;
```

We can now evaluate a simple expression that negates a Boolean value.

```
var prog = parse("if(true, false, true)");
console.log(evaluate(prog, topEnv));
// ▷ false
```

To supply basic arithmetic and comparison operators, we will also add some function values to the environment. In the interest of keeping the code short, we'll use new Function to synthesize a bunch of operator functions in a loop, rather than defining them all individually.

```
["+", "-", "*", "/", "==", "<", ">"].forEach(function(op) {
  topEnv[op] = new Function("a, b", "return a " + op + " b;");
});
```

A way to output values is also very useful, so we'll wrap console.log in a function and call it print.

```
topEnv["print"] = function(value) {
  console.log(value);
  return value;
};
```

That gives us enough elementary tools to write simple programs. The following run function provides a convenient way to write and run them. It creates a fresh environment and parses and evaluates the strings we give it as a single program.

```
function run() {
  var env = Object.create(topEnv);
  var program = Array.prototype.slice.call(arguments, 0).join("\n");
  return evaluate(parse(program), env);
}
```

The use of Array.prototype.slice.call is a trick to turn an array-like object, such as arguments, into a real array so that we can call join on it. It takes all the arguments given to run and treats them as the lines of a program.

```
run("do(define(total, 0),",
    "   define(count, 1),",
    "   while(<(count, 11),",
    "        do(define(total, +(total, count)),",
    "           define(count, +(count, 1)))),",
    "   print(total))");
// ▷ 55
```

This is the program we've seen several times before, which computes the sum of the numbers 1 to 10, expressed in Egg. It is clearly uglier than the equivalent JavaScript program but not bad for a language implemented in less than 150 lines of code.

Functions

A programming language without functions is a poor programming language indeed.

Fortunately, it is not hard to add a fun construct, which treats its last argument as the function's body and treats all the arguments before that as the names of the function's arguments.

```
specialForms["fun"] = function(args, env) {
  if (!args.length)
    throw new SyntaxError("Functions need a body");
  function name(expr) {
    if (expr.type != "word")
      throw new SyntaxError("Arg names must be words");
    return expr.name;
  }
  var argNames = args.slice(0, args.length - 1).map(name);
  var body = args[args.length - 1];

  return function() {
    if (arguments.length != argNames.length)
      throw new TypeError("Wrong number of arguments");
    var localEnv = Object.create(env);
```

```
    for (var i = 0; i < arguments.length; i++)
      localEnv[argNames[i]] = arguments[i];
    return evaluate(body, localEnv);
  };
};
```

Functions in Egg have their own local environment, just like in JavaScript. We use Object.create to make a new object that has access to the variables in the outer environment (its prototype) but that can also contain new variables without modifying that outer scope.

The function created by the fun form creates this local environment and adds the argument variables to it. It then evaluates the function body in this environment and returns the result.

```
run("do(define(plusOne, fun(a, +(a, 1))),",
    "    print(plusOne(10)))");
// ▷ 11

run("do(define(pow, fun(base, exp,",
    "     if(==(exp, 0),",
    "        1,",
    "        *(base, pow(base, -(exp, 1)))))),",
    "   print(pow(2, 10)))");
// ▷ 1024
```

Compilation

What we have built is an interpreter. During evaluation, it acts directly on the representation of the program produced by the parser.

Compilation is the process of adding another step between the parsing and the running of a program, which transforms the program into something that can be evaluated more efficiently by doing as much work as possible in advance. For example, in well-designed languages it is obvious, for each use of a variable, which variable is being referred to, without actually running the program. This can be used to avoid looking up the variable by name every time it is accessed and to directly fetch it from some predetermined memory location.

Traditionally, compilation involves converting the program to machine code, the raw format that a computer's processor can execute. But any process that converts a program to a different representation can be thought of as compilation.

It would be possible to write an alternative evaluation strategy for Egg, one that first converts the program to a JavaScript program, uses new Function to invoke the JavaScript compiler on it, and then runs the result. When done right, this would make Egg run very fast while still being quite simple to implement.

If you are interested in this topic and willing to spend some time on it, I encourage you to try to implement such a compiler as an exercise.

Cheating

When we defined `if` and `while`, you probably noticed that they were more or less trivial wrappers around JavaScript's own `if` and `while`. Similarly, the values in Egg are just regular old JavaScript values.

If you compare the implementation of Egg, built on top of JavaScript, with the amount of work and complexity required to build a programming language directly on the raw functionality provided by a machine, the difference is huge. Regardless, this example hopefully gave you an impression of the way programming languages work.

And when it comes to getting something done, cheating is more effective than doing everything yourself. Though the toy language in this chapter doesn't do anything that couldn't be done better in JavaScript, there *are* situations where writing small languages helps get real work done.

Such a language does not have to resemble a typical programming language. If JavaScript didn't come equipped with regular expressions, you could write your own parser and evaluator for such a sublanguage.

Or imagine you are building a giant robotic dinosaur and need to program its behavior. JavaScript might not be the most effective way to do this. You might instead opt for a language that looks like this:

```
behavior walk
  perform when
    destination ahead
  actions
    move left-foot
    move right-foot

behavior attack
  perform when
    Godzilla in-view
  actions
    fire laser-eyes
    launch arm-rockets
```

This is what is usually called a *domain-specific language*, a language tailored to express a narrow domain of knowledge. Such a language can be more expressive than a general-purpose language because it is designed to express exactly the things that need expressing in its domain and nothing else.

Exercises

Arrays

Add support for arrays to Egg by adding the following three functions to the top scope: array(...) to construct an array containing the argument values, length(array) to get an array's length, and element(array, n) to fetch the *n*th element from an array.

Closure

The way we have defined fun allows functions in Egg to "close over" the surrounding environment, allowing the function's body to use local values that were visible at the time the function was defined, just like JavaScript functions do.

The following program illustrates this: function f returns a function that adds its argument to f's argument, meaning that it needs access to the local scope inside f to be able to use variable a.

```
run("do(define(f, fun(a, fun(b, +(a, b)))),",
    "   print(f(4)(5)))");
// ▷ 9
```

Go back to the definition of the fun form and explain which mechanism causes this to work.

Comments

It would be nice if we could write comments in Egg. For example, whenever we find a hash sign (#), we could treat the rest of the line as a comment and ignore it, similar to // in JavaScript.

We do not have to make any big changes to the parser to support this. We can simply change skipSpace to skip comments like they are whitespace so that all the points where skipSpace is called will now also skip comments. Make this change.

Fixing Scope

Currently, the only way to assign a variable a value is define. This construct acts as a way both to define new variables and to give existing ones a new value.

This ambiguity causes a problem. When you try to give a nonlocal variable a new value, you will end up defining a local one with the same name instead. (Some languages work like this by design, but I've always found it a silly way to handle scope.)

Add a special form set, similar to define, which gives a variable a new value, updating the variable in an outer scope if it doesn't already exist in the inner scope. If the variable is not defined at all, throw a ReferenceError (which is another standard error type).

The technique of representing scopes as simple objects, which has made things convenient so far, will get in your way a little at this point. You might want to use the `Object.getPrototypeOf` function, which returns the prototype of an object. Also remember that scopes do not derive from `Object.prototype`, so if you want to call `hasOwnProperty` on them, you have to use this clumsy expression:

```
Object.prototype.hasOwnProperty.call(scope, name);
```

This fetches the `hasOwnProperty` method from the `Object` prototype and then calls it on a scope object.

PART II

BROWSER

"The browser is a really hostile programming environment."

—Douglas Crockford,
The JavaScript Programming
Language (video lecture)

12

JAVASCRIPT AND THE BROWSER

The next part of this book will talk about web browsers. Without web browsers, there would be no JavaScript. And even if there were, no one would ever have paid any attention to it.

Web technology has, from the start, been decentralized, not just technically but also in the way it has evolved. Various browser vendors have added new functionality in ad hoc and sometimes poorly thought out ways, which then sometimes ended up being adopted by others and finally set down as a standard.

This is both a blessing and a curse. On the one hand, it is empowering to not have a central party control a system but have various parties working in loose collaboration (or occasionally, open hostility). On the other hand, the haphazard way in which the Web was developed means that the resulting system is not exactly a shining example of internal consistency. In fact, some parts of it are downright messy and confusing.

Networks and the Internet

Computer networks have been around since the 1950s. If you put cables between two or more computers and allow them to send data back and forth through these cables, you can do all kinds of wonderful things.

If connecting two machines in the same building allows us to do wonderful things, connecting machines all over the planet should be even better. The technology to start implementing this vision was developed in the 1980s, and the resulting network is called the *Internet*. It has lived up to its promise.

A computer can use this network to spew bits at another computer. For any effective communication to arise out of this bit-spewing, the computers at both ends must know what the bits are supposed to represent. The meaning of any given sequence of bits depends entirely on the kind of thing that it is trying to express and on the encoding mechanism used.

A *network protocol* describes a style of communication over a network. There are protocols for sending email, for fetching email, for sharing files, or even for controlling computers that happen to be infected by malicious software.

For example, a simple chat protocol might consist of one computer sending the bits that represent the text "CHAT?" to another machine and the other responding with "OK!" to confirm that it understands the protocol. They can then proceed to send each other strings of text, read the text sent by the other from the network, and display whatever they receive on their screens.

Most protocols are built on top of other protocols. Our example chat protocol treats the network as a streamlike device into which you can put bits and have them arrive at the correct destination in the correct order. Ensuring those things is already a rather difficult technical problem.

The *Transmission Control Protocol* (TCP) is a protocol that solves this problem. All Internet-connected devices "speak" it, and most communication on the Internet is built on top of it.

A TCP connection works as follows: one computer must be waiting, or *listening*, for other computers to start talking to it. To be able to listen for different kinds of communication at the same time on a single machine, each listener has a number (called a *port*) associated with it. Most protocols specify which port should be used by default. For example, when we want to send an email using the SMTP protocol, the machine through which we send it is expected to be listening on port 25.

Another computer can then establish a connection by connecting to the target machine using the correct port number. If the target machine can be reached and is listening on that port, the connection is successfully created. The listening computer is called the *server*, and the connecting computer is called the *client*.

Such a connection acts as a two-way pipe through which bits can flow—the machines on both ends can put data into it. Once the bits are successfully transmitted, they can be read out again by the machine on the other side. This is a convenient model. You could say that TCP provides an abstraction of the network.

The Web

The *World Wide Web* (not to be confused with the Internet as a whole) is a set of protocols and formats that allow us to visit web pages in a browser. The "Web" part in the name refers to the fact that such pages can easily link to each other, thus connecting into a huge mesh that users can move through.

To add content to the Web, all you need to do is connect a machine to the Internet, and have it listen on port 80, using the *Hypertext Transfer Protocol* (HTTP). This protocol allows other computers to request documents over the network.

Each document on the Web is named by a *Uniform Resource Locator* (URL), which looks something like this:

```
  http://eloquentjavascript.net/12_browser.html
  |       |                      |          |
  protocol   server              path
```

The first part tells us that this URL uses the HTTP protocol (as opposed to, for example, encrypted HTTP, which would be *https://*). Then comes the part that identifies which server we are requesting the document from. Last is a path string that identifies the specific document (or *resource*) we are interested in.

Each machine connected to the Internet gets a unique *IP address*, which looks something like 37.187.37.82. You can use these directly as the server part of a URL. But lists of more or less random numbers are hard to remember and awkward to type, so you can instead register a *domain name* to point toward a specific machine or set of machines. I registered *eloquentjavascript.net* to point at the IP address of a machine I control and can thus use that domain name to serve web pages.

If you type the previous URL into your browser's address bar, it will try to retrieve and display the document at that URL. First, your browser has to find out what address *eloquentjavascript.net* refers to. Then, using the HTTP protocol, it makes a connection to the server at that address and asks for the resource */12_browser.html*.

We will take a closer look at the HTTP protocol in Chapter 17.

HTML

HTML, which stands for *Hypertext Markup Language*, is the document format used for web pages. An HTML document contains text, as well as *tags* that give structure to the text, describing things such as links, paragraphs, and headings.

A simple HTML document looks like this:

```
<!doctype html>
<html>
  <head>
    <title>My home page</title>
  </head>
  <body>
    <h1>My home page</h1>
    <p>Hello, I am Marijn and this is my home page.</p>
    <p>I also wrote a book! Read it
      <a href="http://eloquentjavascript.net">here</a>.</p>
  </body>
</html>
```

This is what such a document would look like in the browser:

My home page

Hello, I am Marijn and this is my home page.

I also wrote a book! Read it here.

The tags, wrapped in angle brackets (< and >), provide information about the structure of the document. The other text is just plaintext.

The document starts with <!doctype html>, which tells the browser to interpret it as *modern* HTML, as opposed to various dialects that were in use in the past.

HTML documents have a head and a body. The head contains information *about* the document, and the body contains the document itself. In this case, we first declared that the title of this document is "My home page" and then gave a document containing a heading (<h1>, meaning "heading 1"—<h2> to <h6> produce more minor headings) and two paragraphs (<p>).

Tags come in several forms. An element, such as the body, a paragraph, or a link, is started by an *opening tag* like <p> and ended by a *closing tag* like </p>. Some opening tags, such as the one for the link (<a>), contain extra information in the form of name="value" pairs. These are called *attributes*. In this case, the destination of the link is indicated with href="http://eloquent javascript.net", where href stands for "hypertext reference."

Some kinds of tags do not enclose anything and thus do not need to be closed. An example of this would be <img src="http://example.com/image.jpg">, which will display the image found at the given source URL.

To be able to include angle brackets in the text of a document, even though they have a special meaning in HTML, yet another form of special notation has to be introduced. A plain opening angle bracket is written as < ("less than"), and a closing bracket is written as > ("greater than"). In

HTML, an ampersand (&) character followed by a word and a semicolon (;) is called an *entity*, and will be replaced by the character it encodes.

This is analogous to the way backslashes are used in JavaScript strings. Since this mechanism gives ampersand characters a special meaning, too, those need to be escaped as &. Inside an attribute, which is wrapped in double quotes, " can be used to insert an actual quote character.

HTML is parsed in a remarkably error-tolerant way. When tags that should be there are missing, the browser reconstructs them. The way in which this is done has been standardized, and you can rely on all modern browsers to do it in the same way.

The following document will be treated just like the one shown previously:

```
<!doctype html>

<title>My home page</title>

<h1>My home page</h1>
<p>Hello, I am Marijn and this is my home page.
<p>I also wrote a book! Read it
  <a href=http://eloquentjavascript.net>here</a>.
```

The `<html>`, `<head>`, and `<body>` tags are gone completely. The browser knows that `<title>` belongs in a head, and that `<h1>` in a body. Furthermore, I am no longer explicitly closing the paragraphs since opening a new paragraph or ending the document will close them implicitly. The quotes around the link target are also gone.

This book will usually omit the `<html>`, `<head>`, and `<body>` tags from examples to keep them short and free of clutter. But I *will* close tags and include quotes around attributes.

I will also usually omit the doctype. This is not to be taken as an encouragement to omit doctype declarations. Browsers will often do ridiculous things when you forget them. You should consider doctypes implicitly present in examples, even when they are not actually shown in the text.

HTML and JavaScript

In the context of this book, the most important HTML tag is `<script>`. This tag allows us to include a piece of JavaScript in a document.

```
<h1>Testing alert</h1>
<script>alert("hello!");</script>
```

Such a script will run as soon as its `<script>` tag is encountered as the browser reads the HTML. The page shown earlier will pop up an `alert` dialog when opened.

Including large programs directly in HTML documents is often impractical. The `<script>` tag can be given an `src` attribute in order to fetch a script file (a text file containing a JavaScript program) from a URL.

```
<h1>Testing alert</h1>
<script src="code/hello.js"></script>
```

The *code/hello.js* file included here contains the same simple program, `alert("hello!")`. When an HTML page references other URLs as part of itself—for example, an image file or a script—web browsers will retrieve them immediately and include them in the page.

A script tag must always be closed with `</script>`, even if it refers to a script file and doesn't contain any code. If you forget this, the rest of the page will be interpreted as part of the script.

Some attributes can also contain a JavaScript program. The `<button>` tag shown next (which shows up as a button) has an `onclick` attribute, whose content will be run whenever the button is clicked.

```
<button onclick="alert('Boom!');">DO NOT PRESS</button>
```

Note that I had to use single quotes for the string in the `onclick` attribute because double quotes are already used to quote the whole attribute. I could also have used `&quot;`, but that'd make the program harder to read.

In the Sandbox

Running programs downloaded from the Internet is potentially dangerous. You do not know much about the people behind most sites you visit, and they do not necessarily mean well. Running programs by people who do not mean well is how you get your computer infected by viruses, your data stolen, and your accounts hacked.

Yet the attraction of the Web is that you can surf it without necessarily trusting all the pages you visit. This is why browsers severely limit the things a JavaScript program may do: it can't look at the files on your computer or modify anything not related to the web page it was embedded in.

Isolating a programming environment in this way is called *sandboxing*, the idea being that the program is harmlessly playing in a sandbox. But you should imagine this particular kind of sandbox as having a cage of thick steel bars over it, which makes it somewhat different from your typical playground sandbox.

The hard part of sandboxing is allowing the programs enough room to be useful yet at the same time restricting them from doing anything dangerous. Lots of useful functionality, such as communicating with other servers or reading the content of the copy-paste clipboard, can also be used to do problematic, privacy-invading things.

Every now and then, someone comes up with a new way to circumvent the limitations of a browser and do something harmful, ranging from leaking minor private information to taking over the whole machine that the browser runs on. The browser developers respond by fixing the hole, and all is well again—that is, until the next problem is discovered, and hopefully publicized, rather than secretly exploited by some government or mafia.

Compatibility and the Browser Wars

In the early stages of the Web, a browser called Mosaic dominated the market. After a few years, the balance had shifted to Netscape, which was then, in turn, largely supplanted by Microsoft's Internet Explorer. At any point where a single browser was dominant, that browser's vendor would feel entitled to unilaterally invent new features for the Web. Since most users used the same browser, websites would simply start using those features—never mind the other browsers.

This was the dark age of compatibility, often called the *browser wars*. Web developers were left with not one unified Web but two or three incompatible platforms. To make things worse, the browsers in use around 2003 were all full of bugs, and of course the bugs were different for each browser. Life was hard for people writing web pages.

Mozilla Firefox, a not-for-profit offshoot of Netscape, challenged Internet Explorer's hegemony in the late 2000s. Because Microsoft was not particularly interested in staying competitive at the time, Firefox took quite a chunk of market share away from it. Around the same time, Google introduced its Chrome browser, and Apple's Safari browser gained popularity, leading to a situation where there were four major players, rather than one.

The new players had a more serious attitude toward standards and better engineering practices, leading to less incompatibility and fewer bugs. Microsoft, seeing its market share crumble, came around and adopted these attitudes. If you are starting to learn web development today, consider yourself lucky. The latest versions of the major browsers behave quite uniformly and have relatively few bugs.

That is not to say that the situation is perfect just yet. Some of the people using the Web are, for reasons of inertia or corporate policy, stuck with very old browsers. Until those browsers die out entirely, writing websites that work for them will require a lot of arcane knowledge about their shortcomings and quirks. This book is not about those quirks. Rather, it aims to present the modern, sane style of web programming.

13

THE DOCUMENT OBJECT MODEL

When you open a web page in your browser, the browser retrieves the page's HTML text and parses it, much like the way our parser from Chapter 11 parsed programs. The browser builds up a model of the document's structure and then uses this model to draw the page on the screen.

This representation of the document is one of the toys that a JavaScript program has available in its sandbox. You can read from the model and also change it. It acts as a *live* data structure: when it is modified, the page on the screen updates to reflect the changes.

Document Structure

You can imagine an HTML document as a nested set of boxes. Tags such as <body> and </body> enclose other tags, which in turn contain other tags or text. Here's the example document from the previous chapter:

```
<!doctype html>
<html>
  <head>
    <title>My home page</title>
```

```
  </head>
  <body>
    <h1>My home page</h1>
    <p>Hello, I am Marijn and this is my home page.</p>
    <p>I also wrote a book! Read it
      <a href="http://eloquentjavascript.net">here</a>.</p>
  </body>
</html>
```

This page has the following structure:

```
html
  ┌─────────────────────────────────────────────┐
  │ head                                        │
  │   ┌───────────────────────────────────────┐ │
  │   │ title                                 │ │
  │   │ My home page                          │ │
  │   └───────────────────────────────────────┘ │
  └─────────────────────────────────────────────┘

  ┌─────────────────────────────────────────────┐
  │ body                                        │
  │   ┌───────────────────────────────────────┐ │
  │   │ h1                                    │ │
  │   │ My home page                          │ │
  │   └───────────────────────────────────────┘ │
  │   ┌───────────────────────────────────────┐ │
  │   │ p                                     │ │
  │   │ Hello, I am Marijn and this is...     │ │
  │   └───────────────────────────────────────┘ │
  │   ┌───────────────────────────────────────┐ │
  │   │ p                        ┌──────────┐ │ │
  │   │                          │ a        │ │ │
  │   │ I also wrote a book! Read it│ here   │ . │ │
  │   │                          └──────────┘ │ │
  │   └───────────────────────────────────────┘ │
  └─────────────────────────────────────────────┘
```

The data structure the browser uses to represent the document follows this shape. For each box, there is an object, which we can interact with to find out things such as what HTML tag it represents and which boxes and text it contains. This representation is called the *Document Object Model*, or DOM for short.

The global variable document gives us access to these objects. Its documentElement property refers to the object representing the <html> tag. It also provides the properties head and body, which hold the objects for those elements.

Trees

Think back to the syntax trees from Chapter 11 for a moment. Their structures are strikingly similar to the structure of a browser's document. Each *node* may refer to other nodes, *children*, which in turn may have their own children. This shape is typical of nested structures where elements can contain subelements that are similar to themselves.

We call a data structure a *tree* when it has a branching structure, has no cycles (a node may not contain itself, directly or indirectly), and has a single, well-defined "root." In the case of the DOM, `document.documentElement` serves as the root.

Trees come up a lot in computer science. In addition to representing recursive structures such as HTML documents or programs, they are often used to maintain sorted sets of data because elements can usually be found or inserted more efficiently in a sorted tree than in a sorted flat array.

A typical tree has different kinds of nodes. The syntax tree for the Egg language had variables, values, and application nodes. Application nodes always have children, whereas variables and values are *leaves*, or nodes without children.

The same goes for the DOM. Nodes for regular *elements*, which represent HTML tags, determine the structure of the document. These can have child nodes. An example of such a node is `document.body`. Some of these children can be leaf nodes, such as pieces of text or comments (comments are written between `<!-` and `->` in HTML).

Each DOM node object has a `nodeType` property, which contains a numeric code that identifies the type of node. Regular elements have the value 1, which is also defined as the constant property `document.ELEMENT_NODE`. Text nodes, representing a section of text in the document, have the value 3 (`document.TEXT_NODE`). Comments have the value 8 (`document.COMMENT_NODE`).

So another way to visualize our document tree is as follows:

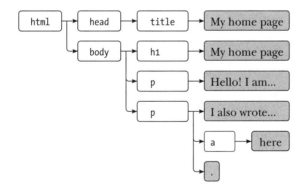

The leaves are text nodes, and the arrows indicate parent-child relationships between nodes.

The Standard

Using cryptic numeric codes to represent node types is not a very JavaScript-like thing to do. Later in this chapter, we'll see that other parts of the DOM interface also feel cumbersome and alien. The reason for this is that the DOM wasn't designed for just JavaScript. Rather, it tries to define a language-neutral interface that can be used in other systems as well—not just HTML but also XML, which is a generic data format with an HTML-like syntax.

This is unfortunate. Standards are often useful. But in this case, the advantage (cross-language consistency) isn't all that compelling. Having an interface that is properly integrated with the language you are using will save you more time than having a familiar interface across languages.

As an example of such poor integration, consider the childNodes property that element nodes in the DOM have. This property holds an array-like object, with a length property and properties labeled by numbers to access the child nodes. But it is an instance of the NodeList type, not a real array, so it does not have methods such as slice and forEach.

Then there are issues that are simply poor design. For example, there is no way to create a new node and immediately add children or attributes to it. Instead, you have to first create it, then add the children one by one, and finally set the attributes one by one, using side effects. Code that interacts heavily with the DOM tends to get long, repetitive, and ugly.

But these flaws aren't fatal. Since JavaScript allows us to create our own abstractions, it is easy to write some helper functions that allow you to express the operations you are performing in a clearer and shorter way. In fact, many libraries intended for browser programming come with such tools.

Moving Through the Tree

DOM nodes contain a wealth of links to other nearby nodes. The following diagram illustrates these:

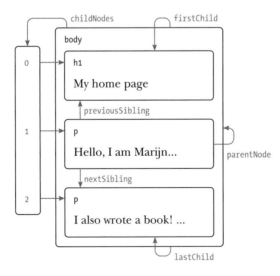

Although the diagram shows only one link of each type, every node has a parentNode property that points to its containing node. Likewise, every element node (node type 1) has a childNodes property that points to an array-like object holding its children.

In theory, you could move anywhere in the tree using just these parent and child links. But JavaScript also gives you access to a number of additional convenience links. The firstChild and lastChild properties point to the first and last child elements or have the value null for nodes without children. Similarly, previousSibling and nextSibling point to adjacent nodes, which are nodes with the same parent that appear immediately before or after the node itself. For a first child, previousSibling will be null, and for a last child, nextSibling will be null.

When dealing with a nested data structure like this one, recursive functions are often useful. The following recursive function scans a document for text nodes containing a given string and returns true when it has found one:

```
function talksAbout(node, string) {
  if (node.nodeType == document.ELEMENT_NODE) {
    for (var i = 0; i < node.childNodes.length; i++) {
      if (talksAbout(node.childNodes[i], string))
        return true;
    }
    return false;
  } else if (node.nodeType == document.TEXT_NODE) {
    return node.nodeValue.indexOf(string) > -1;
  }
}

console.log(talksAbout(document.body, "book"));
// ▷ true
```

The nodeValue property of a text node refers to the string of text that it represents.

Finding Elements

Navigating these links among parents, children, and siblings is often useful, as in the previous function, which runs through the whole document. But if we want to find a specific node in the document, reaching it by starting at document.body and blindly following a hard-coded path of links is a bad idea. Doing so bakes assumptions into our program about the precise structure of the document—a structure we might want to change later. Another complicating factor is that text nodes are created even for the whitespace between nodes. The example document's body tag does not have just three children (<h1> and two <p> elements) but actually has seven: those three, plus the spaces before, after, and between them.

So if we want to get the href attribute of the link in that document, we don't want to say something like "Get the second child of the sixth child of the document body." It'd be better if we could say "Get the first link in the document." And we can.

```
var link = document.body.getElementsByTagName("a")[0];
console.log(link.href);
```

All element nodes have a getElementsByTagName method, which collects all elements with the given tag name that are descendants (direct or indirect children) of the given node and returns them as an array-like object.

To find a specific *single* node, you can give it an id attribute and use document.getElementById instead.

```
<p>My ostrich Gertrude:</p>
<p><img id="gertrude" src="img/ostrich.png"></p>

<script>
  var ostrich = document.getElementById("gertrude");
  console.log(ostrich.src);
</script>
```

A third, similar method is getElementsByClassName, which, like getElementsByTagName, searches through the contents of an element node and retrieves all elements that have the given string in their class attribute.

Changing the Document

Almost everything about the DOM data structure can be changed. Element nodes have a number of methods that can be used to change their content. The removeChild method removes the given child node from the document. To add a child, we can use appendChild, which puts it at the end of the list of children, or insertBefore, which inserts the node given as the first argument before the node given as the second argument.

```
<p>One</p>
<p>Two</p>
<p>Three</p>

<script>
  var paragraphs = document.body.getElementsByTagName("p");
  document.body.insertBefore(paragraphs[2], paragraphs[0]);
</script>
```

A node can exist in the document in only one place. Thus, inserting paragraph "Three" in front of paragraph "One" will first remove it from the end of the document and then insert it at the front, resulting in "Three/One/Two." All operations that insert a node somewhere will, as a side effect, cause it to be removed from its current position (if it has one).

The replaceChild method is used to replace a child node with another one. It takes as arguments two nodes: a new node and the node to be replaced. The replaced node must be a child of the element the method is called on. Note that both `replaceChild` and `insertBefore` expect the *new* node as their first argument.

Creating Nodes

In the following example, we want to write a script that replaces all images (`<img>` tags) in the document with the text held in their `alt` attributes, which specifies an alternative textual representation of the image.

This involves not only removing the images but adding a new text node to replace them. For this, we use the `document.createTextNode` method.

```
<p>The <img src="img/cat.png" alt="Cat"> in the
  <img src="img/hat.png" alt="Hat">.</p>

<p><button onclick="replaceImages()">Replace</button></p>

<script>
  function replaceImages() {
    var images = document.body.getElementsByTagName("img");
    for (var i = images.length - 1; i >= 0; i--) {
      var image = images[i];
      if (image.alt) {
        var text = document.createTextNode(image.alt);
        image.parentNode.replaceChild(text, image);
      }
    }
  }
</script>
```

Given a string, `createTextNode` gives us a type 3 DOM node (a text node), which we can insert into the document to make it show up on the screen.

The loop that goes over the images starts at the end of the list of nodes. This is necessary because the node list returned by a method like `getElementsByTagName` (or a property like `childNodes`) is *live*. That is, it is updated as the document changes. If we started from the front, removing the first image would cause the list to lose its first element so that the second time the loop repeats, where `i` is 1, it would stop because the length of the collection is now also 1.

If you want a *solid* collection of nodes, as opposed to a live one, you can convert the collection to a real array by calling the array `slice` method on it.

```
var arrayish = {0: "one", 1: "two", length: 2};
var real = Array.prototype.slice.call(arrayish, 0);
real.forEach(function(elt) { console.log(elt); });
// ▷ one
//   two
```

To create regular element nodes (type 1), you can use the `document`
`.createElement` method. This method takes a tag name and returns a new
empty node of the given type.

The following example defines a utility `elt`, which creates an element
node and treats the rest of its arguments as children to that node. This function is then used to add a simple attribution to a quote.

```
<blockquote id="quote">
  No book can ever be finished. While working on it we learn
  just enough to find it immature the moment we turn away
  from it.
</blockquote>

<script>
  function elt(type) {
    var node = document.createElement(type);
    for (var i = 1; i < arguments.length; i++) {
      var child = arguments[i];
      if (typeof child == "string")
        child = document.createTextNode(child);
      node.appendChild(child);
    }
    return node;
  }

  document.getElementById("quote").appendChild(
    elt("footer", "--",
        elt("strong", "Karl Popper"),
        ", preface to the second editon of ",
        elt("em", "The Open Society and Its Enemies"),
        ", 1950"));
</script>
```

This is what the resulting document looks like:

No book can ever be finished. While working on it we learn
just enough to find it immature the moment we turn away
from it.
—**Karl Popper**, preface to the second edition of *The Open
Society and Its Enemies*, 1950

Attributes

Some element attributes, such as `href` for links, can be accessed through a
property of the same name on the element's DOM object. This is the case
for a limited set of commonly used standard attributes.

But HTML allows you to set any attribute you want on nodes. This can
be useful because it allows you to store extra information in a document. If

you make up your own attribute names, though, such attributes will not be present as a property on the element's node. Instead, you'll have to use the getAttribute and setAttribute methods to work with them.

```
<p data-classified="secret">The launch code is 00000000.</p>
<p data-classified="unclassified">I have two feet.</p>

<script>
  var paras = document.body.getElementsByTagName("p");
  Array.prototype.forEach.call(paras, function(para) {
    if (para.getAttribute("data-classified") == "secret")
      para.parentNode.removeChild(para);
  });
</script>
```

I recommended prefixing the names of such made-up attributes with data- to ensure they do not conflict with any other attributes.

As a simple example, we'll write a "syntax highlighter" that looks for <pre> tags ("preformatted," used for code and similar plaintext) with a data- language attribute and crudely tries to highlight the keywords for that language.

```
function highlightCode(node, keywords) {
  var text = node.textContent;
  node.textContent = ""; // Clear the node

  var match, pos = 0;
  while (match = keywords.exec(text)) {
    var before = text.slice(pos, match.index);
    node.appendChild(document.createTextNode(before));
    var strong = document.createElement("strong");
    strong.appendChild(document.createTextNode(match[0]));
    node.appendChild(strong);
    pos = keywords.lastIndex;
  }
  var after = text.slice(pos);
  node.appendChild(document.createTextNode(after));
}
```

The function highlightCode takes a <pre> node and a regular expression (with the "global" option turned on) that matches the keywords of the programming language that the element contains.

The textContent property is used to get all the text in the node and is then set to an empty string, which has the effect of emptying the node. We loop over all matches of the keyword expression, appending the text *between* them as regular text nodes, and the text matched (the keywords) as text nodes wrapped in <strong> (bold) elements.

We can automatically highlight all programs on the page by looping over all the <pre> elements that have a data-language attribute and calling highlightCode on each one with the correct regular expression for the language.

```
var languages = {
  javascript: /\b(function|return|var)\b/g /* ... etc */
};

function highlightAllCode() {
  var pres = document.body.getElementsByTagName("pre");
  for (var i = 0; i < pres.length; i++) {
    var pre = pres[i];
    var lang = pre.getAttribute("data-language");
    if (languages.hasOwnProperty(lang))
      highlightCode(pre, languages[lang]);
  }
}
```

Here is an example:

```
<p>Here it is, the identity function:</p>
<pre data-language="javascript">
function id(x) { return x; }
</pre>

<script>highlightAllCode();</script>
```

This produces a page that looks like this:

Here it is, the identity function:

function id(x) { **return** x; }

There is one commonly used attribute, class, which is a reserved word in the JavaScript language. For historical reasons—some old JavaScript implementations could not handle property names that matched keywords or reserved words—the property used to access this attribute is called className. You can also access it under its real name, "class", by using the getAttribute and setAttribute methods.

Layout

You might have noticed that different types of elements are laid out differently. Some, such as paragraphs (<p>) or headings (<h1>), take up the whole width of the document and are rendered on separate lines. These are called *block* elements. Others, such as links (<a>) or the <strong> element used in the previous example, are rendered on the same line with their surrounding text. Such elements are called *inline* elements.

For any given document, browsers are able to compute a layout, which gives each element a size and position based on its type and content. This layout is then used to actually draw the document.

The size and position of an element can be accessed from JavaScript. The offsetWidth and offsetHeight properties give you the space the element takes up in *pixels*. A pixel is the basic unit of measurement in the browser and typically corresponds to the smallest dot that your screen can display. Similarly, clientWidth and clientHeight give you the size of the space *inside* the element, ignoring border width.

```
<p style="border: 3px solid red">
  I'm boxed in
</p>

<script>
  var para = document.body.getElementsByTagName("p")[0];
  console.log("clientHeight:", para.clientHeight);
  console.log("offsetHeight:", para.offsetHeight);
</script>
```

Giving a paragraph a border draws a rectangle around it.

I'm boxed in

The most effective way to find the precise position of an element on the screen is the getBoundingClientRect method. It returns an object with top, bottom, left, and right properties, indicating the pixel positions of the sides of the element relative to the top left of the screen. If you want them relative to the whole document, you must add the current scroll position, found under the global pageXOffset and pageYOffset variables.

Laying out a document can be quite a lot of work. In the interest of speed, browser engines do not immediately re-layout a document every time it is changed but rather wait as long as they can. When a JavaScript program that changed the document finishes running, the browser will have to compute a new layout in order to display the changed document on the screen. When a program *asks* for the position or size of something by reading properties such as offsetHeight or calling getBoundingClientRect, providing correct information also requires computing a layout.

A program that repeatedly alternates between reading DOM layout information and changing the DOM forces a lot of layouts to happen and will consequently run really slowly. The following code shows an example of this. It contains two different programs that build up a line of X characters 2,000 pixels wide and measures the time each one takes.

```
<p><span id="one"></span></p>
<p><span id="two"></span></p>
```

```
<script>
  function time(name, action) {
    var start = Date.now(); // Current time in milliseconds
    action();
    console.log(name, "took", Date.now() - start, "ms");
  }

  time("naive", function() {
    var target = document.getElementById("one");
    while (target.offsetWidth < 2000)
      target.appendChild(document.createTextNode("X"));
  });
  // ▷ naive took 32 ms

  time("clever", function() {
    var target = document.getElementById("two");
    target.appendChild(document.createTextNode("XXXXX"));
    var total = Math.ceil(2000 / (target.offsetWidth / 5));
    for (var i = 5; i < total; i++)
      target.appendChild(document.createTextNode("X"));
  });
  // ▷ clever took 1 ms
</script>
```

Styling

We have seen that different HTML elements display different behavior. Some are displayed as blocks, others inline. Some add styling, such as <strong> making its content bold and <a> making it blue and underlining it.

The way an <img> tag shows an image or an <a> tag causes a link to be followed when it is clicked is strongly tied to the element type. But the default styling associated with an element, such as the text color or underline, can be changed by us. Here is an example using the style property:

```
<p><a href=".">Normal link</a></p>
<p><a href="." style="color: green">Green link</a></p>
```

The second link will be green instead of the default link color.

Normal link

Green link

A style attribute may contain one or more *declarations*, which are a property (such as color) followed by a colon and a value (such as green). When there is more than one declaration, they must be separated by semicolons, as in "color: red; border: none".

There are a lot of aspects that can be influenced by styling. For example, the `display` property controls whether an element is displayed as a block or an inline element.

```
This text is displayed <strong>inline</strong>,
<strong style="display: block">as a block</strong>, and
<strong style="display: none">not at all</strong>.
```

The `block` tag will end up on its own line since block elements are not displayed inline with the text around them. The last tag is not displayed at all—`display: none` prevents an element from showing up on the screen. This is a way to hide elements. It is often preferable to removing them from the document entirely because it makes it easy to reveal them again at a later time.

This text is displayed **inline**,
as a block
, and .

JavaScript code can directly manipulate the style of an element through the node's `style` property. This property holds an object that has properties for all possible style properties. The values of these properties are strings, which we can write to in order to change a particular aspect of the element's style.

```
<p id="para" style="color: purple">
  Pretty text
</p>

<script>
  var para = document.getElementById("para");
  console.log(para.style.color);
  para.style.color = "magenta";
</script>
```

Some style property names contain dashes, such as `font-family`. Because such property names are awkward to work with in JavaScript (you'd have to say `style["font-family"]`), the property names in the style object for such properties have their dashes removed and the letters that follow them capitalized (`style.fontFamily`).

Cascading Styles

The styling system for HTML is called CSS for *Cascading Style Sheets*. A *style sheet* is a set of rules for how to style elements in a document. It can be given inside a `<style>` tag.

```
<style>
  strong {
    font-style: italic;
    color: gray;
  }
</style>
<p>Now <strong>strong text</strong> is italic and gray.</p>
```

The *cascading* in the name refers to the fact that multiple such rules are combined to produce the final style for an element. In the previous example, the default styling for `<strong>` tags, which gives them `font-weight: bold`, is overlaid by the rule in the `<style>` tag, which adds `font-style` and `color`.

When multiple rules define a value for the same property, the most recently read rule gets a higher precedence and wins. So if the rule in the `<style>` tag included `font-weight: normal`, conflicting with the default font- weight rule, the text would be normal, *not* bold. Styles in a style attribute applied directly to the node have the highest precedence and always win.

It is possible to target things other than tag names in CSS rules. A rule for `.abc` applies to all elements with "abc" in their class attributes. A rule for `#xyz` applies to the element with an `id` attribute of "xyz" (which should be unique within the document).

```
.subtle {
  color: gray;
  font-size: 80%;
}
#header {
  background: blue;
  color: white;
}
/* p elements, with classes a and b, and id main */
p.a.b#main {
  margin-bottom: 20px;
}
```

The precedence rule (favoring the most recently defined rule) holds true only when the rules have the same *specificity*. A rule's specificity is a measure of how precisely it describes matching elements, determined by the number and kind (tag, class, or ID) of element aspects it requires. For example, a rule that targets `p.a` is more specific than rules that target just `p` or just `.a` and would thus take precedence over them.

The notation `p > a {...}` applies the given styles to all `<a>` tags that are direct children of `<p>` tags. Similarly, `p a {...}` applies to all `<a>` tags inside `<p>` tags, whether they are direct or indirect children.

Query Selectors

We won't be using style sheets all that much in this book. Although under-standing them is crucial to programming in the browser, properly explain-ing all the properties they support and the interaction among those proper-ties would take two or three books.

The main reason I introduced *selector* syntax—the notation used in style sheets to determine which elements a set of styles apply to—is that we can use this same mini-language as an effective way to find DOM elements.

The querySelectorAll method, which is defined both on the document ob-ject and on element nodes, takes a selector string and returns an array-like object containing all the elements that it matches.

```
<p>And if you go chasing
  <span class="animal">rabbits</span></p>
<p>And you know you're going to fall</p>
<p>Tell 'em a <span class="character">hookah smoking
  <span class="animal">caterpillar</span></span></p>
<p>Has given you the call</p>

<script>
  function count(selector) {
    return document.querySelectorAll(selector).length;
  }
  console.log(count("p"));          // All <p> elements
  // ▷ 4
  console.log(count(".animal"));     // Class animal
  // ▷ 2
  console.log(count("p .animal"));   // Animal inside of <p>
  // ▷ 2
  console.log(count("p > .animal")); // Direct child of <p>
  // ▷ 1
</script>
```

Unlike methods such as getElementsByTagName, the object returned by querySelectorAll is *not* live. It won't change when you change the document.

The querySelector method (without the All part) works in a similar way. This one is useful if you want a specific, single element. It will return only the first matching element or null if no elements match.

Positioning and Animating

The position style property influences layout in a powerful way. By default it has a value of static, meaning the element sits in its normal place in the document. When it is set to relative, the element still takes up space in the document, but now the top and left style properties can be used to move it relative to its normal place. When position is set to absolute, the element is removed from the normal document flow—that is, it no longer takes up space and may overlap with other elements. Also, its top and left properties can be used to absolutely position it relative to the top-left corner of the nearest enclosing element whose position property isn't static, or relative to the document if no such enclosing element exists.

We can use this to create an animation. The following document displays a picture of a cat that floats around in an ellipse:

```
<p style="text-align: center">
  <img src="img/cat.png" style="position: relative">
</p>
<script>
  var cat = document.querySelector("img");
  var angle = 0, lastTime = null;
  function animate(time) {
    if (lastTime != null)
      angle += (time - lastTime) * 0.001;
    lastTime = time;
    cat.style.top = (Math.sin(angle) * 20) + "px";
    cat.style.left = (Math.cos(angle) * 200) + "px";
    requestAnimationFrame(animate);
  }
  requestAnimationFrame(animate);
</script>
```

The gray arrow shows the path along which the image moves.

The picture is centered on the page and given a position of relative. We'll repeatedly update that picture's top and left styles in order to move it.

The script uses requestAnimationFrame to schedule the animate function to run whenever the browser is ready to repaint the screen. The animate function itself again calls requestAnimationFrame to schedule the next update. When the browser window (or tab) is active, this will cause updates to happen at a rate of about 60 per second, which tends to produce a good-looking animation.

If we just updated the DOM in a loop, the page would freeze and nothing would show up on the screen. Browsers do not update their display while a JavaScript program is running, nor do they allow any interaction with the page. This is why we need requestAnimationFrame—it lets the browser know that we are done for now, and it can go ahead and do the things that browsers do, such as updating the screen and responding to user actions.

Our animation function is passed the current time as an argument, which it compares to the time it saw before (the lastTime variable) to ensure the motion of the cat per millisecond is stable, and the animation moves smoothly. If it just moved a fixed amount per step, the motion would stutter if, for example, another heavy task running on the same computer were to prevent the function from running for a fraction of a second.

Moving in circles is done using the trigonometry functions `Math.cos` and `Math.sin`. For those of you who aren't familiar with these, I'll briefly introduce them since we will occasionally need them in this book.

`Math.cos` and `Math.sin` are useful for finding points that lie on a circle around point (0,0) with a radius of one unit. Both functions interpret their argument as the position on this circle, with zero denoting the point on the far right of the circle, going clockwise until 2π (about 6.28) has taken us around the whole circle. `Math.cos` tells you the x-coordinate of the point that corresponds to the given position around the circle, while `Math.sin` yields the y-coordinate. Positions (or angles) greater than 2π or less than 0 are valid—the rotation repeats so that $a+2\pi$ refers to the same angle as a.

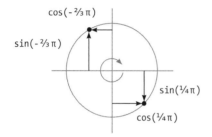

The cat animation code keeps a counter, `angle`, for the current angle of the animation and increments it in proportion to the elapsed time every time the `animate` function is called. It can then use this angle to compute the current position of the image element. The `top` style is computed with `Math.sin` and multiplied by 20, which is the vertical radius of our circle. The `left` style is based on `Math.cos` and multiplied by 200 so that the circle is much wider than it is high, resulting in an elliptic motion.

Note that styles usually need *units*. In this case, we have to append "px" to the number to tell the browser we are counting in pixels (as opposed to centimeters, "ems," or other units). This is easy to forget. Using numbers without units will result in your style being ignored—unless the number is 0, which always means the same thing, regardless of its unit.

Summary

JavaScript programs may inspect and interfere with the current document that a browser is displaying through a data structure called the DOM. This data structure represents the browser's model of the document, and a JavaScript program can modify it to change the visible document.

The DOM is organized like a tree, in which elements are arranged hierarchically according to the structure of the document. The objects representing elements have properties such as `parentNode` and `childNodes`, which can be used to navigate through this tree.

The way a document is displayed can be influenced by *styling*, both by attaching styles to nodes directly and by defining rules that match certain nodes. There are many different style properties, such as color or display. JavaScript can manipulate an element's style directly through its style property.

Exercises

Build a Table

We built plaintext tables in Chapter 6. HTML makes laying out tables quite a bit easier. An HTML table is built with the following tag structure:

```
<table>
  <tr>
    <th>name</th>
    <th>height</th>
    <th>country</th>
  </tr>
  <tr>
    <td>Kilimanjaro</td>
    <td>5895</td>
    <td>Tanzania</td>
  </tr>
</table>
```

For each *row*, the <table> tag contains a <tr> tag. Inside of these <tr> tags, we can put cell elements: either heading cells (<th>) or regular cells (<td>).

The same source data that was used in Chapter 6 is again available in the MOUNTAINS variable in the sandbox. It can also be downloaded from the website (*http://eloquentjavascript.net/code/*).

Write a function buildTable that, given an array of objects that all have the same set of properties, builds up a DOM structure representing a table. The table should have a header row with the property names wrapped in <th> elements and should have one subsequent row per object in the array, with its property values in <td> elements.

The Object.keys function, which returns an array containing the property names that an object has, will probably be helpful here.

Once you have the basics working, right-align cells containing numbers by setting their style.textAlign property to "right".

Elements by Tag Name

The getElementsByTagName method returns all child elements with a given tag name. Implement your own version of it as a regular nonmethod function that takes a node and a string (the tag name) as arguments and returns an array containing all descendant element nodes with the given tag name.

To find the tag name of an element, use its `tagName` property. But note that this will return the tag name in all uppercase. Use the `toLowerCase` or `toUpperCase` string method to compensate for this.

The Cat's Hat

Extend the cat animation defined earlier so that both the cat and his hat (`<img src="img/hat.png">`) orbit at opposite sides of the ellipse.

You can also try to make the hat circle around the cat or alter the animation in some other interesting way.

To make positioning multiple objects easier, it is probably a good idea to switch to absolute positioning. This means that `top` and `left` are counted relative to the top left of the document. To avoid using negative coordinates, you can simply add a fixed number of pixels to the position values.

"You have power over your mind—
not outside events. Realize this,
and you will find strength."
—Marcus Aurelius, *Meditations*

14

HANDLING EVENTS

Some programs work with direct user input, such as mouse and keyboard interaction. The timing and order of such input can't be predicted in advance. This requires a different approach to control flow than the one we have used so far.

Event Handlers

Imagine an interface where the only way to find out whether a key on the keyboard is being pressed is to read the current state of that key. To be able to react to keypresses, you would have to constantly read the key's state so that you'd catch it before it's released again. It would be dangerous to perform other time-intensive computations since you might miss a keypress.

That is how such input was handled on primitive machines. A step up would be for the hardware or operating system to notice the keypress and put it in a queue. A program can then periodically check the queue for new events and react to what it finds there.

Of course, it has to remember to look at the queue, and to do it often, because any time between the key being pressed and the program noticing the event will cause the software to feel unresponsive. This approach is called *polling*. Most programmers avoid it whenever possible.

A better mechanism is for the underlying system to give our code a chance to react to events as they occur. Browsers do this by allowing us to register functions as *handlers* for specific events.

```
<p>Click this document to activate the handler.</p>
<script>
  addEventListener("click", function() {
    console.log("You clicked!");
  });
</script>
```

The addEventListener function registers its second argument to be called whenever the event described by its first argument occurs.

Events and DOM Nodes

Each browser event handler is registered in a context. When you call addEventListener as shown previously, you are calling it as a method on the whole window because in the browser the global scope is equivalent to the window object. Every DOM element has its own addEventListener method, which allows you to listen specifically on that element.

```
<button>Click me</button>
<p>No handler here.</p>
<script>
  var button = document.querySelector("button");
  button.addEventListener("click", function() {
    console.log("Button clicked.");
  });
</script>
```

The example attaches a handler to the button node. Thus, clicks on the button cause that handler to run, whereas clicks on the rest of the document do not.

Giving a node an onclick attribute has a similar effect. But a node has only one onclick attribute, so you can register only one handler per node that way. The addEventListener method allows you to add any number of handlers, so you can't accidentally replace a handler that has already been registered.

The removeEventListener method, called with arguments similar to addEventListener, removes a handler.

```
<button>Act-once button</button>
<script>
  var button = document.querySelector("button");
```

```
  function once() {
    console.log("Done.");
    button.removeEventListener("click", once);
  }
  button.addEventListener("click", once);
</script>
```

To be able to unregister a handler function, we give it a name (such as once) so that we can pass it to both addEventListener and removeEventListener.

Event Objects

Though we have ignored it in the previous examples, event handler functions are passed an argument: the *event object*. This object gives us additional information about the event. For example, if we want to know *which* mouse button was pressed, we can look at the event object's which property.

```
<button>Click me any way you want</button>
<script>
  var button = document.querySelector("button");
  button.addEventListener("mousedown", function(event) {
    if (event.which == 1)
      console.log("Left button");
    else if (event.which == 2)
      console.log("Middle button");
    else if (event.which == 3)
      console.log("Right button");
  });
</script>
```

The information stored in an event object differs per type of event. We'll discuss various types later in this chapter. The object's type property always holds a string identifying the event (for example "click" or "mousedown").

Propagation

Event handlers registered on nodes with children will also receive some events that happen in the children. If a button inside a paragraph is clicked, event handlers on the paragraph will also receive the click event.

But if both the paragraph and the button have a handler, the more specific handler—the one on the button—gets to go first. The event is said to *propagate* outward, from the node where it happened to that node's parent node and on to the root of the document. Finally, after all handlers registered on a specific node have had their turn, handlers registered on the whole window get a chance to respond to the event.

At any point, an event handler can call the `stopPropagation` method on the event object to prevent handlers "further up" from receiving the event. This can be useful when, for example, you have a button inside another clickable element and you don't want clicks on the button to activate the outer element's click behavior.

The following example registers "mousedown" handlers on both a button and the paragraph around it. When clicked with the right mouse button, the handler for the button calls `stopPropagation`, which will prevent the handler on the paragraph from running. When the button is clicked with another mouse button, both handlers will run.

```
<p>A paragraph with a <button>button</button>.</p>
<script>
  var para = document.querySelector("p");
  var button = document.querySelector("button");
  para.addEventListener("mousedown", function() {
    console.log("Handler for paragraph.");
  });
  button.addEventListener("mousedown", function(event) {
    console.log("Handler for button.");
    if (event.which == 3)
      event.stopPropagation();
  });
</script>
```

Most event objects have a target property that refers to the node where they originated. You can use this property to ensure that you're not accidentally handling something that propagated up from a node you do not want to handle.

It is also possible to use the target property to cast a wide net for a specific type of event. For example, if you have a node containing a long list of buttons, it may be more convenient to register a single click handler on the outer node and have it use the target property to figure out whether a button was clicked, rather than register individual handlers on all of the buttons.

```
<button>A</button>
<button>B</button>
<button>C</button>
<script>
  document.body.addEventListener("click", function(event) {
    if (event.target.nodeName == "BUTTON")
      console.log("Clicked", event.target.textContent);
  });
</script>
```

Default Actions

Many events have a default action associated with them. If you click a link, you will be taken to the link's target. If you press the down arrow, the browser will scroll the page down. If you right-click, you'll get a context menu. And so on.

For most types of events, the JavaScript event handlers are called *before* the default behavior is performed. If the handler doesn't want the normal behavior to happen, typically because it has already taken care of handling the event, it can call the `preventDefault` method on the event object.

This can be used to implement your own keyboard shortcuts or context menu. It can also be used to obnoxiously interfere with the behavior that users expect. For example, here is a link that cannot be followed:

```
<a href="https://developer.mozilla.org/">MDN</a>
<script>
  var link = document.querySelector("a");
  link.addEventListener("click", function(event) {
    console.log("Nope.");
    event.preventDefault();
  });
</script>
```

Try not to do such things unless you have a really good reason to. For people using your page, it can be unpleasant when the behavior they expect is broken.

Depending on the browser, some events can't be intercepted. On Chrome, for example, keyboard shortcuts to close the current tab (CTRL-W or COMMAND-W) cannot be handled by JavaScript.

Key Events

When a key on the keyboard is pressed, your browser fires a "keydown" event. When it is released, a "keyup" event is fired.

```
<p>This page turns violet when you hold the V key.</p>
<script>
  addEventListener("keydown", function(event) {
    if (event.keyCode == 86)
      document.body.style.background = "violet";
  });
  addEventListener("keyup", function(event) {
    if (event.keyCode == 86)
      document.body.style.background = "";
  });
</script>
```

Despite its name, "keydown" is fired not only when the key is physically pushed down. When a key is pressed and held, the event is fired again every time the key *repeats*. Sometimes—for example, if you want to increase the acceleration of a game character when an arrow key is pressed and decrease it again when the key is released—you have to be careful not to increase it again every time the key repeats or you'd end up with unintentionally huge values.

The previous example looked at the keyCode property of the event object. This is how you can identify which key is being pressed or released. Unfortunately, it's not always obvious how to translate the numeric key code to an actual key.

For letter and number keys, the associated key code will be the Unicode character code associated with the (uppercase) letter or number printed on the key. The charCodeAt method on strings gives us a way to find this code.

```
console.log("Violet".charCodeAt(0));
// ▷ 86
console.log("1".charCodeAt(0));
// ▷ 49
```

Other keys have less predictable key codes. The best way to find the codes you need is usually by experimenting—register a key event handler that logs the key codes it gets and press the key you are interested in.

Modifier keys such as SHIFT, CTRL, ALT, and META (COMMAND on Mac) generate key events just like normal keys. But when looking for key combinations, you can also find out whether these keys are held down by looking at the shiftKey, ctrlKey, altKey, and metaKey properties of keyboard and mouse events.

```
<p>Press Ctrl-Space to continue.</p>
<script>
  addEventListener("keydown", function(event) {
    if (event.keyCode == 32 && event.ctrlKey)
      console.log("Continuing!");
  });
</script>
```

The "keydown" and "keyup" events give you information about the physical key that is being pressed. But what if you are interested in the actual text being typed? Getting that text from key codes is awkward. Instead, there exists another event, "keypress", which is fired right after "keydown" (and repeated along with "keydown" when the key is held) but only for keys that produce character input. The charCode property in the event object contains a code that can be interpreted as a Unicode character code. We can use the String.fromCharCode function to turn this code into an actual single-character string.

```
<p>Focus this page and type something.</p>
<script>
  addEventListener("keypress", function(event) {
    console.log(String.fromCharCode(event.charCode));
  });
</script>
```

The DOM node where a key event originates depends on the element that has focus when the key is pressed. Normal nodes cannot have focus (unless you give them a `tabindex` attribute), but things such as links, buttons, and form fields can. We'll come back to form fields in Chapter 18. When nothing in particular has focus, `document.body` acts as the target node of key events.

Mouse Clicks

Pressing a mouse button also causes a number of events to fire. The `"mousedown"` and `"mouseup"` events are similar to `"keydown"` and `"keyup"` and fire when the button is pressed and released. These will happen on the DOM nodes that are immediately below the mouse pointer when the event occurs.

After the `"mouseup"` event, a `"click"` event fires on the most specific node that contained both the press and the release of the button. For example, if I press down the mouse button on one paragraph and then move the pointer to another paragraph and release the button, the `"click"` event will happen on the element that contains both those paragraphs.

If two clicks happen close together, a `"dblclick"` (double-click) event also fires, after the second click event.

To get precise information about the place where a mouse event happened, you can look at its `pageX` and `pageY` properties, which contain the event's coordinates (in pixels) relative to the top-left corner of the document.

The following implements a primitive drawing program. Every time you click the document, it adds a dot under your mouse pointer. See Chapter 19 for a less primitive drawing program.

```
<style>
  body {
    height: 200px;
    background: beige;
  }
  .dot {
    height: 8px; width: 8px;
    border-radius: 4px; /* rounds corners */
    background: blue;
    position: absolute;
  }
</style>
```

```
<script>
  addEventListener("click", function(event) {
    var dot = document.createElement("div");
    dot.className = "dot";
    dot.style.left = (event.pageX - 4) + "px";
    dot.style.top = (event.pageY - 4) + "px";
    document.body.appendChild(dot);
  });
</script>
```

The clientX and clientY properties are similar to pageX and pageY but relative to the part of the document that is currently scrolled into view. These can be useful when comparing mouse coordinates with the coordinates returned by getBoundingClientRect, which also returns viewport-relative coordinates.

Mouse Motion

Every time the mouse pointer moves, a "mousemove" event fires. This event can be used to track the position of the mouse. A common situation in which this is useful is when implementing some form of mouse-dragging functionality.

As an example, the following program displays a bar and sets up event handlers so that dragging to the left or right on this bar makes it narrower or wider:

```
<p>Drag the bar to change its width:</p>
<div style="background: orange; width: 60px; height: 20px">
</div>
<script>
  var lastX; // Tracks the last observed mouse X position
  var rect = document.querySelector("div");
  rect.addEventListener("mousedown", function(event) {
    if (event.which == 1) {
      lastX = event.pageX;
      addEventListener("mousemove", moved);
      event.preventDefault(); // Prevent selection
    }
  });

  function buttonPressed(event) {
    if (event.buttons == null)
      return event.which != 0;
    else
      return event.buttons != 0;
  }
```

```
  function moved(event) {
    if (!buttonPressed(event)) {
      removeEventListener("mousemove", moved);
    } else {
      var dist = event.pageX - lastX;
      var newWidth = Math.max(10, rect.offsetWidth + dist);
      rect.style.width = newWidth + "px";
      lastX = event.pageX;
    }
  }
}
</script>
```

The resulting page looks like this:

Drag the bar to change its width:

Note that the "mousemove" handler is registered on the whole window. Even if the mouse goes outside of the bar during resizing, we still want to update its size and stop dragging when the mouse is released.

We must stop resizing the bar when the mouse button is released. Unfortunately, not all browsers give mousemove events a meaningful which property. There is a standard property called buttons that provides similar information, but it is also not supported on all browsers. Fortunately, all major browsers support either buttons or which, so the buttonPressed function in the example first tries buttons and falls back to which when buttons isn't available.

Whenever the mouse pointer enters or leaves a node, a "mouseover" or "mouseout" event is fired. These two events can be used, among other things, to create hover effects, showing or styling something when the mouse is over a given element.

Unfortunately, creating such an effect is not as simple as starting the effect on "mouseover" and ending it on "mouseout". When the mouse moves from a node onto one of its children, "mouseout" is fired on the parent node, though the mouse did not actually leave the node's extent. To make things worse, these events propagate just like other events, and thus you will also receive "mouseout" events when the mouse leaves one of the child nodes of the node on which the handler is registered.

To work around this problem, we can use the relatedTarget property of the event objects created for these events. It tells us, in the case of "mouseover", what element the pointer was over before and, in the case of "mouseout", what element it is going to. We want to change our hover effect only when the relatedTarget is outside of our target node. Only in that case does this event actually represent a *crossing over* from outside to inside the node (or the other way around).

```
<p>Hover over this <strong>paragraph</strong>.</p>
<script>
  var para = document.querySelector("p");
  function isInside(node, target) {
    for (; node != null; node = node.parentNode)
      if (node == target) return true;
  }
  para.addEventListener("mouseover", function(event) {
    if (!isInside(event.relatedTarget, para))
      para.style.color = "red";
  });
  para.addEventListener("mouseout", function(event) {
    if (!isInside(event.relatedTarget, para))
      para.style.color = "";
  });
</script>
```

The isInside function follows the given node's parent links until it either reaches the top of the document (when node becomes null) or finds the parent we are looking for.

I should add that a hover effect like this can be much more easily achieved using the CSS *pseudoselector* :hover, as the next example shows. But when your hover effect involves doing something more complicated than changing a style on the target node, you must use the trick with "mouseover" and "mouseout" events.

```
<style>
  p:hover { color: red }
</style>
<p>Hover over this <strong>paragraph</strong>.</p>
```

Scroll Events

Whenever an element is scrolled, a "scroll" event fires on it. This has various uses, such as knowing what the user is currently looking at (for disabling off-screen animations or sending spy reports to your evil headquarters) or showing some indication of progress (by highlighting part of a table of contents or showing a page number).

The following example draws a progress bar in the top-right corner of the document and updates it to fill up as you scroll down:

```
<style>
  .progress {
    border: 1px solid blue;
    width: 100px;
    position: fixed;
```

```
    top: 10px; right: 10px;
  }
  .progress > div {
    height: 12px;
    background: blue;
    width: 0%;
  }
  body {
    height: 2000px;
  }
</style>
<div class="progress"><div></div></div>
<p>Scroll me...</p>


<script>
  var bar = document.querySelector(".progress div");
  addEventListener("scroll", function() {
    var max = document.body.scrollHeight - innerHeight;
    var percent = (pageYOffset / max) * 100;
    bar.style.width = percent + "%";
  });
</script>
```

Giving an element a position of fixed acts much like an absolute position but also prevents it from scrolling along with the rest of the document. The effect is to make our progress bar stay in its corner. Inside it is another element, which is resized to indicate the current progress. We use %, rather than px, as a unit when setting the width so that the element is sized relative to the whole bar.

The global innerHeight variable gives us the height of the window, which we have to subtract from the total scrollable height—you can't keep scrolling when you hit the bottom of the document. (There's also an innerWidth to go along with innerHeight.) By dividing pageYOffset, the current scroll position, by the maximum scroll position and multiplying by 100, we get the percentage for the progress bar.

Calling preventDefault on a scroll event does not prevent the scrolling from happening. In fact, the event handler is called only *after* the scrolling takes place.

Focus Events

When an element gains focus, the browser fires a "focus" event on it. When it loses focus, a "blur" event fires.

Unlike the events discussed earlier, these two events do not propagate. A handler on a parent element is not notified when a child element gains or loses focus.

The following example displays help text for the text field that currently has focus:

```
<p>Name: <input type="text" data-help="Your full name"></p>
<p>Age: <input type="text" data-help="Age in years"></p>
<p id="help"></p>

<script>
  var help = document.querySelector("#help");
  var fields = document.querySelectorAll("input");
  for (var i = 0; i < fields.length; i++) {
    fields[i].addEventListener("focus", function(event) {
      var text = event.target.getAttribute("data-help");
      help.textContent = text;
    });
    fields[i].addEventListener("blur", function(event) {
      help.textContent = "";
    });
  }
</script>
```

In the following screenshot, help text for the Age field is shown.

Name: Hieronimus

Age: I

Age in years

The window object will receive "focus" and "blur" events when the user moves from or to the browser tab or window in which the document is shown.

Load Event

When a page finishes loading, the "load" event fires on the window and the document body objects. This is often used to schedule initialization actions that require the whole document to have been built. Remember that the content of <script> tags is run immediately when the tag is encountered. This is often too soon, such as when the script needs to do something with parts of the document that appear after the <script> tag.

Elements such as images and script tags that load an external file also have a "load" event that indicates the files they reference were loaded. Like the focus-related events, loading events do not propagate.

When a page is closed or navigated away from (for example by following a link), a "beforeunload" event fires. The main use of this event is to prevent the user from accidentally losing work by closing a document. Preventing the page from unloading is not, as you might expect, done with the preventDefault method. Instead, it is done by returning a string from the handler. The string will be used in a dialog that asks the user if they want to stay on the page or leave it. This mechanism ensures that a user is able to leave the page, even if it is running a malicious script that would prefer to keep them there forever in order to force them to look at dodgy weight loss ads.

Script Execution Timeline

There are various things that can cause a script to start executing. Reading a `<script>` tag is one such thing. An event firing is another. Chapter 13 discussed the `requestAnimationFrame` function, which schedules a function to be called before the next page redraw. That is yet another way in which a script can start running.

It is important to understand that even though events can fire at any time, no two scripts in a single document ever run at the same moment. If a script is already running, event handlers and pieces of code scheduled in other ways have to wait for their turn. This is the reason why a document will freeze when a script runs for a long time. The browser cannot react to clicks and other events inside the document because it can't run event handlers until the current script finishes running.

Some programming environments do allow multiple *threads of execution* to run at the same time. Doing multiple things at the same time can be used to make a program faster. But when you have multiple actors touching the same parts of the system at the same time, thinking about a program becomes at least an order of magnitude harder.

The fact that JavaScript programs do only one thing at a time makes our lives easier. For cases where you *really* do want to do some time-consuming thing in the background without freezing the page, browsers provide something called *web workers*. A worker is an isolated JavaScript environment that runs alongside the main program for a document and can communicate with it only by sending and receiving messages.

Assume we have the following code in a file called code/squareworker.js:

```
addEventListener("message", function(event) {
  postMessage(event.data * event.data);
});
```

Imagine that squaring a number is a heavy, long-running computation that we want to perform in a background thread. This code spawns a worker, sends it a few messages, and outputs the responses.

```
var squareWorker = new Worker("code/squareworker.js");
squareWorker.addEventListener("message", function(event) {
  console.log("The worker responded:", event.data);
});
squareWorker.postMessage(10);
squareWorker.postMessage(24);
```

The postMessage function sends a message, which will cause a "message" event to fire in the receiver. The script that created the worker sends and receives messages through the Worker object, whereas the worker talks to the script that created it by sending and listening directly on its global scope— which is a *new* global scope, not shared with the original script.

Setting Timers

The setTimeout function is similar to requestAnimationFrame. It schedules another function to be called later. But instead of calling the function at the next redraw, it waits for a given amount of milliseconds. This page turns from blue to yellow after two seconds:

```
<script>
  document.body.style.background = "blue";
  setTimeout(function() {
    document.body.style.background = "yellow";
  }, 2000);
</script>
```

Sometimes you need to cancel a function you have scheduled. This is done by storing the value returned by setTimeout and calling clearTimeout on it.

```
var bombTimer = setTimeout(function() {
  console.log("BOOM!");
}, 500);

if (Math.random() < 0.5) { // 50% chance
  console.log("Defused.");
  clearTimeout(bombTimer);
}
```

The cancelAnimationFrame function works in the same way as clearTimeout— calling it on a value returned by requestAnimationFrame will cancel that frame (assuming it hasn't already been called).

A similar set of functions, setInterval and clearInterval are used to set timers that should repeat every *X* milliseconds.

```
var ticks = 0;
var clock = setInterval(function() {
  console.log("tick", ticks++);
  if (ticks == 10) {
    clearInterval(clock);
    console.log("stop.");
  }
}, 200);
```

Debouncing

Some types of events have the potential to fire rapidly, many times in a row (the "mousemove" and "scroll" events, for example). When handling such events, you must be careful not to do anything too time-consuming or your handler will take up so much time that interaction with the document starts to feel slow and choppy.

If you do need to do something nontrivial in such a handler, you can use setTimeout to make sure you are not doing it too often. This is usually called *debouncing* the event. There are several slightly different approaches to this.

In the first example, we want to do something when the user has typed something, but we don't want to do it immediately for every key event. When they are typing quickly, we just want to wait until a pause occurs. Instead of immediately performing an action in the event handler, we set a timeout instead. We also clear the previous timeout (if any) so that when events occur close together (closer than our timeout delay), the timeout from the previous event will be canceled.

```
<textarea>Type something here...</textarea>
<script>
  var textarea = document.querySelector("textarea");
  var timeout;
  textarea.addEventListener("keydown", function() {
    clearTimeout(timeout);
    timeout = setTimeout(function() {
      console.log("You stopped typing.");
    }, 500);
  });
</script>
```

Giving an undefined value to clearTimeout or calling it on a timeout that has already fired has no effect. Thus, we don't have to be careful about when to call it, and we simply do so for every event.

We can use a slightly different pattern if we want to space responses so that they're separated by at least a certain length of time but want to fire them *during* a series of events, not just afterward. For example, we might want to respond to "mousemove" events by showing the current coordinates of the mouse, but only every 250 milliseconds.

```
<script>
  function displayCoords(event) {
    document.body.textContent =
      "Mouse at " + event.pageX + ", " + event.pageY;
  }

  var scheduled = false, lastEvent;
  addEventListener("mousemove", function(event) {
```

```
      lastEvent = event;
      if (!scheduled) {
        scheduled = true;
        setTimeout(function() {
          scheduled = false;
          displayCoords(lastEvent);
        }, 250);
      }
    });
</script>
```

Summary

Event handlers make it possible to detect and react to events we have no direct control over. The addEventListener method is used to register such a handler.

Each event has a type ("keydown", "focus", and so on) that identifies it. Most events are called on a specific DOM element and then *propagate* to that element's ancestors, allowing handlers associated with those elements to handle them.

When an event handler is called, it is passed an event object with additional information about the event. This object also has methods that allow us to stop further propagation (stopPropagation) and prevent the browser's default handling of the event (preventDefault).

Pressing a key fires "keydown", "keypress", and "keyup" events. Pressing a mouse button fires "mousedown", "mouseup", and "click" events. Moving the mouse fires "mousemove" and possibly "mouseenter" and "mouseout" events.

Scrolling can be detected with the "scroll" event, and focus changes can be detected with the "focus" and "blur" events. When the document finishes loading, a "load" event fires on the window.

Only one piece of JavaScript program can run at a time. Thus, event handlers and other scheduled scripts have to wait until other scripts finish before they get their turn.

Exercises

Censored Keyboard

Between 1928 and 2013, Turkish law forbade the use of the letters *Q*, *W*, and *X* in official documents. This was part of a wider initiative to stifle Kurdish culture—those letters occur in the language used by Kurdish people but not in Istanbul Turkish.

As an exercise in doing ridiculous things with technology, I'm asking you to program a text field (an <input type="text"> tag) that these letters cannot be typed into.

(Do not worry about copy and paste and other such loopholes.)

Mouse Trail

In JavaScript's early days, which was the high time of gaudy home pages with lots of animated images, people came up with some truly inspiring ways to use the language.

One of these was the "mouse trail"—a series of images that would follow the mouse pointer as you moved it across the page.

In this exercise, I want you to implement a mouse trail. Use absolutely positioned <div> elements with a fixed size and background color (refer to the code in the "Mouse Clicks" section for an example). Create a bunch of such elements and, when the mouse moves, display them in the wake of the mouse pointer.

There are various possible approaches here. You can make your solution as simple or as complex as you want. A simple solution to start with is to keep a fixed number of trail elements and cycle through them, moving the next one to the mouse's current position every time a "mousemove" event occurs.

Tabs

A tabbed interface is a common design pattern. It allows you to select an interface panel by choosing from a number of tabs "sticking out" above an element.

In this exercise you'll implement a simple tabbed interface. Write a function, asTabs, that takes a DOM node and creates a tabbed interface showing the child elements of that node. It should insert a list of <button> elements at the top of the node, one for each child element, containing text retrieved from the data-tabname attribute of the child. All but one of the original children should be hidden (given a display style of none), and the currently visible node can be selected by clicking the buttons.

When it works, extend it to also style the currently active button differently.

"All reality is a game."
—Iain Banks, *The Player of Games*

15

PROJECT: A PLATFORM GAME

My initial fascination with computers, like that of many kids, originated with computer games. I was drawn into the tiny computer-simulated worlds that I could manipulate and in which stories (sort of) unfolded—more, I suppose, because of the way I could project my imagination into them than because of the possibilities they actually offered.

I wouldn't wish a career in game programming on anyone. Much like the music industry, the discrepancy between the many eager young people wanting to work in it and the actual demand for such people creates a rather unhealthy environment. But writing games for fun is amusing.

This chapter will walk through the implementation of a simple platform game. Platform games (or "jump and run" games) are games that expect the player to move a figure through a world, which is often two-dimensional and viewed from the side, and do lots of jumping onto and over things.

The Game

Our game will be roughly based on Dark Blue (*www.lessmilk.com/games/10*) by Thomas Palef. I chose this game because it is both entertaining and minimalist, and because it can be built without too much code. It looks like this:

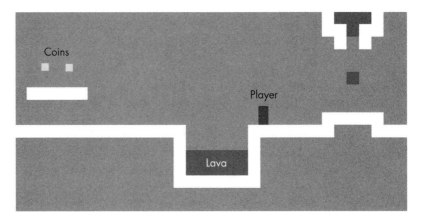

The dark box represents the player, whose task is to collect the yellow boxes (coins) while avoiding the red stuff (which I'll call lava). A level is completed when all coins have been collected.

The player can walk around with the left and right arrow keys and jump with the up arrow. Jumping is a specialty of this game character. It can reach several times its own height and is able to change direction in midair. This may not be entirely realistic, but it helps give the player the feeling of being in direct control of the onscreen avatar.

The game consists of a fixed background, laid out like a grid, with the moving elements overlaid on that background. Each field on the grid is either empty, solid, or lava. The moving elements are the player, coins, and certain pieces of lava. Unlike the artificial life simulation from Chapter 7, the positions of these elements are not constrained to the grid—their coordinates may be fractional, allowing smooth motion.

The Technology

We will use the browser DOM to display the game, and we'll read user input by handling key events.

The screen- and keyboard-related code is only a tiny part of the work we need to do to build this game. Since everything looks like colored boxes, drawing is uncomplicated: we create DOM elements and use styling to give them a background color, size, and position.

We can represent the background as a table since it is an unchanging grid of squares. The free-moving elements can be overlaid on top of that, using absolutely positioned elements.

In games and other programs that have to animate graphics and respond to user input without noticeable delay, efficiency is important. Although the DOM was not originally designed for high-performance graphics, it is actually better at this than you would expect. You saw some animations in Chapter 13. On a modern machine, a simple game like this performs well, even if we don't think about optimization much.

In the next chapter, we will explore another browser technology, the <canvas> tag, which provides a more traditional way to draw graphics, working in terms of shapes and pixels rather than DOM elements.

Levels

In Chapter 7 we used arrays of strings to describe a two-dimensional grid. We can do the same here. It will allow us to design levels without first building a level editor.

A simple level would look like this:

```
var simpleLevelPlan = [
  "                      ",
  "                      ",
  "  x              = x  ",
  "  x         o o    x  ",
  "  x @      xxxxx    x  ",
  "  xxxxx            x  ",
  "      x!!!!!!!!!!!!!x  ",
  "      xxxxxxxxxxxxx  ",
  "                      "
];
```

Both the fixed grid and the moving elements are included in the plan. The *x* characters stand for walls, the space characters for empty space, and the exclamation marks represent fixed, nonmoving lava tiles.

The @ defines the place where the player starts. Every o is a coin, and the equal sign (=) stands for a block of lava that moves back and forth horizontally. Note that the grid for these positions will be set to contain empty space, and another data structure is used to track the position of such moving elements.

We'll support two other kinds of moving lava: the pipe character (|) for vertically moving blobs, and v for *dripping* lava—vertically moving lava that doesn't bounce back and forth but only moves down, jumping back to its start position when it hits the floor.

A whole game consists of multiple levels that the player must complete. A level is completed when all coins have been collected. If the player touches lava, the current level is restored to its starting position, and the player may try again.

Reading a Level

The following constructor builds a Level object. Its argument should be the array of strings that define the level.

```
function Level(plan) {
  this.width = plan[0].length;
  this.height = plan.length;
  this.grid = [];
  this.actors = [];

  for (var y = 0; y < this.height; y++) {
    var line = plan[y], gridLine = [];
    for (var x = 0; x < this.width; x++) {
      var ch = line[x], fieldType = null;
      var Actor = actorChars[ch];
      if (Actor)
        this.actors.push(new Actor(new Vector(x, y), ch));
      else if (ch == "x")
        fieldType = "wall";
      else if (ch == "!")
        fieldType = "lava";
      gridLine.push(fieldType);
    }
    this.grid.push(gridLine);
  }

  this.player = this.actors.filter(function(actor) {
    return actor.type == "player";
  })[0];
  this.status = this.finishDelay = null;
}
```

For brevity, the code does not check for malformed input. It assumes that you've given it a proper level plan, complete with a player start position and other essentials.

A level stores its width and height, along with two arrays—one for the grid and one for the *actors*, which are the dynamic elements. The grid is represented as an array of arrays, where each of the inner arrays represents a horizontal line and each square contains either null, for empty squares, or a string indicating the type of the square—"wall" or "lava".

The actors array holds objects that track the current position and state of the dynamic elements in the level. Each of these is expected to have a pos property that gives its position (the coordinates of its top-left corner), a size property that gives its size, and a type property that holds a string identifying the element ("lava", "coin", or "player").

After building the grid, we use the `filter` method to find the "player" actor object, which we store in a property of the level. The `status` property tracks whether the player has won or lost. When this happens, `finishDelay` is used to keep the level active for a short period of time so that a simple animation can be shown. (Immediately resetting or advancing the level would look cheap.) This method can be used to find out whether a level is finished:

```
Level.prototype.isFinished = function() {
  return this.status != null && this.finishDelay < 0;
};
```

Actors

To store the position and size of an actor, we will return to our trusty `Vector` type, which groups an x-coordinate and a y-coordinate into an object.

```
function Vector(x, y) {
  this.x = x; this.y = y;
}
Vector.prototype.plus = function(other) {
  return new Vector(this.x + other.x, this.y + other.y);
};
Vector.prototype.times = function(factor) {
  return new Vector(this.x * factor, this.y * factor);
};
```

The `times` method scales a vector by a given amount. It will be useful when we need to multiply a speed vector by a time interval to get the distance traveled during that time.

In the previous section, the `actorChars` object was used by the `Level` constructor to associate characters with constructor functions. The object looks like this:

```
var actorChars = {
  "@": Player,
  "o": Coin,
  "=": Lava, "|": Lava, "v": Lava
};
```

Three characters map to `Lava`. The `Level` constructor passes the actor's source character as the second argument to the constructor, and the `Lava` constructor uses that to adjust its behavior (bouncing horizontally, bouncing vertically, or dripping).

The player type is built with the following constructor. It has a property `speed` that stores its current speed, which will help simulate momentum and gravity.

```
function Player(pos) {
  this.pos = pos.plus(new Vector(0, -0.5));
  this.size = new Vector(0.8, 1.5);
  this.speed = new Vector(0, 0);
}
Player.prototype.type = "player";
```

Because a player is one-and-a-half squares high, its initial position is set to be half a square above the position where the @ character appeared. This way, its bottom aligns with the bottom of the square it appeared in.

When constructing a dynamic Lava object, we need to initialize the object differently depending on the character it is based on. Dynamic lava moves along at its given speed until it hits an obstacle. At that point, if it has a repeatPos property, it will jump back to its start position (dripping). If it does not, it will invert its speed and continue in the other direction (bouncing). The constructor only sets up the necessary properties. The method that does the actual moving will be written later.

```
function Lava(pos, ch) {
  this.pos = pos;
  this.size = new Vector(1, 1);
  if (ch == "=") {
    this.speed = new Vector(2, 0);
  } else if (ch == "|") {
    this.speed = new Vector(0, 2);
  } else if (ch == "v") {
    this.speed = new Vector(0, 3);
    this.repeatPos = pos;
  }
}
Lava.prototype.type = "lava";
```

Coin actors are simple. They mostly just sit in their place. But to liven up the game a little, they are given a "wobble," a slight vertical motion back and forth. To track this, a coin object stores a base position as well as a wobble property that tracks the phase of the bouncing motion. Together, these determine the coin's actual position (stored in the pos property).

```
function Coin(pos) {
  this.basePos = this.pos = pos.plus(new Vector(0.2, 0.1));
  this.size = new Vector(0.6, 0.6);
  this.wobble = Math.random() * Math.PI * 2;
}
Coin.prototype.type = "coin";
```

In Chapter 13, we saw that `Math.sin` gives us the y-coordinate of a point on a circle. That coordinate goes back and forth in a smooth wave form as we move along the circle, which makes the sine function useful for modeling a wavy motion.

To avoid a situation where all coins move up and down synchronously, the starting phase of each coin is randomized. The *phase* of `Math.sin`'s wave, the width of a wave it produces, is 2π. We multiply the value returned by `Math.random` by that number to give the coin a random starting position on the wave.

We have now written all the parts needed to represent the state of a level.

```
var simpleLevel = new Level(simpleLevelPlan);
console.log(simpleLevel.width, "by", simpleLevel.height);
// ▷ 22 by 9
```

The task ahead is to display such levels on the screen and to model time and motion inside them.

Encapsulation as a Burden

Most of the code in this chapter does not worry about encapsulation for two reasons. First, encapsulation takes extra effort. It makes programs bigger and requires additional concepts and interfaces to be introduced. Since there is only so much code you can throw at a reader before their eyes glaze over, I've made an effort to keep the program small.

Second, the various elements in this game are so closely tied together that if the behavior of one of them changed, it is unlikely that any of the others would be able to stay the same. Interfaces between the elements would end up encoding a lot of assumptions about the way the game works. This makes them a lot less effective—whenever you change one part of the system, you still have to worry about the way it impacts the other parts because their interfaces wouldn't cover the new situation.

Some *cutting points* in a system lend themselves well to separation through rigorous interfaces, but others don't. Trying to encapsulate something that isn't a suitable boundary is a sure way to waste a lot of energy. When you are making this mistake, you'll usually notice that your interfaces are getting awkwardly large and detailed and that they need to be modified often, as the program evolves.

There is one thing that we *will* encapsulate in this chapter, and that is the drawing subsystem. The reason for this is that we will display the same game in a different way in the next chapter. By putting the drawing behind an interface, we can simply load the same game program there and plug in a new display module.

Drawing

The encapsulation of the drawing code is done by defining a *display* object, which displays a given level. The display type we define in this chapter is called DOMDisplay because it uses simple DOM elements to show the level.

We will be using a style sheet to set the actual colors and other fixed properties of the elements that make up the game. It would also be possible to directly assign to the elements' style property when we create them, but that would produce more verbose programs.

The following helper function provides a short way to create an element and give it a class:

```
function elt(name, className) {
  var elt = document.createElement(name);
  if (className) elt.className = className;
  return elt;
}
```

A display is created by giving it a parent element to which it should append itself and a level object.

```
function DOMDisplay(parent, level) {
  this.wrap = parent.appendChild(elt("div", "game"));
  this.level = level;

  this.wrap.appendChild(this.drawBackground());
  this.actorLayer = null;
  this.drawFrame();
}
```

We used the fact that appendChild returns the appended element to create the wrapper element and store it in the wrap property in a single statement.

The level's background, which never changes, is drawn once. The actors are redrawn every time the display is updated. The actorLayer property will be used by drawFrame to track the element that holds the actors so that they can be easily removed and replaced.

Our coordinates and sizes are tracked in units relative to the grid size, where a size or distance of 1 means 1 grid unit. When setting pixel sizes, we will have to scale these coordinates up—everything in the game would be ridiculously small at a single pixel per square. The scale variable gives the number of pixels that a single unit takes up on the screen.

```
var scale = 20;

DOMDisplay.prototype.drawBackground = function() {
  var table = elt("table", "background");
  table.style.width = this.level.width * scale + "px";
```

```
this.level.grid.forEach(function(row) {
  var rowElt = table.appendChild(elt("tr"));
  rowElt.style.height = scale + "px";
  row.forEach(function(type) {
    rowElt.appendChild(elt("td", type));
  });
});
return table;
};
```

As mentioned earlier, the background is drawn as a `<table>` element. This nicely corresponds to the structure of the grid property in the level—each row of the grid is turned into a table row (`<tr>` element). The strings in the grid are used as class names for the table cell (`<td>`) elements. The following CSS helps the resulting table look like the background we want:

```
.background    { background: rgb(52, 166, 251);
                 border-spacing: 0;             }
.background td { padding: 0;                    }
.lava          { background: rgb(255, 100, 100); }
.wall          { background: white;            }
```

Some of these (`border-spacing` and `padding`) are simply used to suppress unwanted default behavior. We don't want space between the table cells or padding inside them.

The `background` rule sets the background color. CSS allows colors to be specified both as words (`white`) and with a format such as `rgb(R, G, B)`, where the red, green, and blue components of the color are separated into three numbers from 0 to 255. So, in `rgb(52, 166, 251)`, the red component is 52, green is 166, and blue is 251. Since the blue component is the largest, the resulting color will be bluish. You can see that in the `.lava` rule, the first number (red) is the largest.

We draw each actor by creating a DOM element for it and setting that element's position and size based on the actor's properties. The values have to be multiplied by `scale` to go from game units to pixels.

```
DOMDisplay.prototype.drawActors = function() {
  var wrap = elt("div");
  this.level.actors.forEach(function(actor) {
    var rect = wrap.appendChild(elt("div", "actor " + actor.type));
    rect.style.width = actor.size.x * scale + "px";
    rect.style.height = actor.size.y * scale + "px";
    rect.style.left = actor.pos.x * scale + "px";
    rect.style.top = actor.pos.y * scale + "px";
  });
  return wrap;
};
```

To give an element more than one class, we separate the class names by spaces. In the CSS code shown next, the actor class gives the actors their absolute position. Their type name is used as an extra class to give them a color. We don't have to define the lava class again because we reuse it for the lava grid squares, which we defined earlier.

```
.actor  { position: absolute;              }
.coin   { background: rgb(241, 229, 89); }
.player { background: rgb(64, 64, 64);   }
```

When it updates the display, the drawFrame method first removes the old actor graphics, if any, and then redraws them in their new positions. It may be tempting to try to reuse the DOM elements for actors, but to make that work, we would need a lot of additional information flow between the display code and the simulation code. We'd need to associate actors with DOM elements, and the drawing code must remove elements when their actors vanish. Since there will typically be only a handful of actors in the game, redrawing all of them is not expensive.

```
DOMDisplay.prototype.drawFrame = function() {
  if (this.actorLayer)
    this.wrap.removeChild(this.actorLayer);
  this.actorLayer = this.wrap.appendChild(this.drawActors());
  this.wrap.className = "game " + (this.level.status || "");
  this.scrollPlayerIntoView();
};
```

By adding the level's current status as a class name to the wrapper, we can style the player actor slightly differently when the game is won or lost by adding a CSS rule that takes effect only when the player has an ancestor element with a given class.

```
.lost .player {
  background: rgb(160, 64, 64);
}
.won .player {
  box-shadow: -4px -7px 8px white, 4px -7px 8px white;
}
```

After touching lava, the player's color turns dark red, suggesting scorching. When the last coin has been collected, we use two blurred white box shadows, one to the top left and one to the top right, to create a white halo effect.

We can't assume that levels always fit in the viewport. That is why the scrollPlayerIntoView call is needed—it ensures that if the level is protruding outside the viewport, we scroll that viewport to make sure the player is near its center. The following CSS gives the game's wrapping DOM element a maximum size and ensures that anything that sticks out of the element's box is not visible. We also give the outer element a relative position so that the actors inside it are positioned relative to the level's top-left corner.

```
.game {
  overflow: hidden;
  max-width: 600px;
  max-height: 450px;
  position: relative;
}
```

In the `scrollPlayerIntoView` method, we find the player's position and update the wrapping element's scroll position. We change the scroll position by manipulating that element's `scrollLeft` and `scrollTop` properties when the player is too close to the edge.

```
DOMDisplay.prototype.scrollPlayerIntoView = function() {
  var width = this.wrap.clientWidth;
  var height = this.wrap.clientHeight;
  var margin = width / 3;

  // The viewport
  var left = this.wrap.scrollLeft, right = left + width;
  var top = this.wrap.scrollTop, bottom = top + height;

  var player = this.level.player;
  var center = player.pos.plus(player.size.times(0.5))
                 .times(scale);

  if (center.x < left + margin)
    this.wrap.scrollLeft = center.x - margin;
  else if (center.x > right - margin)
    this.wrap.scrollLeft = center.x + margin - width;
  if (center.y < top + margin)
    this.wrap.scrollTop = center.y - margin;
  else if (center.y > bottom - margin)
    this.wrap.scrollTop = center.y + margin - height;
};
```

The way the player's center is found shows how the methods on our Vector type allow computations with objects to be written in a readable way. To find the actor's center, we add its position (its top-left corner) and half its size. That is the center in level coordinates, but we need it in pixel coordinates, so we then multiply the resulting vector by our display scale.

Next, a series of checks verify that the player position isn't outside of the allowed range. Note that sometimes this will set nonsense scroll coordinates, below zero or beyond the element's scrollable area. This is okay—the DOM will constrain them to sane values. Setting `scrollLeft` to −10 will cause it to become 0.

It would have been slightly simpler to always try to scroll the player to the center of the viewport. But this creates a rather jarring effect. As you are jumping, the view will constantly shift up and down. It is more pleasant to have a "neutral" area in the middle of the screen where you can move around without causing any scrolling.

Finally, we'll need a way to clear a displayed level, to be used when the game moves to the next level or resets a level.

```
DOMDisplay.prototype.clear = function() {
  this.wrap.parentNode.removeChild(this.wrap);
};
```

We are now able to display our tiny level.

```
<link rel="stylesheet" href="css/game.css">

<script>
  var simpleLevel = new Level(simpleLevelPlan);
  var display = new DOMDisplay(document.body, simpleLevel);
</script>
```

The `<link>` tag, when used with `rel="stylesheet"`, is a way to load a CSS file into a page. The file `game.css` contains the styles necessary for our game.

Motion and Collision

Now we're at the point where we can start adding motion—the most interesting aspect of the game. The basic approach, taken by most games like this, is to split time into small steps and, for each step, move the actors by a distance corresponding to their speed (distance moved per second) multiplied by the size of the time step (in seconds).

That is easy. The difficult part is dealing with the interactions between the elements. When the player hits a wall or floor, they should not simply move through it. The game must notice when a given motion causes an object to hit another object and respond accordingly. For walls, the motion must be stopped. For coins, the coin must be collected, and so on.

Solving this for the general case is a big task. You can find libraries, usually called *physics engines*, that simulate interaction between physical objects in two or three dimensions. We'll take a more modest approach in this chapter, handling only collisions between rectangular objects and handling them in a rather simplistic way.

Before moving the player or a block of lava, we test whether the motion would take it inside of a nonempty part of the background. If it does, we simply cancel the motion altogether. The response to such a collision depends on the type of actor—the player will stop, whereas a lava block will bounce back.

This approach requires our time steps to be rather small since it will cause motion to stop before the objects actually touch. If the time steps (and thus the motion steps) are too big, the player would end up hovering a noticeable distance above the ground. Another approach, arguably better but more complicated, would be to find the exact collision spot and move there. We will take the simple approach and hide its problems by ensuring the animation proceeds in small steps.

This method tells us whether a rectangle (specified by a position and a size) overlaps with any nonempty space on the background grid:

```
Level.prototype.obstacleAt = function(pos, size) {
  var xStart = Math.floor(pos.x);
  var xEnd = Math.ceil(pos.x + size.x);
  var yStart = Math.floor(pos.y);
  var yEnd = Math.ceil(pos.y + size.y);

  if (xStart < 0 || xEnd > this.width || yStart < 0)
    return "wall";
  if (yEnd > this.height)
    return "lava";
  for (var y = yStart; y < yEnd; y++) {
    for (var x = xStart; x < xEnd; x++) {
      var fieldType = this.grid[y][x];
      if (fieldType) return fieldType;
    }
  }
};
```

This method computes the set of grid squares that the body overlaps with by using Math.floor and Math.ceil on the body's coordinates. Remember that grid squares are 1×1 units in size. By rounding the sides of a box up and down, we get the range of background squares that the box touches.

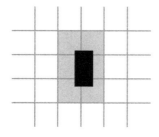

If the body sticks out of the level, we always return "wall" for the sides and top and "lava" for the bottom. This ensures that the player dies when falling out of the world. When the body is fully inside the grid, we loop over the block of grid squares found by rounding the coordinates and return the content of the first nonempty square we find.

Collisions between the player and other dynamic actors (coins, moving lava) are handled *after* the player moved. When the motion has taken the player into another actor, the appropriate effect—collecting a coin or dying—is activated.

This method scans the array of actors, looking for an actor that overlaps the one given as an argument:

```
Level.prototype.actorAt = function(actor) {
  for (var i = 0; i < this.actors.length; i++) {
    var other = this.actors[i];
    if (other != actor &&
        actor.pos.x + actor.size.x > other.pos.x &&
        actor.pos.x < other.pos.x + other.size.x &&
        actor.pos.y + actor.size.y > other.pos.y &&
        actor.pos.y < other.pos.y + other.size.y)
      return other;
  }
};
```

Actors and Actions

The animate method on the Level type gives all actors in the level a chance to move. Its step argument is the time step in seconds. The keys object contains information about the arrow keys the player has pressed.

```
var maxStep = 0.05;

Level.prototype.animate = function(step, keys) {
  if (this.status != null)
    this.finishDelay -= step;

  while (step > 0) {
    var thisStep = Math.min(step, maxStep);
```

```
  this.actors.forEach(function(actor) {
    actor.act(thisStep, this, keys);
  }, this);

  step -= thisStep;
  }
};
```

When the level's status property has a non-null value (which is the case when the player has won or lost), we must count down the finishDelay property, which tracks the time between the point where winning or losing happens and the point where we want to stop showing the level.

The while loop cuts the time step we are animating into suitably small pieces. It ensures that no step larger than maxStep is taken. For example, a step of 0.12 second would be cut into two steps of 0.05 second and one step of 0.02.

Actor objects have an act method, which takes as arguments the time step, the level object, and the keys object. Here is one, for the Lava actor type, which ignores the keys object:

```
Lava.prototype.act = function(step, level) {
  var newPos = this.pos.plus(this.speed.times(step));
  if (!level.obstacleAt(newPos, this.size))
    this.pos = newPos;
  else if (this.repeatPos)
    this.pos = this.repeatPos;
  else
    this.speed = this.speed.times(-1);
};
```

It computes a new position by adding the product of the time step and its current speed to its old position. If no obstacle blocks that new position, it moves there. If there is an obstacle, the behavior depends on the type of the lava block—dripping lava has a repeatPos property, to which it jumps back when it hits something. Bouncing lava simply inverts its speed (multiplies it by −1) in order to start moving in the other direction.

Coins use their act method to wobble. They ignore collisions since they are simply wobbling around inside of their own square, and collisions with the player will be handled by the *player*'s act method.

```
var wobbleSpeed = 8, wobbleDist = 0.07;

Coin.prototype.act = function(step) {
  this.wobble += step * wobbleSpeed;
  var wobblePos = Math.sin(this.wobble) * wobbleDist;
  this.pos = this.basePos.plus(new Vector(0, wobblePos));
};
```

The wobble property is updated to track time and then used as an argument to Math.sin to create a wave, which is used to compute a new position.

That leaves the player itself. Player motion is handled separately per axis because hitting the floor should not prevent horizontal motion, and hitting a wall should not stop falling or jumping motion. This method implements the horizontal part:

```
var playerXSpeed = 7;

Player.prototype.moveX = function(step, level, keys) {
  this.speed.x = 0;
  if (keys.left) this.speed.x -= playerXSpeed;
  if (keys.right) this.speed.x += playerXSpeed;

  var motion = new Vector(this.speed.x * step, 0);
  var newPos = this.pos.plus(motion);
  var obstacle = level.obstacleAt(newPos, this.size);
  if (obstacle)
    level.playerTouched(obstacle);
  else
    this.pos = newPos;
};
```

The horizontal motion is computed based on the state of the left and right arrow keys. When a motion causes the player to hit something, the level's playerTouched method, which handles things like dying in lava and collecting coins, is called. Otherwise, the object updates its position.

Vertical motion works in a similar way but for jumping and gravity.

```
var gravity = 30;
var jumpSpeed = 17;

Player.prototype.moveY = function(step, level, keys) {
  this.speed.y += step * gravity;
  var motion = new Vector(0, this.speed.y * step);
  var newPos = this.pos.plus(motion);
  var obstacle = level.obstacleAt(newPos, this.size);
  if (obstacle) {
    level.playerTouched(obstacle);
    if (keys.up && this.speed.y > 0)
      this.speed.y = -jumpSpeed;
    else
      this.speed.y = 0;
  } else {
    this.pos = newPos;
  }
};
```

At the start of the method, the player is accelerated vertically to account for gravity. The gravity, jumping speed, and pretty much all other constants in this game have been set by trial and error. I tested various values until I found a combination I liked.

Next, we check for obstacles again. If we hit an obstacle, there are two possible outcomes. When the up arrow is pressed *and* we are moving down (meaning the thing we hit is below us), the speed is set to a relatively large, negative value. This causes the player to jump. If that is not the case, we simply bumped into something, and the speed is reset to zero.

The actual act method looks like this:

```
Player.prototype.act = function(step, level, keys) {
  this.moveX(step, level, keys);
  this.moveY(step, level, keys);

  var otherActor = level.actorAt(this);
  if (otherActor)
    level.playerTouched(otherActor.type, otherActor);

  // Losing animation
  if (level.status == "lost") {
    this.pos.y += step;
    this.size.y -= step;
  }
};
```

After moving, the method checks for other actors that the player is colliding with and again calls `playerTouched` when it finds one. This time, it passes the actor object as the second argument because if the other actor is a coin, `playerTouched` needs to know *which* coin is being collected.

Finally, when the player dies (touches lava), we set up a little animation that causes them to "shrink" or "sink" down by reducing the height of the player object.

And here is the method that handles collisions between the player and other objects:

```
Level.prototype.playerTouched = function(type, actor) {
  if (type == "lava" && this.status == null) {
    this.status = "lost";
    this.finishDelay = 1;
  } else if (type == "coin") {
    this.actors = this.actors.filter(function(other) {
      return other != actor;
    });
    if (!this.actors.some(function(actor) {
      return actor.type == "coin";
    })) {
```

```
        this.status = "won";
        this.finishDelay = 1;
      }
    }
};
```

When lava is touched, the game's status is set to "lost". When a coin is touched, that coin is removed from the array of actors, and if it was the last one, the game's status is set to "won".

This gives us a level that can actually be animated. All that is missing now is the code that *drives* the animation.

Tracking Keys

For a game like this, we do not want keys to take effect once per keypress. Rather, we want their effect (moving the player figure) to continue happening as long as they are pressed.

We need to set up a key handler that stores the current state of the left, right, and up arrow keys. We will also want to call preventDefault for those keys so that they don't end up scrolling the page.

The following function, when given an object with key codes as property names and key names as values, will return an object that tracks the current position of those keys. It registers event handlers for "keydown" and "keyup" events and, when the key code in the event is present in the set of codes that it is tracking, updates the object.

```
var arrowCodes = {37: "left", 38: "up", 39: "right"};

function trackKeys(codes) {
  var pressed = Object.create(null);
  function handler(event) {
    if (codes.hasOwnProperty(event.keyCode)) {
      var down = event.type == "keydown";
      pressed[codes[event.keyCode]] = down;
      event.preventDefault();
    }
  }
  addEventListener("keydown", handler);
  addEventListener("keyup", handler);
  return pressed;
}
```

Note how the same handler function is used for both event types. It looks at the event object's type property to determine whether the key state should be updated to true ("keydown") or false ("keyup").

Running the Game

The `requestAnimationFrame` function, which we saw in Chapter 13, provides a good way to animate a game. But its interface is quite primitive—using it requires us to track the time at which our function was called the last time around and call `requestAnimationFrame` again after every frame.

Let's define a helper function that wraps those boring parts in a convenient interface and allows us to simply call `runAnimation`, giving it a function that expects a time difference as an argument and draws a single frame. When the frame function returns the value `false`, the animation stops.

```
function runAnimation(frameFunc) {
  var lastTime = null;
  function frame(time) {
    var stop = false;
    if (lastTime != null) {
      var timeStep = Math.min(time - lastTime, 100) / 1000;
      stop = frameFunc(timeStep) === false;
    }
    lastTime = time;
    if (!stop)
      requestAnimationFrame(frame);
  }
  requestAnimationFrame(frame);
}
```

I have set a maximum frame step of 100 milliseconds (one-tenth of a second). When the browser tab or window with our page is hidden, `requestAnimationFrame` calls will be suspended until the tab or window is shown again. In this case, the difference between `lastTime` and `time` will be the entire time in which the page was hidden. Advancing the game by that much in a single step will look silly and might be a lot of work (remember the time-splitting in the `animate` method).

The function also converts the time steps to seconds, which are an easier quantity to think about than milliseconds.

The `runLevel` function takes a `Level` object, a constructor for a display, and, optionally, a function. It displays the level (in `document.body`) and lets the user play through it. When the level is finished (lost or won), `runLevel` clears the display, stops the animation, and, if an `andThen` function was given, calls that function with the level's status.

```
var arrows = trackKeys(arrowCodes);

function runLevel(level, Display, andThen) {
  var display = new Display(document.body, level);
  runAnimation(function(step) {
    level.animate(step, arrows);
    display.drawFrame(step);
```

```
    if (level.isFinished()) {
      display.clear();
      if (andThen)
        andThen(level.status);
      return false;
    }
  });
}
```

A game is a sequence of levels. Whenever the player dies, the current level is restarted. When a level is completed, we move on to the next level. This can be expressed by the following function, which takes an array of level plans (arrays of strings) and a display constructor:

```
function runGame(plans, Display) {
  function startLevel(n) {
    runLevel(new Level(plans[n]), Display, function(status) {
      if (status == "lost")
        startLevel(n);
      else if (n < plans.length - 1)
        startLevel(n + 1);
      else
        console.log("You win!");
    });
  }
  startLevel(0);
}
```

These functions show a peculiar style of programming. Both runAnimation and runLevel are higher-order functions but are not in the style we saw in Chapter 5. The function argument is used to arrange things to happen at some time in the future, and neither of the functions returns anything useful. Their task is, in a way, to schedule actions. Wrapping these actions in functions gives us a way to store them as a value so that they can be called at the right moment.

This programming style is usually called *asynchronous* programming. Event handling is also an instance of this style, and we will see much more of it when working with tasks that can take an arbitrary amount of time, such as network requests in Chapter 17 and input and output in general in Chapter 20.

There is a set of level plans available in the GAME_LEVELS variable (downloadable from *http://eloquentjavascript.net/code#15*). This page feeds them to runGame, starting an actual game:

```
<link rel="stylesheet" href="css/game.css">

<script>
  runGame(GAME_LEVELS, DOMDisplay);
</script>
```

Exercises

Game Over

It's traditional for platform games to have the player start with a limited number of *lives* and subtract one life each time they die. When the player is out of lives, the game restarts from the beginning.

Adjust runGame to implement lives. Have the player start with three.

Pausing the Game

Make it possible to pause (suspend) and unpause the game by pressing the ESC key.

This can be done by changing the runLevel function to use another keyboard event handler and interrupting or resuming the animation whenever the ESC key is hit.

The runAnimation interface may not look like it is suitable for this at first glance, but it is, if you rearrange the way runLevel calls it.

When you have that working, there is something else you could try. The way we have been registering keyboard event handlers is somewhat problematic. The arrows object is currently a global variable, and its event handlers are kept around even when no game is running. You could say they *leak* out of our system. Extend trackKeys to provide a way to unregister its handlers, and then change runLevel to register its handlers when it starts and unregister them again when it is finished.

"Drawing is deception."

—M.C. Escher, cited by Bruno Ernst
in *The Magic Mirror of M.C. Escher*

16

DRAWING ON CANVAS

Browsers give us several ways to display graphics. The simplest way is to use styles to position and color regular DOM elements. This can get you quite far, as the game in the previous chapter showed. By adding partially transparent background images to the nodes, we can make them look exactly the way we want. It is even possible to rotate or skew nodes by using the `transform` style.

But we'd be using the DOM for something that it wasn't originally designed for. Some tasks, such as drawing a line between arbitrary points, are extremely awkward to do with regular HTML elements.

There are two alternatives. The first is DOM-based but utilizes *Scalable Vector Graphics (SVG)*, rather than HTML elements. Think of SVG as a dialect for describing documents that focuses on shapes rather than text. You can embed an SVG document in an HTML document, or you can include it through an `<img>` tag.

The second alternative is called a *canvas*. A canvas is a single DOM element that encapsulates a picture. It provides a programming interface for drawing shapes onto the space taken up by the node. The main difference between a canvas and an SVG picture is that in SVG the original description of the shapes is preserved so that they can be moved or resized at any time.

A canvas, on the other hand, converts the shapes to pixels (colored dots on a raster) as soon as they are drawn and does not remember what these pixels represent. The only way to move a shape on a canvas is to clear the canvas (or the part of the canvas around the shape) and redraw it with the shape in a new position.

SVG

This book will not go into SVG in detail, but I will briefly explain how it works. At the end of the chapter, I'll come back to the trade-offs that you must consider when deciding which drawing mechanism is appropriate for a given application.

This is an HTML document with a simple SVG picture in it:

```
<p>Normal HTML here.</p>
<svg xmlns="http://www.w3.org/2000/svg">
  <circle r="50" cx="50" cy="50" fill="red"/>
  <rect x="120" y="5" width="90" height="90"
        stroke="blue" fill="none"/>
</svg>
```

The xmlns attribute changes an element (and its children) to a different *XML namespace*. This namespace, identified by a URL, specifies the dialect that we are currently speaking. The <circle> and <rect> tags, which do not exist in HTML, do have a meaning in SVG—they draw shapes using the style and position specified by their attributes.

The document is displayed like this:

Normal HTML here.

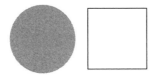

These tags create DOM elements, just like HTML tags. For example, this changes the <circle> element to be colored cyan instead:

```
var circle = document.querySelector("circle");
circle.setAttribute("fill", "cyan");
```

The Canvas Element

Canvas graphics can be drawn onto a <canvas> element. You can give such an element width and height attributes to determine its size in pixels.

A new canvas is empty, meaning it is entirely transparent and thus shows up simply as empty space in the document.

The <canvas> tag is intended to support different styles of drawing. To get access to an actual drawing interface, we first need to create a *context*, which is an object whose methods provide the drawing interface. There are currently two widely supported drawing styles: "2d" for two-dimensional graphics and "webgl" for three-dimensional graphics through the OpenGL interface.

This book won't discuss WebGL. We stick to two dimensions. But if you are interested in three-dimensional graphics, I do encourage you to look into WebGL. It provides a very direct interface to modern graphics hardware and thus allows you to render even complicated scenes efficiently from JavaScript.

A context is created through the getContext method on the <canvas> element.

```
<p>Before canvas.</p>
<canvas width="120" height="60"></canvas>
<p>After canvas.</p>
<script>
  var canvas = document.querySelector("canvas");
  var context = canvas.getContext("2d");
  context.fillStyle = "red";
  context.fillRect(10, 10, 100, 50);
</script>
```

After creating the context object, the example draws a red rectangle 100 pixels wide and 50 pixels high, with its top-left corner at coordinates (10,10).

Before canvas.

After canvas.

Just like in HTML (and SVG), the coordinate system that the canvas uses puts (0,0) at the top-left corner, and the positive y-axis goes down from there. So (10,10) is 10 pixels below and to the right of the top-left corner.

Filling and Stroking

In the canvas interface, a shape can be *filled*, meaning its area is given a certain color or pattern, or it can be *stroked*, which means a line is drawn along its edge. The same terminology is used by SVG.

The fillRect method fills a rectangle. It takes first the x- and y-coordinates of the rectangle's top-left corner, then its width, and then its height. A similar method, strokeRect, draws the outline of a rectangle.

Neither method takes any further parameters. The color of the fill, thickness of the stroke, and so on are not determined by an argument to the method (as you might justly expect) but rather by properties of the context object.

Setting fillStyle changes the way shapes are filled. It can be set to a string that specifies a color, and any color understood by CSS can also be used here.

The strokeStyle property works similarly but determines the color used for a stroked line. The width of that line is determined by the lineWidth property, which may contain any positive number.

```
<canvas></canvas>
<script>
  var cx = document.querySelector("canvas").getContext("2d");
  cx.strokeStyle = "blue";
  cx.strokeRect(5, 5, 50, 50);
  cx.lineWidth = 5;
  cx.strokeRect(135, 5, 50, 50);
</script>
```

This code draws two blue squares, using a thicker line for the second one.

When no width or height attribute is specified, as in the previous example, a canvas element gets a default width of 300 pixels and height of 150 pixels.

Paths

A path is a sequence of lines. The 2D canvas interface takes a peculiar approach to describing such a path. It is done entirely through side effects. Paths are not values that can be stored and passed around. Instead, if you want to do something with a path, you make a sequence of method calls to describe its shape.

```
<canvas></canvas>
<script>
  var cx = document.querySelector("canvas").getContext("2d");
  cx.beginPath();
  for (var y = 10; y < 100; y += 10) {
    cx.moveTo(10, y);
    cx.lineTo(90, y);
  }
  cx.stroke();
</script>
```

The path described by the previous program looks like this:

This example creates a path with a number of horizontal line segments and then strokes it using the stroke method. Each segment created with lineTo starts at the path's *current* position. That position is usually the end of the last segment, unless moveTo was called. In that case, the next segment would start at the position passed to moveTo.

When filling a path (using the fill method), each shape is filled separately. A path can contain multiple shapes—each moveTo motion starts a new one. But the path needs to be *closed* (meaning its start and end are in the same position) before it can be filled. If the path is not already closed, a line is added from its end to its start, and the shape enclosed by the completed path is filled.

```
<canvas></canvas>
<script>
  var cx = document.querySelector("canvas").getContext("2d");
  cx.beginPath();
  cx.moveTo(50, 10);
  cx.lineTo(10, 70);
  cx.lineTo(90, 70);
  cx.fill();
</script>
```

This example draws a filled triangle. Note that only two of the triangle's sides are explicitly drawn. The third, from the bottom-right corner back to the top, is implied and won't be there when you stroke the path.

You could also use the `closePath` method to explicitly close a path by adding an actual line segment back to the path's start. This segment *is* drawn when stroking the path.

Curves

A path may also contain curved lines. These are, unfortunately, a bit more involved to draw than straight lines.

The `quadraticCurveTo` method draws a curve to a given point. To determine the curvature of the line, the method is given a control point as well as a destination point. Imagine this control point as *attracting* the line, giving the line its curve. The line won't go through the control point. Rather, the direction of the line at its start and end points will be such that it aligns with the line from there to the control point. The following example illustrates this:

```
<canvas></canvas>
<script>
  var cx = document.querySelector("canvas").getContext("2d");
  cx.beginPath();
  cx.moveTo(10, 90);
  // control=(60,10) goal=(90,90)
  cx.quadraticCurveTo(60, 10, 90, 90);
  cx.lineTo(60, 10);
  cx.closePath();
  cx.stroke();
</script>
```

The program produces a path that looks like this:

We draw a quadratic curve from the left to the right, with (60,10) as control point, and then draw two line segments going through that control point and back to the start of the line. The result somewhat resembles a *Star Trek* insignia. You can see the effect of the control point: the lines leaving the lower corners start off in the direction of the control point and then curve toward their target.

The bezierCurveTo method draws a similar kind of curve. Instead of a single control point, this one has two—one for each of the line's endpoints. Here is a similar sketch to illustrate the behavior of such a curve:

```
<canvas></canvas>
<script>
  var cx = document.querySelector("canvas").getContext("2d");
  cx.beginPath();
  cx.moveTo(10, 90);
  // control1=(10,10) control2=(90,10) goal=(50,90)
  cx.bezierCurveTo(10, 10, 90, 10, 50, 90);
  cx.lineTo(90, 10);
  cx.lineTo(10, 10);
  cx.closePath();
  cx.stroke();
</script>
```

The two control points specify the direction at both ends of the curve. The further they are away from their corresponding point, the more the curve will "bulge" in that direction.

Such curves can be hard to work with—it's not always clear how to find the control points that provide the shape you are looking for. Sometimes you can compute them, and sometimes you'll just have to find a suitable value by trial and error.

Arcs—fragments of a circle—are easier to reason about. The arcTo method takes no less than five arguments. The first four arguments act somewhat like the arguments to quadraticCurveTo. The first pair provides a sort of control point, and the second pair gives the line's destination. The fifth argument provides the radius of the arc. The method will conceptually project a corner—a line going to the control point and then to the destination point—and round the corner's point so that it forms part of a circle with the given radius. The arcTo method then draws the rounded part, as well as a line from the starting position to the start of the rounded part.

```
<canvas></canvas>
<script>
  var cx = document.querySelector("canvas").getContext("2d");
  cx.beginPath();
```

```
  cx.moveTo(10, 10);
  // control=(90,10) goal=(90,90) radius=20
  cx.arcTo(90, 10, 90, 90, 20);
  cx.moveTo(10, 10);
  // control=(90,10) goal=(90,90) radius=80
  cx.arcTo(90, 10, 90, 90, 80);
  cx.stroke();
</script>
```

This produces two rounded corners with different radii.

The arcTo method won't draw the line from the end of the rounded part to the goal position, though the word *to* in its name would suggest it does. You can follow up with a call to lineTo with the same goal coordinates to add that part of the line.

To draw a circle, you could use four calls to arcTo (each turning 90 degrees). But the arc method provides a simpler way. It takes a pair of coordinates for the arc's center, a radius, and then a start and end angle.

Those last two parameters make it possible to draw only part of circle. The angles are measured in radians, not degrees. This means a full circle has an angle of 2π, or 2 * Math.PI, which is about 6.28. The angle starts counting at the point to the right of the circle's center and goes clockwise from there. You can use a start of 0 and an end bigger than 2π (say, 7) to draw a full circle.

```
<canvas></canvas>
<script>
  var cx = document.querySelector("canvas").getContext("2d");
  cx.beginPath();
  // center=(50,50) radius=40 angle=0 to 7
  cx.arc(50, 50, 40, 0, 7);
  // center=(150,50) radius=40 angle=0 to ½π
  cx.arc(150, 50, 40, 0, 0.5 * Math.PI);
  cx.stroke();
</script>
```

The resulting picture contains a line from the right of the full circle (first call to arc) to the right of the quarter-circle (second call). Like other path-drawing methods, a line drawn with arc is connected to the previous path segment by default. You'd have to call moveTo or start a new path if you want to avoid this.

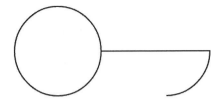

Drawing a Pie Chart

Imagine you've just taken a job at EconomiCorp, Inc., and your first assignment is to draw a pie chart of their customer satisfaction survey results.

The results variable contains an array of objects that represent the survey responses.

```
var results = [
  {name: "Satisfied", count: 1043, color: "lightblue"},
  {name: "Neutral", count: 563, color: "lightgreen"},
  {name: "Unsatisfied", count: 510, color: "pink"},
  {name: "No comment", count: 175, color: "silver"}
];
```

To draw a pie chart, we draw a number of pie slices, each made up of an arc and a pair of lines to the center of that arc. We can compute the angle taken up by each arc by dividing a full circle (2π) by the total number of responses and then multiplying that number (the angle per response) by the number of people who picked a given choice.

```
<canvas width="200" height="200"></canvas>
<script>
  var cx = document.querySelector("canvas").getContext("2d");
  var total = results.reduce(function(sum, choice) {
    return sum + choice.count;
  }, 0);
  // Start at the top
  var currentAngle = -0.5 * Math.PI;
  results.forEach(function(result) {
    var sliceAngle = (result.count / total) * 2 * Math.PI;
    cx.beginPath();
    // center=100,100, radius=100
    // from current angle, clockwise by slice's angle
    cx.arc(100, 100, 100,
           currentAngle, currentAngle + sliceAngle);
    currentAngle += sliceAngle;
    cx.lineTo(100, 100);
    cx.fillStyle = result.color;
    cx.fill();
  });
</script>
```

This draws the following chart:

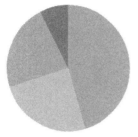

But a chart that doesn't tell us what it means isn't very helpful. We need a way to draw text to the canvas.

Text

A 2D canvas drawing context provides the methods `fillText` and `strokeText`. The latter can be useful for outlining letters, but usually `fillText` is what you need. It will fill the given text with the current `fillColor`.

```
<canvas></canvas>
<script>
  var cx = document.querySelector("canvas").getContext("2d");
  cx.font = "28px Georgia";
  cx.fillStyle = "fuchsia";
  cx.fillText("I can draw text, too!", 10, 50);
</script>
```

You can specify the size, style, and font of the text with the `font` property. This example just gives a font size and family name. You can add `italic` or `bold` to the start of the string to select a style.

The last two arguments to `fillText` (and `strokeText`) provide the position at which the font is drawn. By default, they indicate the position of the start of the text's alphabetic baseline, which is the line that letters "stand" on, not counting hanging parts in letters like *j* or *p*. You can change the horizontal position by setting the `textAlign` property to `"end"` or `"center"` and the vertical position by setting `textBaseline` to `"top"`, `"middle"`, or `"bottom"`.

We will come back to our pie chart, and the problem of labeling the slices, in the exercises at the end of the chapter.

Images

In computer graphics, a distinction is often made between *vector* graphics and *bitmap* graphics. The first is what we have been doing so far in this chapter—specifying a picture by giving a logical description of shapes. Bitmap graphics, on the other hand, don't specify actual shapes but rather work with pixel data (rasters of colored dots).

The `drawImage` method allows us to draw pixel data onto a canvas. This pixel data can originate from an <img> element or from another canvas, and neither has to be visible in the actual document. The following example creates a detached <img> element and loads an image file into it. But it cannot immediately start drawing from this picture because the browser may not have fetched it yet. To deal with this, we register a "load" event handler and do the drawing after the image has loaded.

```
<canvas></canvas>
<script>
  var cx = document.querySelector("canvas").getContext("2d");
  var img = document.createElement("img");
  img.src = "img/hat.png";
  img.addEventListener("load", function() {
    for (var x = 10; x < 200; x += 30)
      cx.drawImage(img, x, 10);
  });
</script>
```

By default, `drawImage` will draw the image at its original size. You can also give it two additional arguments to dictate a different width and height.

When `drawImage` is given *nine* arguments, it can be used to draw only a fragment of an image. The second through fifth arguments indicate the rectangle (*x*, *y*, width, and height) in the source image that should be copied, and the sixth to ninth arguments give the rectangle (on the canvas) into which it should be copied.

This can be used to pack multiple *sprites* (image elements) into a single image file and then draw only the part you need. For example, we have this picture containing a game character in multiple poses:

By alternating which pose we draw, we can show an animation that looks like a walking character.

To animate the picture on a canvas, the `clearRect` method is useful. It resembles `fillRect`, but instead of coloring the rectangle, it makes it transparent, removing the previously drawn pixels.

We know that each *sprite*, each subpicture, is 24 pixels wide and 30 pixels high. The following code loads the image and then sets up an interval (repeated timer) to draw the next *frame*:

```
<canvas></canvas>
<script>
  var cx = document.querySelector("canvas").getContext("2d");
  var img = document.createElement("img");
  img.src = "img/player.png";
  var spriteW = 24, spriteH = 30;
```

```
    img.addEventListener("load", function() {
      var cycle = 0;
      setInterval(function() {
        cx.clearRect(0, 0, spriteW, spriteH);
        cx.drawImage(img,
                     // source rectangle
                     cycle * spriteW, 0, spriteW, spriteH,
                     // destination rectangle
                     0,              0, spriteW, spriteH);
        cycle = (cycle + 1) % 8;
      }, 120);
    });
</script>
```

The cycle variable tracks our position in the animation. Each frame, it is incremented and then clipped back to the 0 to 7 range by using the remainder operator. This variable is then used to compute the x-coordinate that the sprite for the current pose has in the picture.

Transformation

But what if we want our character to walk to the left instead of to the right? We could add another set of sprites, of course. But we can also instruct the canvas to draw the picture the other way round.

Calling the scale method will cause anything drawn after it to be scaled. This method takes two parameters, one to set a horizontal scale and one to set a vertical scale.

```
<canvas></canvas>
<script>
  var cx = document.querySelector("canvas").getContext("2d");
  cx.scale(3, .5);
  cx.beginPath();
  cx.arc(50, 50, 40, 0, 7);
  cx.lineWidth = 3;
  cx.stroke();
</script>
```

Due to the call to scale, the circle is drawn three times as wide and half as high.

Scaling will cause everything about the drawn image, including the line width, to be stretched out or squeezed together as specified. Scaling by a negative amount will flip the picture around. The flipping happens around point (0,0), which means it will also flip the direction of the coordinate system. When a horizontal scaling of −1 is applied, a shape drawn at *x* position 100 will end up at what used to be position −100.

So to turn a picture around, we can't simply add cx.scale(-1, 1) before the call to drawImage since that would move our picture outside of the canvas, where it won't be visible. You could adjust the coordinates given to drawImage to compensate for this by drawing the image at *x* position −50 instead of 0. Another solution, which doesn't require the code that does the drawing to know about the scale change, is to adjust the axis around which the scaling happens.

There are several other methods besides scale that influence the coordinate system for a canvas. You can rotate subsequently drawn shapes with the rotate method and move them with the translate method. The interesting—and confusing—thing is that these transformations *stack*, meaning that each one happens relative to the previous transformations.

So if we translate by 10 horizontal pixels twice, everything will be drawn 20 pixels to the right. If we first move the center of the coordinate system to (50,50) and then rotate by 20 degrees (0.1π in radians), that rotation will happen *around* point (50,50).

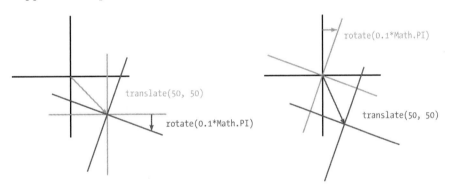

But if we *first* rotate by 20 degrees and *then* translate by (50,50), the translation will happen in the rotated coordinate system and thus produce a different orientation. The order in which transformations are applied matters.

To flip a picture around the vertical line at a given x position, we can do the following:

```
function flipHorizontally(context, around) {
  context.translate(around, 0);
  context.scale(-1, 1);
  context.translate(-around, 0);
}
```

We move the y-axis to where we want our mirror to be, apply the mirroring, and finally move the y-axis back to its proper place in the mirrored universe. The following picture explains why this works:

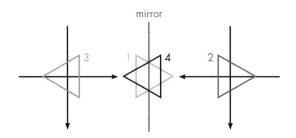

This shows the coordinate systems before and after mirroring across the central line. If we draw a triangle at a positive *x* position, it would, by default, be in the place where triangle 1 is. A call to flipHorizontally first does a translation to the right, which gets us to triangle 2. It then scales, flipping the triangle back to position 3. This is not where it should be, if it were mirrored in the given line. The second translate call fixes this—it "cancels" the initial translation and makes triangle 4 appear exactly where it should.

We can now draw a mirrored character at position (100,0) by flipping the world around the character's vertical center.

```
<canvas></canvas>
<script>
  var cx = document.querySelector("canvas").getContext("2d");
  var img = document.createElement("img");
  img.src = "img/player.png";
  var spriteW = 24, spriteH = 30;
  img.addEventListener("load", function() {
    flipHorizontally(cx, 100 + spriteW / 2);
    cx.drawImage(img, 0, 0, spriteW, spriteH,
                 100, 0, spriteW, spriteH);
  });
</script>
```

Storing and Clearing Transformations

Transformations stick around. Everything else we draw after drawing that mirrored character would also be mirrored. That might be a problem.

It is possible to save the current transformation, do some drawing and transforming, and then restore the old transformation. This is usually the proper thing to do for a function that needs to temporarily transform the coordinate system. First, we save whatever transformation the code that called the function was using. Then, the function does its thing (on top of the existing transformation), possibly adding more transformations. And finally, we revert to the transformation that we started with.

The save and restore methods on the 2D canvas context perform this kind of transformation management. They conceptually keep a stack of transformation states. When you call save, the current state is pushed onto the stack, and when you call restore, the state on top of the stack is taken off and used as the context's current transformation.

The branch function in the following example illustrates what you can do with a function that changes the transformation and then calls another function (in this case itself), which continues drawing with the given transformation.

This function draws a treelike shape by drawing a line, moving the center of the coordinate system to the end of the line, and calling itself twice—first rotated to the left and then rotated to the right. Every call reduces the length of the branch drawn, and the recursion stops when the length drops below 8.

```
<canvas width="600" height="300"></canvas>
<script>
  var cx = document.querySelector("canvas").getContext("2d");
  function branch(length, angle, scale) {
    cx.fillRect(0, 0, 1, length);
    if (length < 8) return;
    cx.save();
    cx.translate(0, length);
    cx.rotate(-angle);
    branch(length * scale, angle, scale);
    cx.rotate(2 * angle);
    branch(length * scale, angle, scale);
    cx.restore();
  }
  cx.translate(300, 0);
  branch(60, 0.5, 0.8);
</script>
```

The result is a simple fractal.

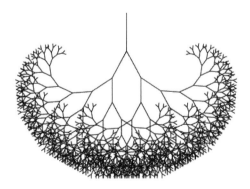

If the calls to save and restore were not there, the second recursive call to branch would end up with the position and rotation created by the first call. It wouldn't be connected to the current branch but rather to the innermost, rightmost branch drawn by the first call. The resulting shape might also be interesting, but it is definitely not a tree.

Back to the Game

We now know enough about canvas drawing to start working on a canvas-based display system for the game from the previous chapter. The new display will no longer be showing just colored boxes. Instead, we'll use drawImage to draw pictures that represent the game's elements.

We will define an object type CanvasDisplay, supporting the same interface as DOMDisplay from Chapter 15, namely, the methods drawFrame and clear.

This object keeps a little more information than DOMDisplay. Rather than using the scroll position of its DOM element, it tracks its own viewport, which tells us what part of the level we are currently looking at. It also tracks time and uses that to decide which animation frame to use. And finally, it keeps a flipPlayer property so that even when the player is standing still, it keeps facing the direction it last moved in.

```
function CanvasDisplay(parent, level) {
  this.canvas = document.createElement("canvas");
  this.canvas.width = Math.min(600, level.width * scale);
  this.canvas.height = Math.min(450, level.height * scale);
  parent.appendChild(this.canvas);
  this.cx = this.canvas.getContext("2d");

  this.level = level;
  this.animationTime = 0;
  this.flipPlayer = false;

  this.viewport = {
    left: 0,
    top: 0,
    width: this.canvas.width / scale,
    height: this.canvas.height / scale
  };

  this.drawFrame(0);
}

CanvasDisplay.prototype.clear = function() {
  this.canvas.parentNode.removeChild(this.canvas);
};
```

The `animationTime` counter is the reason we passed the step size to `drawFrame` in Chapter 15, even though `DOMDisplay` does not use it. Our new `drawFrame` function uses the counter to track time so that it can switch between animation frames based on the current time.

```
CanvasDisplay.prototype.drawFrame = function(step) {
  this.animationTime += step;

  this.updateViewport();
  this.clearDisplay();
  this.drawBackground();
  this.drawActors();
};
```

Other than tracking time, the method updates the viewport for the current player position, fills the whole canvas with a background color, and draws the background and actors onto that. Note that this is different from the approach in Chapter 15, where we drew the background once and scrolled the wrapping DOM element to move it.

Because shapes on a canvas are just pixels, after we draw them, there is no way to move them (or remove them). The only way to update the canvas display is to clear it and redraw the scene.

The `updateViewport` method is similar to `DOMDisplay`'s `scrollPlayerIntoView` method. It checks whether the player is too close to the edge of the screen and moves the viewport when this is the case.

```
CanvasDisplay.prototype.updateViewport = function() {
  var view = this.viewport, margin = view.width / 3;
  var player = this.level.player;
  var center = player.pos.plus(player.size.times(0.5));

  if (center.x < view.left + margin)
    view.left = Math.max(center.x - margin, 0);
  else if (center.x > view.left + view.width - margin)
    view.left = Math.min(center.x + margin - view.width,
                         this.level.width - view.width);
  if (center.y < view.top + margin)
    view.top = Math.max(center.y - margin, 0);
  else if (center.y > view.top + view.height - margin)
    view.top = Math.min(center.y + margin - view.height,
                        this.level.height - view.height);
};
```

The calls to `Math.max` and `Math.min` ensure that the viewport does not end up showing space outside of the level. `Math.max(x, 0)` ensures that the resulting number is not less than zero. `Math.min`, similarly, ensures a value stays below a given bound.

When clearing the display, we'll use a slightly different color depending on whether the game is won (brighter) or lost (darker).

```
CanvasDisplay.prototype.clearDisplay = function() {
  if (this.level.status == "won")
    this.cx.fillStyle = "rgb(68, 191, 255)";
  else if (this.level.status == "lost")
    this.cx.fillStyle = "rgb(44, 136, 214)";
  else
    this.cx.fillStyle = "rgb(52, 166, 251)";
  this.cx.fillRect(0, 0,
                   this.canvas.width, this.canvas.height);
};
```

To draw the background, we run through the tiles that are visible in the current viewport, using the same trick used in obstacleAt in the previous chapter.

```
var otherSprites = document.createElement("img");
otherSprites.src = "img/sprites.png";

CanvasDisplay.prototype.drawBackground = function() {
  var view = this.viewport;
  var xStart = Math.floor(view.left);
  var xEnd = Math.ceil(view.left + view.width);
  var yStart = Math.floor(view.top);
  var yEnd = Math.ceil(view.top + view.height);

  for (var y = yStart; y < yEnd; y++) {
    for (var x = xStart; x < xEnd; x++) {
      var tile = this.level.grid[y][x];
      if (tile == null) continue;
      var screenX = (x - view.left) * scale;
      var screenY = (y - view.top) * scale;
      var tileX = tile == "lava" ? scale : 0;
      this.cx.drawImage(otherSprites,
                        tileX,         0, scale, scale,
                        screenX, screenY, scale, scale);
    }
  }
};
```

Tiles that are not empty (null) are drawn with drawImage. The otherSprites image contains the pictures used for elements other than the player. It contains, from left to right, the wall tile, the lava tile, and the sprite for a coin.

Background tiles are 20 by 20 pixels, since we will use the same scale that we used in DOMDisplay. Thus, the offset for lava tiles is 20 (the value of the scale variable), and the offset for walls is 0.

We don't bother waiting for the sprite image to load. Calling drawImage with an image that hasn't been loaded yet will simply do nothing. Thus, we might fail to draw the game properly for the first few frames, while the image is still loading, but that is not a serious problem. Since we keep updating the screen, the correct scene will appear as soon as the loading finishes.

The walking character shown earlier will be used to represent the player. The code that draws it needs to pick the right sprite and direction based on the player's current motion. The first eight sprites contain a walking animation. When the player is moving along a floor, we cycle through them based on the display's animationTime property. This is measured in seconds, and we want to switch frames 12 times per second, so the time is multiplied by 12 first. When the player is standing still, we draw the ninth sprite. During jumps, which are recognized by the fact that the vertical speed is not zero, we use the tenth, rightmost sprite.

Because the sprites are slightly wider than the player object—24 instead of 16 pixels, to allow some space for feet and arms—the method has to adjust the x-coordinate and width by a given amount (playerXOverlap).

```
var playerSprites = document.createElement("img");
playerSprites.src = "img/player.png";
var playerXOverlap = 4;

CanvasDisplay.prototype.drawPlayer = function(x, y, width, height) {
  var sprite = 8, player = this.level.player;
  width += playerXOverlap * 2;
  x -= playerXOverlap;
  if (player.speed.x != 0)
    this.flipPlayer = player.speed.x < 0;

  if (player.speed.y != 0)
    sprite = 9;
  else if (player.speed.x != 0)
    sprite = Math.floor(this.animationTime * 12) % 8;

  this.cx.save();
  if (this.flipPlayer)
    flipHorizontally(this.cx, x + width / 2);

  this.cx.drawImage(playerSprites,
                    sprite * width, 0, width, height,
                    x,                y, width, height);

  this.cx.restore();
};
```

The `drawPlayer` method is called by `drawActors`, which is responsible for drawing all the actors in the game.

```
CanvasDisplay.prototype.drawActors = function() {
  this.level.actors.forEach(function(actor) {
    var width = actor.size.x * scale;
    var height = actor.size.y * scale;
    var x = (actor.pos.x - this.viewport.left) * scale;
    var y = (actor.pos.y - this.viewport.top) * scale;
    if (actor.type == "player") {
      this.drawPlayer(x, y, width, height);
    } else {
      var tileX = (actor.type == "coin" ? 2 : 1) * scale;
      this.cx.drawImage(otherSprites,
                        tileX, 0, width, height,
                        x,     y, width, height);
    }
  }, this);
};
```

When drawing something that is not the player, we look at its type to find the offset of the correct sprite. The lava tile is found at offset 20, and the coin sprite is found at 40 (two times scale).

We have to subtract the viewport's position when computing the actor's position since (0,0) on our canvas corresponds to the top left of the viewport, not the top left of the level. We could also have used `translate` for this. Either way works.

That concludes the new display system. The resulting game looks something like this:

Choosing a Graphics Interface

Whenever you need to generate graphics in the browser, you can choose between plain HTML, SVG, and canvas. There is no single *best* approach that works in all situations. Each option has strengths and weaknesses.

Plain HTML has the advantage of being simple. It also integrates well with text. Both SVG and canvas allow you to draw text, but they won't help you position that text or wrap it when it takes up more than one line. In an HTML-based picture, it is easy to include blocks of text.

SVG can be used to produce crisp graphics that look good at any zoom level. It is more difficult to use than plain HTML but also much more powerful.

Both SVG and HTML build up a data structure (the DOM) that represents the picture. This makes it possible to modify elements after they are drawn. If you need to repeatedly change a small part of a big picture in response to what the user is doing or as part of an animation, doing it in a canvas can be needlessly expensive. The DOM also allows us to register mouse event handlers on every element in the picture (even on shapes drawn with SVG). You can't do that with canvas.

But canvas's pixel-oriented approach can be an advantage when drawing a huge amount of tiny elements. The fact that it does not build up a data structure but only repeatedly draws onto the same pixel surface gives canvas a lower cost per shape.

There are also effects, such as rendering a scene one pixel at a time (for example, using a ray tracer) or postprocessing an image with JavaScript (blurring or distorting it), that can only be realistically handled by a pixel-based technique.

In some cases, you may want to combine several of these techniques. For example, you might draw a graph with SVG or canvas but show textual information by positioning an HTML element on top of the picture.

For nondemanding applications, it really doesn't matter much which interface you choose. The second display we built for our game in this chapter could have been implemented using any of these three graphics technologies since it does not need to draw text, handle mouse interaction, or work with an extraordinarily large amount of elements.

Summary

In this chapter, we discussed techniques for drawing graphics in the browser, focusing on the <canvas> element.

A canvas node represents an area in a document that our program may draw on. This drawing is done through a drawing context object, created with the getContext method.

The 2D drawing interface allows us to fill and stroke various shapes. The context's fillStyle property determines how shapes are filled. The strokeStyle and lineWidth properties control the way lines are drawn.

Rectangles and pieces of text can be drawn with a single method call. The `fillRect` and `strokeRect` methods draw rectangles, and the `fillText` and `strokeText` methods draw text. To create custom shapes, we must first build up a path.

Calling `beginPath` starts a new path. A number of other methods add lines and curves to the current path. For example, `lineTo` can add a straight line. When a path is finished, it can be filled with the `fill` method or stroked with the `stroke` method.

Moving pixels from an image or another canvas onto our canvas is done with the `drawImage` method. By default, this method draws the whole source image, but by giving it more parameters, you can copy a specific area of the image. We used this for our game by copying individual poses of the game character out of an image that contained many such poses.

Transformations allow you to draw a shape in multiple orientations. A 2D drawing context has a current transformation that can be changed with the `translate`, `scale`, and `rotate` methods. These will affect all subsequent drawing operations. A transformation state can be saved with the save method and restored with the `restore` method.

When drawing an animation on a canvas, the `clearRect` method can be used to clear part of the canvas before redrawing it.

Exercises

Shapes

Write a program that draws the following shapes on a canvas:

1. A trapezoid (a rectangle that is wider on one side)
2. A red diamond (a rectangle rotated 45 degrees or $\frac{1}{4}\pi$ radians)
3. A zigzagging line
4. A spiral made up of 100 straight line segments
5. A yellow star

When drawing the last two, you may want to refer to the explanation of `Math.cos` and `Math.sin` in Chapter 13, which describes how to get coordinates on a circle using these functions.

I recommend creating a function for each shape. Pass the position, and optionally other properties, such as the size or the number of points, as parameters. The alternative, which is to hard-code numbers all over your code, tends to make the code needlessly hard to read and modify.

The Pie Chart

Earlier in the chapter, we saw an example program that drew a pie chart. Modify this program so that the name of each category is shown next to the slice that represents it. Try to find a pleasing-looking way to automatically position this text, which would work for other data sets as well. You may assume that categories are no smaller than 5 percent (that is, there won't be a bunch of tiny ones next to each other).

You might again need `Math.sin` and `Math.cos`, as described in the previous exercise.

A Bouncing Ball

Use the `requestAnimationFrame` technique that we saw in Chapter 13 and Chapter 15 to draw a box with a bouncing ball in it. The ball moves at a constant speed and bounces off the box's sides when it hits them.

Precomputed Mirroring

One unfortunate thing about transformations is that they slow down drawing of bitmaps. For vector graphics, the effect is less serious since only a few points (for example, the center of a circle) need to be transformed, after which drawing can happen as normal. For a bitmap image, the position of each pixel has to be transformed, and though it is possible that browsers will get more clever about this in the future, this currently causes a measurable increase in the time it takes to draw a bitmap.

In a game like ours, where we are drawing only a single transformed sprite, this is a nonissue. But imagine that we need to draw hundreds of characters or thousands of rotating particles from an explosion.

Think of a way to allow us to draw an inverted character without loading additional image files and without having to make transformed `drawImage` calls every frame.

"The dream behind the Web is of a common information space in which we communicate by sharing information. Its universality is essential: the fact that a hypertext link can point to anything, be it personal, local or global, be it draft or highly polished."

—Tim Berners-Lee,
The World Wide Web: A very short personal history

17

HTTP

The *Hypertext Transfer Protocol,* already mentioned in Chapter 12, is the mechanism through which data is requested and provided on the World Wide Web. This chapter describes the protocol in more detail and explains the way browser JavaScript has access to it.

The Protocol

If you type *eloquentjavascript.net/17_http.html* into your browser's address bar, the browser first looks up the address of the server associated with *eloquentjavascript.net* and tries to open a TCP connection to it on port 80, the default port for HTTP traffic. If the server exists and accepts the connection, the browser sends something like this:

```
GET /17_http.html HTTP/1.1
Host: eloquentjavascript.net
User-Agent: Your browser's name
```

Then the server responds, through that same connection.

```
HTTP/1.1 200 OK
Content-Length: 65585
```

```
Content-Type: text/html
Last-Modified: Wed, 09 Apr 2014 10:48:09 GMT

<!doctype html>
... the rest of the document
```

The browser then takes the part of the response after the blank line and displays it as an HTML document.

The information sent by the client is called the *request*. It starts with this line:

```
GET /17_http.html HTTP/1.1
```

The first word is the *method* of the request. GET means that we want to *get* the specified resource. Other common methods are DELETE to delete a resource, PUT to replace it, and POST to send information to it. Note that the server is not obliged to carry out every request it gets. If you walk up to a random website and tell it to DELETE its main page, it'll probably refuse.

The part after the method name is the path of the resource the request applies to. In the simplest case, a resource is simply a file on the server, but the protocol doesn't require it to be. A resource may be anything that can be transferred *as if* it is a file. Many servers generate the responses they produce on the fly. For example, if you open *twitter.com/marijnjh*, the server looks in its database for a user named *marijnjh*, and if it finds one, it will generate a profile page for that user.

After the resource path, the first line of the request mentions HTTP/1.1 to indicate the version of the HTTP protocol it is using.

The server's response will start with a version as well, followed by the status of the response, first as a three-digit status code and then as a human-readable string.

```
HTTP/1.1 200 OK
```

Status codes starting with a 2 indicate that the request succeeded. Codes starting with 4 mean there was something wrong with the request. 404 is probably the most famous HTTP status code—it means that the resource that was requested could not be found. Codes that start with 5 mean an error happened on the server and the request is not to blame.

The first line of a request or response may be followed by any number of *headers*. These are lines in the form "name: value" that specify extra information about the request or response. These headers were part of the example response:

```
Content-Length: 65585
Content-Type: text/html
Last-Modified: Wed, 09 Apr 2014 10:48:09 GMT
```

This tells us the size and type of the response document. In this case, it is an HTML document of 65,585 bytes. It also tells us when that document was last modified.

For the most part, a client or server decides which headers to include in a request or response, though a few headers are required. For example, the Host header, which specifies the hostname, should be included in a request because a server might be serving multiple hostnames on a single IP address, and without that header, the server won't know which host the client is trying to talk to.

After the headers, both requests and responses may include a blank line followed by a *body*, which contains the data being sent. GET and DELETE requests don't send along any data, but PUT and POST requests do. Similarly, some response types, such as error responses, do not require a body.

Browsers and HTTP

As we saw in the example, a browser will make a request when we enter a URL in its address bar. When the resulting HTML page references other files, such as images and JavaScript files, those are also fetched.

A moderately complicated website can easily include anywhere from 10 to 200 resources. To be able to fetch those quickly, browsers will make several requests simultaneously, rather than waiting for the responses one at a time. Such documents are always fetched using GET requests.

HTML pages may include *forms*, which allow the user to fill out information and send it to the server. This is an example of a form:

```
<form method="GET" action="example/message.html">
  <p>Name: <input type="text" name="name"></p>
  <p>Message:<br><textarea name="message"></textarea></p>
  <p><button type="submit">Send</button></p>
</form>
```

This code describes a form with two fields: a small one asking for a name and a larger one to write a message in. When you click the Send button, the information in those fields will be encoded into a *query string*. When the <form> element's method attribute is GET (or is omitted), that query string is tacked onto the action URL, and the browser makes a GET request to that URL.

```
GET /example/message.html?name=Jean&message=Yes%3F HTTP/1.1
```

The start of a query string is indicated by a question mark. After that follow pairs of names and values, corresponding to the name attribute on the form field elements and the content of those elements, respectively. An ampersand character (&) is used to separate the pairs.

The actual message encoded in the previous URL is "Yes?," even though the question mark is replaced by a strange code. Some characters in query strings must be escaped. The question mark, represented as %3F, is one of those. There seems to be an unwritten rule that every format needs its own way of escaping characters. This one, called *URL encoding*, uses a percent sign followed by two hexadecimal digits that encode the character code. In this case, 3F, which is 63 in decimal notation, is the code of a question mark character. JavaScript provides the `encodeURIComponent` and `decodeURIComponent` functions to encode and decode this format.

```
console.log(encodeURIComponent("Hello & goodbye"));
// ▷ Hello%20%26%20goodbye
console.log(decodeURIComponent("Hello%20%26%20goodbye"));
// ▷ Hello & goodbye
```

If we change the `method` attribute of the HTML form in the example we saw earlier to POST, the HTTP request made to submit the form will use the POST method and put the query string in body of the request, rather than adding it to the URL.

```
POST /example/message.html HTTP/1.1
Content-length: 24
Content-type: application/x-www-form-urlencoded

name=Jean&message=Yes%3F
```

By convention, the GET method is used for requests that do not have side effects, such as doing a search. Requests that change something on the server, such as creating a new account or posting a message, should be expressed with other methods, such as POST. Client-side software, such as a browser, knows that it shouldn't blindly make POST requests but will often implicitly make GET requests—for example, to prefetch a resource it believes the user will soon need.

The next chapter will return to forms and talk about how we can script them with JavaScript.

XMLHttpRequest

The interface through which browser JavaScript can make HTTP requests is called XMLHttpRequest (note the inconsistent capitalization). It was designed by Microsoft, for its Internet Explorer browser, in the late 1990s. During this time, the XML file format was *very* popular in the world of business software—a world where Microsoft has always been at home. In fact, it was so popular that the acronym XML was tacked onto the front of the name of an interface for HTTP, which is in no way tied to XML.

The name isn't completely nonsensical, though. The interface allows you to parse response documents as XML if you want. Conflating two distinct concepts (making a request and parsing the response) makes for terrible design, of course, but so it goes.

When the XMLHttpRequest interface was added to Internet Explorer, it allowed people to do things with JavaScript that had been very hard before. For example, websites started showing lists of suggestions when the user was typing something into a text field. The script would send the text to the server over HTTP as the user typed. The server, which had some database of possible inputs, would match the database entries against the partial input and send back possible completions to show the user. This was considered spectacular—people were used to waiting for a full page reload for every interaction with a website.

The other significant browser at that time, Mozilla (later Firefox), did not want to be left behind. To allow people to do similarly neat things in *its* browser, Mozilla copied the interface, including the bogus name. The next generation of browsers followed this example, and today XMLHttpRequest is a de facto standard interface.

Sending a Request

To make a simple request, we create a request object with the XMLHttpRequest constructor and call its open and send methods.

```
var req = new XMLHttpRequest();
req.open("GET", "example/data.txt", false);
req.send(null);
console.log(req.responseText);
// ▷ This is the content of data.txt
```

The open method configures the request. In this case, we choose to make a GET request for the *example/data.txt* file. URLs that don't start with a protocol name (such as *http:*) are relative, which means that they are interpreted relative to the current document. When they start with a slash (/), they replace the current path, which is the part after the server name. When they do not, the part of the current path up to and including its last slash character is put in front of the relative URL.

After opening the request, we can send it with the send method. The argument to send is the request body. For GET requests, we can pass null. If the third argument to open was false, send will return only after the response to our request was received. We can read the request object's responseText property to get the response body.

The other information included in the response can also be extracted from this object. The status code is accessible through the status property, and the human-readable status text is accessible through statusText. Headers can be read with getResponseHeader.

```
var req = new XMLHttpRequest();
req.open("GET", "example/data.txt", false);
req.send(null);
console.log(req.status, req.statusText);
// ▷ 200 OK
```

```
console.log(req.getResponseHeader("content-type"));
// ▷ text/plain
```

Header names are case insensitive. They are usually written with a capital letter at the start of each word, such as "Content-Type," but "content-type" and "cOnTeNt-TyPe" refer to the same header.

The browser will automatically add some request headers, such as "Host" and those needed for the server to figure out the size of the body. But you can add your own headers with the setRequestHeader method. This is needed only for advanced uses and requires the cooperation of the server you are talking to—a server is free to ignore headers it does not know how to handle.

Asynchronous Requests

In the examples we saw, the request has finished when the call to send returns. This is convenient because it means properties such as responseText are available immediately. But it also means that our program is suspended as long as the browser and server are communicating. When the connection is bad, the server is slow, or the file is big, that might take quite a while. Worse, because no event handlers can fire while our program is suspended, the whole document will become unresponsive.

If we pass true as the third argument to open, the request is *asynchronous*. This means that when we call send, the only thing that happens right away is that the request is scheduled to be sent. Our program can continue, and the browser will take care of the sending and receiving of data in the background.

But as long as the request is running, we won't be able to access the response. We need a mechanism that will notify us when the data is available. For this, we must listen for the "load" event on the request object.

```
var req = new XMLHttpRequest();
req.open("GET", "example/data.txt", true);
req.addEventListener("load", function() {
  console.log("Done:", req.status);
});
req.send(null);
```

Just like the use of requestAnimationFrame in Chapter 15, this forces us to use an asynchronous style of programming, wrapping the things that have to be done after the request in a function and arranging for that to be called at the appropriate time. We will come back to this later.

Fetching XML Data

When the resource retrieved by an XMLHttpRequest object is an XML document, the object's responseXML property will hold a parsed representation of this document. This representation works much like the DOM discussed in Chapter 13, except that it doesn't have HTML-specific functionality like the style property. The object that responseXML holds corresponds to the document object. Its documentElement property refers to the outer tag of the XML document. In the following document (*example/fruit.xml*), that would would be the <fruits> tag:

```
<fruits>
  <fruit name="banana" color="yellow"/>
  <fruit name="lemon" color="yellow"/>
  <fruit name="cherry" color="red"/>
</fruits>
```

We can retrieve such a file like this:

```
var req = new XMLHttpRequest();
req.open("GET", "example/fruit.xml", false);
req.send(null);
console.log(req.responseXML.querySelectorAll("fruit").length);
// ▷ 3
```

XML documents can be used to exchange structured information with the server. Their form—tags nested inside other tags—lends itself well to storing most types of data, at least better than flat text files. The DOM interface is rather clumsy for extracting information, though, and XML documents tend to be verbose. It is often a better idea to communicate using JSON data, which is easier to read and write, both for programs and for humans.

```
var req = new XMLHttpRequest();
req.open("GET", "example/fruit.json", false);
req.send(null);
console.log(JSON.parse(req.responseText));
// ▷ {banana: "yellow", lemon: "yellow", cherry: "red"}
```

HTTP Sandboxing

Making HTTP requests in web page scripts once again raises concerns about security. The person who controls the script might not have the same interests as the person on whose computer it is running. More specifically, if I visit *themafia.org*, I do not want its scripts to be able to make a request to *mybank.com*, using identifying information from my browser, with instructions to transfer all my money to some random mafia account.

It is possible for websites to protect themselves against such attacks, but that requires effort, and many websites fail to do it. For this reason, browsers protect us by disallowing scripts to make HTTP requests to other *domains* (names such as *themafia.org* and *mybank.com*).

This can be an annoying problem when building systems that want to access several domains for legitimate reasons. Fortunately, servers can include a header like this in their response to explicitly indicate to browsers that it is okay for the request to come from other domains:

```
Access-Control-Allow-Origin: *
```

Abstracting Requests

In Chapter 10, in our implementation of the AMD module system, we used a hypothetical function called `backgroundReadFile`. It took a filename and a function and called that function with the contents of the file when it had finished fetching it. Here's a simple implementation of that function:

```
function backgroundReadFile(url, callback) {
  var req = new XMLHttpRequest();
  req.open("GET", url, true);
  req.addEventListener("load", function() {
    if (req.status < 400)
      callback(req.responseText);
  });
  req.send(null);
}
```

This simple abstraction makes it easier to use `XMLHttpRequest` for simple `GET` requests. If you are writing a program that has to make HTTP requests, it is a good idea to use a helper function so that you don't end up repeating the ugly `XMLHttpRequest` pattern all through your code.

The function argument's name, `callback`, is a term that is often used to describe functions like this. A callback function is given to other code to provide that code with a way to "call us back" later.

It is not hard to write an HTTP utility function tailored to what your application is doing. The previous one does only `GET` requests and doesn't give us control over the headers or the request body. You could write another variant for `POST` requests or a more generic one that supports various kinds of requests. Many JavaScript libraries also provide wrappers for `XMLHttpRequest`.

The main problem with the previous wrapper is its handling of failure. When the request returns a status code that indicates an error (400 and up), it does nothing. This might be okay, in some circumstances, but imagine we put a "loading" indicator on the page to indicate that we are fetching information. If the request fails because the server crashed or the connection is briefly interrupted, the page will just sit there, misleadingly looking like it is doing something. The user will wait for a while, get impatient, and consider the site uselessly flaky.

We should also have an option to be notified when the request fails so that we can take appropriate action. For example, we could remove the "loading" message and inform the user that something went wrong.

Error handling in asynchronous code is even trickier than error handling in synchronous code. Because we often need to defer part of our work, putting it in a callback function, the scope of a try block becomes meaningless. In the following code, the exception will *not* be caught because the call to backgroundReadFile returns immediately. Control then leaves the try block, and the function it was given won't be called until later.

```
try {
  backgroundReadFile("example/data.txt", function(text) {
    if (text != "expected")
      throw new Error("That was unexpected");
  });
} catch (e) {
  console.log("Hello from the catch block");
}
```

To handle failing requests, we have to allow an additional function to be passed to our wrapper and call that when a request goes wrong. Alternatively, we can use the convention that if the request fails, an additional argument describing the problem is passed to the regular callback function. Here's an example:

```
function getURL(url, callback) {
  var req = new XMLHttpRequest();
  req.open("GET", url, true);
  req.addEventListener("load", function() {
    if (req.status < 400)
      callback(req.responseText);
    else
      callback(null, new Error("Request failed: " +
                               req.statusText));
  });
  req.addEventListener("error", function() {
    callback(null, new Error("Network error"));
  });
  req.send(null);
}
```

We have added a handler for the "error" event, which will be signaled when the request fails entirely. We also call the callback function with an error argument when the request completes with a status code that indicates an error.

Code using getURL must then check whether an error was given and, if it finds one, handle it.

```
getURL("data/nonsense.txt", function(content, error) {
  if (error != null)
    console.log("Failed to fetch nonsense.txt: " + error);
  else
    console.log("nonsense.txt: " + content);
});
```

This does not help when it comes to exceptions. When chaining several asynchronous actions together, an exception at any point of the chain will still (unless you wrap each handling function in its own try/catch block) land at the top level and abort your chain of actions.

Promises

For complicated projects, writing asynchronous code in plain callback style is hard to do correctly. It is easy to forget to check for an error or to allow an unexpected exception to cut the program short in a crude way. Additionally, arranging for correct error handling when the error has to flow through multiple callback functions and catch blocks is tedious.

There have been a lot of attempts to solve this with extra abstractions. One of the more successful ones is called *promises*. Promises wrap an asynchronous action in an object, which can be passed around and told to do certain things when the action finishes or fails. This interface is set to become part of the next version of the JavaScript language but can already be used as a library.

The interface for promises isn't entirely intuitive, but it is powerful. This chapter will only roughly describe it. You can find a more thorough treatment at *http://www.promisejs.org/*.

To create a promise object, we call the Promise constructor, giving it a function that initializes the asynchronous action. The constructor calls that function, passing it two arguments, which are themselves functions. The first should be called when the action finishes successfully, and the second should be called when it fails.

Once again, here is our wrapper for GET requests, this time returning a promise. We'll simply call it get this time.

```
function get(url) {
  return new Promise(function(succeed, fail) {
    var req = new XMLHttpRequest();
    req.open("GET", url, true);
    req.addEventListener("load", function() {
      if (req.status < 400)
        succeed(req.responseText);
      else
        fail(new Error("Request failed: " + req.statusText));
```

```
    });
    req.addEventListener("error", function() {
      fail(new Error("Network error"));
    });
    req.send(null);
  });
}
```

Note that the interface to the function itself is now a lot simpler. You give it a URL, and it returns a promise. That promise acts as a *handle* to the request's outcome. It has a then method that you can call with two functions: one to handle success and one to handle failure.

```
get("example/data.txt").then(function(text) {
  console.log("data.txt: " + text);
}, function(error) {
  console.log("Failed to fetch data.txt: " + error);
});
```

So far, this is just another way to express the same thing we already expressed. It is only when you need to chain actions together that promises make a significant difference.

Calling then produces a new promise, whose result (the value passed to success handlers) depends on the return value of the first function we passed to then. This function may return another promise to indicate that more asynchronous work is being done. In this case, the promise returned by then itself will wait for the promise returned by the handler function, succeeding or failing with the same value when it is resolved. When the handler function returns a nonpromise value, the promise returned by then immediately succeeds with that value as its result.

This means you can use then to transform the result of a promise. For example, this returns a promise whose result is the content of the given URL, parsed as JSON:

```
function getJSON(url) {
  return get(url).then(JSON.parse);
}
```

That last call to then did not specify a failure handler. This is allowed. The error will be passed to the promise returned by then, which is exactly what we want—getJSON does not know what to do when something goes wrong, but hopefully its caller does.

As an example that shows the use of promises, we will build a program that fetches a number of JSON files from the server and, while it is doing that, shows the word *loading*. The JSON files contain information about people, with links to files that represent other people in properties such as father, mother, or spouse.

We want to get the name of the mother of the spouse of *example/bert.json*. And if something goes wrong, we want to remove the *loading* text and show an error message instead. Here is how that might be done with promises:

```
<script>
  function showMessage(msg) {
    var elt = document.createElement("div");
    elt.textContent = msg;
    return document.body.appendChild(elt);
  }

  var loading = showMessage("Loading...");
  getJSON("example/bert.json").then(function(bert) {
    return getJSON(bert.spouse);
  }).then(function(spouse) {
    return getJSON(spouse.mother);
  }).then(function(mother) {
    showMessage("The name is " + mother.name);
  }).catch(function(error) {
    showMessage(String(error));
  }).then(function() {
    document.body.removeChild(loading);
  });
</script>
```

The resulting program is relatively compact and readable. The catch method is similar to then, except that it only expects a failure handler and will pass through the result unmodified in case of success. Much like with the catch clause for the try statement, control will continue as normal after the failure is caught. That way, the final then, which removes the loading message, is always executed, even if something went wrong.

You can think of the promise interface as implementing its own language for asynchronous control flow. The extra method calls and function expressions needed to achieve this make the code look somewhat awkward but not remotely as awkward as it would look if we took care of all the error handling ourselves.

Appreciating HTTP

When building a system that requires communication between a JavaScript program running in the browser (client-side) and a program on a server (server-side), there are several different ways to model this communication.

A commonly used model is that of *remote procedure calls*. In this model, communication follows the patterns of normal function calls, except that the function is actually running on another machine. Calling it involves making a request to the server that includes the function's name and arguments. The response to that request contains the returned value.

When thinking in terms of remote procedure calls, HTTP is just a vehicle for communication, and you will most likely write an abstraction layer that hides it entirely.

Another approach is to build your communication around the concept of resources and HTTP methods. Instead of a remote procedure called addUser, you use a PUT request to /users/larry. Instead of encoding that user's properties in function arguments, you define a document format or use an existing format that represents a user. The body of the PUT request to create a new resource is then simply such a document. A resource is fetched by making a GET request to the resource's URL (for example, /user/larry), which returns the document representing the resource.

This second approach makes it easier to use some of the features that HTTP provides, such as support for caching resources (keeping a copy on the client side). It can also help the coherence of your interface since resources are easier to reason about than a jumble of functions.

Security and HTTPS

Data traveling over the Internet tends to follow a long, dangerous road. To get to its destination, it must hop through anything from coffee-shop Wi-Fi networks to networks controlled by various companies and states. At any point along its route it may be inspected or even modified.

If it is important that something remain secret, such as the password to your email account, or that it arrive at its destination unmodified, such as the account number you transfer money to from your bank's website, plain HTTP is not good enough.

The secure HTTP protocol, whose URLs start with *https://*, wraps HTTP traffic in a way that makes it harder to read and tamper with. First, the client verifies that the server is who it claims to be by requiring that server to prove that it has a cryptographic certificate issued by a certificate authority that the browser recognizes. Next, all data going over the connection is encrypted in a way that should prevent eavesdropping and tampering.

Thus, when it works right, HTTPS prevents both someone impersonating the website you were trying to talk to and someone snooping on your communication. It is not perfect, and there have been various incidents where HTTPS failed because of forged or stolen certificates and broken software. Still, plain HTTP is trivial to mess with, whereas breaking HTTPS requires the kind of effort that only states or sophisticated criminal organizations can hope to make.

Summary

In this chapter, we saw that HTTP is a protocol for accessing resources over the Internet. A *client* sends a request, which contains a method (usually GET) and a path that identifies a resource. The *server* then decides what to do with the request and responds with a status code and a response body. Both requests and responses may contain headers that provide additional information.

Browsers make GET requests to fetch the resources needed to display a web page. A web page may also contain forms, which allow information entered by the user to be sent along in the request made when the form is submitted. You will learn more about that in the next chapter.

The interface through which browser JavaScript can make HTTP requests is called XMLHttpRequest. You can usually ignore the "XML" part of that name (but you still have to type it). There are two ways in which it can be used—synchronous, which blocks everything until the request finishes, and asynchronous, which requires an event handler to notice that the response came in. In almost all cases, asynchronous is preferable. Making a request looks like this:

```
var req = new XMLHttpRequest();
req.open("GET", "example/data.txt", true);
req.addEventListener("load", function() {
  console.log(req.status);
});
req.send(null);
```

Asynchronous programming is tricky. *Promises* are an interface that makes it slightly easier by helping route error conditions and exceptions to the right handler and by abstracting away some of the more repetitive and error-prone elements in this style of programming.

Exercises

Content Negotiation

One of the things that HTTP can do, but that we have not discussed yet in this chapter, is called *content negotiation*. The Accept header for a request can be used to tell the server what type of document the client would like to get. Many servers ignore this header, but when a server knows of various ways to encode a resource, it can look at this header and send the one that the client prefers.

The URL *eloquentjavascript.net/author* is configured to respond with either plaintext, HTML, or JSON, depending on what the client asks for. These formats are identified by the standardized *media types* text/plain, text/html, and application/json.

Send requests to fetch all three formats of this resource. Use the setRequestHeader method of your XMLHttpRequest object to set the header named Accept to one of the media types given earlier. Make sure you set the header *after* calling open but before calling send.

Finally, try asking for the media type application/rainbows+unicorns and see what happens.

Waiting for Multiple Promises

The Promise constructor has an all method that, given an array of promises, returns a promise that waits for all of the promises in the array to finish. It then succeeds, yielding an array of result values. If any of the promises in the array fail, the promise returned by all fails too (with the failure value from the failing promise).

Try to implement something like this yourself as a regular function called all.

Note that after a promise is resolved (has succeeded or failed), it can't succeed or fail again, and further calls to the functions that resolve it are ignored. This can simplify the way you handle failure of your promise.

"I shall this very day, at Doctor's feast,
My bounden service duly pay thee.
But one thing!—For insurance' sake, I pray thee,
Grant me a line or two, at least."

—Mephistopheles, in *Goethe's Faust*

18

FORMS AND FORM FIELDS

Forms were introduced briefly in the previous chapter as a way to *submit* information provided by the user over HTTP. They were designed for a pre-JavaScript Web, assuming that interaction with the server always happens by navigating to a new page.

But their elements are part of the DOM like the rest of the page, and the DOM elements that represent form fields support a number of properties and events that are not present on other elements. These make it possible to inspect and control such input fields with JavaScript programs and do things such as adding functionality to a traditional form or using forms and fields as building blocks in a JavaScript application.

Fields

A web form consists of any number of input fields grouped in a `<form>` tag. HTML allows a number of different styles of fields, ranging from simple on/off checkboxes to drop-down menus and fields for text input. This book won't try to comprehensively discuss all field types, but we will start with a rough overview.

A lot of field types use the `<input>` tag. This tag's type attribute is used to select the field's style. These are some commonly used `<input>` types:

text A single-line text field

password Same as text but hides the text that is typed

checkbox An on/off switch

radio (Part of) a multiple-choice field

file Allows the user to choose a file from their computer

Form fields do not necessarily have to appear in a `<form>` tag. You can put them anywhere in a page. Such fields cannot be submitted (only a form as a whole can), but when responding to input with JavaScript, we often do not want to submit our fields normally anyway.

```
<p><input type="text" value="abc"> (text)</p>
<p><input type="password" value="abc"> (password)</p>
<p><input type="checkbox" checked> (checkbox)</p>
<p><input type="radio" value="A" name="choice">
   <input type="radio" value="B" name="choice">
   <input type="radio" value="C" name="choice" checked> (radio)</p>
<p><input type="file"> (file)</p>
```

The fields created with this HTML code look like this:

abc   (text)

•••   (password)

☑ (checkbox)

◯ ◯ ◉ (radio)

Choose File   snippets.txt   (file)

The JavaScript interface for such elements differs with the type of the element. We'll go over each of them later in the chapter.

Multiline text fields have their own tag, `<textarea>`, mostly because using an attribute to specify a multiline starting value would be awkward. The `<textarea>` requires a matching `</textarea>` closing tag and uses the text between those two, instead of using its value attribute, as starting text.

```
<textarea>
one
two
three
</textarea>
```

Finally, the `<select>` tag is used to create a field that allows the user to select from a number of predefined options.

```
<select>
  <option>Pancakes</option>
  <option>Pudding</option>
  <option>Ice cream</option>
</select>
```

Such a field looks like this:

Whenever the value of a form field changes, it fires a "change" event.

Focus

Unlike most elements in an HTML document, form fields can get *keyboard focus*. When clicked—or activated in some other way—they become the currently active element, the main recipient of keyboard input.

If a document has a text field, text typed will end up in there only when the field is focused. Other fields respond differently to keyboard events. For example, a <select> menu tries to move to the option that contains the text the user typed and responds to the arrow keys by moving its selection up and down.

We can control focus from JavaScript with the focus and blur methods. The first moves focus to the DOM element it is called on, and the second removes focus. The value in document.activeElement corresponds to the currently focused element.

```
<input type="text">
<script>
  document.querySelector("input").focus();
  console.log(document.activeElement.tagName);
  // ▷ INPUT
  document.querySelector("input").blur();
  console.log(document.activeElement.tagName);
  // ▷ BODY
</script>
```

For some pages, the user is expected to want to interact with a form field immediately. JavaScript can be used to focus this field when the document is loaded, but HTML also provides the autofocus attribute, which produces the same effect but lets the browser know what we are trying to achieve. This makes it possible for the browser to disable the behavior when it is not appropriate, such as when the user has focused on something else.

```
<input type="text" autofocus>
```

Browsers traditionally also allow the user to move the focus through the document by pressing the TAB key. We can influence the order in which elements receive focus with the `tabindex` attribute. The following example document will let focus jump from the text input to the OK button, rather than going through the help link first:

```
<input type="text" tabindex=1> <a href=".">(help)</a>
<button onclick="console.log('ok')" tabindex=2>OK</button>
```

By default, most types of HTML elements cannot be focused. But you can add a `tabindex` attribute to any element, which will make it focusable.

Disabled Fields

All form fields can be *disabled* through their `disabled` attribute, which also exists as a property on the element's DOM object.

```
<button>I'm all right</button>
<button disabled>I'm out</button>
```

Disabled fields cannot be focused or changed, and unlike active fields, they usually look gray and faded.

When a program is in the process of handling an action caused by some button or other control, which might require communication with the server and thus take a while, it can be a good idea to disable the control until the action finishes. That way, when the user gets impatient and clicks it again, they don't accidentally repeat their action.

The Form as a Whole

When a field is contained in a `<form>` element, its DOM element will have a property `form` linking back to the form's DOM element. The `<form>` element, in turn, has a property called `elements` that contains an array-like collection of the fields inside it.

The `name` attribute of a form field determines the way its value will be identified when the form is submitted. It can also be used as a property name when accessing the form's `elements` property, which acts both as an array-like object (accessible by number) and a map (accessible by name).

```
<form action="example/submit.html">
  Name: <input type="text" name="name"><br>
  Password: <input type="password" name="password"><br>
  <button type="submit">Log in</button>
</form>
<script>
```

```
    var form = document.querySelector("form");
    console.log(form.elements[1].type);
    // ▷ password
    console.log(form.elements.password.type);
    // ▷ password
    console.log(form.elements.name.form == form);
    // ▷ true
</script>
```

A button with a type attribute of submit will, when pressed, cause the form to be submitted. Pressing ENTER when a form field is focused has the same effect.

Submitting a form normally means that the browser navigates to the page indicated by the form's action attribute, using either a GET or a POST request. But before that happens, a "submit" event is fired. This event can be handled by JavaScript, and the handler can prevent the default behavior by calling preventDefault on the event object.

```
<form action="example/submit.html">
  Value: <input type="text" name="value">
  <button type="submit">Save</button>
</form>
<script>
  var form = document.querySelector("form");
  form.addEventListener("submit", function(event) {
    console.log("Saving value", form.elements.value.value);
    event.preventDefault();
  });
</script>
```

Intercepting "submit" events in JavaScript has various uses. We can write code to verify that the values the user entered make sense and immediately show an error message instead of submitting the form when they don't. Or we can disable the regular way of submitting the form entirely, as in the previous example, and have our program handle the input, possibly using XMLHttpRequest to send it over to a server without reloading the page.

Text Fields

Fields created by <input> tags with a type of text or password, as well as textarea tags, share a common interface. Their DOM elements have a value property that holds their current content as a string value. Setting this property to another string changes the field's content.

The selectionStart and selectionEnd properties of text fields give us information about the cursor and selection in the text. When nothing is selected, these two properties hold the same number, indicating the position of the cursor. For example, 0 indicates the start of the text, and 10 indicates that the cursor is after the 10th character. When part of the field is selected, the two properties will differ, giving us the start and end of the selected text. Like value, these properties may also be written to.

As an example, imagine you are writing an article about Khasekhemwy but have some trouble spelling his name. The following code wires up a <textarea> tag with an event handler that, when you press F2, inserts the string "Khasekhemwy" for you.

```
<textarea></textarea>
<script>
  var textarea = document.querySelector("textarea");
  textarea.addEventListener("keydown", function(event) {
    // The key code for F2 happens to be 113
    if (event.keyCode == 113) {
      replaceSelection(textarea, "Khasekhemwy");
      event.preventDefault();
    }
  });
  function replaceSelection(field, word) {
    var from = field.selectionStart, to = field.selectionEnd;
    field.value = field.value.slice(0, from) + word +
                  field.value.slice(to);
    // Put the cursor after the word
    field.selectionStart = field.selectionEnd =
      from + word.length;
  };
</script>
```

The replaceSelection function replaces the currently selected part of a text field's content with the given word and then moves the cursor after that word so that the user can continue typing.

The "change" event for a text field does not fire every time something is typed. Rather, it fires when the field loses focus after its content was changed. To respond immediately to changes in a text field, you should register a handler for the "input" event instead, which fires for every time the user types a character, deletes text, or otherwise manipulates the field's content.

The following example shows a text field and a counter showing the current length of the text entered:

```
<input type="text"> length: <span id="length">0</span>
<script>
  var text = document.querySelector("input");
  var output = document.querySelector("#length");
  text.addEventListener("input", function() {
    output.textContent = text.value.length;
  });
</script>
```

Checkboxes and Radio Buttons

A checkbox field is a simple binary toggle. Its value can be extracted or changed through its checked property, which holds a Boolean value.

```
<input type="checkbox" id="purple">
<label for="purple">Make this page purple</label>
<script>
  var checkbox = document.querySelector("#purple");
  checkbox.addEventListener("change", function() {
    document.body.style.background =
      checkbox.checked ? "mediumpurple" : "";
  });
</script>
```

The <label> tag is used to associate a piece of text with an input field. Its for attribute should refer to the id of the field. Clicking the label will activate the field, which focuses it and toggles its value when it is a checkbox or radio button.

A radio button is similar to a checkbox, but it's implicitly linked to other radio buttons with the same name attribute so that only one of them can be active at any time.

```
Color:
<input type="radio" name="color" value="mediumpurple"> Purple
<input type="radio" name="color" value="lightgreen"> Green
<input type="radio" name="color" value="lightblue"> Blue
<script>
  var buttons = document.getElementsByName("color");
  function setColor(event) {
    document.body.style.background = event.target.value;
  }
  for (var i = 0; i < buttons.length; i++)
    buttons[i].addEventListener("change", setColor);
</script>
```

The document.getElementsByName method gives us all elements with a given name attribute. The example loops over those (with a regular for loop, not forEach, because the returned collection is not a real array) and registers an event handler for each element. Remember that event objects have a target property referring to the element that triggered the event. This is often useful in event handlers like this one, which will be called on different elements and need some way to access the current target.

Select Fields

Select fields are conceptually similar to radio buttons—they also allow the user to choose from a set of options. But where a radio button puts the layout of the options under our control, the appearance of a `<select>` tag is determined by the browser.

Select fields also have a variant that is more akin to a list of checkboxes, rather than radio boxes. When given the `multiple` attribute, a `<select>` tag will allow the user to select any number of options, rather than just a single option.

```
<select multiple>
  <option>Pancakes</option>
  <option>Pudding</option>
  <option>Ice cream</option>
</select>
```

This will, in most browsers, show up differently than a non-multiple select field, which is commonly drawn as a *drop-down* control that shows the options only when you open it.

The `size` attribute to the `<select>` tag is used to set the number of options that are visible at the same time, which gives you explicit control over the drop-down's appearance. For example, setting the `size` attribute to `"3"` will make the field show three lines, whether it has the `multiple` option enabled or not.

Each `<option>` tag has a value. This value can be defined with a `value` attribute, but when that is not given, the text inside the option will count as the option's value. The `value` property of a `<select>` element reflects the currently selected option. For a `multiple` field, though, this property doesn't mean much since it will give the value of only *one* of the currently selected options.

The `<option>` tags for a `<select>` field can be accessed as an array-like object through the field's `options` property. Each option has a property called `selected`, which indicates whether that option is currently selected. The property can also be written to select or deselect an option.

The following example extracts the selected values from a `multiple` select field and uses them to compose a binary number from individual bits. Hold CTRL (or COMMAND on a Mac) to select multiple options.

```
<select multiple>
  <option value="1">0001</option>
  <option value="2">0010</option>
  <option value="4">0100</option>
  <option value="8">1000</option>
```

```
</select> = <span id="output">0</span>
<script>
  var select = document.querySelector("select");
  var output = document.querySelector("#output");
  select.addEventListener("change", function() {
    var number = 0;
    for (var i = 0; i < select.options.length; i++) {
      var option = select.options[i];
      if (option.selected)
        number += Number(option.value);
    }
    output.textContent = number;
  });
</script>
```

File Fields

File fields were originally designed as a way to upload files from the browser's machine through a form. In modern browsers, they also provide a way to read such files from JavaScript programs. The field acts as a manner of gate-keeper. The script cannot simply start reading private files from the user's computer, but if the user selects a file in such a field, the browser interprets that action to mean that the script may read the file.

A file field usually looks like a button labeled with something like "choose file" or "browse," with information about the chosen file next to it.

```
<input type="file">
<script>
  var input = document.querySelector("input");
  input.addEventListener("change", function() {
    if (input.files.length > 0) {
      var file = input.files[0];
      console.log("You chose", file.name);
      if (file.type)
        console.log("It has type", file.type);
    }
  });
</script>
```

The files property of a file field element is an array-like object (again, not a real array) containing the files chosen in the field. It is initially empty. The reason there isn't simply a file property is that file fields also support a multiple attribute, which makes it possible to select multiple files at the same time.

Objects in the files property have properties such as name (the filename), size (the file's size in bytes), and type (the media type of the file, such as text/plain or image/jpeg).

What it does not have is a property that contains the content of the file. Getting at that is a little more involved. Since reading a file from disk can take time, the interface will have to be asynchronous to avoid freezing the document. You can think of the `FileReader` constructor as being similar to `XMLHttpRequest` but for files.

```
<input type="file" multiple>
<script>
  var input = document.querySelector("input");
  input.addEventListener("change", function() {
    Array.prototype.forEach.call(input.files, function(file) {
      var reader = new FileReader();
      reader.addEventListener("load", function() {
        console.log("File", file.name, "starts with",
                    reader.result.slice(0, 20));
      });
      reader.readAsText(file);
    });
  });
</script>
```

Reading a file is done by creating a `FileReader` object, registering a `"load"` event handler for it, and calling its `readAsText` method, giving it the file we want to read. Once loading finishes, the reader's `result` property contains the file's content.

The example uses `Array.prototype.forEach` to iterate over the array since in a normal loop it would be awkward to get the correct `file` and `reader` objects from the event handler. The variables would be shared by all iterations of the loop.

FileReaders also fire an `"error"` event when reading the file fails for any reason. The error object itself will end up in the reader's `error` property. If you don't want to remember the details of yet another inconsistent asynchronous interface, you could wrap it in a `Promise` (see Chapter 17) like this:

```
function readFile(file) {
  return new Promise(function(succeed, fail) {
    var reader = new FileReader();
    reader.addEventListener("load", function() {
      succeed(reader.result);
    });
    reader.addEventListener("error", function() {
      fail(reader.error);
    });
    reader.readAsText(file);
  });
}
```

It is possible to read only part of a file by calling slice on it and passing the result (a so-called *blob* object) to the file reader.

Storing Data Client-Side

Simple HTML pages with a bit of JavaScript can be a great medium for "mini applications"—small helper programs that automate everyday things. By connecting a few form fields with event handlers, you can do anything from converting between degrees Celsius and Fahrenheit to computing passwords from a master password and a website name.

When such an application needs to remember something between sessions, you cannot use JavaScript variables since those are thrown away every time a page is closed. You could set up a server, connect it to the Internet, and have your application store something there. We will see how to do that in Chapter 20. But this adds a lot of extra work and complexity. Sometimes it is enough to just keep the data in the browser. But how?

You can store string data in a way that survives page reloads by putting it in the localStorage object. This object allows you to file string values under names (also strings), as in this example:

```
localStorage.setItem("username", "marijn");
console.log(localStorage.getItem("username"));
// ▷ marijn
localStorage.removeItem("username");
```

A value in localStorage sticks around until it is overwritten, it is removed with removeItem, or the user clears their local data.

Sites from different domains get different storage compartments. That means data stored in localStorage by a given website can, in principle, only be read (and overwritten) by scripts on that same site.

Browsers also enforce a limit on the size of the data a site can store in localStorage, typically on the order of a few megabytes. That restriction, along with the fact that filling up people's hard drives with junk is not really profitable, prevents this feature from eating up too much space.

The following code implements a simple note-taking application. It keeps the user's notes as an object, associating note titles with content strings. This object is encoded as JSON and stored in localStorage. The user can select a note from a <select> field and change that note's text in a <textarea>. A note can be added by clicking a button.

```
Notes: <select id="list"></select>
<button onclick="addNote()">new</button><br>
<textarea id="currentnote" style="width: 100%; height: 10em">
</textarea>

<script>
  var list = document.querySelector("#list");
```

```
function addToList(name) {
  var option = document.createElement("option");
  option.textContent = name;
  list.appendChild(option);
}

// Initialize the list from localStorage
var notes = JSON.parse(localStorage.getItem("notes")) ||
            {"shopping list": ""};
for (var name in notes)
  if (notes.hasOwnProperty(name))
    addToList(name);

function saveToStorage() {
  localStorage.setItem("notes", JSON.stringify(notes));
}

var current = document.querySelector("#currentnote");
current.value = notes[list.value];

list.addEventListener("change", function() {
  current.value = notes[list.value];
});
current.addEventListener("change", function() {
  notes[list.value] = current.value;
  saveToStorage();
});

function addNote() {
  var name = prompt("Note name", "");
  if (!name) return;
  if (!notes.hasOwnProperty(name)) {
    notes[name] = "";
    addToList(name);
    saveToStorage();
  }
  list.value = name;
  current.value = notes[name];
}
</script>
```

The script initializes the notes variable to the value stored in localStorage or, if that is missing, to a simple object with only an empty "shopping list" note in it. Reading a field that does not exist from localStorage will yield null. Passing null to JSON.parse will make it parse the string "null" and return null. Thus, the || operator can be used to provide a default value in a situation like this.

Whenever the note data changes (when a new note is added or an existing note changed), the saveToStorage function is called to update the storage field. If this application was intended to handle thousands of notes, rather than a handful, this would be too expensive, and we'd have to come up with a more complicated way to store them, such as giving each note its own storage field.

When the user adds a new note, the code must update the text field explicitly, even though the <select> field has a "change" handler that does the same thing. This is necessary because "change" events fire only when the *user* changes the field's value, not when a script does it.

There is another object similar to localStorage called sessionStorage. The difference between the two is that the content of sessionStorage is forgotten at the end of each session, which for most browsers means whenever the browser is closed.

Summary

HTML can express various types of form fields, such as text fields, checkboxes, multiple-choice fields, and file pickers.

Such fields can be inspected and manipulated with JavaScript. They fire the "change" event when changed, the "input" event when text is typed, and various keyboard events. These events allow us to notice when the user is interacting with the fields. Properties like value (for text and select fields) or checked (for checkboxes and radio buttons) are used to read or set the field's content.

When a form is submitted, its "submit" event fires. A JavaScript handler can call preventDefault on that event to prevent the submission from happening. Form field elements do not have to be wrapped in <form> tags.

When the user has selected a file from their local filesystem in a file picker field, the FileReader interface can be used to access the content of this file from a JavaScript program.

The localStorage and sessionStorage objects can be used to save information in a way that survives page reloads. The first saves the data forever (or until the user decides to clear it), and the second saves it until the browser is closed.

Exercises

A JavaScript Workbench

Build an interface that allows people to type and run pieces of JavaScript code.

Put a button next to a <textarea> field, which, when pressed, uses the Function constructor we saw in Chapter 10 to wrap the text in a function and call it. Convert the return value of the function, or any error it raised, to a string and display it after the text field.

Autocompletion

Extend a text field so that when the user types, a list of suggested values is shown below the field. You have an array of possible values available and should show those that start with the text that was typed. When a suggestion is clicked, replace the text field's current value with it.

Conway's Game of Life

Conway's Game of Life is a simple simulation that creates artificial life on a grid, each cell of which is either live or not. Each generation (turn), the following rules are applied:

- Any live cell with fewer than two or more than three live neighbors dies.
- Any live cell with two or three live neighbors lives on to the next generation.
- Any dead cell with exactly three live neighbors becomes a live cell.

A neighbor is defined as any adjacent cell, including diagonally adjacent ones.

Note that these rules are applied to the whole grid at once, not one square at a time. That means the counting of neighbors is based on the situation at the start of the generation, and changes happening to neighbor cells during this generation should not influence the new state of a given cell.

Implement this game using whichever data structure you find appropriate. Use `Math.random` to populate the grid with a random pattern initially. Display it as a grid of checkbox fields, with a button next to it to advance to the next generation. When the user checks or unchecks the checkboxes, their changes should be included when computing the next generation.

"I look at the many colors before me. I look at my blank canvas. Then, I try to apply colors like words that shape poems, like notes that shape music."

—Joan Miro

19

PROJECT: A PAINT PROGRAM

The material from the previous chapters gives you all the elements you need to build a simple web application. In this chapter, we will do just that.

Our application will be a web-based drawing program, along the lines of Microsoft Paint. You can use it to open image files, scribble on them with your mouse, and save them. This is what it will look like:

Painting on a computer is great. You don't need to worry about materials, skill, or talent. You just start smearing.

Implementation

The interface for the paint program shows a big <canvas> element on top, with a number of form fields below it. The user draws on the picture by selecting a tool from a <select> field and then clicking or dragging across the canvas. There are tools for drawing lines, erasing parts of the picture, adding text, and so on.

Clicking the canvas will hand off the "mousedown" event to the currently selected tool, which can handle it in whichever way it chooses. The line drawing tool, for example, will listen for "mousemove" events until the mouse button is released and draw lines along the mouse's path using the current color and brush size.

Color and brush size are selected with additional form fields. These are hooked up to update the canvas drawing context's fillStyle, strokeStyle, and lineWidth whenever they are changed.

You can load an image into the program in two ways. The first uses a file field, where the user can select a file on their own filesystem. The second asks for a URL and will fetch an image from the Web.

Images are saved in a somewhat atypical way. The save link at the right side points at the current image. It can be followed, shared, or saved. I will explain how this is achieved in a moment.

Building the DOM

Our program's interface is built from more than 30 DOM elements. We need to construct these somehow.

HTML is the most obvious format for defining complex DOM structures. But separating the program into a piece of HTML and a script is made difficult by the fact that many of the DOM elements need event handlers or have to be touched by the script in some other way. Thus, our script would have to make lots of querySelector (or similar) calls in order to find the DOM elements that it needs to act on.

It would be nice if the DOM structure for each part of our interface is defined close to the JavaScript code that drives it. Thus, I've chosen to do all creation of DOM nodes in JavaScript. As we saw in Chapter 13, the built-in interface for building up a DOM structure is horrendously verbose. If we are going to do a lot of DOM construction, we need a helper function.

This helper function is an extended version of the elt function from Chapter 13. It creates an element with the given name and attributes and appends all further arguments it gets as child nodes, automatically converting strings to text nodes.

```
function elt(name, attributes) {
  var node = document.createElement(name);
```

```
  if (attributes) {
    for (var attr in attributes)
      if (attributes.hasOwnProperty(attr))
        node.setAttribute(attr, attributes[attr]);
  }
  for (var i = 2; i < arguments.length; i++) {
    var child = arguments[i];
    if (typeof child == "string")
      child = document.createTextNode(child);
    node.appendChild(child);
  }
  return node;
}
```

This allows us to create elements easily, without making our source code as long and dull as a corporate end-user agreement.

The Foundation

The core of our program is the createPaint function, which appends the paint interface to the DOM element it is given as an argument. Because we want to build our program piece by piece, we define an object called controls, which will hold functions to initialize the various controls below the image.

```
var controls = Object.create(null);

function createPaint(parent) {
  var canvas = elt("canvas", {width: 500, height: 300});
  var cx = canvas.getContext("2d");
  var toolbar = elt("div", {class: "toolbar"});
  for (var name in controls)
    toolbar.appendChild(controls[name](cx));

  var panel = elt("div", {class: "picturepanel"}, canvas);
  parent.appendChild(elt("div", null, panel, toolbar));
}
```

Each control has access to the canvas drawing context and, through that context's canvas property, to the <canvas> element. Most of the program's state lives in this canvas—it contains the current picture as well as the selected color (in its fillStyle property) and brush size (in its lineWidth property).

We wrap the canvas and the controls in <div> elements with classes so we can add some styling, such as a gray border around the picture.

Tool Selection

The first control we add is the <select> element that allows the user to pick a drawing tool. As with controls, we will use an object to collect the various tools so that we do not have to hard-code them all in one place and can add more tools later. This object associates the names of the tools with the function that should be called when they are selected and the canvas is clicked.

```
var tools = Object.create(null);

controls.tool = function(cx) {
  var select = elt("select");
  for (var name in tools)
    select.appendChild(elt("option", null, name));

  cx.canvas.addEventListener("mousedown", function(event) {
    if (event.which == 1) {
      tools[select.value](event, cx);
      event.preventDefault();
    }
  });

  return elt("span", null, "Tool: ", select);
};
```

The tool field is populated with <option> elements for all tools that have been defined, and a "mousedown" handler on the canvas element takes care of calling the function for the current tool, passing it both the event object and the drawing context as arguments. It also calls preventDefault so that holding the mouse button and dragging does not cause the browser to select parts of the page.

The most basic tool is the line tool, which allows the user to draw lines with the mouse. To put the line ends in the right place, we need to find the canvas-relative coordinates that a given mouse event corresponds to. The getBoundingClientRect method, briefly mentioned in Chapter 13, can help us here. It tells us where an element is shown, relative to the top-left corner of the screen. The clientX and clientY properties on mouse events are also relative to this corner, so we can subtract the top-left corner of the canvas from them to get a position relative to that corner.

```
function relativePos(event, element) {
  var rect = element.getBoundingClientRect();
  return {x: Math.floor(event.clientX - rect.left),
          y: Math.floor(event.clientY - rect.top)};
}
```

Several of the drawing tools need to listen for "mousemove" events as long as the mouse button is held down. The trackDrag function takes care of the event registration and unregistration for such situations.

```
function trackDrag(onMove, onEnd) {
  function end(event) {
    removeEventListener("mousemove", onMove);
    removeEventListener("mouseup", end);
    if (onEnd)
      onEnd(event);
  }
  addEventListener("mousemove", onMove);
  addEventListener("mouseup", end);
}
```

This function takes two arguments. One is a function to call for each "mousemove" event, and the other is a function to call when the mouse button is released. Either argument can be omitted when it is not needed.

The line tool uses these two helpers to do the actual drawing.

```
tools.Line = function(event, cx, onEnd) {
  cx.lineCap = "round";

  var pos = relativePos(event, cx.canvas);
  trackDrag(function(event) {
    cx.beginPath();
    cx.moveTo(pos.x, pos.y);
    pos = relativePos(event, cx.canvas);
    cx.lineTo(pos.x, pos.y);
    cx.stroke();
  }, onEnd);
};
```

The function starts by setting the drawing context's lineCap property to "round", which causes both ends of a stroked path to be round rather than the default square form. This is a trick to make sure that multiple separate lines, drawn in response to separate events, look like a single, coherent line. With bigger line widths, you will see gaps at corners if you use the default flat line caps.

Then, for every "mousemove" event that occurs as long as the mouse button is down, a simple line segment is drawn between the mouse's old and new position, using whatever strokeStyle and lineWidth happen to be currently set.

The onEnd argument to tools.Line is simply passed through to trackDrag. The normal way to run tools won't pass a third argument, so when using the line tool, that argument will hold undefined, and nothing happens at the end of the mouse drag. The argument is there to allow us to implement the erase tool on top of the line tool with very little additional code.

```
tools.Erase = function(event, cx) {
  cx.globalCompositeOperation = "destination-out";
  tools.Line(event, cx, function() {
    cx.globalCompositeOperation = "source-over";
  });
};
```

The `globalCompositeOperation` property influences the way drawing operations on a canvas change the color of the pixels they touch. By default, the property's value is "source-over", which means that the drawn color is overlaid on the existing color at that spot. If the color is opaque, it will simply replace the old color, but if it is partially transparent, the two will be mixed.

The erase tool sets `globalCompositeOperation` to "destination-out", which has the effect of erasing the pixels we touch, making them transparent again.

That gives us two tools in our paint program. We can draw black lines a single pixel wide (the default `strokeStyle` and `lineWidth` for a canvas) and erase them again. It is a working, albeit rather limited, paint program.

Color and Brush Size

Assuming that users will want to draw in colors other than black and use different brush sizes, let's add controls for those two settings.

In Chapter 18, I discussed a number of different form fields. Color fields were not among those. Traditionally, browsers don't have built-in support for color pickers, but in the past few years, a number of new form field types have been standardized. One of those is `<input type="color">`. Others include "date", "email", "url", and "number". Not all browsers support them yet—at the time of writing, no version of Internet Explorer supports color fields. The default type of an `<input>` tag is "text", and when an unsupported type is used, browsers will treat it as a text field. This means that Internet Explorer users running our paint program will have to type in the name of the color they want, rather than select it from a convenient widget.

This is what a color picker may look like:

```
controls.color = function(cx) {
  var input = elt("input", {type: "color"});
  input.addEventListener("change", function() {
    cx.fillStyle = input.value;
    cx.strokeStyle = input.value;
  });
  return elt("span", null, "Color: ", input);
};
```

Whenever the value of the color field changes, the drawing context's fillStyle and strokeStyle are updated to hold the new value.

The field for configuring the brush size works similarly.

```
controls.brushSize = function(cx) {
  var select = elt("select");
  var sizes = [1, 2, 3, 5, 8, 12, 25, 35, 50, 75, 100];
  sizes.forEach(function(size) {
    select.appendChild(elt("option", {value: size},
                           size + " pixels"));
  });
  select.addEventListener("change", function() {
    cx.lineWidth = select.value;
  });
  return elt("span", null, "Brush size: ", select);
};
```

The code generates options from an array of brush sizes, and again ensures that the canvas's lineWidth updates when a brush size is chosen.

Saving

To explain the implementation of the save link, I must first tell you about *data URLs*. A data URL is a URL with *data:* as its protocol. Unlike regular *http:* and *https:* URLs, data URLs don't point at a resource but rather contain the entire resource in them. This is a data URL containing a simple HTML document:

```
data:text/html,<h1 style="color:red">Hello!</h1>
```

Data URLs are useful for various tasks, such as including small images directly in a style sheet file. They also allow us to link to files that we created on the client side, in the browser, without first moving them to some server.

Canvas elements have a convenient method, called toDataURL, which will return a data URL that contains the picture on the canvas as an image file. We don't want to update our save link every time the picture is changed, however. For big pictures, that involves moving quite a lot of data into a link and would be noticeably slow. Instead, we rig the link to update its `href` attribute whenever it is focused with the keyboard or the mouse is moved over it.

```
controls.save = function(cx) {
  var link = elt("a", {href: "/"}, "Save");
  function update() {
    try {
      link.href = cx.canvas.toDataURL();
    } catch (e) {
      if (e instanceof SecurityError)
        link.href = "javascript:alert(" +
          JSON.stringify("Can't save: " + e.toString()) + ")";
      else
        throw e;
    }
  }
  link.addEventListener("mouseover", update);
  link.addEventListener("focus", update);
  return link;
};
```

Thus, the link just quietly sits there, pointing at the wrong thing, but when the user approaches it, it magically updates itself to point at the current picture.

If you load a big image, some browsers will choke on the giant data URLs that this produces. For small pictures, this approach works without problem.

But here we once again run into the subtleties of browser sandboxing. When an image is loaded from a URL on another domain, if the server's response doesn't include a header that tells the browser the resource may be used from other domains (see Chapter 17), then the canvas will contain information that the *user* may look at but that the *script* may not.

We may have requested a picture that contains private information (for example, a graph showing the user's bank account balance) using the user's session. If scripts could get information out of that picture, they could snoop on the user in undesirable ways.

To prevent these kinds of information leaks, browsers will mark a canvas as *tainted* when an image that the script may not see is drawn onto it. Pixel data, including data URLs, may not be extracted from a tainted canvas. You can write to it, but you can no longer read it.

This is why we need the try/catch statement in the `update` function for the save link. When the canvas has become tainted, calling `toDataURL` will raise an exception that is an instance of `SecurityError`. When that happens, we set the link to point at yet another kind of URL, using the *javascript:* protocol. Such links simply execute the script given after the colon when they are followed so that the link will show an `alert` window informing the user of the problem when it is clicked.

Loading Image Files

The final two controls are used to load images from local files and from URLs. We'll need the following helper function, which tries to load an image file from a URL and replace the contents of the canvas with it:

```
function loadImageURL(cx, url) {
  var image = document.createElement("img");
  image.addEventListener("load", function() {
    var color = cx.fillStyle, size = cx.lineWidth;
    cx.canvas.width = image.width;
    cx.canvas.height = image.height;
    cx.drawImage(image, 0, 0);
    cx.fillStyle = color;
    cx.strokeStyle = color;
    cx.lineWidth = size;
  });
  image.src = url;
}
```

We want to change the size of the canvas to precisely fit the image. For some reason, changing the size of a canvas will cause its drawing context to forget configuration properties such as fillStyle and lineWidth, so the function saves those and restores them after it has updated the canvas size.

The control for loading a local file uses the FileReader technique from Chapter 18. Apart from the readAsText method we used there, such reader objects also have a method called readAsDataURL, which is exactly what we need here. We load the file that the user chose as a data URL and pass it to loadImageURL to put it into the canvas.

```
controls.openFile = function(cx) {
  var input = elt("input", {type: "file"});
  input.addEventListener("change", function() {
    if (input.files.length == 0) return;
    var reader = new FileReader();
    reader.addEventListener("load", function() {
      loadImageURL(cx, reader.result);
    });
    reader.readAsDataURL(input.files[0]);
  });
  return elt("div", null, "Open file: ", input);
};
```

Loading a file from a URL is even simpler. But with a text field, it is less clear when the user has finished writing the URL, so we can't simply listen for "change" events. Instead, we will wrap the field in a form and respond when the form is submitted, either because the user pressed ENTER or because they clicked the load button.

```
controls.openURL = function(cx) {
  var input = elt("input", {type: "text"});
  var form = elt("form", null,
                 "Open URL: ", input,
                 elt("button", {type: "submit"}, "load"));
  form.addEventListener("submit", function(event) {
    event.preventDefault();
    loadImageURL(cx, form.querySelector("input").value);
  });
  return form;
};
```

We have now defined all the controls that our simple paint program needs, but it could still use a few more tools.

Finishing Up

We can easily add a text tool that uses prompt to ask the user which string it should draw.

```
tools.Text = function(event, cx) {
  var text = prompt("Text:", "");
  if (text) {
    var pos = relativePos(event, cx.canvas);
    cx.font = Math.max(7, cx.lineWidth) + "px sans-serif";
    cx.fillText(text, pos.x, pos.y);
  }
};
```

You could add extra fields for the font size and the font, but for simplicity's sake, we always use a sans-serif font and base the font size on the current brush size. The minimum size is 7 pixels because text smaller than that is unreadable.

Another indispensable tool for drawing amateurish computer graphics is the spray paint tool. This one draws dots in random locations under the brush as long as the mouse is held down, creating denser or less dense speckling based on how fast or slow the mouse moves.

```
tools.Spray = function(event, cx) {
  var radius = cx.lineWidth / 2;
  var area = radius * radius * Math.PI;
  var dotsPerTick = Math.ceil(area / 30);

  var currentPos = relativePos(event, cx.canvas);
  var spray = setInterval(function() {
    for (var i = 0; i < dotsPerTick; i++) {
      var offset = randomPointInRadius(radius);
```

```
      cx.fillRect(currentPos.x + offset.x,
                  currentPos.y + offset.y, 1, 1);
    }
  }, 25);
  trackDrag(function(event) {
    currentPos = relativePos(event, cx.canvas);
  }, function() {
    clearInterval(spray);
  });
};
```

The spray tool uses `setInterval` to spit out colored dots every 25 milliseconds as long as the mouse button is held down. The `trackDrag` function is used to keep `currentPos` pointing at the current mouse position and to turn off the interval when the mouse button is released.

To determine how many dots to draw every time the interval fires, the function computes the area of the current brush and divides that by 30. To find a random position under the brush, the `randomPointInRadius` function is used.

```
function randomPointInRadius(radius) {
  for (;;) {
    var x = Math.random() * 2 - 1;
    var y = Math.random() * 2 - 1;
    if (x * x + y * y <= 1)
      return {x: x * radius, y: y * radius};
  }
}
```

This function generates points in the square between $(-1,-1)$ and $(1,1)$. Using the Pythagorean theorem, it tests whether the generated point lies within a circle of radius 1. As soon as the function finds such a point, it returns the point multiplied by the radius argument.

The loop is necessary for a uniform distribution of dots. The straightforward way of generating a random point within a circle would be to use a random angle and distance and call `Math.sin` and `Math.cos` to create the corresponding point. But with that method, the dots are more likely to appear near the center of the circle. There are other ways around that, but they're more complicated than the previous loop.

We now have a functioning paint program.

Exercises

There is still plenty of room for improvement in this program. Let's add a few more features as exercises.

Rectangles

Define a tool called `Rectangle` that fills a rectangle (see the `fillRect` method from Chapter 16) with the current color. The rectangle should span from the point where the user pressed the mouse button to the point where they released it. Note that the latter might be above or to the left of the former.

Once it works, you'll notice that it is somewhat jarring to not see the rectangle as you are dragging the mouse to select its size. Can you come up with a way to show some kind of rectangle during the dragging, without actually drawing to the canvas until the mouse button is released?

If nothing comes to mind, think back to the `position: absolute` style discussed in Chapter 13, which can be used to overlay a node on the rest of the document. The `pageX` and `pageY` properties of a mouse event can be used to position an element precisely under the mouse, by setting the `left`, `top`, `width`, and `height` styles to the correct pixel values.

Color Picker

Another tool that is commonly found in graphics programs is a color picker, which allows the user to click the picture and selects the color under the mouse pointer. Build this.

For this tool, we need a way to access the content of the canvas. The `toDataURL` method more or less did that, but getting pixel information out of such a data URL is hard. Instead, we'll use the `getImageData` method on the drawing context, which returns a rectangular piece of the image as an object with `width`, `height`, and `data` properties. The `data` property holds an array of numbers from 0 to 255, using four numbers to represent each pixel's red, green, blue, and alpha (opaqueness) components.

This example retrieves the numbers for a single pixel from a canvas once when the canvas is blank (all pixels are transparent black) and once when the pixel has been colored red.

```
function pixelAt(cx, x, y) {
  var data = cx.getImageData(x, y, 1, 1);
  console.log(data.data);
}

var canvas = document.createElement("canvas");
var cx = canvas.getContext("2d");
pixelAt(cx, 10, 10);
// ▷ [0, 0, 0, 0]

cx.fillStyle = "red";
cx.fillRect(10, 10, 1, 1);
pixelAt(cx, 10, 10);
// ▷ [255, 0, 0, 255]
```

The arguments to getImageData indicate the starting x- and y-coordinates of the rectangle we want to retrieve, followed by its width and height.

Ignore transparency during this exercise and look only at the first three values for a given pixel. Also, do not worry about updating the color field when the user picks a color. Just make sure that the drawing context's fillStyle and strokeStyle are set to the color under the mouse cursor.

Remember that these properties accept any color that CSS understands, which includes the rgb(R, G, B) style you saw in Chapter 15.

The getImageData method is subject to the same restrictions as toDataURL—it will raise an error when the canvas contains pixels that originate from another domain. Use a try/catch statement to report such errors with an alert dialog.

Flood Fill

This is a more advanced exercise than the preceding two, and it will require you to design a nontrivial solution to a tricky problem. Make sure you have plenty of time and patience before starting to work on this exercise, and do not get discouraged by initial failures.

A flood fill tool colors the pixel under the mouse and the surrounding pixels of the same color. For the purpose of this exercise, we will consider such a group to include all pixels that can be reached from our starting pixel by moving in single-pixel horizontal and vertical steps (not diagonal), without ever touching a pixel that has a color different from the starting pixel.

The following image illustrates the set of pixels colored when the flood fill tool is used at the marked pixel:

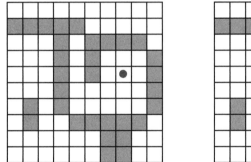 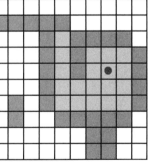

The flood fill does not leak through diagonal gaps and does not touch pixels that are not reachable, even if they have the same color as the target pixel.

You will once again need getImageData to find out the color for each pixel. It is probably a good idea to fetch the whole image in one go and then pick out pixel data from the resulting array. The pixels are organized in this array in a similar way to the grid elements in Chapter 7, one row at a time, except that each pixel is represented by four values. The first value for the pixel at (x,y) is at position $(x + y \times \text{width}) \times 4$.

Do include the fourth (alpha) value this time since we want to be able to tell the difference between empty and black pixels.

Finding all adjacent pixels with the same color requires you to "walk" over the pixel surface, one pixel up, down, left, or right, as long as new same-colored pixels can be found. But you won't find all pixels in a group on the first walk. Rather, you have to do something similar to the backtracking done by the regular expression matcher, described in Chapter 9. Whenever more than one possible direction to proceed is seen, you must store all the directions you do not take immediately and look at them later, when you finish your current walk.

In a normal-sized picture, there are a *lot* of pixels. Thus, you must take care to do the minimal amount of work required or your program will take a very long time to run. For example, every walk must ignore pixels seen by previous walks so that it does not redo work that has already been done.

I recommend calling fillRect for individual pixels when a pixel that should be colored is found, and keeping some data structure that tells you about all the pixels that have already been looked at.

PART III

BEYOND

"A student asked 'The programmers of old used only simple machines and no programming languages, yet they made beautiful programs. Why do we use complicated machines and programming languages?' Fu-Tzu replied 'The builders of old used only sticks and clay, yet they made beautiful huts.'"

—Master Yuan-Ma, *The Book of Programming*

20

NODE.JS

So far, you have learned the JavaScript language and used it within a single environment: the browser. This chapter and the next one will briefly introduce you to Node.js, a program that allows you to apply your JavaScript skills outside of the browser. With it, you can build anything from simple command-line tools to dynamic HTTP servers.

These chapters aim to teach you the important ideas that Node.js builds on and to give you enough information to write some useful programs for it. They do not try to be a complete, or even a thorough, treatment of Node.

If you want to follow along and run the code in this chapter, start by going to *http://nodejs.org/* and following the installation instructions for your operating system. Also refer to that website for further documentation about Node and its built-in modules.

Background

One of the more difficult problems with writing systems that communicate over the network is managing input and output—that is, the reading and writing of data to and from the network, the hard drive, and other such devices. Moving data around takes time, and scheduling it cleverly can make a big difference in how quickly a system responds to the user or to network requests.

The traditional way to handle input and output is to have a function, such as `readFile`, start reading a file and return only when the file has been fully read. This is called *synchronous I/O* (I/O stands for input/output).

Node was initially conceived for the purpose of making *asynchronous* I/O easy and convenient. We have seen asynchronous interfaces before, such as a browser's `XMLHttpRequest` object, discussed in Chapter 17. An asynchronous interface allows the script to continue running while it does its work and calls a callback function when it's done. This is the way Node does all its I/O.

JavaScript lends itself well to a system like Node. It is one of the few programming languages that does not have a built-in way to do I/O. Thus, JavaScript could be fit onto Node's rather eccentric approach to I/O without ending up with two inconsistent interfaces. In 2009, when Node was being designed, people were already doing callback-based I/O in the browser, so the community around the language was used to an asynchronous programming style.

Asynchronicity

I'll try to illustrate synchronous versus asynchronous I/O with a small example, where a program needs to fetch two resources from the Internet and then do some simple processing with the result.

In a synchronous environment, the obvious way to perform this task is to make the requests one after the other. This method has the drawback that the second request will be started only when the first has finished. The total time taken will be at least the sum of the two response times. This is not an effective use of the machine, which will be mostly idle when it is transmitting and receiving data over the network.

The solution to this problem, in a synchronous system, is to start additional threads of control. (Refer to Chapter 14 for a previous discussion of threads.) A second thread could start the second request, and then both threads wait for their results to come back, after which they resynchronize to combine their results.

In the following diagram, the thick lines represent time the program spends running normally, and the thin lines represent time spent waiting for I/O. In the synchronous model, the time taken by I/O is *part* of the timeline for a given thread of control. In the asynchronous model, starting an I/O action conceptually causes a *split* in the timeline. The thread that initiated the I/O continues running, and the I/O itself is done alongside it, finally calling a callback function when it is finished.

Synchronous, single thread of control

Synchronous, two threads of control

Asynchronous

Another way to express this difference is that waiting for I/O to finish is *implicit* in the synchronous model, while it is *explicit*, directly under our control, in the asynchronous one. But asynchronicity cuts both ways. It makes expressing programs that do not fit the straight-line model of control easier, but it also makes expressing programs that do follow a straight line more awkward.

In Chapter 17, I already touched on the fact that all those callbacks add quite a lot of noise and indirection to a program. Whether this style of asynchronicity is a good idea in general can be debated. In any case, it takes some getting used to.

But for a JavaScript-based system, I would argue that callback-style asynchronicity is a sensible choice. One of the strengths of JavaScript is its simplicity, and trying to add multiple threads of control to it would add a lot of complexity. Though callbacks don't tend to lead to simple *code*, as a *concept*, they're pleasantly simple yet powerful enough to write high-performance web servers.

The node Command

When Node.js is installed on a system, it provides a program called node, which is used to run JavaScript files. Say you have a file hello.js, containing this code:

```
var message = "Hello world";
console.log(message);
```

You can then run node from the command line like this to execute the program:

```
$ node hello.js
Hello world
```

The console.log method in Node does something similar to what it does in the browser. It prints out a piece of text. But in Node, the text will go to the process's standard output stream, rather than to a browser's JavaScript console.

If you run `node` without giving it a file, it provides you with a prompt at which you can type JavaScript code and immediately see the result.

```
$ node
> 1 + 1
2
> [-1, -2, -3].map(Math.abs)
[1, 2, 3]
> process.exit(0)
$
```

The `process` variable, just like the `console` variable, is available globally in Node. It provides various ways to inspect and manipulate the current program. The `exit` method ends the process and can be given an exit status code, which tells the program that started `node` (in this case, the command-line shell) whether the program completed successfully (code zero) or encountered an error (any other code).

To find the command-line arguments given to your script, you can read `process.argv`, which is an array of strings. Note that it also includes the name of the `node` commands and your script name, so the actual arguments start at index 2. If `showargv.js` simply contains the statement `console.log(process.argv)`, you could run it like this:

```
$ node showargv.js one --and two
["node", "/home/marijn/showargv.js", "one", "--and", "two"]
```

All the standard JavaScript global variables, such as `Array`, `Math`, and `JSON`, are also present in Node's environment. Browser-related functionality, such as `document` and `alert`, is absent.

The global scope object, which is called `window` in the browser, has the more sensible name `global` in Node.

Modules

Beyond the few variables I mentioned, such as `console` and `process`, Node puts little functionality in the global scope. If you want to access other built-in functionality, you have to ask the module system for it.

The CommonJS module system, based on the `require` function, was described in Chapter 10. This system is built into Node and is used to load anything from built-in modules to downloaded libraries to files that are part of your own program.

When `require` is called, Node has to resolve the given string to an actual file to load. Pathnames that start with "/", "./", or "../" are resolved relative to the current module's path, where "./" stands for the current directory, "../" for one directory up, and "/" for the root of the filesystem. So if you ask for "./world/world" from the file /home/marijn/elife/run.js, Node will try to load the file /home/marijn/elife/world/world.js. The .js extension may be omitted.

When a string that does not look like a relative or absolute path is given to require, it is assumed to refer to either a built-in module or a module installed in a node_modules directory. For example, require("fs") will give you Node's built-in filesystem module, and require("elife") will try to load the library found in node_modules/elife/. A common way to install such libraries is by using NPM, which I will discuss in a moment.

To illustrate the use of require, let's set up a simple project consisting of two files. The first one is called main.js, which defines a script that can be called from the command line to garble a string.

```
var garble = require("./garble");

// Index 2 holds the first actual command-line argument
var argument = process.argv[2];

console.log(garble(argument));
```

The file garble.js defines a library for garbling strings, which can be used both by the command-line tool defined earlier and by other scripts that need direct access to a garbling function.

```
module.exports = function(string) {
  return string.split("").map(function(ch) {
    return String.fromCharCode(ch.charCodeAt(0) + 5);
  }).join("");
};
```

Remember that replacing module.exports, rather than adding properties to it, allows us to export a specific value from a module. In this case, we make the result of requiring our garble file the garbling function itself.

The function splits the string it is given into single characters by splitting on the empty string and then replaces each character with the character whose code is five points higher. Finally, it joins the result back into a string.

We can now call our tool like this:

```
$ node main.js JavaScript
Of{fXhwnuy
```

Installing with NPM

NPM, which was briefly discussed in Chapter 10, is an online repository of JavaScript modules, many of which are specifically written for Node. When you install Node on your computer, you also get a program called npm, which provides a convenient interface to this repository.

For example, one module you will find on NPM is `figlet`, which can convert text into *ASCII art*—drawings made out of text characters. The following transcript shows how to install and use it:

```
$ npm install figlet
npm GET https://registry.npmjs.org/figlet
npm 200 https://registry.npmjs.org/figlet
npm GET https://registry.npmjs.org/figlet/-/figlet-1.0.9.tgz
npm 200 https://registry.npmjs.org/figlet/-/figlet-1.0.9.tgz
figlet@1.0.9 node_modules/figlet
$ node
> var figlet = require("figlet");
> figlet.text("Hello world!", function(error, data) {
    if (error)
      console.error(error);
    else
      console.log(data);
  });

 _   _          _   _                       _       _   _ _
| | | |  ___  | | | |  ___     _    _      __      __   _  _  _| | _| | |
| | |_| |/ _ \ | | |/ _ \    \ \  /\ / /  _  \ | '_  \ |  / _ `  | |
|  _  | |  _/ | | (_) |   \ V  V / (_) |  | |  | | (_|  |_|
|_| |_|\___|_|_|\___/     \_/\_/ \___/|_|  |_|\_,_(_)
```

After running `npm install`, NPM will have created a directory called `node_modules`. Inside that directory will be a `figlet` directory, which contains the library. When we run `node` and call `require("figlet")`, this library is loaded, and we can call its `text` method to draw some big letters.

Somewhat unexpectedly perhaps, instead of simply returning the string that makes up the big letters, `figlet.text` takes a callback function that it passes its result to. It also passes the callback another argument, `error`, which will hold an error object when something goes wrong or null when everything is all right.

This is a common pattern in Node code. Rendering something with `figlet` requires the library to read a file that contains the letter shapes. Reading that file from disk is an asynchronous operation in Node, so `figlet.text` can't immediately return its result. Asynchronicity is infectious, in a way—every function that calls an asynchronous function must itself become asynchronous.

There is much more to NPM than `npm install`. It reads `package.json` files, which contain JSON-encoded information about a program or library, such as which other libraries it depends on. Doing `npm install` in a directory that contains such a file will automatically install all dependencies, as well as *their* dependencies. The `npm` tool is also used to publish libraries to NPM's online repository of packages so that other people can find, download, and use them.

This book won't delve further into the details of NPM usage. Refer to *http://npmjs.org/* for further documentation and for an easy way to search for libraries.

The Filesystem Module

One of the most commonly used built-in modules that comes with Node is the "fs" module, which stands for *filesystem*. This module provides functions for working with files and directories.

For example, there is a function called readFile, which reads a file and then calls a callback with the file's contents.

```
var fs = require("fs");
fs.readFile("file.txt", "utf8", function(error, text) {
  if (error)
    throw error;
  console.log("The file contained:", text);
});
```

The second argument to readFile indicates the *character encoding* used to decode the file into a string. There are several ways in which text can be encoded to binary data, but most modern systems use UTF-8 to encode text, so unless you have reasons to believe another encoding is used, passing "utf8" when reading a text file is a safe bet. If you do not pass an encoding, Node will assume you are interested in the binary data and will give you a Buffer object instead of a string. This is an array-like object that contains numbers representing the bytes in the files.

```
var fs = require("fs");
fs.readFile("file.txt", function(error, buffer) {
  if (error)
    throw error;
  console.log("The file contained", buffer.length, "bytes.",
              "The first byte is:", buffer[0]);
});
```

A similar function, writeFile, is used to write a file to disk.

```
var fs = require("fs");
fs.writeFile("graffiti.txt", "Node was here", function(err) {
  if (err)
    console.log("Failed to write file:", err);
  else
    console.log("File written.");
});
```

Here, it was not necessary to specify the encoding since writeFile will assume that if it is given a string to write, rather than a Buffer object, it should write it out as text using its default character encoding, which is UTF-8.

The "fs" module contains many other useful functions: readdir will return the files in a directory as an array of strings, stat will retrieve information about a file, rename will rename a file, unlink will remove one, and so on. See the documentation at *http://nodejs.org/* for specifics.

Many of the functions in "fs" come in both synchronous and asynchronous variants. For example, there is a synchronous version of readFile called readFileSync.

```
var fs = require("fs");
console.log(fs.readFileSync("file.txt", "utf8"));
```

Synchronous functions require less ceremony to use and can be useful in simple scripts, where the extra speed provided by asynchronous I/O is irrelevant. But note that while such a synchronous operation is being performed, your program will be stopped entirely. If it should be responding to the user or to other machines on the network, being stuck on synchronous I/O might produce annoying delays.

The HTTP Module

Another central module is called "http". It provides functionality for running HTTP servers and making HTTP requests.

This is all it takes to start a simple HTTP server:

```
var http = require("http");
var server = http.createServer(function(request, response) {
  response.writeHead(200, {"Content-Type": "text/html"});
  response.write("<h1>Hello!</h1><p>You asked for <code>" +
                 request.url + "</code></p>");
  response.end();
});
server.listen(8000);
```

If you run this script on your own machine, you can point your web browser at *http://localhost:8000/hello* to make a request to your server. It will respond with a small HTML page.

The function passed as an argument to createServer is called every time a client tries to connect to the server. The request and response variables are objects representing the incoming and outgoing data. The first contains information about the request, such as its url property, which tells us to what URL the request was made.

To send something back, you call methods on the response object. The first, writeHead, will write out the response headers (see Chapter 17). You give it the status code (200 for "OK" in this case) and an object that contains header values. Here we tell the client that we will be sending back an HTML document.

Next, the actual response body (the document itself) is sent with `response` `.write`. You are allowed to call this method multiple times if you want to send the response piece by piece, possibly streaming data to the client as it becomes available. Finally, `response.end` signals the end of the response.

The call to `server.listen` causes the server to start waiting for connections on port 8000. This is the reason you have to connect to *localhost:8000*, rather than just *localhost* (which would use the default port, 80), to speak to this server.

To stop running a Node script like this, which doesn't finish automatically because it is waiting for further events (in this case, network connections), press CTRL-C.

A real web server usually does more than the one in the previous example—it looks at the request's method (the `method` property) to see what action the client is trying to perform and at the request's URL to find out which resource this action is being performed on. You'll see a more advanced server later in this chapter.

To act as an HTTP *client*, we can use the `request` function in the `"http"` module.

```
var http = require("http");
var request = http.request({
  hostname: "eloquentjavascript.net",
  path: "/20_node.html",
  method: "GET",
  headers: {Accept: "text/html"}
}, function(response) {
  console.log("Server responded with status code",
              response.statusCode);
});
request.end();
```

The first argument to `request` configures the request, telling Node what server to talk to, what path to request from that server, which method to use, and so on. The second argument is the function that should be called when a response comes in. It is given an object that allows us to inspect the response, for example to find out its status code.

Just like the `response` object we saw in the server, the object returned by `request` allows us to stream data into the request with the `write` method and finish the request with the `end` method. The example does not use `write` because GET requests should not contain data in their request body.

To make requests to secure HTTP (HTTPS) URLs, Node provides a package called `https`, which contains its own `request` function, similar to `http.request`.

Streams

We have seen two examples of writable streams in HTTP—namely, the response object that the server could write to and the request object that was returned from `http.request`.

Writable streams are a widely used concept in Node interfaces. All writable streams have a `write` method, which can be passed a string or a `Buffer` object. Their `end` method closes the stream and, if given an argument, will also write out a piece of data before it does so. Both of these methods can also be given a callback as an additional argument, which they will call when the writing to or closing of the stream has finished.

It is possible to create a writable stream that points at a file with the `fs.createWriteStream` function. Then you can use the `write` method on the resulting object to write the file one piece at a time, rather than in one shot as with `fs.writeFile`.

Readable streams are a little more involved. Both the request variable that was passed to the HTTP server's callback function and the response variable passed to the HTTP client are readable streams. (A server reads requests and then writes responses, whereas a client first writes a request and then reads a response.) Reading from a stream is done using event handlers, rather than methods.

Objects that emit events in Node have a method called `on` that is similar to the `addEventListener` method in the browser. You give it an event name and then a function, and it will register that function to be called whenever the given event occurs.

Readable streams have `"data"` and `"end"` events. The first is fired every time some data comes in, and the second is called whenever the stream is at its end. This model is most suited for "streaming" data, which can be immediately processed, even when the whole document isn't available yet. A file can be read as a readable stream by using the `fs.createReadStream` function.

The following code creates a server that reads request bodies and streams them back to the client as all-uppercase text:

```
var http = require("http");
http.createServer(function(request, response) {
  response.writeHead(200, {"Content-Type": "text/plain"});
  request.on("data", function(chunk) {
    response.write(chunk.toString().toUpperCase());
  });
  request.on("end", function() {
    response.end();
  });
}).listen(8000);
```

The `chunk` variable passed to the data handler will be a binary `Buffer`, which we can convert to a string by calling `toString` on it, which will decode the variable using the default encoding (UTF-8).

The following piece of code, if run while the uppercasing server is running, will send a request to that server and write out the response it gets:

```
var http = require("http");
var request = http.request({
  hostname: "localhost",
  port: 8000,
  method: "POST"
}, function(response) {
  response.on("data", function(chunk) {
    process.stdout.write(chunk.toString());
  });
});
request.end("Hello server");
```

The example writes to process.stdout (the process's standard output, as a writable stream) instead of using console.log. We can't use console.log because it adds an extra newline character after each piece of text that it writes, which isn't appropriate here.

A Simple File Server

Let's combine our newfound knowledge about HTTP servers and talking to the filesystem and create a bridge between them: an HTTP server that allows remote access to a filesystem. Such a server has many uses. It allows web applications to store and share data or give a group of people shared access to a bunch of files.

When we treat files as HTTP resources, the HTTP methods GET, PUT, and DELETE can be used to read, write, and delete the files, respectively. We will interpret the path in the request as the path of the file that the request refers to.

We probably don't want to share our whole filesystem, so we'll interpret these paths as starting in the server's working directory, which is the directory in which it was started. If I ran the server from /home/marijn/public/ (or C:\Users\marijn\public\ on Windows), then a request for /file.txt should refer to /home/marijn/public/file.txt (or C:\Users\marijn\public\file.txt).

We'll build the program piece by piece, using an object called methods to store the functions that handle the various HTTP methods.

```
var http = require("http"), fs = require("fs");

var methods = Object.create(null);

http.createServer(function(request, response) {
  function respond(code, body, type) {
    if (!type) type = "text/plain";
    response.writeHead(code, {"Content-Type": type});
```

```
    if (body && body.pipe)
      body.pipe(response);
    else
      response.end(body);
  }
  if (request.method in methods)
    methods[request.method](urlToPath(request.url),
                            respond, request);
  else
    respond(405, "Method " + request.method +
            " not allowed.");
}).listen(8000);
```

This starts a server that just returns 405 error responses, which is the code used to indicate that a given method isn't handled by the server.

The respond function is passed to the functions that handle the various methods and acts as a callback to finish the request. It takes an HTTP status code, a body, and optionally a content type as arguments. If the value passed as the body is a readable stream, it will have a pipe method, which is used to forward a readable stream to a writable stream. If not, it is assumed to be either null (no body) or a string and is passed directly to the response's end method.

To get a path from the URL in the request, the urlToPath function uses Node's built-in "url" module to parse the URL. It takes its pathname, which will be something like /file.txt, decodes that to get rid of the %20-style escape codes, and prefixes a single dot to produce a path relative to the current directory.

```
function urlToPath(url) {
  var path = require("url").parse(url).pathname;
  return "." + decodeURIComponent(path);
}
```

If you are worried about the security of the urlToPath function, you are right. We will return to that in the exercises.

We will set up the GET method to return a list of files when reading a directory and to return the file's content when reading a regular file.

One tricky question is what kind of Content-Type header we should add when returning a file's content. Since these files could be anything, our server can't simply return the same type for all of them. But NPM can help with that. The mime package (content type indicators like text/plain are also called *MIME types*) knows the correct type for a huge number of file extensions.

If you run the following npm command in the directory where the server script lives, you'll be able to use require("mime") to get access to the library:

```
$ npm install mime
npm http GET https://registry.npmjs.org/mime
```

```
npm http 304 https://registry.npmjs.org/mime
mime@1.2.11 node_modules/mime
```

When a requested file does not exist, the correct HTTP error code to return is 404. We will use fs.stat, which looks up information on a file, to find out both whether the file exists and whether it is a directory.

```
methods.GET = function(path, respond) {
  fs.stat(path, function(error, stats) {
    if (error && error.code == "ENOENT")
      respond(404, "File not found");
    else if (error)
      respond(500, error.toString());
    else if (stats.isDirectory())
      fs.readdir(path, function(error, files) {
        if (error)
          respond(500, error.toString());
        else
          respond(200, files.join("\n"));
      });
    else
      respond(200, fs.createReadStream(path),
              require("mime").lookup(path));
  });
};
```

Because it has to touch the disk and thus might take a while, fs.stat is asynchronous. When the file does not exist, fs.stat will pass an error object with a code property of "ENOENT" to its callback. It would be nice if Node defined different subtypes of Error for different types of error, but it doesn't. Instead, it just puts obscure, Unix-inspired codes in there.

We are going to report any errors we didn't expect with status code 500, which indicates that the problem exists in the server, as opposed to codes starting with 4 (such as 404), which refer to bad requests. There are some situations in which this is not entirely accurate, but for a small example program like this, it will have to be good enough.

The stats object returned by fs.stat tells us a number of things about a file, such as its size (size property) and its modification date (mtime property). Here we are interested in the question of whether it is a directory or a regular file, which the isDirectory method tells us.

We use fs.readdir to read the list of files in a directory and, in yet another callback, return it to the user. For normal files, we create a readable stream with fs.createReadStream and pass it to respond, along with the content type that the "mime" module gives us for the file's name.

The code to handle DELETE requests is slightly simpler.

```
methods.DELETE = function(path, respond) {
  fs.stat(path, function(error, stats) {
```

```
    if (error && error.code == "ENOENT")
      respond(204);
    else if (error)
      respond(500, error.toString());
    else if (stats.isDirectory())
      fs.rmdir(path, respondErrorOrNothing(respond));
    else
      fs.unlink(path, respondErrorOrNothing(respond));
  });
};
```

You may be wondering why trying to delete a nonexistent file returns a 204 status, rather than an error. When the file that is being deleted is not there, you could say that the request's objective is already fulfilled. The HTTP standard encourages people to make requests *idempotent*, which means that applying them multiple times does not produce a different result.

```
function respondErrorOrNothing(respond) {
  return function(error) {
    if (error)
      respond(500, error.toString());
    else
      respond(204);
  };
}
```

When an HTTP response does not contain any data, the status code 204 ("no content") can be used to indicate this. Since we need to provide callbacks that either report an error or return a 204 response in a few different situations, I wrote a respondErrorOrNothing function that creates such a callback.

This is the handler for PUT requests:

```
methods.PUT = function(path, respond, request) {
  var outStream = fs.createWriteStream(path);
  outStream.on("error", function(error) {
    respond(500, error.toString());
  });
  outStream.on("finish", function() {
    respond(204);
  });
  request.pipe(outStream);
};
```

Here, we don't need to check whether the file exists—if it does, we'll just overwrite it. We again use pipe to move data from a readable stream to a writable one, in this case from the request to the file. If creating the stream fails, an "error" event is raised for it, which we report in our response. When the data is transferred successfully, pipe will close both streams, which will cause a "finish" event to fire on the writable stream. When that happens, we can report success to the client with a 204 response.

The full script for the server is available at *http://eloquentjavascript.net/ code/file_server.js*. You can download that and run it with Node to start your own file server. And of course, you can modify and extend it to solve this chapter's exercises or to experiment.

The command-line tool curl, widely available on Unix-like systems, can be used to make HTTP requests. The following session briefly tests our server. Note that -X is used to set the request's method and -d is used to include a request body.

```
$ curl http://localhost:8000/file.txt
File not found
$ curl -X PUT -d hello http://localhost:8000/file.txt
$ curl http://localhost:8000/file.txt
hello
$ curl -X DELETE http://localhost:8000/file.txt
$ curl http://localhost:8000/file.txt
File not found
```

The first request for file.txt fails since the file does not exist yet. The PUT request creates the file, and behold, the next request successfully retrieves it. After deleting it with a DELETE request, the file is again missing.

Error Handling

In the code for the file server, there are *six* places where we are explicitly routing exceptions for which we don't know how to handle error responses. Because exceptions aren't automatically propagated to callbacks but rather passed to them as arguments, they have to be handled explicitly every time. This completely defeats the advantage of exception handling, namely, the ability to centralize the handling of failure conditions.

What happens when something actually *throws* an exception in this system? Since we are not using any try blocks, the exception will propagate to the top of the call stack. In Node, that aborts the program and writes information about the exception (including a stack trace) to the program's standard error stream.

This means that our server will crash whenever a problem is encountered in the server's code itself, as opposed to asynchronous problems, which will be passed as arguments to the callbacks. If we wanted to handle all exceptions raised during the handling of a request, to make sure we send a response, we would have to add try/catch blocks to *every* callback.

This is not workable. Many Node programs are written to make as little use of exceptions as possible, with the assumption that if an exception is raised, it is not something the program can handle, and crashing is the right response.

Another approach is to use promises, which were introduced in Chapter 17. Those catch exceptions raised by callback functions and propagate them as failures. It is possible to load a promise library in Node and use that to manage your asynchronous control. Few Node libraries integrate promises, but it is often trivial to wrap them. The excellent "promise" module from NPM contains a function called denodeify, which takes an asynchronous function like fs.readFile and converts it to a promise-returning function.

```
var Promise = require("promise");
var fs = require("fs");

var readFile = Promise.denodeify(fs.readFile);
readFile("file.txt", "utf8").then(function(content) {
  console.log("The file contained: " + content);
}, function(error) {
  console.log("Failed to read file: " + error);
});
```

For comparison, I've written another version of the file server based on promises, which you can find at *http://eloquentjavascript.net/code/file_server _promises.js*. It is slightly cleaner because functions can now *return* their results, rather than having to call callbacks, and the routing of exceptions is implicit, rather than explicit.

I'll list a few lines from the promise-based file server to illustrate the difference in the style of programming.

The fsp object that is used by this code contains promise-style variants of a number of fs functions, wrapped by Promise.denodeify. The object returned from the method handler, with code and body properties, will become the final result of the chain of promises, and it will be used to determine what kind of response to send to the client.

```
methods.GET = function(path) {
  return inspectPath(path).then(function(stats) {
    if (!stats) // Does not exist
      return {code: 404, body: "File not found"};
    else if (stats.isDirectory())
      return fsp.readdir(path).then(function(files) {
        return {code: 200, body: files.join("\n")};
      });
    else
      return {code: 200,
              type: require("mime").lookup(path),
              body: fs.createReadStream(path)};
  });
};
```

```
function inspectPath(path) {
  return fsp.stat(path).then(null, function(error) {
    if (error.code == "ENOENT") return null;
    else throw error;
  });
}
```

The inspectPath function is a simple wrapper around fs.stat, which handles the case where the file is not found. In that case, we replace the failure with a success that yields null. All other errors are allowed to propagate. When the promise that is returned from these handlers fails, the HTTP server responds with a 500 status code.

Summary

Node is a nice, straightforward system that lets us run JavaScript in a non-browser context. It was originally designed for network tasks to play the role of a *node* in a network. But it lends itself to all kinds of scripting tasks, and if writing JavaScript is something you enjoy, automating everyday tasks with Node works wonderfully.

NPM provides libraries for everything you can think of (and quite a few things you'd probably never think of), and it allows you to fetch and install those libraries by running a simple command. Node also comes with a number of built-in modules, including the "fs" module, for working with the filesystem, and the "http" module, for running HTTP servers and making HTTP requests.

All input and output in Node is done asynchronously, unless you explicitly use a synchronous variant of a function, such as fs.readFileSync. You provide callback functions, and Node will call them at the appropriate time, when the I/O you asked for has finished.

Exercises

Content Negotiation, Again

In Chapter 17, the first exercise was to make several requests to *http://eloquentjavascript.net/author/*, asking for different types of content by passing different Accept headers.

Do this again, using Node's http.request function. Ask for at least the media types text/plain, text/html, and application/json. Remember that headers to a request can be given as an object, in the headers property of http.request's first argument.

Write out the content of the responses to each request.

Fixing a Leak

For easy remote access to some files, I might get into the habit of having the file server defined in this chapter running on my machine, in the /home/marijn/public directory. Then, one day, I find that someone has gained access to all the passwords I stored in my browser.

What happened?

If it isn't clear to you yet, think back to the urlToPath function, defined like this:

```
function urlToPath(url) {
  var path = require("url").parse(url).pathname;
  return "." + decodeURIComponent(path);
}
```

Now consider the fact that paths passed to the "fs" functions can be relative—they may contain "../" to go up a directory. What happens when a client sends requests to URLs like the ones shown here?

```
http://myhostname:8000/../.config/config/google-chrome/Default/Web%20Data
http://myhostname:8000/../.ssh/id_dsa
http://myhostname:8000/../../../etc/passwd
```

Change urlToPath to fix this problem. Take into account the fact that Node on Windows allows both forward slashes and backslashes to separate directories.

Also, meditate on the fact that as soon as you expose some half-baked system on the Internet, the bugs in that system might be used to do bad things to your machine.

Creating Directories

Though the DELETE method is wired up to delete directories (using fs.rmdir), the file server currently does not provide any way to *create* a directory.

Add support for a method MKCOL, which should create a directory by calling fs.mkdir. MKCOL is not one of the basic HTTP methods, but it does exist, for this same purpose, in the *WebDAV* standard, which specifies a set of extensions to HTTP, making it suitable for writing resources, not just reading them.

A Public Space on the Web

Since the file server serves up any kind of file and even includes the right Content-Type header, you can use it to serve a website. Since it allows everybody to delete and replace files, it would be an interesting kind of website: one that can be modified, vandalized, and destroyed by everybody who takes the time to create the right HTTP request. Still, it would be a website.

Write a basic HTML page that includes a simple JavaScript file. Put the files in a directory served by the file server and open them in your browser.

Next, as an advanced exercise or even a weekend project, combine all the knowledge you gained from this book to build a more user-friendly interface for modifying the website from *inside* the website.

Use an HTML form (Chapter 18) to edit the content of the files that make up the website, allowing the user to update them on the server by using HTTP requests as described in Chapter 17.

Start by making only a single file editable. Then make it so that the user can select which file to edit. Use the fact that our file server returns lists of files when reading a directory.

Don't work directly in the code on the file server; if you make a mistake, you are likely to damage the files there. Instead, keep your work outside of the publicly accessible directory and copy it there when testing.

If your computer is directly connected to the Internet, without a firewall, router, or other interfering device in between, you might be able to invite a friend to use your website. To check, go to *http://whatismyip.com/*, copy the IP address it gives you into the address bar of your browser, and add :8000 after it to select the right port. If that brings you to your site, it is online for everybody to see.

21

PROJECT: SKILL-SHARING WEBSITE

A *skill-sharing* meeting is an event where people with a shared interest come together and give small, informal presentations about things they know. At a gardening skill-sharing meeting, someone might explain how to cultivate celery. Or in a programming-oriented skill-sharing group, you could drop by and tell everybody about Node.js.

Such meetups, also often called *users' groups* when they are about computers, are a great way to broaden your horizon, learn about new developments, or simply meet people with similar interests. Many large cities have a JavaScript meetup. They are typically free to attend, and I've found the ones I've visited to be friendly and welcoming.

In this final project chapter, our goal is to set up a website for managing talks given at a skill-sharing meeting. Imagine a small group of people meeting up regularly in a member's office to talk about unicycling. The problem is that when the previous organizer of the meetings moved to another town, nobody stepped forward to take over this task. We want a system that will let the participants propose and discuss talks among themselves, without a central organizer.

The full code for the project can be downloaded from *http:// eloquentjavascript.net/code/skillsharing.zip*.

Design

There is a *server* part to this project, written for Node.js, and a *client* part, written for the browser. The server stores the system's data and provides it to the client. It also serves the HTML and JavaScript files that implement the client-side system.

The server keeps a list of talks proposed for the next meeting, and the client shows this list. Each talk has a presenter name, a title, a summary, and a list of comments associated with it. The client allows users to propose new talks (adding them to the list), delete talks, and comment on existing talks. Whenever the user makes such a change, the client makes an HTTP request to tell the server about it.

Your name: `Bob`

Unituning
by **Carlos**

Modifying your cycle for extra style

Alice: Will you talk about raising a cycle?
Carlos: Definitely!
Alice: I'll be there

`[          ]` `Add comment` `Delete talk`

Submit a talk
Title: `[                                            ]`
Summary: `[                                       ]` `Send`

The application will be set up to show a *live* view of the current proposed talks and their comments. Whenever someone, somewhere, submits a new talk or adds a comment, all people who have the page open in their browsers should immediately see the change. This poses a bit of a challenge since there is no way for a web server to open up a connection to a client, nor is there a good way to know which clients currently are looking at a given website.

A common solution to this problem is called *long polling*, which happens to be one of the motivations for Node's design.

Long Polling

To be able to immediately notify a client that something changed, we need a connection to that client. Since web browsers do not traditionally accept connections and clients are usually behind devices that would block such connections anyway, having the server initiate this connection is not practical.

We can arrange for the client to open the connection and keep it around so that the server can use it to send information when it needs to do so.

But an HTTP request allows only a simple flow of information, where the client sends a request, the server comes back with a single response, and that is it. There is a technology called *web sockets*, supported by modern browsers, which makes it possible to open connections for arbitrary data exchange. But using them properly is somewhat tricky.

In this chapter, we will use a relatively simple technique, long polling, where clients continuously ask the server for new information using regular HTTP requests, and the server simply stalls its answer when it has nothing new to report.

As long as the client makes sure it constantly has a polling request open, it will receive information from the server immediately. For example, if Alice has our skill-sharing application open in her browser, that browser will have made a request for updates and be waiting for a response to that request. When Bob submits a talk on Extreme Downhill Unicycling from his own browser, the server will notice that Alice is waiting for updates and send information about the new talk as a response to her pending request. Alice's browser will receive the data and update the screen to show the talk.

To prevent connections from timing out (being aborted because of a lack of activity), long-polling techniques usually set a maximum time for each request, after which the server will respond anyway, even though it has nothing to report, and the client will start a new request. Periodically restarting the request also makes the technique more robust, allowing clients to recover from temporary connection failures or server problems.

A busy server that is using long polling may have thousands of waiting requests, and thus TCP connections, open. Node, which makes it easy to manage many connections without creating a separate thread of control for each one, is a good fit for such a system.

HTTP Interface

Before we start fleshing out either the server or the client, let's think about the point where they touch: the HTTP interface over which they communicate.

We will base our interface on JSON, and like in the file server from Chapter 20, we'll try to make good use of HTTP methods. The interface is centered around the /talks path. Paths that do not start with /talks will be used for serving static files—the HTML and JavaScript code that implements the client-side system.

A GET request to /talks returns a JSON document like this:

```
{"serverTime": 1405438911833,
 "talks": [{"title": "Unituning",
            "presenter": "Carlos",
            "summary": "Modifying your cycle for extra style",
            "comment": []}]}
```

The serverTime field will be used to make reliable long polling possible. I will return to it later.

Creating a new talk is done by making a PUT request to a URL like /talks/Unituning, where the part after the second slash is the title of the talk. The PUT request's body should contain a JSON object that has presenter and summary properties.

Since talk titles may contain spaces and other characters that may not appear normally in a URL, title strings must be encoded with the encodeURIComponent function when building up such a URL.

```
console.log("/talks/" + encodeURIComponent("How to Idle"));
// ▷ /talks/How%20to%20Idle
```

A request to create a talk about idling might look something like this:

```
PUT /talks/How%20to%20Idle HTTP/1.1
Content-Type: application/json
Content-Length: 92

{"presenter": "Dana",
 "summary": "Standing still on a unicycle"}
```

Such URLs also support GET requests to retrieve the JSON representation of a talk and DELETE requests to delete a talk.

Adding a comment to a talk is done with a POST request to a URL like /talks/Unituning/comments, with a JSON object that has author and message properties as the body of the request.

```
POST /talks/Unituning/comments HTTP/1.1
Content-Type: application/json
Content-Length: 72

{"author": "Alice",
 "message": "Will you talk about raising a cycle?"}
```

To support long polling, GET requests to /talks may include a query parameter called changesSince, which is used to indicate that the client is interested in updates that happened since a given point in time. When there are such changes, they are immediately returned. When there aren't, the response is delayed until something happens or until a given time period (we will use 90 seconds) has elapsed.

The time must be indicated as the number of milliseconds elapsed since the start of 1970, the same type of number that is returned by Date.now(). To ensure that it receives all updates and doesn't receive the same update more than once, the client must pass the time at which it last received information from the server. The server's clock might not be exactly in sync with the client's clock, and even if it were, it would be impossible for the client to know the precise time at which the server sent a response because transferring data over the network takes time.

This is the reason for the existence of the serverTime property in responses sent to GET requests to /talks. That property tells the client the precise time, from the server's perspective, at which the data it receives was created. The client can then simply store this time and pass it along in its next polling request to make sure that it receives exactly the updates that it has not seen before.

```
GET /talks?changesSince=1405438911833 HTTP/1.1

(time passes)

HTTP/1.1 200 OK
Content-Type: application/json
Content-Length: 95

{"serverTime": 1405438913401,
 "talks": [{"title": "Unituning",
            "deleted": true}]}
```

When a talk has been changed, has been newly created, or has a comment added, the full representation of the talk is included in the response to the client's next polling request. When a talk is deleted, only its title and the property deleted are included. The client can then add talks with titles it has not seen before to its display, update talks that it was already showing, and remove those that were deleted.

The protocol described in this chapter does not do any access control. Everybody can comment, modify talks, and even delete them. Since the Internet is filled with hooligans, putting such a system online without further protection is likely to end in disaster.

A simple solution would be to put the system behind a *reverse proxy*, which is an HTTP server that accepts connections from outside the system and forwards them to HTTP servers that are running locally. Such a proxy can be configured to require a username and password, and you could make sure only the participants in the skill-sharing group have this password.

The Server

Let's start by writing the server-side part of the program. The code in this section runs on Node.js.

Routing

Our server will use http.createServer to start an HTTP server. In the function that handles a new request, we must distinguish between the various kinds of requests (as determined by the method and the path) that we support. This can be done with a long chain of if statements, but there is a nicer way.

A *router* is a component that helps dispatch a request to the function that can handle it. You can tell the router, for example, that PUT requests with a path that matches the regular expression /^\/talks\/([^\/]+)$/ (which matches /talks/ followed by a talk title) can be handled by a given function. In addition, it can help extract the meaningful parts of the path, in this case the talk title, wrapped in parentheses in the regular expression and pass those to the handler function.

There are a number of good router packages on NPM, but here we will write one ourselves to illustrate the principle.

This is router.js, which we will later require from our server module:

```
var Router = module.exports = function() {
  this.routes = [];
};

Router.prototype.add = function(method, url, handler) {
  this.routes.push({method: method,
                    url: url,
                    handler: handler});
};

Router.prototype.resolve = function(request, response) {
  var path = require("url").parse(request.url).pathname;

  return this.routes.some(function(route) {
    var match = route.url.exec(path);
    if (!match || route.method != request.method)
      return false;

    var urlParts = match.slice(1).map(decodeURIComponent);
    route.handler.apply(null, [request, response]
                              .concat(urlParts));
    return true;
  });
};
```

The module exports the Router constructor. A router object allows new handlers to be registered with the add method and can resolve requests with its resolve method.

The latter will return a Boolean that indicates whether a handler was found. The some method on the array of routes will try the routes one at a time (in the order in which they were defined) and stop, returning true, when a matching one is found.

The handler functions are called with the request and response objects. When the regular expression that matches the URL contains any groups, the strings they match are passed to the handler as extra arguments. These strings have to be URL-decoded since the raw URL contains %20-style codes.

Serving Files

When a request matches none of the request types defined in our router, the server must interpret it as a request for a file in the public directory. It would be possible to use the file server defined in Chapter 20 to serve such files, but we neither need nor want to support PUT and DELETE requests on files, and we would like to have advanced features such as support for caching. So let's use a solid, well-tested static file server from NPM instead.

I opted for ecstatic. This isn't the only such server on NPM, but it works well and fits our purposes. The ecstatic module exports a function that can be called with a configuration object to produce a request handler function. We use the root option to tell the server where it should look for files. The handler function accepts request and response parameters and can be passed directly to createServer to create a server that serves *only* files. We want to first check for requests that we handle specially, though, so we wrap it in another function.

```
var http = require("http");
var Router = require("./router");
var ecstatic = require("ecstatic");

var fileServer = ecstatic({root: "./public"});
var router = new Router();

http.createServer(function(request, response) {
  if (!router.resolve(request, response))
    fileServer(request, response);
}).listen(8000);
```

The respond and respondJSON helper functions are used throughout the server code to send off responses with a single function call.

```
function respond(response, status, data, type) {
  response.writeHead(status, {
    "Content-Type": type || "text/plain"
  });
```

```
    response.end(data);
}

function respondJSON(response, status, data) {
  respond(response, status, JSON.stringify(data),
          "application/json");
}
```

Talks as Resources

The server keeps the talks that have been proposed in an object called talks, whose property names are the talk titles. These will be exposed as HTTP resources under /talks/[title], so we need to add handlers to our router that implement the various methods that clients can use to work with them.

The handler for requests that GET a single talk must look up the talk and respond either with the talk's JSON data or with a 404 error response.

```
var talks = Object.create(null);

router.add("GET", /^\/talks\/([^\/]+)$/,
           function(request, response, title) {
  if (title in talks)
    respondJSON(response, 200, talks[title]);
  else
    respond(response, 404, "No talk '" + title + "' found");
});
```

Deleting a talk is done by removing it from the talks object.

```
router.add("DELETE", /^\/talks\/([^\/]+)$/,
           function(request, response, title) {
  if (title in talks) {
    delete talks[title];
    registerChange(title);
  }
  respond(response, 204, null);
});
```

The registerChange function, which we will define later, notifies waiting long-polling requests about the change.

To retrieve the content of JSON-encoded request bodies, we define a function called readStreamAsJSON, which reads all content from a stream, parses it as JSON, and then calls a callback function.

```
function readStreamAsJSON(stream, callback) {
  var data = "";
  stream.on("data", function(chunk) {
    data += chunk;
  });
  stream.on("end", function() {
    var result, error;
    try { result = JSON.parse(data); }
    catch (e) { error = e; }
    callback(error, result);
  });
  stream.on("error", function(error) {
    callback(error);
  });
}
```

One handler that needs to read JSON responses is the PUT handler, which is used to create new talks. It has to check whether the data it was given has presenter and summary properties, which are strings. Any data coming from outside the system might be nonsense, and we don't want to corrupt our internal data model, or even crash, when bad requests come in.

If the data looks valid, the handler stores an object that represents the new talk in the talks object, possibly overwriting an existing talk with this title, and again calls registerChange.

```
router.add("PUT", /^\/talks\/([^\/]+)$/,
           function(request, response, title) {
  readStreamAsJSON(request, function(error, talk) {
    if (error) {
      respond(response, 400, error.toString());
    } else if (!talk ||
               typeof talk.presenter != "string" ||
               typeof talk.summary != "string") {
      respond(response, 400, "Bad talk data");
    } else {
      talks[title] = {title: title,
                      presenter: talk.presenter,
                      summary: talk.summary,
                      comments: []};
      registerChange(title);
      respond(response, 204, null);
    }
  });
});
```

Adding a comment to a talk works similarly. We use `readStreamAsJSON` to get the content of the request, validate the resulting data, and store it as a comment when it looks valid.

```
router.add("POST", /^\/talks\/([^\/]+)\/comments$/,
           function(request, response, title) {
  readStreamAsJSON(request, function(error, comment) {
    if (error) {
      respond(response, 400, error.toString());
    } else if (!comment ||
               typeof comment.author != "string" ||
               typeof comment.message != "string") {
      respond(response, 400, "Bad comment data");
    } else if (title in talks) {
      talks[title].comments.push(comment);
      registerChange(title);
      respond(response, 204, null);
    } else {
      respond(response, 404, "No talk '" + title + "' found");
    }
  });
});
```

Trying to add a comment to a nonexistent talk should return a 404 error, of course.

Long-Polling Support

The most interesting aspect of the server is the part that handles long polling. When a GET request comes in for /talks, it can be either a simple request for all talks or a request for updates, with a changesSince parameter.

There will be various situations in which we have to send a list of talks to the client, so we first define a small helper function that attaches the serverTime field to such responses.

```
function sendTalks(talks, response) {
  respondJSON(response, 200, {
    serverTime: Date.now(),
    talks: talks
  });
}
```

The handler itself needs to look at the query parameters in the request's URL to see whether a changesSince parameter is given. If you give the "url" module's parse function a second argument of true, it will also parse the query part of a URL. The object it returns will have a query property, which holds another object that maps parameter names to values.

```
router.add("GET", /^\/talks$/, function(request, response) {
  var query = require("url").parse(request.url, true).query;
  if (query.changesSince == null) {
    var list = [];
    for (var title in talks)
      list.push(talks[title]);
    sendTalks(list, response);
  } else {
    var since = Number(query.changesSince);
    if (isNaN(since)) {
      respond(response, 400, "Invalid parameter");
    } else {
      var changed = getChangedTalks(since);
      if (changed.length > 0)
        sendTalks(changed, response);
      else
        waitForChanges(since, response);
    }
  }
});
```

When the changesSince parameter is missing, the handler simply builds
up a list of all talks and returns that.

Otherwise, the changeSince parameter first has to be checked to make
sure that it is a valid number. The getChangedTalks function, to be defined
shortly, returns an array of changed talks since a given point in time. If it
returns an empty array, the server does not yet have anything to send back
to the client, so it stores the response object (using waitForChanges) to be responded to at a later time.

```
var waiting = [];

function waitForChanges(since, response) {
  var waiter = {since: since, response: response};
  waiting.push(waiter);
  setTimeout(function() {
    var found = waiting.indexOf(waiter);
    if (found > -1) {
      waiting.splice(found, 1);
      sendTalks([], response);
    }
  }, 90 * 1000);
}
```

The splice method is used to cut a piece out of an array. You give it
an index and a number of elements, and it *mutates* the array, removing
that many elements after the given index. In this case, we remove a single

element, the object that tracks the waiting response, whose index we found by calling indexOf. If you pass additional arguments to splice, their values will be inserted into the array at the given position, replacing the removed elements.

When a response object is stored in the waiting array, a timeout is immediately set. After 90 seconds, this timeout sees whether the request is still waiting and, if it is, sends an empty response and removes it from the waiting array.

To be able to find exactly those talks that have been changed since a given point in time, we need to keep track of the history of changes. Registering a change with registerChange will remember that change, along with the current time, in an array called changes. When a change occurs, that means there is new data, so all waiting requests can be responded to immediately.

```
var changes = [];

function registerChange(title) {
  changes.push({title: title, time: Date.now()});
  waiting.forEach(function(waiter) {
    sendTalks(getChangedTalks(waiter.since), waiter.response);
  });
  waiting = [];
}
```

Finally, getChangedTalks uses the changes array to build up an array of changed talks, including objects with a deleted property for talks that no longer exist. When building that array, getChangedTalks has to ensure that it doesn't include the same talk twice since there might have been multiple changes to a talk since the given time.

```
function getChangedTalks(since) {
  var found = [];
  function alreadySeen(title) {
    return found.some(function(f) {return f.title == title;});
  }
  for (var i = changes.length - 1; i >= 0; i--) {
    var change = changes[i];
    if (change.time <= since)
      break;
    else if (alreadySeen(change.title))
      continue;
    else if (change.title in talks)
      found.push(talks[change.title]);
    else
      found.push({title: change.title, deleted: true});
  }
```

```
  return found;
}
```

That concludes the server code. Running the program defined so far will get you a server running on port 8000, which serves files from the public subdirectory alongside a talk-managing interface under the /talks URL.

The Client

The client-side part of the talk-managing website consists of three files: an HTML page, a style sheet, and a JavaScript file.

HTML

It is a widely used convention for web servers to try to serve a file named index.html when a request is made directly to a path that corresponds to a directory. The file server module we use, ecstatic, supports this convention. When a request is made to the path /, the server looks for the file ./public/index.html (./public being the root we gave it) and returns that file if found.

Thus, if we want a page to show up when a browser is pointed at our server, we should put it in public/index.html. This is how our index file starts:

```html
<!doctype html>

<title>Skill Sharing</title>
<link rel="stylesheet" href="skillsharing.css">

<h1>Skill sharing</h1>

<p>Your name: <input type="text" id="name"></p>

<div id="talks"></div>
```

It defines the document title and includes a style sheet, which defines a few styles to, among other things, add a border around talks. Then it adds a heading and a name field. The user is expected to put their name in the latter so that it can be attached to talks and comments they submit.

The <div> element with the ID "talks" will contain the current list of talks. The script fills the list in when it receives talks from the server.

Next comes the form that is used to create a new talk.

```html
<form id="newtalk">
  <h3>Submit a talk</h3>
  Title: <input type="text" style="width: 40em" name="title">
  <br>
  Summary: <input type="text" style="width: 40em" name="summary">
  <button type="submit">Send</button>
</form>
```

The script will add a "submit" event handler to this form, from which it can make the HTTP request that tells the server about the talk.

Next comes a rather mysterious block, which has its display style set to none, preventing it from actually showing up on the page. Can you guess what it is for?

```
<div id="template" style="display: none">
  <div class="talk">
    <h2>{{title}}</h2>
    <div>by <span class="name">{{presenter}}</span></div>
    <p>{{summary}}</p>
    <div class="comments"></div>
    <form>
      <input type="text" name="comment">
      <button type="submit">Add comment</button>
      <button type="button" class="del">Delete talk</button>
    </form>
  </div>
  <div class="comment">
    <span class="name">{{author}}</span>: {{message}}
  </div>
</div>
```

Creating complicated DOM structures with JavaScript code produces ugly code. You can make the code slightly better by introducing helper functions like the elt function from Chapter 13, but the result will still look worse than HTML, which can be thought of as a domain-specific language for expressing DOM structures.

To create DOM structures for the talks, our program will define a simple *templating* system, which uses hidden DOM structures included in the document to instantiate new DOM structures, replacing the placeholders between double braces with the values of a specific talk.

Finally, the HTML document includes the script file that contains the client-side code.

```
<script src="skillsharing_client.js"></script>
```

Starting up

The first thing the client has to do when the page is loaded is ask the server for the current set of talks. Since we are going to make a lot of HTTP requests, we will again define a small wrapper around XMLHttpRequest, which accepts an object to configure the request as well as a callback to call when the request finishes.

```
function request(options, callback) {
  var req = new XMLHttpRequest();
  req.open(options.method || "GET", options.pathname, true);
  req.addEventListener("load", function() {
    if (req.status < 400)
      callback(null, req.responseText);
    else
      callback(new Error("Request failed: " + req.statusText));
  });
  req.addEventListener("error", function() {
    callback(new Error("Network error"));
  });
  req.send(options.body || null);
}
```

The initial request displays the talks it receives on the screen and starts the long-polling process by calling waitForChanges.

```
var lastServerTime = 0;

request({pathname: "talks"}, function(error, response) {
  if (error) {
    reportError(error);
  } else {
    response = JSON.parse(response);
    displayTalks(response.talks);
    lastServerTime = response.serverTime;
    waitForChanges();
  }
});
```

The lastServerTime variable is used to track the time of the last update that was received from the server. After the initial request, the client's view of the talks corresponds to the view that the server had when it responded to that request. Thus, the serverTime property included in the response provides an appropriate initial value for lastServerTime.

When the request fails, we don't want to have our page just sit there, doing nothing without explanation. So we define a simple function called reportError, which at least shows the user a dialog that tells them something went wrong.

```
function reportError(error) {
  if (error)
    alert(error.toString());
}
```

The function checks whether there *is* an actual error, and it alerts only when there is one. That way, we can also directly pass this function to request for requests where we can ignore the response. This makes sure that if the request fails, the error is reported to the user.

Displaying Talks

To be able to update the view of the talks when changes come in, the client must keep track of the talks that it is currently showing. That way, when a new version of a talk that is already on the screen comes in, the talk can be replaced (in place) with its updated form. Similarly, when information comes in that a talk is being deleted, the right DOM element can be removed from the document.

The function displayTalks is used both to build up the initial display and to update it when something changes. It will use the shownTalks object, which associates talk titles with DOM nodes, to remember the talks it currently has on the screen.

```
var talkDiv = document.querySelector("#talks");
var shownTalks = Object.create(null);

function displayTalks(talks) {
  talks.forEach(function(talk) {
    var shown = shownTalks[talk.title];
    if (talk.deleted) {
      if (shown) {
        talkDiv.removeChild(shown);
        delete shownTalks[talk.title];
      }
    } else {
      var node = drawTalk(talk);
      if (shown)
        talkDiv.replaceChild(node, shown);
      else
        talkDiv.appendChild(node);
      shownTalks[talk.title] = node;
    }
  });
}
```

Building up the DOM structure for talks is done using the templates that were included in the HTML document. First, we must define instantiateTemplate, which looks up and fills in a template.

The name parameter is the template's name. To look up the template element, we search for an element whose class name matches the template name, which is a child of the element with ID "template". Using the querySelector method makes this easy. There were templates named "talk" and "comment" in the HTML page.

```
function instantiateTemplate(name, values) {
  function instantiateText(text) {
    return text.replace(/\{\{(\w+)\}\}/g, function(_, name) {
      return values[name];
    });
  }
  function instantiate(node) {
    if (node.nodeType == document.ELEMENT_NODE) {
      var copy = node.cloneNode();
      for (var i = 0; i < node.childNodes.length; i++)
        copy.appendChild(instantiate(node.childNodes[i]));
      return copy;
    } else if (node.nodeType == document.TEXT_NODE) {
      return document.createTextNode(
              instantiateText(node.nodeValue));
    }
  }

  var template = document.querySelector("#template ." + name);
  return instantiate(template);
}
```

The cloneNode method, which all DOM nodes have, creates a copy of a node. It won't copy the node's child nodes unless true is given as a first argument. The instantiate function recursively builds up a copy of the template, filling in the template as it goes.

The second argument to instantiateTemplate should be an object, whose properties hold the strings that are to be filled into the template. A placeholder like {{title}} will be replaced with the value of values' title property.

This is a crude approach to templating, but it is enough to implement drawTalk.

```
function drawTalk(talk) {
  var node = instantiateTemplate("talk", talk);
  var comments = node.querySelector(".comments");
  talk.comments.forEach(function(comment) {
    comments.appendChild(
      instantiateTemplate("comment", comment));
  });

  node.querySelector("button.del").addEventListener(
    "click", deleteTalk.bind(null, talk.title));

  var form = node.querySelector("form");
  form.addEventListener("submit", function(event) {
    event.preventDefault();
    addComment(talk.title, form.elements.comment.value);
```

```
    form.reset();
  });
  return node;
}
```

After instantiating the "talk" template, there are various things that need to be patched up. First, the comments have to be filled in by repeatedly instantiating the "comment" template and appending the results to the node with class "comments". Next, event handlers have to be attached to the button that deletes the task and the form that adds a new comment.

Updating the Server

The event handlers registered by drawTalk call the function deleteTalk and addComment to perform the actual actions required to delete a talk or add a comment. These will need to build up URLs that refer to talks with a given title, for which we define the talkURL helper function.

```
function talkURL(title) {
  return "talks/" + encodeURIComponent(title);
}
```

The deleteTalk function fires off a DELETE request and reports the error when that fails.

```
function deleteTalk(title) {
  request({pathname: talkURL(title), method: "DELETE"},
          reportError);
}
```

Adding a comment requires building up a JSON representation of the comment and submitting that as part of a POST request.

```
function addComment(title, comment) {
  var comment = {author: nameField.value, message: comment};
  request({pathname: talkURL(title) + "/comments",
          body: JSON.stringify(comment),
          method: "POST"},
          reportError);
}
```

The nameField variable used to set the comment's author property is a reference to the <input> field at the top of the page that allows the user to specify their name. We also wire up that field to localStorage so that it does not have to be filled in again every time the page is reloaded.

```
var nameField = document.querySelector("#name");

nameField.value = localStorage.getItem("name") || "";

nameField.addEventListener("change", function() {
  localStorage.setItem("name", nameField.value);
});
```

The form at the bottom of the page, for proposing a new talk, gets a "submit" event handler. This handler prevents the event's default effect (which would cause a page reload), clears the form, and fires off a PUT request to create the talk.

```
var talkForm = document.querySelector("#newtalk");

talkForm.addEventListener("submit", function(event) {
  event.preventDefault();
  request({pathname: talkURL(talkForm.elements.title.value),
           method: "PUT",
           body: JSON.stringify({
             presenter: nameField.value,
             summary: talkForm.elements.summary.value
           })}, reportError);
  talkForm.reset();
});
```

Noticing Changes

I should point out that the various functions that change the state of the application by creating or deleting talks or adding a comment do absolutely nothing to ensure that the changes they make are visible on the screen. They simply tell the server and rely on the long-polling mechanism to trigger the appropriate updates to the page.

Given the mechanism that we implemented in our server and the way we defined displayTalks to handle updates of talks that are already on the page, the actual long polling is surprisingly simple.

```
function waitForChanges() {
  request({pathname: "talks?changesSince=" + lastServerTime},
          function(error, response) {
    if (error) {
      setTimeout(waitForChanges, 2500);
      console.error(error.stack);
    } else {
      response = JSON.parse(response);
```

```
        displayTalks(response.talks);
        lastServerTime = response.serverTime;
        waitForChanges();
      }
    });
}
```

This function is called once when the program starts up and then keeps calling itself to ensure that a polling request is always active. When the request fails, we don't call reportError since popping up a dialog every time we fail to reach the server would get annoying when the server is down. Instead, the error is written to the console (to ease debugging), and another attempt is made 2.5 seconds later.

When the request succeeds, the new data is put onto the screen, and lastServerTime is updated to reflect the fact that we received data corresponding to this new point in time. The request is immediately restarted to wait for the next update.

If you run the server and open two browser windows for *localhost:8000/* next to each other, you can see that the actions you perform in one window are immediately visible in the other.

Exercises

The following exercises will involve modifying the system defined in this chapter. To work on them, make sure you download the code first (*http://eloquentjavascript.net/code/skillshare.zip*) and have Node installed (*http://nodejs.org/*).

Disk Persistence

The skill-sharing server keeps its data purely in memory. This means that when it crashes or is restarted for any reason, all talks and comments are lost.

Extend the server so that it stores the talk data to disk and automatically reloads the data when it is restarted. Do not worry about efficiency—do the simplest thing that works.

Comment Field Resets

The wholesale redrawing of talks works pretty well because you usually can't tell the difference between a DOM node and its identical replacement. But there are exceptions. If you start typing something in the comment field for a talk in one browser window and then, in another, add a comment to that talk, the field in the first window will be redrawn, removing both its content and its focus.

In a heated discussion, where multiple people are adding comments to a single talk, this would be very annoying. Can you come up with a way to avoid it?

Better Templates

Most templating systems do more than just fill in some strings. At the very least, they also allow conditional inclusion of parts of the template, analogous to `if` statements, and repetition of parts of a template, similar to a loop.

If we were able to repeat a piece of template for each element in an array, we would not need the second template (`"comment"`). Rather, we could specify the `"talk"` template to loop over the array held in a talk's `comments` property and render the nodes that make up a comment for every element in the array.

It could look like this:

```
<div class="comments">
  <div class="comment" template-repeat="comments">
    <span class="name">{{author}}</span>: {{message}}
  </div>
</div>
```

The idea is that whenever a node with a `template-repeat` attribute is found during template instantiation, the instantiating code loops over the array held in the property named by that attribute. For each element in the array, it adds an instance of the node. The template's context (the `values` variable in `instantiateTemplate`) would, during this loop, point at the current element of the array so that `{{author}}` would be looked up in the comment object rather than in the original context (the talk).

Rewrite `instantiateTemplate` to implement this and then change the templates to use this feature and remove the explicit rendering of comments from the `drawTalk` function.

How would you add conditional instantiation of nodes, making it possible to omit parts of the template when a given value is true or false?

The Unscriptables

When someone visits our website with a browser that has JavaScript disabled or is simply not capable of displaying JavaScript, they will get a completely broken, inoperable page. This is not nice.

Some types of web applications really can't be done without JavaScript. For others, you just don't have the budget or patience to bother about clients that can't run scripts. But for pages with a wide audience, it is polite to support scriptless users.

Try to think of a way the skill-sharing website could be set up to preserve basic functionality when run without JavaScript. The automatic updates will have to go, and people will have to refresh their page the old-fashioned way. But being able to see existing talks, create new ones, and submit comments would be nice.

Don't feel obliged to actually implement this. Outlining a solution is enough. Does the revised approach strike you as more or less elegant than what we did initially?

22

JAVASCRIPT AND PERFORMANCE

Running a computer program on a machine requires bridging the gap between the programming language and the machine's own instruction format. This can be done by writing a program that *interprets* other programs, as we did in Chapter 11, but it is usually done by *compiling* (translating) the program to machine code.

Some programming languages, such as C, are designed to express exactly those things that the machine is known to be good at. This makes them easy to compile efficiently. But JavaScript is designed in an entirely different way, with a focus on simplicity and ease of use instead, and almost none of its features correspond directly to features of the machine. That makes JavaScript difficult to execute efficiently.

Yet somehow modern JavaScript *engines* (the programs that compile and run JavaScript) manage to run scripts at a surprising speed. It is possible to write JavaScript programs that are less than 10 times slower than the speed of an equivalent C program. That may sound like a huge gap, but older JavaScript engines (as well as contemporary implementations of languages with a similar design, such as Python and Ruby) tend to be closer to 100 times slower than C. Compared to these, modern JavaScript is strikingly fast—so fast that you will rarely be forced to switch to another language because of performance problems.

Still, you may occasionally need to rewrite your code to avoid aspects of JavaScript that remain slow. As an example of that, this chapter will work through a speed-hungry program and make it faster. In the process, we will discuss the way JavaScript engines compile your programs.

Staged Compilation

First, you must understand that JavaScript compilers do not simply compile a program once—the way classical compilers for languages like C do. Instead, code is compiled and recompiled as needed, while the program is running.

Traditionally, compiling a big program takes a while. That has usually been acceptable because with traditional languages, a program is compiled ahead of time and distributed in compiled form.

For JavaScript, the situation is different. A website might include a huge amount of code, which is retrieved in text form, and that code must be compiled every time the website is opened. If that took five minutes, the user would not be happy. A JavaScript compiler must be able to start running a program, even a big program, almost instantaneously.

To do this, JavaScript compilers contain multiple compilation strategies. When a website is opened, the scripts are first compiled in a cheap, superficial way. This doesn't result in very fast execution, but it happens quickly. In fact, some JavaScript engines don't compile functions at all until the first time they are called. Each major browser has its own JavaScript engine, and each engine has its own compilation strategies.

In a typical program, most code is run only a handful of times (or not at all). For these parts of the program, the cheap compilation strategy is sufficient since they won't take up much time anyway. But functions that are called often, or that contain loops that do a lot of work, have to be treated differently. While running the program, the JavaScript engine observes how often each piece of code is run. When it looks like the code in a function might consume a serious amount of time (this is called *hot* code), the function is recompiled with an advanced (but slower) compiler. This compiler performs more *optimizations* and will thus produce faster code. Some engines have a third, even more advanced (and thus even slower) compiler to use on *very* hot code.

Interleaving running and compiling code means that by the time the clever compiler starts working with a piece of code, it has already been run multiple times. This makes it possible to *observe* the running code and gather information about it. Later in the chapter, we'll see how that can allow the compiler to create more efficient code.

Graph Layout

Our example problem for this chapter concerns graphs. A *graph* is a set of points (nodes) with connections (edges) between them. It can be used to describe networks of roads, family trees, the way control flows through a computer program, and so on. The following picture shows a graph representing some countries in the Middle East, with edges between those that share land borders:

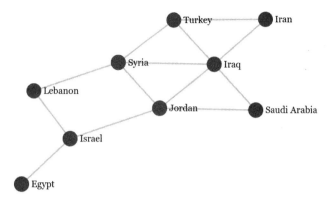

Deriving a picture like this from the definition of a graph is called *graph layout*. It involves assigning a place to each node in such a way that connected nodes are near each other but don't crowd into each other. A random layout of the same graph is a lot harder to interpret.

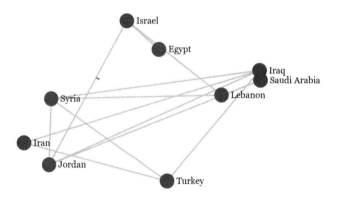

Finding a nice-looking layout for a given graph is a notoriously difficult problem. For big graphs with lots of edges, there is no known solution that works well for all types of graphs—though there are solutions for graphs with a specific form.

To lay out a small graph (say, up to 100 nodes) that is not too tangled, we can apply an approach called *force-directed graph layout*. This runs a simple physics simulation on the nodes of the graph, treating edges between nodes as if they are springs and having the nodes themselves repel each other as if electrically charged.

In this chapter, we will implement a force-directed graph layout and observe its performance. We can run such a physical simulation by repeatedly computing the forces that act on each node and moving the nodes around in response to those forces. Performance of such a program is important since it might take a lot of iterations to reach a good-looking, stable layout, and each iteration has to compute a lot of forces.

Defining a Graph

We can represent a graph as an array of GraphNode objects, each of which carries its current position and an array of the other nodes to which it has edges. The starting positions of nodes are randomized.

```
function GraphNode() {
  this.pos = new Vector(Math.random() * 1000,
                        Math.random() * 1000);
  this.edges = [];
}
GraphNode.prototype.connect = function(other) {
  this.edges.push(other);
  other.edges.push(this);
};
GraphNode.prototype.hasEdge = function(other) {
  for (var i = 0; i < this.edges.length; i++)
    if (this.edges[i] == other)
      return true;
};
```

We use the familiar Vector type from previous chapters to represent positions and forces.

The connect and hasEdge methods provide a way to connect a node to another node when building up a graph and to test whether two nodes are connected.

The treeGraph function builds a simple graph on which we can test our layout program. It takes two parameters—the depth of the tree and the number of branches to create at each level—and recursively constructs a tree-shaped graph with the specified shape.

```
function treeGraph(depth, branches) {
  var graph = [];
  function buildNode(depth) {
    var node = new GraphNode();
    graph.push(node);
    if (depth > 1)
      for (var i = 0; i < branches; i++)
        node.connect(buildNode(depth - 1));
    return node;
  }
  buildNode(depth);
  return graph;
}
```

Tree-shaped graphs don't contain cycles, which makes them relatively easy to lay out and allows even the unsophisticated program we'll use in this chapter to produce good-looking shapes.

The graph created by `treeGraph(3, 5)` would be a tree of depth 3, with five branches.

So you can inspect the layouts produced by the code in this chapter, I've defined a `drawGraph` function that draws the graph onto a canvas. This function is defined in the code at *http://eloquentjavascript.net/code/draw_graph.js* and is available in the online sandbox.

A First Force-Directed Layout Function

We will move nodes one at a time, computing the forces that act on the current node and immediately moving that node according to these forces.

The force that an (idealized) spring applies can be approximated with Hooke's law, which says that this force is proportional to the difference between the spring's resting length and its current length. The variable `springLength` defines the resting length of our edge springs, and the variable `springStrength` defines a constant that is used to model the rigidity of the spring, which we'll multiply by the length difference to determine the resulting force.

```
var springLength = 40;
var springStrength = 0.1;
```

To model the repulsion between nodes, we use another physical law, Coulomb's law, which states that the repulsion between two electrically charged particles is inversely proportional to the square of the distance between them. When two nodes are almost on top of each other, the squared distance is tiny, so the resulting force is gigantic. As the nodes move further apart, the squared distance grows rapidly, and the repelling force quickly weakens.

We'll again multiply by an experimentally determined constant, `repulsionStrength`, which defines the degree to which nodes repel each other.

```
var repulsionStrength = 1500;
```

The force that acts on a given node is computed by looping over all other nodes and applying the repelling force for each of them. When another node shares an edge with the current node, the spring's force is also applied.

Both of these forces depend on the distance between the two nodes. The function computes a vector named apart that represents the path from the current node to the other node. The function then takes the length of the vector to find the actual distance. When the distance is less than one, we set it to one to prevent dividing by zero or by very small numbers because that will produce NaN values or forces so gigantic they catapult the node into outer space.

Using this distance, we can compute the magnitude of the force that acts between these two given nodes. To go from a magnitude to a force vector, we must multiply the magnitude by a normalized version of the apart vector. Normalizing a vector means creating a vector with the same direction but with a length of one, and it can be done by dividing a vector by its own length.

```
function forceDirected_simple(graph) {
  graph.forEach(function(node) {
    graph.forEach(function(other) {
      if (other == node) return;
      var apart = other.pos.minus(node.pos);
      var distance = Math.max(1, apart.length);
      var forceSize = -repulsionStrength / (distance * distance);
      if (node.hasEdge(other))
        forceSize += (distance - springLength) * springStrength;
      var normalized = apart.times(1 / distance);
      node.pos = node.pos.plus(normalized.times(forceSize));
    });
  });
}
```

We will use the runLayout function to test a given implementation of our graph layout system. It runs the model for 4,000 steps and tracks the time this takes. To give us something to look at while the code runs, it will draw the current layout of the graph after every 100 steps.

```
function runLayout(implementation, graph) {
  var totalSteps = 0, time = 0;
  function step() {
    var startTime = Date.now();
    for (var i = 0; i < 100; i++)
      implementation(graph);
    totalSteps += 100;
    time += Date.now() - startTime;
    drawGraph(graph);
```

```
    if (totalSteps < 4000)
      requestAnimationFrame(step);
    else
      console.log(time);
  }
  step();
}
```

We can now run our first implementation and see how much time it takes.

```
<script>
  runLayout(forceDirected_simple, treeGraph(4, 4));
</script>
```

My machine, using version 38 of the Chrome browser, reports that those 4,000 iterations took a little more than four seconds. That's a lot. Let's see if we can do better.

Profiling

So our code is slow. You may already have some theories on why that is. But performance problems can come from unexpected corners, and if you just start changing code on the *assumption* that your idea will make your code run faster, you are likely to waste a lot of time on changes that don't actually help.

Our runLayout function measures the time the program currently takes. That's already a good start. To improve something, you must first measure it so that you can get useful feedback on whether a change you make is actually having an effect.

The developer tools in modern browsers provide an even better way to measure the time used by your program. The *profiler* tool will, while a program is running, gather information on how much time the various parts of the program take to run.

When your browser has a profiler, it will be available from the developer tool interface, probably as a tab listed in the top bar. The profiler in Chrome spits out a three-column table for our program.

Self		Total		Function
3787.5 ms	47.48 %	5015.4 ms	62.87 %	(anonymous function)
2528.3 ms	31.70 %	7545.7 ms	94.60 %	(anonymous function)
1229.9 ms	15.42 %	1229.9 ms	15.42 %	Vector
188.4 ms	2.36 %	188.4 ms	2.36 %	(garbage collector)
44.3 ms	0.56 %	7590.1 ms	95.15 %	forceDirected_simple
39.3 ms	0.49 %	39.3 ms	0.49 %	stroke
22.2 ms	0.28 %	22.2 ms	0.28 %	fill
11.1 ms	0.14 %	11.1 ms	0.14 %	clearRect

```
6.0 ms  0.08 %      6.0 ms  0.08 %    arc
4.0 ms  0.05 %     88.6 ms  1.11 %    drawGraph
2.0 ms  0.03 %   7680.7 ms 96.29 %    step
```

The numbers give us the time spent executing a given function, both in milliseconds and as a percentage of the total time taken. The first column shows only the time that control was actually in the function, while the second column includes time spent in functions called by this function.

From this data, we can tell that the time spent drawing the graph is tiny compared to the time spent running the simulation. In the browser, we can click through to the definition of each function. This allows us to confirm that the two anonymous functions at the top of the profile are the functions passed to forEach in forceDirected_simple. As expected, the bulk of the time the program takes is spent computing forces.

The row labeled (garbage collector) gives us the time spent cleaning up memory that is no longer being used. Given that our program creates a huge number of vector objects, the 2.36 percent of time spent reclaiming memory is strikingly low. Chrome has an advanced garbage collector. But note that we *are* spending more than 15 percent of our time creating vector objects. This is definitely an opportunity for optimization, which we will explore later in the chapter. But first, we will address another source of slowness.

Function Inlining

Not one of the vector methods, such as plus, shows up in the profile we saw, even though they are being used heavily. This is because the engine *inlined* them. This means that rather than having the code in the inner function call an actual method to add vectors, the vector-adding code is put directly inside the function, and no actual method call happens in the compiled code.

There are various ways in which inlining helps make code fast. Functions and methods are, at the machine level, called using a protocol, which requires putting the arguments and the return address (the place where execution must continue when the function returns) somewhere the function can find them. The way a function call gives control to another part of the program also often requires saving some of the processor's state so that the called function can use the processor without interfering with data that the caller still needs. All of this becomes unnecessary when a function is inlined.

Furthermore, a good compiler will do its best to find ways to simplify the code it generates. If functions are treated as black boxes that might do anything, the compiler does not have a lot to work with. On the other hand, if it can see and include the function body in its analysis, it might find additional opportunities to optimize the resulting code.

For example, a JavaScript engine could avoid creating some of the vector objects in our code altogether. In an expression like the following one, if we can see through the methods, it is clear that the resulting vector's coordinates are the result of adding force's coordinates to the product of normalized's coordinates and the `forceSize` variable. Thus, there is no need to create the intermediate object produced by the `times` method.

```
force.plus(normalized.times(forceSize))
```

But JavaScript is a dynamic language. How does the compiler figure out which function this `plus` method actually is? And what if someone changes the value stored in `Vector.prototype.plus` later? The next time code that has inlined that function runs, it might continue to use the old definition, violating the programmer's assumptions about the way their program behaves.

This is where the interleaving of execution and compilation starts to pay off. When a hot function is compiled, it has already run a number of times. If, during those runs, it always called the same function, it is reasonable to try inlining that function. The code is optimistically compiled with the assumption that, in the future, the same function is going to be called here.

To handle the pessimistic case, where another function ends up being called, the compiler inserts a test that compares the called function to the one that was inlined. If the two do not match, the optimistically compiled code is useless, and the JavaScript engine must *deoptimize*, meaning it falls back to a less optimized version of the code.

Going Back to Old-school Loops

The fact that the two anonymous functions passed to `forEach` in our simulation function show up at the top of the profile tells us that those were not inlined. These are called *very* often, and we would really like the compiler to optimize the body of the simulation function as tightly as possible.

At the time of writing, no JavaScript engine seems capable of inlining `forEach` calls. This means that a function object has to be created for each call, that the closed-over variables (`graph` and `node`) have to be put in a special shared piece of memory, and that there are a *lot* function calls happening.

The solution is easy. Use a traditional `for` loop instead. It makes the code a little less pleasant to look at, but for my inner loops, I am willing to pay that price.

```
function forceDirected_forloop(graph) {
  for (var i = 0; i < graph.length; i++) {
    var node = graph[i];
    for (var j = 0; j < graph.length; j++) {
      if (i == j) continue;
      var other = graph[j];
      var apart = other.pos.minus(node.pos);
      var distance = Math.max(1, apart.length);
      var forceSize = -1 * repulsionStrength / (distance * distance);
      if (node.hasEdge(other))
        forceSize += (distance - springLength) * springStrength;
      var normalized = apart.times(1 / distance);
```

```
      node.pos = node.pos.plus(normalized.times(forceSize));
    }
  }
}
```

The result is that the code is about 30 percent faster both in Chrome 38 and in Firefox 32. If I profile again, the forceDirected_forloop function takes up most of the time. Interestingly, the Vector constructor also disappears from the profile, suggesting that the engine either avoided creating vectors or inlined the constructor.

Avoiding Work

You can make code faster by finding a cheaper way to do the work the code is already doing, as we did earlier. But sometimes you can also find ways to avoid doing some of the work altogether. There are cases where this can improve your code's performance by orders of magnitude, without doing the finicky *micro-optimizing* work like replacing forEach loops with for loops.

In the case of our example project, there is a modest opportunity for doing less work. Every pair of nodes has the forces between them computed twice, once when moving the first node and once when moving the second. Since the force that node X exerts on node Y is exactly the opposite of the force Y exerts on X, we do not need to compute these forces twice.

The next version of the function changes the inner loop to loop over only the nodes that come after the current one so that each pair of nodes is looked at only once. At the end of that loop, it updates the position of both nodes.

```
function forceDirected_norepeat(graph) {
  for (var i = 0; i < graph.length; i++) {
    var node = graph[i];
    for (var j = i + 1; j < graph.length; j++) {
      var other = graph[j];
      var apart = other.pos.minus(node.pos);
      var distance = Math.max(1, apart.length);
      var forceSize = -1 * repulsionStrength / (distance * distance);
      if (node.hasEdge(other))
        forceSize += (distance - springLength) * springStrength;
      var applied = apart.times(forceSize / distance);
      node.pos = node.pos.plus(applied);
      other.pos = other.pos.minus(applied);
    }
  }
}
```

If I measure this code, I see another big speed boost compared to the version before it—over 40 percent less time taken on Chrome 38, and around 30 percent less on Firefox 32 and Internet Explorer 11.

Creating Less Garbage

Though some of the vector objects that we are using to do two-dimensional arithmetic might be optimized away entirely by some engines, there is likely still a cost to creating all those objects. To estimate the size of this cost, let's write a version of the code that does the vector computations "by hand," using local variables for both dimensions.

```
function forceDirected_novector(graph) {
  for (var i = 0; i < graph.length; i++) {
    var node = graph[i];
    for (var j = i + 1; j < graph.length; j++) {
      var other = graph[j];
      var apartX = other.pos.x - node.pos.x;
      var apartY = other.pos.y - node.pos.y;
      var distance = Math.max(1, Math.sqrt(apartX * apartX + apartY * apartY));
      var forceSize = -repulsionStrength / (distance * distance);
      if (node.hasEdge(other))
        forceSize += (distance - springLength) * springStrength;

      var forceX = apartX * forceSize / distance;
      var forceY = apartY * forceSize / distance;
      node.pos.x  += forceX; node.pos.y  += forceY;
      other.pos.x -= forceX; other.pos.y -= forceY;
    }
  }
}
```

The new code is wordier and more repetitive, but if I measure it, the improvement is large enough to consider doing this kind of manual object flattening in performance-sensitive code. Chrome 38 appears to be quite good at optimizing object creation, and the new code produces a speedup of approximately 40 percent compared to the version that came before. On Firefox 32, the speedup is more than 60 percent. And on Internet Explorer 11, this piece of manual optimization makes the code run 80 percent faster!

This disparity makes it clear that the speed at which a piece of JavaScript executes is very much tied to the engine that is running it. JavaScript, because of its hard-to-compile nature, forces compilers to be extremely complicated pieces of software. This complexity makes them unpredictable. Small changes in your code, the way the code is used, or the version of the engine that you are running it on can cause big fluctuations in its performance.

Garbage Collection

So why are objects expensive? There are two reasons. First, the engine has to find a place to store them, and second, it has to figure out when they are no longer used and reclaim them. Both are tricky to do.

Imagine memory, again, as a long, long series of bits. When the program starts, it might receive an empty piece of memory and just start putting the objects it creates in there, one after the other. But at some point, the space is full, and some of the objects in it are no longer used by the program. The JavaScript engine has to figure out which objects are used and which are not, and then mark the unused pieces of memory as ready to be reused.

Now the program's memory space is a bit of a mess, containing living objects interspersed with free space. Creating a new object involves finding a piece of free space large enough for the object, which might require some searching. Alternatively, the engine could move all live objects to the start of the memory space, which makes creating new objects cheaper (they can just be put one after the other again) but requires more work when moving the old objects.

In principle, figuring out which objects are still used requires tracing through all reachable objects, starting from the global scope and the currently active local scope. Any object referenced from those scopes, directly or indirectly, is still alive. If your program has a lot of data in memory, this is quite a lot of work.

A technique called *generational garbage collection* can help reduce these costs. Chrome uses this technique, which is probably the main reason why getting rid of the intermediate vector objects made a smaller difference in that browser than in other browsers. Firefox is, at the time of writing, working on moving to this approach as well.

Generational garbage collection exploits the fact that most objects have short lives. It splits the memory available to the JavaScript program into two or more *generations*. New objects are created in the space reserved for the young generation. When this space is full, the engine figures out which of the objects in it are still alive and moves those to the next generation. If only a small fraction of the objects in the young generation are still alive when this occurs, only a small amount of work has to be done to move these objects.

Of course, figuring out which objects are alive requires knowing about all references to objects in the live generation. The engine wants to avoid looking through all the objects in the older generations every time the young generation is collected. For this reason, when a reference is created from an old object to a new object, this reference must be recorded so that it can be taken into account during the next collection. This makes writing to old objects slightly more expensive, but that cost is more than compensated for by the time saved during garbage collection.

Writing to Objects

Given that writing to old objects might incur a cost, you can rightly feel a bit worried about the way our code is applying forces. The inner loop updates the x and y properties of the long-lived node position objects. For a graph with N nodes, the inner loop runs N^2 times. For our 85-node test graph, this is 7,225 times for every iteration of the simulation.

Computing the forces locally and updating the node positions only after all forces have been fully computed might help. This requires some additional code to build up the arrays that hold the forces and to apply those forces at the end of the function.

```
function forceDirected_localforce(graph) {
  var forcesX = [], forcesY = [];
  for (var i = 0; i < graph.length; i++)
   forcesX[i] = forcesY[i] = 0;

  for (var i = 0; i < graph.length; i++) {
    var node = graph[i];
    for (var j = i + 1; j < graph.length; j++) {
      var other = graph[j];
      var apartX = other.pos.x - node.pos.x;
      var apartY = other.pos.y - node.pos.y;
      var distance = Math.max(1, Math.sqrt(apartX * apartX + apartY * apartY));
      var forceSize = -repulsionStrength / (distance * distance);
      if (node.hasEdge(other))
        forceSize += (distance - springLength) * springStrength;

      var forceX = apartX * forceSize / distance;
      var forceY = apartY * forceSize / distance;
      forcesX[i] += forceX; forcesY[i] += forceY;
      forcesX[j] -= forceX; forcesY[j] -= forceY;
    }
  }

  for (var i = 0; i < graph.length; i++) {
    graph[i].pos.x += forcesX[i];
    graph[i].pos.y += forcesY[i];
  }
}
```

Batching position updates like this improves the program's speed by another 20 percent. Interestingly, this improvement is consistently visible on all three browsers I tested on, even though two of them supposedly don't use generational garbage collection. This most likely has to do with the way they do their garbage collection *incrementally*, cutting up the work of tracing all live memory into small chunks, rather than doing it all at once, which could cause noticeable pauses in the program's execution. This technique also requires keeping track of newly created references.

Step by step, we've transformed our small program, making it less pretty but about 85 percent faster (the last version takes about 15 percent of the time that the first version took).

I want to urge you again to not apply these techniques to all code you write. For most code, it won't make a difference. Only code in inner loops that runs *very* often benefits from this kind of tweaking.

Dynamic Types

JavaScript expressions that fetch a property from an object, like node.pos, are far from trivial to compile. In many languages, *variables* have a type, and thus, when you perform an operation on the value they hold, the compiler already knows what kind of operation you need. In JavaScript, only *values* have types, and a variable can end up holding values of different types.

This means that, initially, the compiler knows little about the property the code might be trying to access and has to produce code that handles all possible types. If node holds an undefined value, the code must throw an error. If it holds a string, it must look up pos in String.prototype. If it holds an object, the way the pos property is extracted from it depends on the type of object. And so on.

Fortunately, variables in most programs *do* have a single type, though JavaScript does not require it. And if the compiler knows the variable type, it can use this information to create more efficient code. If node has always been an object with pos and edges properties so far, the optimizing compiler code can simply create code that fetches the property from its known position in such an object, which is simple and fast.

But events observed in the past do not give any guarantees about events that will occur in the future. Some piece of code that hasn't run yet might still pass another type of value to our function—a different kind of node object, for example, which also has an id property.

So the compiled code still has to *check* whether its assumptions hold and take an appropriate action if they do not. An engine could deoptimize entirely, falling back to the unoptimized version of the function. Or it could compile a new version of the function that also handles the newly observed type.

You can observe the slowdown caused by the failure to predict object types by intentionally messing up the uniformity of the input objects for our graph layout function, as in this example:

```
var mangledGraph = treeGraph(4, 4);
mangledGraph.forEach(function(node) {
  var letter = Math.floor(Math.random() * 26);
```

```
    node[String.fromCharCode("A".charCodeAt(0) + letter)] = true;
});

runLayout(forceDirected_localforce, mangledGraph);
```

Every node gets an extra property, named with a random uppercase letter. The letter is computed by taking the character code of the *A* character and adding a random number to it.

If we run our fast simulation code on the resulting graph, it becomes three times as slow on Chrome 38 and nine (!) times as slow on Firefox 32. Now that object types vary, the code has to look up the properties without prior knowledge about the shape of the object, which is a lot more expensive to do.

A similar technique is used for things other than property access. The + operator, for example, means different things depending on what kind of values it is applied to. Instead of always running the full code that handles all these meanings, a smart JavaScript compiler will use previous observations to build up some expectation of the type that the operator is probably being applied to. If it is applied only to numbers, a much simpler piece of machine code can be generated to handle it. But again, such assumptions must be checked every time the function runs.

The moral of the story is that if a piece of code needs to be fast, you can help by feeding it consistent types. JavaScript engines can handle cases where a handful of different types occur relatively well—they will generate code that handles all of these types and deoptimizes only when a new type is seen. But the resulting code is still slower than what you would get for a single type.

Summary

Thanks to the enormous amount of money being poured into the Web, as well as the rivalry between the different browsers, JavaScript compilers are good at what they do: making code run fast.

But sometimes you have to help them a little and rewrite your inner loops to avoid more expensive JavaScript features. Higher-order functions are one such feature. Creating fewer objects (and arrays and strings) can also help.

Before you start mangling your code to make it faster, think about ways to make it do less work. The biggest opportunities for optimization are often found in this direction.

JavaScript engines compile hot code multiple times and will use information gathered during previous execution to compile more efficient code. You can help by giving your variables a consistent type.

Exercises

Pathfinding

Write a function `findPath` that tries to find the shortest path between two nodes in a graph. It takes two `GraphNode` objects (as used throughout this chapter) as arguments and returns either `null`, if no path could be found, or an array of nodes that represents a path through the graph. Nodes that occur next to each other in this array should have an edge between them.

A good approach for finding a path in a graph goes like this:

1. Create a work list that contains a single, single-node path that consists of the starting node.

2. Start with the first path in the work list.

3. If the node at the end of the current path is the goal node, return this path.

4. Otherwise, for each neighbor of the node at the end of the path, if that node has not been looked at before (does not occur at the end of any paths in the work list), create a new path by extending the current path with that neighbor and add the path to the work list.

5. If there are more paths in the work list, go to the next path and continue at step 3.

6. Otherwise, there is no path.

By "spreading out" paths from the start node, this approach ensures that it always reaches a given other node by the shortest path since longer paths are considered only after all shorter paths have been tried.

Implement this program and test it on some simple tree graphs. Construct a graph with a cycle in it (for example, by adding edges to a tree graph with the `connect` method) and see whether your function can find the shortest path when there are multiple possibilities.

Timing

Use `Date.now()` to measure the time it takes your `findPath` function to find a path in a more complicated graph. Since `treeGraph` always puts the root at the start of the graph array and a leaf at the end, you can give your function a nontrivial task by doing something like this:

```
var graph = treeGraph(5, 3);
console.log(findPath(graph[0], graph[graph.length - 1]).length);
// ▷ 5
```

Create a test case that has a running time of around half a second. Be careful with passing larger numbers to `treeGraph`—the size of the graph increases exponentially, so you can easily make your graph so big that it'll take huge amounts of time and memory to find a path through them.

Optimizing

Now that you have a measured test case, find ways to make your `findPath` function faster.

Think both about macro-optimization (doing less work) and micro-optimization (doing the given work in a cheaper way). Also, consider ways to use less memory and allocate fewer or smaller data structures.

If you need to, you can start by adding `id` properties to nodes to make it easier to store information about them in a map. Use a function like this one:

```
function withIDs(graph) {
  for (var i = 0; i < graph.length; i++) graph[i].id = i;
  return graph;
}
```

EXERCISE HINTS

The hints below might help when you are stuck with one of the exercises in this book. They don't give away the entire solution, but rather try to help you find it yourself.

Program Structure

Looping a Triangle

You can start with a program that simply prints out the numbers 1 to 7, which you can derive by making a few modifications to the even number printing example given earlier in the chapter, where the for loop was introduced.

Now consider the equivalence between numbers and strings of hash characters. Similarly, you can go from 1 to 2 by adding 1 (+= 1). You can go from "#" to "##" by adding a character (+= "#"). Thus, your solution can closely follow the number printing program.

FizzBuzz

Going over the numbers is clearly a looping job, and selecting what to print is a matter of conditional execution. Remember the trick of using the remainder (%) operator for checking whether a number is divisible by another number (has a remainder of zero).

In the first version, there are three possible outcomes for every number, so you'll have to create an if/else if/else chain.

The second version of the program has a straightforward solution and a clever one. The simple way is to add another "branch" to precisely test the given condition. For the clever method, build up a string containing the word or words to output and print either this word or the number if there is no word, potentially by making elegant use of the || operator.

Chess Board

The string can be built by starting with an empty one ("") and repeatedly adding characters. A newline character is written "\n".

Use console.log to inspect the output of your program.

To work with two dimensions, you will need a loop inside of a loop. Put braces around the bodies of both loops to make it easy to see where they start and end. Try to properly indent these bodies. The order of the loops must follow the order in which we build up the string (line by line, left to right, top to bottom). So the outer loop handles the lines, and the inner loop handles the characters on a line.

You'll need two variables to track your progress. To know whether to put a space or a hash sign at a given position, you could test whether the sum of the two counters is even (% 2).

Terminating a line by adding a newline character happens after the line has been built up, so do this after the inner loop but inside of the outer loop.

Functions

Minimum

If you have trouble putting braces and parentheses in the right place to get a valid function definition, start by copying one of the examples in this chapter and modifying it.

A function may contain multiple return statements.

Recursion

Your function will likely look somewhat similar to the inner find function in the recursive findSolution example in this chapter, with an if/else if/else chain that tests which of the three cases applies. The final else, corresponding to the third case, makes the recursive call. Each of the branches should contain a return statement or in some other way arrange for a specific value to be returned.

When given a negative number, the function will recurse again and again, passing itself an ever more negative number, thus getting further and further away from returning a result. It will eventually run out of stack space and abort.

Bean Counting

A loop in your function will have to look at every character in the string by running an index from zero to one below its length (< string.length). If the character at the current position is the same as the one the function is looking for, it adds 1 to a counter variable. Once the loop has finished, the counter can be returned.

Take care to make all the variables used in the function *local* to the function by using the var keyword.

Data Structures: Objects and Arrays

The Sum of a Range

Building up an array is most easily done by first initializing a variable to [] (a fresh, empty array) and repeatedly calling its push method to add a value. Don't forget to return the array at the end of the function.

Since the end boundary is inclusive, you'll need to use the <= operator rather than simply < to check for the end of your loop.

To check whether the optional step argument was given, either check arguments.length or compare the value of the argument to undefined. If it wasn't given, simply set it to its default value (1) at the top of the function.

Having range understand negative step values is probably best done by writing two separate loops—one for counting up and one for counting down—because the comparison that checks whether the loop is finished needs to be >= rather than <= when counting down.

It might also be worthwhile to use a different default step, namely, -1, when the end of the range is smaller than the start. That way, range(5, 2) returns something meaningful, rather than getting stuck in an infinite loop.

Reversing an Array

There are two obvious ways to implement reverseArray. The first is to simply go over the input array from front to back and use the unshift method on the new array to insert each element at its start. The second is to loop over the input array backward and use the push method. Iterating over an array backward requires a (somewhat awkward) for specification like (var i = array.length - 1; i \textgreater{}= 0; i--).

Reversing the array in place is harder. You have to be careful not to overwrite elements that you will need later. Using reverseArray or otherwise copying the whole array (`array.slice(0)` is a good way to copy an array) works but is cheating.

The trick is to *swap* the first and last elements, then the second and second-to-last, and so on. You can do this by looping over half the length of the array (use `Math.floor` to round down—you don't need to touch the middle element in an array with an odd length) and swapping the element at position i with the one at position `array.length - 1 - i`. You can use a local variable to briefly hold on to one of the elements, overwrite that one with its mirror image, and then put the value from the local variable in the place where the mirror image used to be.

A List

Building up a list is best done back to front. So `arrayToList` could iterate over the array backward (see previous exercise) and, for each element, add an object to the list. You can use a local variable to hold the part of the list that was built so far and use a pattern like `list = {value: X, rest: list}` to add an element.

To run over a list (in `listToArray` and `nth`), a `for` loop specification like this can be used:

```
for (var node = list; node; node = node.rest) {}
```

Can you see how that works? Every iteration of the loop, `node` points to the current sublist, and the body can read its `value` property to get the current element. At the end of an iteration, `node` moves to the next sublist. When that is null, we have reached the end of the list and the loop is finished.

The recursive version of `nth` will, similarly, look at an ever smaller part of the "tail" of the list and at the same time count down the index until it reaches zero, at which point it can return the `value` property of the node it is looking at. To get the zeroeth element of a list, you simply take the `value` property of its head node. To get element $N + 1$, you take the Nth element of the list that's in this list's rest property.

Deep Comparison

Your test for whether you are dealing with a real object will look something like `typeof x == "object" && x != null`. Be careful to compare properties only when *both* arguments are objects. In all other cases you can just immediately return the result of applying `===`.

Use a `for/in` loop to go over the properties. You need to test whether both objects have the same set of property names and whether those properties have identical values. The first test can be done by counting the properties in both objects and returning `false` if the numbers of properties are different. If they're the same, then go over the properties of one object, and for each of them, verify that the other object also has the property. The values of the properties are compared by a recursive call to `deepEqual`.

Returning the correct value from the function is best done by immediately returning `false` when a mismatch is noticed and returning `true` at the end of the function.

Higher-Order Functions

Mother-Child Age Difference

Because not all elements in the `ancestry` array produce useful data (we can't compute the age difference unless we know the birth date of the mother), we will have to apply `filter` in some manner before calling `average`. You could do it as a first pass, by defining a `hasKnownMother` function and filtering on that first. Alternatively, you could start by calling `map` and in your mapping function return either the age difference or `null` if no mother is known. Then, you can call `filter` to remove the `null` elements before passing the array to `average`.

Historical Life Expectancy

The essence of this example lies in grouping the elements of a collection by some common aspect. Here, we want to split the array of ancestors into smaller arrays, grouping ancestors by century.

During the grouping process, keep an object that associates century names (numbers) with arrays of either person objects or ages. Since we do not know in advance what categories we will find, we'll have to create them on the fly. For each person, after computing their century, we test whether that century was already known. If not, add an array for it. Then add the person (or age) to the array for the proper century.

Finally, a `for/in` loop can be used to print the average ages for the individual centuries.

Every and Then Some

The functions can follow a similar pattern to the definition of `forEach` at the start of the chapter, except that they must return immediately (with the right value) when the predicate function returns `false`—or `true`. Don't forget to put another `return` statement after the loop so that the function also returns the correct value when it reaches the end of the array.

The Secret Life of Objects

A Vector Type

Your solution can follow the pattern of the `Rabbit` constructor from this chapter quite closely.

Adding a getter property to the constructor can be done with the `Object.defineProperty` function. To compute the distance from $(0, 0)$ to (x, y), you can use the Pythagorean theorem, which says that the square of the distance we are looking for is equal to the square of the x-coordinate plus the square of the y-coordinate. Thus, $\sqrt{x^2 + y^2}$ is the number you want, and `Math.sqrt` is the way you compute a square root in JavaScript.

Another Cell

You'll have to store all three constructor arguments in the instance object. The `minWidth` and `minHeight` methods should call through to the corresponding methods in the inner cell but ensure that no number less than the given size is returned (possibly using `Math.max`).

Don't forget to add a `draw` method that simply forwards the call to the inner cell.

Sequence Interface

One way to solve this is to give the sequence objects *state*, meaning their properties are changed in the process of using them. You could store a counter that indicates how far the sequence object has advanced.

At least, your interface will need to expose a way to get the next element and to find out whether the iteration has reached the end of the sequence yet. It is tempting to roll these into one method, `next`, which returns `null` or `undefined` when the sequence is at its end. But now you have a problem when a sequence actually contains `null`. So a separate method (or getter property) to find out whether the end has been reached is probably preferable.

Another solution is to avoid changing state in the object. You can expose a method for getting the current element (without advancing any counter) and another for getting a new sequence that represents the remaining elements after the current one (or a special value if the end of the sequence is reached). This is quite elegant—a sequence value will "stay itself" even after it is used and can thus be shared with other code without worrying about what might happen to it. It is, unfortunately, also somewhat inefficient in a language like JavaScript because it involves creating a lot of objects during iteration.

Project: Electronic Life

Artificial Stupidity

The greediness problem can be attacked in several ways. The critters could stop eating when they reach a certain energy level. Or they could eat only every N turns (by keeping a counter of the turns since their last meal in a property on the critter object). Or to make sure plants never go entirely extinct, the critters could refuse to eat a plant unless they see at least one other plant nearby (using the `findAll` method on the view). A combination of these, or some entirely different strategy, might also work.

Making the critters move more effectively could be done by stealing one of the movement strategies from the critters in our old, energyless world. Both the bouncing behavior and the wall-following behavior showed a much wider range of movement than completely random staggering.

Making critters breed more slowly is trivial. Just increase the minimum energy level at which they reproduce. Of course, making the ecosystem more stable also makes it more boring. If you have a handful of fat, immobile critters forever munching on a sea of plants and never reproducing, that makes for a very stable ecosystem. But no one wants to watch that.

Predators

Many of the same tricks that worked for the previous exercise also apply here. Making the predators big (lots of energy) and having them reproduce slowly is recommended. That'll make them less vulnerable to periods of starvation when the herbivores are scarce.

Beyond staying alive, keeping its food stock alive is a predator's main objective. Find some way to make predators hunt more aggressively when there are a lot of herbivores and hunt more slowly (or not at all) when prey is rare. Since herbivores move around, the simple trick of eating one only when others are nearby is unlikely to work—that'll happen so rarely that your predator will starve. But you could keep track of observations in previous turns, in some data structure kept on the predator objects, and have it base its behavior on what it has seen recently.

Bugs and Error Handling

Retry

The call to `primitiveMultiply` should obviously happen in a try block. The corresponding catch block should rethrow the exception when it is not an instance of `MultiplicatorUnitFailure` and ensure the call is retried when it is.

To do the retrying, you can either use a loop that breaks only when a call succeeds—as in the `look` example earlier in this chapter—or use recursion and hope you don't get a string of failures so long that it overflows the stack (which is a pretty safe bet).

The Locked Box

This exercise calls for a `finally` block, as you probably guessed. Your function should first unlock the box and then call the argument function from inside a try body. The `finally` block after it should lock the box again.

To make sure we don't lock the box when it wasn't already locked, check its lock at the start of the function and unlock and lock it only when it started out locked.

Regular Expressions

Quoting Style

The most obvious solution is to only replace quotes with a nonword character on at least one side. Something like /\W'|'\W/. But you also have to take the start and end of the line into account.

In addition, you must ensure that the replacement also includes the characters that were matched by the \W pattern so that those are not dropped. This can be done by wrapping them in parentheses and including their groups in the replacement string ($1, $2). Groups that are not matched will be replaced by nothing.

Numbers Again

First, do not forget the backslash in front of the dot.

Matching the optional sign in front of the number, as well as in front of the exponent, can be done with [+\-]? or (\+|-|) (plus, minus, or nothing). The more complicated part of the exercise is the problem of matching both "5." and ".5" without also matching ".". For this, a good solution is to use the | operator to separate the two cases—either one or more digits optionally followed by a dot and zero or more digits *or* a dot followed by one or more digits.

Finally, to make the *e* case insensitive, either add an i option to the regular expression or use [eE].

Modules

Month Names

This follows the weekDay module almost exactly. A function expression, called immediately, wraps the variable that holds the array of names, along with the two functions that must be exported. The functions are put in an object and returned. The returned interface object is stored in the month variable.

A Return to Electronic Life

Here is what I came up with. I've put parentheses around internal functions.

```
Module "grid"
  Vector
  Grid
  directions
  directionNames

Module "world"
  (randomElement)
  (elementFromChar)
  (charFromElement)
```

```
View
World
LifelikeWorld
directions [reexported]

Module "simple_ecosystem"
  (randomElement) [duplicated]
  (dirPlus)
  Wall
  BouncingCritter
  WallFollower

Module "ecosystem"
  Wall [duplicated]
  Plant
  PlantEater
  SmartPlantEater
  Tiger
```

I have reexported the directions array from the grid module from world so that modules built on that (the ecosystems) don't have to know or worry about the existence of the grid module.

I also duplicated two generic and tiny helper values (randomElement and Wall) since they are used as internal details in different contexts and do not belong in the interfaces for these modules.

Circular Dependencies

The trick is to add the exports object created for a module to require's cache *before* actually running the module. This means the module will not yet have had a chance to override module.exports, so we do not know whether it wants to export some other value. After loading, the cache object is overridden with module.exports, which may be a different value.

But if in the course of loading the module, a second module is loaded that asks for the first module, its default exports object, which is likely still empty at this point, will be in the cache, and the second module will receive a reference to it. If it doesn't try to do anything with the object until the first module has finished loading, things will work.

Project: A Programming Language

Arrays

The easiest way to do this is to represent Egg arrays with JavaScript arrays.

The values added to the top environment must be functions. Array.prototype.slice can be used to convert an arguments array-like object into a regular array.

Closure

Again, we are riding along on a JavaScript mechanism to get the equivalent feature in Egg. Special forms are passed the local environment in which they are evaluated so that they can evaluate their subforms in that environment. The function returned by fun closes over the env argument given to its enclosing function and uses that to create the function's local environment when it is called.

This means that the prototype of the local environment will be the environment in which the function was created, which makes it possible to access variables in that environment from the function. This is all there is to implementing closure (though to compile it in a way that is actually efficient, you'd need to do some more work).

Comments

Make sure your solution handles multiple comments in a row, with whitespace potentially between or after them.

A regular expression is probably the easiest way to solve this. Write something that matches "whitespace or a comment, zero or more times." Use the exec or match method and look at the length of the first element in the returned array (the whole match) to find out how many characters to slice off.

Fixing Scope

You will have to loop through one scope at a time, using Object.getPrototypeOf to go the next outer scope. For each scope, use hasOwnProperty to find out whether the variable, indicated by the name property of the first argument to set, exists in that scope. If it does, set it to the result of evaluating the second argument to set and then return that value.

If the outermost scope is reached (Object.getPrototypeOf returns null) and we haven't found the variable yet, it doesn't exist, and an error should be thrown.

The Document Object Model

Build a Table

Use document.createElement to create new element nodes, document .createTextNode to create text nodes, and the appendChild method to put nodes into other nodes.

You should loop over the key names once to fill in the top row and then again for each object in the array to construct the data rows.

Don't forget to return the enclosing <table> element at the end of the function.

Elements by Tag Name

The solution is most easily expressed with a recursive function, similar to the talksAbout function defined earlier in this chapter.

You could call byTagname itself recursively, concatenating the resulting arrays to produce the output. For a more efficient approach, define an inner function that calls itself recursively and that has access to an array variable defined in the outer function to which it can add the matching elements it finds. Don't forget to call the inner function once from the outer function.

The recursive function must check the node type. Here we are interested only in node type 1 (document.ELEMENT_NODE). For such nodes, we must loop over their children and, for each child, see whether the child matches the query while also doing a recursive call on it to inspect its own children.

Handling Events

Censored Keyboard

The solution to this exercise involves preventing the default behavior of key events. You can handle either "keypress" or "keydown". If either of them has preventDefault called on it, the letter will not appear.

Identifying the letter typed requires looking at the keyCode or charCode property and comparing that with the codes for the letters you want to filter. In "keydown", you do not have to worry about lowercase and uppercase letters, since it identifies only the key pressed. If you decide to handle "keypress" instead, which identifies the actual character typed, you have to make sure you test for both cases. Here's one way to do that:

```
/[qwx]/i.test(String.fromCharCode(event.charCode))
```

Mouse Trail

Creating the elements is best done in a loop. Append them to the document to make them show up. Store the trail elements in an array, so you can access them later to change their position.

Cycling through them can be done by keeping a counter variable and adding 1 to it every time the "mousemove" event fires. The remainder operator (% 10) can then be used to get a valid array index to pick the element you want to position during a given event.

Another interesting effect can be achieved by modeling a simple physics system. Use only the "mousemove" event to update a pair of variables that track the mouse position. Then use requestAnimationFrame to simulate the trailing elements being attracted to the position of the mouse pointer. At every animation step, update their position based on their position relative to the pointer (and optionally, a speed that is stored for each element). Figuring out a good way to do this is up to you.

Tabs

One pitfall you'll probably run into is that you can't directly use the node's childNodes property as a collection of tab nodes. For one thing, when you add the buttons, they will also become child nodes and end up in this object because it is live. For another, the text nodes created for the whitespace between the nodes are also in there and should not get their own tabs.

To work around this, start by building up a real array of all the children in the wrapper that have a nodeType of 1.

When registering event handlers on the buttons, the handler functions will need to know which tab element is associated with the button. If they are created in a normal loop, you can access the loop index variable from inside the function, but it won't give you the correct number because that variable will have been further changed by the loop.

A simple workaround is to use the forEach method and create the handler functions from inside the function passed to forEach. The loop index, which is passed as a second argument to that function, will be a normal local variable there and won't be overwritten by further iterations.

Project: A Platform Game

Game Over

The most obvious solution would be to make lives a variable that lives in runGame and is thus visible to the startLevel closure.

Another approach, which fits nicely with the spirit of the rest of the function, would be to add a second parameter to startLevel that gives the number of lives. When the whole state of a system is stored in the arguments to a function, calling that function provides an elegant way to transition to a new state.

In any case, when a level is lost, there should now be two possible state transitions. If that was the last life, we go back to level zero with the starting amount of lives. If not, we repeat the current level with one less life remaining.

Pausing the Game

An animation can be interrupted by returning false from the function given to runAnimation. It can be continued by calling runAnimation again.

To communicate that the animation should be interrupted to the function passed to runAnimation so that it can return false, you can use a variable that both the event handler and that function have access to.

When finding a way to unregister the handlers registered by trackKeys, remember that the *exact* same function value that was passed to addEventListener must be passed to removeEventListener to successfully remove a handler. Thus, the handler function value created in trackKeys must be available to the code that unregisters the handlers.

You can add a property to the object returned by trackKeys, which contains either that function value or a method that handles the unregistering directly.

Drawing on Canvas

Shapes

The trapezoid (1) is easy to draw using a path. Pick suitable center coordinates and add each of the four corners around that.

The diamond (2) can be drawn the easy way, with a path, or the interesting way, with a rotate transformation. To use rotation, you will have to apply a trick similar to what we did in the flipHorizontally function. Because you want to rotate around the center of your rectangle and not around the point (0,0), you must first translate to there, then rotate, and then translate back.

For the zigzag (3) it becomes impractical to write a new call to lineTo for each line segment. Instead, you should use a loop. You can have each iteration draw either two line segments (right and then left again) or one, in which case you must use the evenness (% 2) of the loop index to determine whether to go left or right.

You'll also need a loop for the spiral (4). If you draw a series of points, with each point moving further along a circle around the spiral's center, you get a circle. If, during the loop, you vary the radius of the circle on which you are putting the current point and go around more than once, the result is a spiral.

The star (5) depicted is built out of quadraticCurveTo lines. You could also draw one with straight lines. Divide a circle into eight pieces, or a piece for each point you want your star to have. Draw lines between these points, making them curve toward the center of the star. With quadraticCurveTo, you can use the center as the control point.

The Pie Chart

You will need to call fillText and set the context's textAlign and textBaseline properties in such a way that the text ends up where you want it.

A sensible way to position the labels would be to put the text on the line going from the center of the pie through the middle of the slice. You don't want to put the text directly against the side of the pie but rather move the text out to the side of the pie by a given number of pixels.

The angle of this line is currentAngle + 0.5 * sliceAngle. The following code finds a position on this line, 120 pixels from the center:

```
var middleAngle = currentAngle + 0.5 * sliceAngle;
var textX = Math.cos(middleAngle) * 120 + centerX;
var textY = Math.sin(middleAngle) * 120 + centerY;
```

For textBaseline, the value "middle" is probably appropriate when using this approach. What to use for textAlign depends on the side of the circle we are on. On the left, it should be "right", and on the right, it should be "left" so that the text is positioned away from the pie.

If you are not sure how to find out which side of the circle a given angle is on, look to the explanation of Math.cos in the previous exercise. The cosine of an angle tells us which x-coordinate it corresponds to, which in turn tells us exactly which side of the circle we are on.

A Bouncing Ball

A box is easy to draw with strokeRect. Define a variable that holds its size or define two variables if your box's width and height differ. To create a round ball, start a path, call arc(x, y, radius, 0, 7), which creates an arc going from zero to more than a whole circle, and fill it.

To model the ball's position and speed, you can use the Vector type from Chapter 15. Give it a starting speed, preferably one that is not purely vertical or horizontal, and every frame, multiply that speed by the amount of time that elapsed. When the ball gets too close to a vertical wall, invert the x component in its speed. Likewise, invert the y component when it hits a horizontal wall.

After finding the ball's new position and speed, use clearRect to delete the scene and redraw it using the new position.

Precomputed Mirroring

The key to the solution is the fact that we can use a canvas element as a source image when using drawImage. It is possible to create an extra <canvas> element, without adding it to the document, and draw our inverted sprites to it once. When drawing an actual frame, we just copy the already inverted sprites to the main canvas.

Some care would be required because images do not load instantly. We do the inverted drawing only once, and if we do it before the image loads, it won't draw anything. A "load" handler on the image can be used to draw the inverted images to the extra canvas. This canvas can be used as a drawing source immediately (it'll simply be blank until we draw the character onto it).

HTTP

Content Negotiation

Look at the various examples of using an XMLHttpRequest in this chapter to see the method calls involved in making a request. You can use a synchronous request (by setting the third parameter to open to false) if you want.

Asking for a bogus media type will return a response with code 406, "Not acceptable," which is the code a server should return when it can't fulfill the Accept header.

Waiting for Multiple Promises

The function passed to the `Promise` constructor will have to call `then` on each of the promises in the given array. When one of them succeeds, two things need to happen. The resulting value needs to be stored in the correct position of a result array, and we must check whether this was the last pending promise and finish our own promise if it was.

The latter can be done with a counter, which is initialized to the length of the input array and from which we subtract 1 every time a promise succeeds. When it reaches 0, we are done. Make sure you take the situation where the input array is empty (and thus no promise will ever resolve) into account.

Handling failure requires some thought but turns out to be extremely simple. Just pass the failure function of the wrapping promise to each of the promises in the array so that a failure in one of them triggers the failure of the whole wrapper.

Forms and Form Fields

A JavaScript Workbench

Use `document.querySelector` or `document.getElementById` to get access to the elements defined in your HTML. An event handler for `"click"` or `"mousedown"` events on the button can get the `value` property of the text field and call `new Function` on it.

Make sure you wrap both the call to `new Function` and the call to its result in a `try` block so that you can catch exceptions that it produces. In this case, we really don't know what type of exception we are looking for, so catch everything.

The `textContent` property of the output element can be used to fill it with a string message. Or if you want to keep the old content around, create a new text node using `document.createTextNode` and append it to the element. Remember to add a newline character to the end so that not all output appears on a single line.

Autocompletion

The best event for updating the suggestion list is `"input"` since that will fire immediately when the content of the field is changed.

Then loop over the array of terms and see whether they start with the given string. For example, you could call `indexOf` and see whether the result is zero. For each matching string, add an element to the suggestions `<div>`. You should probably also empty that each time you start updating the suggestions, for example, by setting its `textContent` to the empty string.

You could either add a `"click"` event handler to every suggestion element or add a single one to the outer `<div>` that holds them and look at the `target` property of the event to find out which suggestion was clicked.

To get the suggestion text out of a DOM node, you could look at its textContent or set an attribute to explicitly store the text when you create the element.

Conway's Game of Life

To solve the problem of having the changes conceptually happen at the same time, try to see the computation of a generation as a pure function, which takes one grid and produces a new grid that represents the next turn.

Representing the grid can be done in any of the ways shown in Chapters 7 and 15. Counting live neighbors can be done with two nested loops, looping over adjacent coordinates. Take care not to count cells outside of the field and to ignore the cell in the center, whose neighbors we are counting.

Making changes to checkboxes that will take effect on the next generation can be done in two ways. An event handler could notice these changes and update the current grid to reflect them, or you could generate a fresh grid from the values in the checkboxes before computing the next turn.

If you choose to go with event handlers, you might want to attach attributes that identify the position that each checkbox corresponds to so that it is easy to find out which cell to change.

To draw the grid of checkboxes, you either can use a <table> element (see Chapter 13) or simply put them all in the same element with
 (line break) elements between the rows.

Project: A Paint Program

Rectangles

You can use relativePos to find the corner corresponding to the start of the mouse drag. Figuring out where the drag ends can be done with trackDrag or by registering your own event handler.

When you have two corners of the rectangle, you must somehow translate these into the arguments that fillRect expects: the top-left corner, width, and height of the rectangle. Math.min can be used to find the leftmost x-coordinate and topmost y-coordinate. To get the width or height, you can call Math.abs (the absolute value) on the difference between two sides.

Showing the rectangle during the mouse drag requires a similar set of numbers but in the context of the whole page rather than relative to the canvas. Consider writing a function findRect, which converts two points into an object with top, left, width, and height properties so that you don't have to write the same logic twice.

You can then create a <div> node and set its style.position to absolute. When setting positioning styles, do not forget to append "px" to the numbers. The node must be added to the document (you can append it to document.body) and also removed again when the drag ends and the actual rectangle is drawn onto the canvas.

Color Picker

You'll again need to use relativePos to find out which pixel was clicked. The pixelAt function in the example demonstrates how to get the values for a given pixel. Putting those into an rgb string merely requires some string concatenation.

Make sure you verify that the exception you catch is an instance of SecurityError so that you don't accidentally handle the wrong kind of exception.

Flood Fill

Given a pair of starting coordinates and the image data for the whole canvas, this approach should work:

1. Create an array to hold information about already colored coordinates.

2. Create a work list array to hold coordinates that must be looked at. Put the start position in it.

3. When the work list is empty, we are done.

4. Remove one pair of coordinates from the work list.

5. If those coordinates are already in our array of colored pixels, go back to step 3.

6. Color the pixel at the current coordinates and add the coordinates to the array of colored pixels.

7. Add the coordinates of each adjacent pixel whose color is the same as the starting pixel's original color to the work list.

8. Return to step 3.

The work list can simply be an array of vector objects. The data structure that tracks colored pixels will be consulted *very* often. Searching through the whole thing every time a new pixel is visited will take a lot of time. You could instead create an array that has a value in it for every pixel, using again the $x + y \times$ width scheme for associating positions with pixels. When checking whether a pixel has been colored already, you could directly access the field corresponding to the current pixel.

You can compare colors by running over the relevant part of the data array, comparing one field at a time. Or you can "condense" a color to a single number or string and compare those. When doing this, ensure that every color produces a unique value. For example, simply adding the color's components is not safe since multiple colors will have the same sum.

When enumerating the neighbors of a given point, take care to exclude neighbors that are not inside of the canvas or your program might run off into one direction forever.

Node.js

Content Negotiation, Again

Don't forget to call the `end` method on the object returned by `http.request` in order to actually fire off the request.

The response object passed to `http.request`'s callback is a readable stream. This means that it is not entirely trivial to get the whole response body from it. The following utility function reads a whole stream and calls a callback function with the result, using the usual pattern of passing any errors it encounters as the first argument to the callback:

```javascript
function readStreamAsString(stream, callback) {
  var data = "";
  stream.on("data", function(chunk) {
    data += chunk;
  });
  stream.on("end", function() {
    callback(null, data);
  });
  stream.on("error", function(error) {
    callback(error);
  });
}
```

Fixing a Leak

It is enough to strip out all occurrences of two dots that have a slash, a backslash, or the end of the string on both sides. Using the `replace` method with a regular expression is the easiest way to do this. Do not forget the g flag on the expression, or `replace` will replace only a single instance, and people could still get around this safety measure by including additional double dots in their paths! Also, make sure you do the replace *after* decoding the string, or it would be possible to foil the check by encoding a dot or a slash.

Another potentially worrying case is when paths start with a slash, which are interpreted as absolute paths. But because `urlToPath` puts a dot character in front of the path, it is impossible to create requests that result in such a path. Multiple slashes in a row, inside the path, are odd but will be treated as a single slash by the filesystem.

Creating Directories

You can use the function that implements the `DELETE` method as a blueprint for the `MKCOL` method. When no file is found, try to create a directory with `fs.mkdir`. When a directory exists at that path, you can return a 204 response so that directory creation requests are idempotent. If a nondirectory file exists here, return an error code. The code 400 ("bad request") would be appropriate here.

A Public Space on the Web

You can create a `<textarea>` element to hold the content of the file that is being edited. A GET request, using `XMLHttpRequest`, can be used to get the current content of the file. You can use relative URLs like *index.html*, instead of *http://localhost:8000/index.html*, to refer to files on the same server as the running script.

Then, when the user clicks a button (you can use a `<form>` element and `"submit"` event or simply a `"click"` handler), make a PUT request to the same URL, with the content of the `<textarea>` as request body, to save the file.

You can then add a `<select>` element that contains all the files in the server's root directory by adding `<option>` elements containing the lines returned by a GET request to the URL /. When the user selects another file (a `"change"` event on the field), the script must fetch and display that file. Also, make sure that when saving a file, you use the currently selected filename.

Unfortunately, the server is too simplistic to be able to reliably read files from subdirectories since it does not tell us whether the thing we fetched with a GET request is a regular file or a directory. Can you think of a way to extend the server to address this?

Project: Skill-Sharing Website

Disk Persistence

The simplest solution I can come up with is to encode the whole `talks` object as JSON and dump it to a file with `fs.writeFile`. There is already a function (`registerChange`) that is called every time the server's data changes. It can be extended to write the new data to disk.

Pick a filename, for example, `./talks.json`. When the server starts, it can try to read that file with `fs.readFile`, and if that succeeds, the server can use the file's contents as its starting data.

Beware, though. The `talks` object started as a prototype-less object so that the `in` operator could be sanely used. `JSON.parse` will return regular objects with `Object.prototype` as their prototype. If you use JSON as your file format, you'll have to copy the properties of the object returned by `JSON.parse` into a new, prototype-less object.

Comment Field Resets

The ad hoc approach is to simply store the state of a talk's comment field (its content and whether it is focused) before redrawing the talk and then reset the field to its old state afterward.

Another solution would be to not simply replace the old DOM structure with the new one but recursively compare them, node by node, and update only the parts that actually changed. This is a lot harder to implement, but it's more general and continues working even if we add another text field.

Better Templates

You could change instantiateTemplate so that its inner function takes not just a node but also a current context as an argument. You can then, when looping over a node's child nodes, check whether the child has a template-repeat attribute. If it does, don't instantiate it once but instead loop over the array indicated by the attribute's value and instantiate it once for every element in the array, passing the current array element as context.

Conditionals can be implemented in a similar way, with attributes called, for example, template-when and template-unless, which cause a node to be instantiated only when a given property is true (or false).

The Unscriptables

Two central aspects of the approach taken in this chapter—a clean HTTP interface and client-side template rendering—don't work without JavaScript. Normal HTML forms can send GET and POST requests but not PUT or DELETE requests and can send their data only to a fixed URL.

Thus, the server would have to be revised to accept comments, new talks, and deleted talks through POST requests, whose bodies aren't JSON but rather use the URL-encoded format that HTML forms use (see Chapter 17). These requests would have to return the full new page so that users see the new state of the site after they make a change. This would not be too hard to engineer and could be implemented alongside the "clean" HTTP interface.

The code for rendering talks would have to be duplicated on the server. The index.html file, rather than being a static file, would have to be generated dynamically by adding a handler for it to the router. That way, it already includes the current talks and comments when it gets served.

JavaScript and Performance

Pathfinding

The work list can be an array, and you can add paths to it with the push method. You cannot use the built-in forEach method to loop over the work items since that uses the initial length of the array to bound the loop. We will be adding new items to the array from inside the loop, so its length has to be checked again on every iteration.

If you use arrays to represent paths, you can extend them with the concat method, as in path.concat([node]).

To find out whether a node has already been seen, you can loop over the existing work list normally or use the some method.

Optimizing

The main opportunity for macro-optimization is to get rid of the inner loop that figures out whether a node has already been looked at. Looking this up in an object is much faster than iterating over the work list to search for the node. But since JavaScript map objects require strings, not objects, as property names, we need a trick like withIDs to be able to use a map to associate information with a given object. (The next version of JavaScript defines an object type Map, which is a *real* map, whose keys can be any JavaScript values, not just strings.)

Another improvement can be made by changing the way paths are stored. Extending an array with a new element without modifying the existing array requires copying the whole array. A data structure like the list from Chapter 4 does not have this problem—it allows multiple extensions of a list to share the data that they have in common.

You can make your function internally store paths as objects with last and via properties, where last is the last node in the path and via is either null or another such object. This way, extending a path only requires creating an object with two properties, rather than copying a whole array. Make sure you convert the list to an actual array before returning it.

INDEX

Symbols

&& operator, 17, 20, 96
* operator, 13, 18, 156
*= operator, 34
{} (block), 31, 44, 85
{} (object), 63, 113
- operator, 14, 15, 18
-= operator, 34
= operator, 25, 64, 168, 170, 197
== operator, 16, 19, 66, 79
=== operator, 19, 79, 410
/ operator, 14
/= operator, 34
> operator, 16
>= operator, 16
< operator, 16
<= operator, 16
− operator, 34
% operator, 14, 34, 286, 408, 417, 419
+ operator, 13, 15, 18, 156, 403
++ operator, 34
+= operator, 34
?: operator, 17, 20
[] (array), 60
[] (subscript), 61
|| operator, 17, 19, 51, 96, 123, 326, 408
200 (HTTP status code), 300, 354
204 (HTTP status code), 360
2d (canvas context), 277
400 (HTTP status code), 424
404 (HTTP status code), 300, 359, 374, 376
405 (HTTP status code), 358
406 (HTTP status code), 420
500 (HTTP status code), 359, 363

A

a (HTML tag), 210, 224, 226, 318
Abelson, Hal, 190
absolute path, 424
absolute positioning, 229, 233, 241, 245, 250
abstract syntax tree, *see* syntax tree
abstraction, 82, 84, 85, 91, 191, 208, 218
acceleration, 268
Accept header, 312, 363, 420
access control, 127, 151, 178, 371
Access-Control-Allow-Origin header, 305
actionTypes object, 130
activeElement property, 317
actor, 256, 261, 266–267, 291
actorAt method, 266
addEntry function, 66
addEventListener method, 236, 270, 356
addition, 13, 117
address, 299
address bar, 209, 299, 301
adoption, 153
age difference (exercise), 95, 411
alert function, 27, 47, 211
algorithm, 423
algorithmic optimization, 398, 405
alignment, 114
all function, 313, 421
alpha, 343
alphanumeric character, 155
alt attribute, 221
ALT key, 240
altKey property, 240
ambiguity, 202
AMD, 183, 185
American English, 156
ampersand character, 211, 301
analysis, 139, 143
ancestor element, 262
ancestry example, 87–90, 92–95
ANCESTRY_FILE data set, 88
angle, 231, 282–283, 341, 419
angle brackets, 210
animate method, 266

module object, 182
modulo operator, 14
Mongolian vowel separator, 171
month name (exercise), 187, 414
Mosaic, 213
motion, 254
MOUNTAINS data set, 108, 111, 232
mouse, 26, 332, 334, 342, 421
   button, 237, 238, 241
   cursor, 241
mouse trail (exercise), 250, 417
mousedown event, 238, 241, 332, 334, 421
mousemove event, 242–243, 248, 334–335, 417
mouseout event, 243
mouseover event, 243, 338
mouseup event, 241, 243, 332, 334
moveTo method, 279, 282
Mozilla, 213, 303
multiple attribute, 322, 323
multiple-choice, 316, 321, 322
multiplication, 13, 257, 267
multiplier function, 49
mutability, 64, 65, 105
mutation, 412

N

name attribute, 318, 321
namespace, 75, 176, 177, 180, 181
namespace pollution, 75, 176, 179
naming, 4, 6
NaN, 14, 17, 18, 140
negation, 15, 17
neighbor, 328, 422
nerd, 166
nesting
   of arrays, 68
   of expressions, 23, 193
   of functions, 44, 85, 110
   of loops, 38, 91, 124, 408
   of objects, 216, 219
   in regular expressions, 163
   of scope, 44
Netscape, 6, 213
network, 207–209, 311, 371
new operator, 103
newline character, 14, 38, 155, 165, 169, 421

nextSibling property, 218
node, 216–217
node program, 349, 350
Node.js
   asynchronous programming and, 352
   console.log and, 27
   DELETE method, 359
   file server example, 361
   fs module, 353
   GET method, 358
   HTTP module, 354
   long polling and, 368–370
   module system, 182, 350–351
   NPM, 177, 351
   overview, 347–349, 363
   PUT method, 360
   stopping script, 355
   streams and, 356
node_modules directory, 351–352
NodeList type, 218
nodeType property, 217, 417, 418
nodeValue property, 219
nonbreaking space, 171
normalizing, 394
not a number, 14
note-taking example, 325
notification, 369
NPM, 177, 351–353, 358, 362, 372–373
null, 18, 19, 79, 95, 144, 411
number
   conversion to, 18, 29
   immutable types, 65
   matching with regular expression, 155, 173
   notation, 12, 13
   precision of, 13
   representation, 12
   special values, 14
number field, 336
Number function, 29, 36
number puzzle example, 51

O

object
   creation, 103
   DOM and, 216
   global, 77
   identity, 65

Why's Poignant Guide to Ruby, 22
width (CSS), 342
window, 236, 237, 243, 246, 350
window variable, 77
Windows, 364
with statement, 141
withContext function, 146–147
word boundary, 160
word character, 155, 160, 170
work list, 423
workbench (exercise), 327, 421
world, 119, 120, 253
World type, 12–124, 126–127, 130
World Wide Web, 6, 87, 183, 207, 209,
    212–213, 299
writable stream, 355–358
write method, 355, 356
writeFile function, 353, 356, 425
writeHead method, 354
writing code, 7, 119
WWW, *see* World Wide Web

X

XML, 218, 276, 302, 304, 305
XML namespace, 276
XMLHttpRequest, 302–304, 306, 312,
    319, 425
xmlns attribute, 276

Y

yield (reserved word), 26
Yuan-Ma, 10, 346

Z

Zawinski, Jamie, 152
zero-based counting, 56, 61, 159
zeroPad function, 54
zigzag shape, 419
zooming, 295

UPDATES

Visit *http://nostarch.com/ejs2/* for updates, errata, and other information.

More no-nonsense books from  **NO STARCH PRESS**

THE BOOK OF CSS3,
2ND EDITION
**A Developer's Guide to
the Future of Web Design**
by PETER GASSTON
NOVEMBER 2014, 304 PP., $34.95
ISBN 978-1-59327-580-8

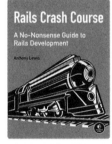

RAILS CRASH COURSE
**A No-Nonsense Guide to
Rails Development**
by ANTHONY LEWIS
OCTOBER 2014, 296 PP., $34.95
ISBN 978-1-59327-572-3

IF HEMINGWAY
WROTE JAVASCRIPT
by ANGUS CROLL
OCTOBER 2014, 192 PP., $19.95
ISBN 978-1-59327-585-3

PYTHON FOR KIDS
A Playful Introduction to Programming
by JASON R. BRIGGS
DECEMBER 2012, 344 PP., $34.95
ISBN 978-1-59327-407-8
full color

JAVASCRIPT FOR KIDS
A Playful Introduction to Programming
by NICK MORGAN
DECEMBER 2014, 348 PP., $34.95
ISBN 978-1-59327-408-5
full color

THE PRINCIPLES OF
OBJECT-ORIENTED JAVASCRIPT
by NICHOLAS C. ZAKAS
FEBRUARY 2014, 120 PP., $24.95
ISBN 978-1-59327-540-2

PHONE:
800.420.7240 OR
415.863.9900

EMAIL:
SALES@NOSTARCH.COM

WEB:
WWW.NOSTARCH.COM